PATHS ALONG THE HUDSON

PART II ALONG THE HUDSON

Paths along the Hudson

A GUIDE TO WALKING AND BIKING

JEFFREY PERLS

RUTGERS UNIVERSITY PRESS
New Brunswick, New Jersey, and London

To my parents, who raised me and instilled in me a sense of adventure; and to my wife, Robin, who shares my experiences on the trail

Library of Congress Cataloging-in-Publication Data
Perls, Jeffrey, 1954–
Paths along the Hudson : a guide to walking and biking / Jeffrey Perls.
    p.   cm.
Includes bibliographical references (p.   ) and index.
ISBN 0-8135-2657-4 (paper : alk. paper)
1. Hiking—Hudson River Valley (N.Y. and N.J.)—Guidebooks.
2. Walking—Huson River Valley (N.Y. and N.J.)—Guidebooks.
3. Cycling—Hudson River Valley (N.Y. and N.J.)—Guidebooks.
4. Hudson River Valley (N.Y. and N.J.)—Guidebooks. I. Title.
GV199.42.H83P47   1999
917.47'304'43—dc21   99-11393
                                                        CIP

British Cataloging-in-Publication data for this book is available from the British Library

Maps by Margaret Westergaard

Second printing, 2001

Copyright © 1999 by Jeffrey Perls
All rights reserved

Manufactured in the United States of America

CONTENTS

ACKNOWLEDGMENTS

I would personally like to thank for their assistance with this project: Doreen Valentine, Helen Hsu, Marilyn Campbell, and the staff of Rutgers University Press; Maggie Westergaard for maps and Susan H. Llewellyn for copyediting; Frances Dunwell and Betsy Blair of the New York State Department of Environmental Conservation (NYSDEC) Hudson River Programs; Fred Gerde of the NYSDEC; Seth McKee, Rita Shaheen, and Jeff Anzevino of Scenic Hudson; Steve Stanne and the staff of Clearwater; Eric Kiviat and Gretchen Stevens of Hudsonia; Brian Goodman, superintendent of the Old Croton Aqueduct Trailway; Joann Dolan, Jane Daniels, and Gary Haugland of the New York/New Jersey Trail Conference; Dave Sampson, Maggie Vinciguerra, and Kevin McLoughlin of the Hudson River Valley Greenway Conservancy; Karl Beard, director of the Rivers and Trails Program of the National Park Service's New York field office; Daniel Luciano of the Open Space Institute; Sue Cahill of the City of Kingston Planning Department; Tom Cordier, deputy mayor of the village of Tivoli; Todd Dreyer of the City of Poughkeepsie Planning Department; Lynette Thorne of the Dutchess County Planning Department; Ed Phillips, recreation director of the Town of Poughkeepsie Parks and Recreation Department; Carla Decker of the Newburgh Historical Society; the staffs of the Town of Marlboro and the Town of Esopus Libraries; Fred Schaeffer of the Dutchess and Beyond Bicycle Club; and the Mid-Hudson Sierra Club.

I'd also like to thank Peter Kick, Steve Kasdin, Kate Folkers, and Craig Apololito. And special thanks are due all my friends and family, especially my nieces, Ashli and Alexandra, and my nephews, Joseph and Richard, for accompanying me on the trails.

PATHS ALONG THE HUDSON

Introduction

The Hudson River is one of the great wonders of the eastern United States. From the rugged topography of the Hudson Highlands Gorge, to the towers and crowded ethnic neighborhoods of Manhattan, to sections so wide it seems more like a lake than a river, to rolling pastoral countryside with distant mountain views, the Hudson has been an inspiration for poets, writers, artists, and countless others.

As a guide to walking and biking, this book focuses on the areas in the immediate vicinity of the Hudson, those areas that are within view of the river or that have a strong connection to it. It also covers only the 150-mile section from New York Harbor north to Albany—the part of the river that is a tidal estuary, an arm of the sea. It is that section—to which I refer as the Hudson region, and which has the most magnificent scenery—that is really unique among great American rivers.

More than just the concrete jungle many people picture, the region around the Hudson Estuary is notable for its incredible diversity of landscapes, cultures, and life forms. The Hudson's long geologic history has created an eclectic landscape of interesting and distinct structures such as the towering Catskills, the Hudson Highlands, and the Palisades. The region's varied habitats support incredibly rich flora and fauna. Commercially valuable fish depend on the estuary for spawning and as a nursery for their young, and numerous bird species utilize the Hudson as a major seasonal migration route. The Hudson is also home to such rare and endangered species as the peregrine falcon and the shortnose sturgeon. The region's temperate climate provides an endless parade of seasonal changes.

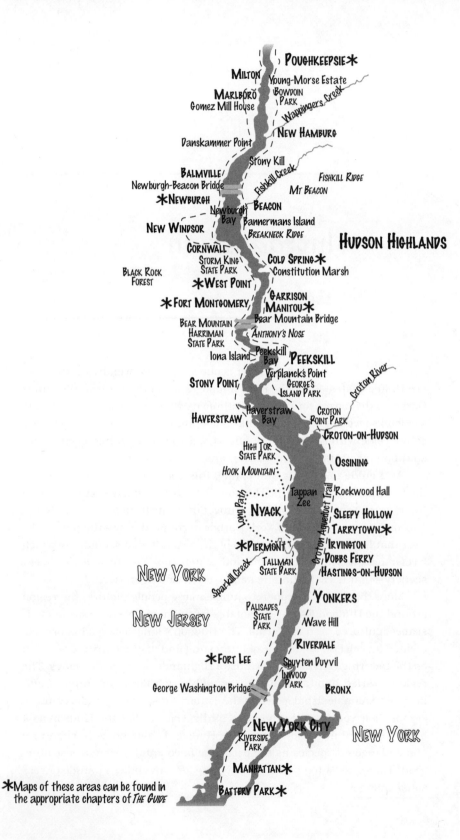

POUGHKEEPSIE ✳

MILTON

Young-Morse Estate

BOWDOIN PARK

MARLBORO

Gomez Mill House

Wappingers Creek

NEW HAMBURG

Danskammer Point

Stony Kill

BALMVILLE

Fishkill Creek

FISHKILL RIDGE

Newburgh-Beacon Bridge

MT BEACON

✳ NEWBURGH

Newburgh Bay

BEACON

NEW WINDSOR

Bannermans Island

BREAKNECK RIDGE

HUDSON HIGHLANDS

CORNWALL

STORM KING STATE PARK

COLD SPRING ✳

Constitution Marsh

BLACK ROCK FOREST

✳ WEST POINT

GARRISON

✳ FORT MONTGOMERY

MANITOU ✳

Bear Mountain Bridge

BEAR MOUNTAIN

HARRIMAN STATE PARK

ANTHONY'S NOSE

Iona Island

Peekskill Bay

PEEKSKILL

STONY POINT

Verplanck's Point

GEORGE'S ISLAND PARK

Croton River

HAVERSTRAW

Haverstraw Bay

CROTON POINT PARK

CROTON-ON-HUDSON

HIGH TOR STATE PARK

OSSINING

Hook Mountain

Rockwood Hall

Tappan Zee

Long Path

NYACK

SLEEPY HOLLOW

TARRYTOWN ✳

✳ PIERMONT

IRVINGTON

DOBBS FERRY

Croton Aqueduct Trail

Sparkill Creek

TALLMAN STATE PARK

HASTINGS-ON-HUDSON

NEW YORK

YONKERS

NEW JERSEY

PALISADES STATE PARK

Wave Hill

RIVERDALE

✳ FORT LEE

Spuyten Duyvil

INWOOD PARK

BRONX

George Washington Bridge

NEW YORK CITY

RIVERSIDE PARK

NEW YORK

MANHATTAN ✳

BATTERY PARK ✳

✳ Maps of these areas can be found in
the appropriate chapters of THE GUIDE

A primary force affecting the Hudson region's landscape is human development, which to a large degree has shaped what we encounter today. In addition to forests, fields, and wetlands, the region also supports farms, small communities, suburbs, and cities, including the nation's largest and most vibrant urban metropolis. While suburban development is rapidly spreading up the valley, and once-agrarian landscapes are being transformed into subdivisions and malls, much of the area's rural charm remains. It can be said that the Hudson region has the best of what civilization and nature have to offer.

The Hudson has played a pivotal role in the history of this country, and today—fittingly—the region has the nation's largest concentration of historic sites. The Hudson was the only region in North America settled by the Dutch, which made it distinct culturally and commercially from the other American colonies. The Hudson region also played a significant strategic role in America's War of Independence and was heavily contested by both sides, who saw control of the river as essential for winning the war. After the completion of the Erie Canal in 1825, the Hudson served as the gateway to the West and as the nation's primary transportation corridor. The Hudson River played a critical role in the nation's industrial and commercial development. Steamships, railroads, and such monumental engineering feats as bridges and tunnels, aqueducts, and skyscrapers became key features of the Hudson's landscape. The river has traditionally been the nation's primary entry point for immigrants to this country, many of whom settled nearby. The region's current social topography is characterized by cultural and ethnic diversity: The Hudson region certainly has one of the most heterogeneous and cosmopolitan populations in the world.

As home to both the Hudson River painters and Knickerbocker writers, the region played a leading role in the nation's early cultural, intellectual, and artistic development, and it remains the nation's preeminent center for culture and the arts. The Hudson's physical and cultural landscapes have been the setting for many major works of literature and art as well as of architecture and landscape design. Appreciation of the Hudson region as a scenic resource helped to promote efforts to protect the land, establish parks, and clean up the river. Such regional efforts have provided a useful model for environmental activism in other parts of the country and around the world. Today the Hudson region is home to a number of active environmental organizations.

Right now the region is in the throes of many profound economic, social, and technological changes. Among these is a growing awareness and appreciation of the Hudson's importance as a scenic, recreational,

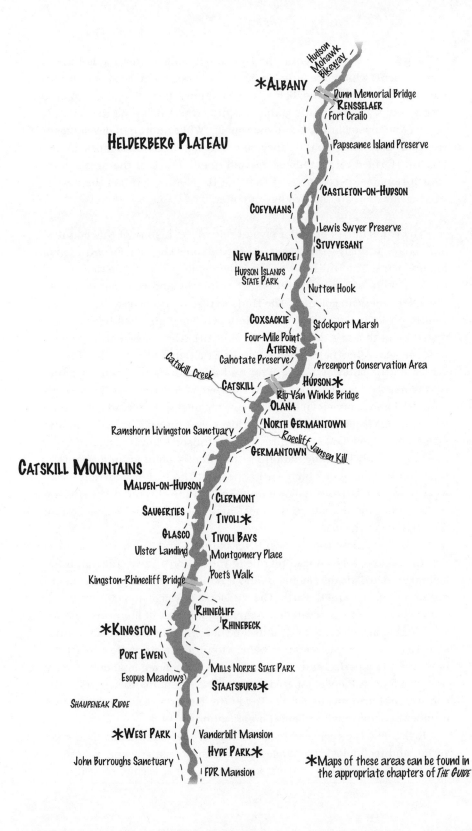

Hudson Mohawk Bikeway

✳ALBANY

Dunn Memorial Bridge
RENSSELAER
Fort Crailo

HELDERBERG PLATEAU

Papscanee Island Preserve

CASTLETON-ON-HUDSON

COEYMANS

Lewis Swyer Preserve

STUYVESANT

NEW BALTIMORE

HUDSON ISLANDS
STATE PARK

Nutten Hook

COXSACKIE

Stockport Marsh

Four-Mile Point
ATHENS
Cahotate Preserve

Catskill Creek

CATSKILL

Greenport Conservation Area

HUDSON✳

Rip Van Winkle Bridge

OLANA

NORTH GERMANTOWN

Ramshorn Livingston Sanctuary

Roecliff Jansen Kill

GERMANTOWN

CATSKILL MOUNTAINS

MALDEN-ON-HUDSON

CLERMONT

SAUGERTIES

TIVOLI✳

GLASCO

TIVOLI BAYS

Ulster Landing

Montgomery Place

Kingston-Rhinecliff Bridge

Poet's Walk

RHINECLIFF

✳KINGSTON

RHINEBECK

PORT EWEN

Esopus Meadows

Mills Norrie State Park

STAATSBURG✳

SHAUPENEAK RIDGE

✳WEST PARK

Vanderbilt Mansion

HYDE PARK✳

John Burroughs Sanctuary

FDR Mansion

✳Maps of these areas can be found in
the appropriate chapters of *THE GUIDE*

and biological resource. The creation in 1991 of the Hudson River Valley Greenway, plus the Hudson's recent designation as a National Heritage Area and as one of the nation's ten leading heritage rivers, are just some of the ways its significance is now being recognized. There is a literal renaissance of activity along the river: the state and private groups protecting land, creating parks, restoring historic sites and riverfronts, and building trails, many of which have only appeared in the past year or two. Even Metro-North is working on ways to increase safe public access to the Hudson's shores. The river has become a focal point around which the region's communities can plan cooperatively for their future.

Although one can gain a lot by reading, experiencing the region at first hand is the ultimate way to appreciate it. Walking and biking are two outdoor activities that provide rewarding, healthy ways to explore the region and feel a greater sense of connectedness to it. A continuous linear network of scenic trails lines both sides of the Hudson between New York and Albany, with a tremendous variety of walking and biking adventures possible. Included are such famous long-distance trails as the Appalachian Trail and the Long Path, but also many excellent examples that are not well known or publicized. Regardless of tastes or abilities, though, there's something for practically everyone.

The trail routes described in the book aim to bring the reader as close to the river as possible as well as affording him or her a sample of the region's diverse attractions. The trails visit rewarding vistas, nature preserves, and historic landmarks. While *Paths Along the Hudson* should be a useful guide for visitors to the Hudson region, the book's main focus is to acquaint local residents with the wonderful things in their own backyards.

Walking and biking along the Hudson helped me appreciate that the region is really one diverse community, physically and spiritually linked by the river. I hope *Paths along the Hudson* fills the need for a useful, practical guide to experiencing the river and the land that surrounds it.

Please join me, and let the adventure begin.

BACKGROUND

1 The Natural Landscape

Topography and Climate

RIVER OR ESTUARY?

From the very top of Mount Marcy, the tallest peak in the Adirondack Mountains and the highest in New York State, water streams down the bare summit rocks and alpine vegetation toward tiny Lake Tear in the Clouds, a thousand feet below. From there it tumbles several miles descending to the Hudson River, eventually flowing to New York Harbor, 306 miles away. Although the Hudson is only 71st among the 135 U.S. rivers more than 100 miles long, its greatness cannot be measured in length.

For 150 miles, from the tip of Manhattan up to the Federal Dam in Troy, several miles north of Albany, the Hudson is not really a river but an estuary; an arm of the sea. Three factors distinguish an estuary from river: elevation, tides, and salinity. To all intents and purposes the elevation of the river at Troy is sea level. Freshwater flow from the Hudson's numerous tributaries accounts for less than 10 percent of the river's total flow; the rest is the result of tidal actions. In the Hudson River there are roughly three to four feet of difference between high and low tides. Tides occur on a twenty-five-hour cycle, with six and a quarter hours between tides.

The lower part of the estuary consists of brackish water—that is, water that contains a fair amount of salt, though less than that in the ocean. In New York Harbor the salinity of the water is approximately thirty parts per thousand (ppt). As one moves north, the salinity gradually decreases to 14 ppt at Piermont Marsh and finally 0.05 ppt north of Albany. The position of the salt line (the official demarcation between freshwater and salt water), varies depending on conditions. Typically it is located in the vicinity of Newburgh Bay. However, during spring runoff the salt line can occur farther south, even as far south as Yonkers or Manhattan. During periods of extended drought, it can reach as far north as Poughkeepsie.

The river channel between New York and Albany is maintained, through dredging, at a constant depth of at least 32 feet. This ensures the river can be navigated by large oceangoing ships as far north as the Port of Albany. However, the river depth varies considerably. At the deepest spot, World's End, located off Gees Point, between West Point and Constitution Island, the river is 216 feet deep. Actually, the original channel is even deeper than that. Much of it is filled with sediment and debris left behind by glaciers during the Ice Age. Excavations for the Catskill Aqueduct near Storm King didn't reach solid bedrock until workers had drilled more than 700 feet below the surface of the water.

The width of the river also varies considerably. At Haverstraw Bay it is more than three and half miles wide. Other wide sections—though they tend to be rather shallow—are the Tappan Zee and Newburgh Bay. North of Kingston the width is generally less than a mile.

Tributary streams carry large amounts of silt down into the river, giving the Hudson its often muddy, or turbid, appearance ("turbidity" refers to the amount of suspended sediment in water). Underwater visibility, except in early fall, is usually less than a foot. Much of the silt is the result of soil erosion from land that has been cleared for residential or commercial development.

As fascinating as the estuary is, the varied landscape of mountains and low-lying areas through which it flows is just as interesting. The Catskills, the broad marshes, and the cliffs of the Palisades are some of the more noteworthy features, but the most magnificent of them all is the spectacular fifteen-mile gorge where the river slices through the Appalachians. There, in an area called the Hudson Highlands, steep rocky peaks rise more than a thousand feet, practically from the river's edge in some places. Inspired by this landscape, the English navigator Henry Hudson called it "the river of the mountains." Many believe that this gorge is actually a fjord, one of only two on the East Coast of the United States. A fjord is a deep valley, carved by glaciers, that has been flooded. Whether by strict definition the Hudson Highlands Gorge is a true fjord or not, I've been to Somes Sound in Maine, the East Coast's other fjord, and I have to say that the Hudson Highlands are far more impressive.

A TEMPERATE CLIMATE

Climate is the average weather conditions of an area over an extended period of time. The climate of the Hudson region may be categorized as temperate, which means that it has moderately cold winters and warm, humid summers. Weather conditions can be quite variable day to day, but in a temperate climate overall variation depends primarily on season.

Latitude—distance from the poles and the equator—and position of the earth in relation to the sun are two important factors affecting climate. As expected, the farther north, the colder it gets. Albany's growing season is more than twenty days shorter than New York City's. Species diversity also tends to decrease the farther north you go. This is probably due to the rigors of winter, which fewer species can endure. The lower reaches of the river are affected by warm sea breezes, which penetrate as far north as the Hudson Highlands, stopping at Iona Island. This may explain the presence of some more typically southern plants and animals along this section of the river.

Another major factor affecting climate is elevation. The varied topography of the Hudson region has elevation ranges from sea level to more than fifteen hundred feet (more than thirty-five hundred feet in the neighboring Catskills). Generally the higher up you go, the thinner and colder the air gets, a phenomenon that explains the presence of snow on mountaintops long after it has melted in the valleys and lowlands. Even a difference of a few hundred feet in elevation can have a profound impact on an area's climate and the kinds of plants and animals found there. Areas of higher elevation can sometimes support species of plants and animals south of their normal ranges. Mountains also block the passage of air, forcing it to rise, which cools it and causes condensation and the formation of clouds and precipitation. As a result the Catskill Mountains get twice as much precipitation as the adjacent Hudson Valley.

As a large body of water, the Hudson warms more slowly than the surrounding land, and it cools more slowly as well. This lag in temperature change has a slight moderating effect on climate in the immediate vicinity of the river.

In addition to the factors mentioned above, human beings also have an impact on climate. One that is causing a great deal of concern is global warming. According to some theories, the large-scale emission of greenhouse gases such as carbon dioxide and ozone (primarily from the burning of fossil fuels), is causing the earth's atmosphere to warm. This warming effect may eventually induce parts of the polar icecaps to melt, which could, in turn, cause the oceans to rise, flooding large sections of coastal plain. When these changes might take place and whether they are already happening, is hotly debated, but such questions have certainly raised awareness of the effects of human activity on climate and other natural phenomena.

SEASONS

Seasonal changes in conditions present a huge challenge for plant and animal life, which must be able to adapt in order to survive and grow. The effects of seasonal changes on plants and animals are one of the most fascinating aspects of the Hudson region's natural history and ecology.

In the spring large amounts of rain and snowmelt from the mountains enter the estuary and flush sediment and pollution out to sea. Spring arrives early in large river valleys like the Hudson. It brings new green buds to the forest. The entire sequence of greening may take from five to seven weeks in any particular location. Skunk cabbage blooms at the beginning of March, generating so much heat that it can literally melt its way through the snow. The noxious odor of the skunk cabbage attracts flies, the only pollinators available so early in the season. Many species of trees flower before their leaves emerge in order to take full advantage of wind for seed dispersal. Late April to early May is the prime time for most woodland flowers, which bloom while sunlight can still penetrate to the forest floor.

Spring is when many animals emerge from months of wintertime hibernation. Shad spawn in April and May. In mid-March amphibians begin their spring migration to swamps and vernal pools—temporary bodies of water located in shallow depressions, the result of spring rains and snowmelt—to mate and reproduce. Juvenile frogs and toads, called tadpoles, live in water, breathing through gills, switching to lungs when they become adults. Vernal pools dry up during the summer, so the young must reach maturity before this happens.

Spring is the time of the great bird migration north. The presence of abundant insect food, less competition, fewer predators, and longer days make the Hudson region, like much of the Northeast, attractive for birds migrating up from the tropics. The Hudson is part of a major bird migration route in the spring and fall.

The warmer conditions, clear skies, and the presence of fresh greenery also make spring a favorite time for outdoor enthusiasts. Conditions can vary, however. Snow can occur in March and even April in some places. Rainstorms are a common feature, and the ground recently liberated from its mantle of snow can be quite muddy in places.

In early summer, flowering plants in fields and wetlands begin to blossom when insect activity is at its peak and competition for pollinators is greatest. In the forests mountain laurel and wild azaleas bloom. Summer and fall are times when wild berries appear, as well as many wild and cultivated fruits. Birds and other creatures consume the fruits, then later defecate the indigestible seeds, spreading them around. The larger, more numerous, and palatable fruits are the ones birds and insects are attracted to.

Outdoor activity in summer has its drawbacks. Summer days can be sultry, making strenuous activity unbearable. Heat cramps, heat exhaustion, and heat stroke are potential risks for those who overexert themselves or don't drink enough fluids. Sunburn may afflict the unwary. Views may be obscured by pollution. Biting insects are at their peak, and so is poison ivy. Fast-growing vegetation can overwhelm trails, making them impassable. However, pleasant summer days are not uncommon. There's plenty of wildlife to see. Waterborne activities like swimming, sailing, canoeing, and kayaking are enjoyable ways to experience the river in summertime. Festivals of all kinds also seem to take place just about every weekend.

The most dramatic and spectacular event in the fall is the annual change of colors that takes place in October and continues into early November in the southernmost parts of the region (the farther south, the longer the transition). This occurs at roughly the same time every year regardless of climatic conditions. To conserve moisture for the winter, trees cease photosynthesizing and transpiring water through their leaves. Trees withdraw their sap reserves into the trunk and roots. No longer a part of the tree's life activity, the leaves slowly die. The dramatic color changes are the result of the deterioration of green chlorophyll pigments, a process that reveals the other pigments present in the leaf. These also decay, and the leaf eventually turns brown and falls off. Temperature seems to have little effect on this change process.

In the fall many species of birds migrate south, to avoid the rigors of winter and the reduced food supply. Monarch butterflies and red bats also migrate south in the fall. The shortening day length appears to be a signal that it's time to migrate. Some birds feed and forage during the day and migrate at night, when the air is cooler and flight requires less expense of energy. Some, such as hawks, prefer the day in order to take advantage of thermal currents. To prepare for the arduous journey or for the hardships of winter, many birds will fatten up on a diet of fruit. (The availability of insects declines in the fall at the same time as many trees are bearing fruit.) Hibernating mammals also build up their fat reserves prior to winter.

Because of the cooler, drier weather, the apple harvest, and the spectacular color changes, fall is one of the most popular times of the year for outdoor activities, and many places become crowded with visitors. Recently fallen damp leaves can make trails slick and hazardous for walking. One should also be mindful of deer-hunting season, which takes place in late fall.

In winter most of the river freezes, though Coast Guard icebreakers keep a channel open for ships. Days are shorter in winter. Birds have very high body temperatures and thick coverings of feathers, which provide effective insulation from the cold. Many also roost in tree cavities protected from wind chill. In the worst weather they become inactive, conserving energy. Mammals are afforded similar protection by their coats of fur, enabling some, such as deer, squirrels, and snowshoe rabbits, to remain active throughout the winter.

Many plants and animals of temperate regions have evolved dormancy mechanisms to adapt to the cold and the extreme fluctuations in conditions. Animals that are endothermic are unable to generate their own heat and therefore must hibernate in the winter because they cannot keep themselves warm. This includes reptiles, amphibians, and insects. Hibernating animals decrease their respiration, heart rates, and body temperature, expending as little energy as possible. To all intents and purposes they exist in a state of suspended animation. Certain mammals like chipmunks and bears partially hibernate. They do not decrease their body temperature much and are easily aroused, becoming active again during warm spells.

During winter most moisture is frozen and unavailable for life-sustaining activity. This lack of moisture is another serious challenge plants and animals must face. Though broad-leafed hardwoods shed their leaves prior to the onset of winter, evergreens, on the other hand, have reduced water loss because their tiny needles have a waxy coating and relatively small surface area, hence they shed enough snow so that it doesn't build up and weigh down the branches, damaging the tree. Evergreen needles are also filled with a resin that protects them from freezing. The leaves of evergreen shrubs like mountain laurel curl up and point downward, reducing their surface areas and conserving moisture. Mosses and lichens become active during intermittent warm spells, drawing moisture from the thin layers of soil that have temporarily thawed.

The cold and the presence of snow and ice tend to discourage most outdoor enthusiasts in the winter. However, if the snow is good, snowshoeing, downhill, or crosscountry skiing are rewarding ways to experience the outdoors. If there isn't much snow on the ground, one can still bundle up and hike the trails. (Be sure to read the section on hypothermia first, however.) Forests are more open in winter, and there are certainly more views at that time of year. Places that are normally crowded may be quite serene.

Geology

The Hudson region is an area of great geological diversity. More than a billion years of shifting continents, volcanic activity, deposits of sediments, erosion, and glaciation have shaped the region's varied topography. Based on a number of factors, including geologic history and rock types, the Hudson region can be divided into five separate areas: the Reading Prong, the Manhattan Prong, the Hudson/Mohawk Lowlands, the Allegheny Plateau, and the Newark Lowlands.

THE READING PRONG

The Reading Prong forms a relatively narrow twenty-mile-wide band of very ancient rocks underlying the Hudson Highlands. It extends all the way from Reading, Pennsylvania, to western Connecticut. The Reading Prong is part of the Appalachian Cordillera, an area of geologically similar rock that underlies the Appalachian Mountains.

During the Proterozoic era, 1.3 billion years ago, sediments were deposited in shallow seas that covered the area. The sediments were buried deep under many layers of newer sediment, gradually hardening into sedimentary rocks. About 1.1 billion years ago, the continents collided. The force of the collision (which took millions of years), created tremendous pressure. Rock layers trapped between the two continents, having no where else to go, were pushed upward, forming a huge range of mountains that stretched from Georgia to Labrador. During this collision and mountain-building event, which is called the Grenville Orogeny, there were intrusions of magma (hot liquid rock from beneath the earth's crust), which later hardened into granite, an igneous rock. The earlier sediments were buried deep below the earth's surface, where intense heat and pressure altered the granular structure of the rocks and turned them into gneiss, a metamorphic rock. Metamorphic rocks have been transformed by forces underneath the surface of the earth. Eventually the mountains of the Grenville Orogeny eroded down to a flat plain, exposing the older rocks.

During the early Paleozoic era, 600 to 500 million years ago, the entire Hudson region was flooded by an ancient sea. New sediments were deposited on top of the older rocks. In the Ordovician period, 450 million years ago, another collision of the continents occurred, called the Taconian Orogeny. This collision formed a tall mountain range that covered almost the entire Hudson region as well as western New England. The rocks of the Reading Prong were again buried deep below the earth's surface and subjected to more heat and pressure. As the Taconic Mountains gradually eroded away, the original rocks were exposed once more.

During the Permian period, 300 million to 250 million years ago, the collision of North America and Africa in the Alleghenian Orogeny caused the entire Appalachian mountain range to be uplifted, including the rocks of the Reading Prong. They were probably uplifted again, more than once, but evidence of these later uplifts has been erased by erosion.

THE MANHATTAN PRONG

The Manhattan Prong comprises most of Westchester County south of the Hudson Highlands, as well as most of the Bronx and all of Manhattan Island. It is also part of a larger region called the New England Uplands, centered in western New England. In the Cambrian period, 600 to 500 million years ago, thick layers of sediment were deposited in shallow seas that bordered the edge of the continent. This sediment later hardened into sedimentary rock, becoming limestone, sandstone, and shale. The collision of continents during the Taconian Orogeny buried the rocks deep beneath mountains that were once possibly as tall as the Himalayas. Subjected to intense heat and pressure, the rocks in many cases became like plastic and were folded and squeezed. This drastically altered the granular structure of the rocks and turned them into metamorphic rocks: gneiss, schist, and marble.

Over the next 50 million years the Taconic Mountains gradually wore down. The original rocks were probably buried under additional sediment, which eventually eroded away, exposing the ancient rocks we see today.

THE HUDSON/MOHAWK LOWLANDS

The area of mostly gentle topography north of the Hudson Highlands is part of the Ridge and Valley Province of the Appalachian Cordillera, which stretches between Alabama and Newfoundland. This valley comprises sedimentary rocks (sandstone, shale, and limestone), deposited during the Ordovician period, 500 to 450 million years ago, to the east of what was then the coast of North America. These rocks are slightly younger than those of the Manhattan Prong. During the Taconian and Acadian Orogenies the rocks of the Hudson/Mohawk Lowlands were intensely folded but were not as deformed as those in the Manhattan Prong.

Animal life was present in the Ordovician seas and left its remains behind in the form of fossils. Fossils are often the cast or impression left of the hard parts of an animal or plant after it dies and is buried in mud, which later hardens into sedimentary rock. In some cases the animal or plant remains are replaced by mineral deposits. In other cases traces of animals are found, as in the case of worm burrows and animal footprints. Among the common fossils found in the Hudson/Mohawk Lowlands are graptolites. These were lightweight colonies, similar in form to modern-day jellyfish, which floated on the surface of the ocean, drifting with the currents. Their fossils can be found in shale in the form of carbonized remains that resemble pencil marks.

THE ALLEGHENY PLATEAU

The Allegheny Plateau consists of mostly undisturbed layers of sedimentary rock from the late Silurian to the Upper Devonian age. This area extends into western New York State and northern Pennsylvania. The northeastern boundary is the prominent Helderberg Escarpment, a few miles southwest of Albany. The southeastern boundary is the Shawangunk Ridge, which extends from Rosendale in the north, south through New Jersey as the Kittatinny Ridge, and then into Pennsylvania. An extension of this plateau occurs in south-central Orange County and includes Schunemunk Mountain, while two small "islands" occur east of the Hudson in Columbia County.

The most prominent topographical feature of this area is the Catskill Mountains. From Kingston north to just south of Albany, the plateau makes its farthest extension east, coming within a mile of the Hudson in a number of places. It is likely that much of the region, including areas east of the Hudson River, was once covered by sedimentary rocks of the Allegheny Plateau, though most of it has eroded away. (Limestones of the Allegheny Plateau—the primary source of cement in the Hudson Region— have been quarried extensively.)

Most of the rocks of the Allegheny Plateau are from the Devonian period, 408 to 360 million years old. These rocks reach their greatest thickness, over ten thousand feet, south of the Catskill Mountains. During the Devonian Period the Taconic Mountains had already worn down, and the much of the region was covered with warm shallow seas. The older Devonian rocks contain the richest fossil deposits in the region. By far the most common fossils are brachiopods, a marine shellfish, once abundant but now largely extinct except for a few deep-water species. There were also trilobites, an extinct order of arthropods that superficially resembled modern horseshoe crabs. Other fossils include corals, crinoids (sea lilies), and various mollusks, especially the squidlike shelled cephalopods (nautilus).

During the Middle Devonian period, there was another collision— known as the Acadian Orogeny—between the continents which caused the Acadian Mountains to rise in what is now New England and the Canadian Maritime Provinces. As the Acadian Mountains grew in the east, however, they were also eroding. Between the mountains and the sea, sediment was deposited by ancient rivers, forming an alluvial plain, and deltas grew out into the sea. The sediment accumulated till it was thousands of feet thick. Later it hardened into the red, green, and gray shales, sandstones, and pebblestones (conglomerates), we now see in the Catskills. The Catskill deltas, which may have resembled present-day

Louisiana, were inhabited by the world's oldest known trees and by some of the oldest creatures to inhabit the land: Microscopic remains of rare mites, ticks, and spiders have been unearthed in the Catskills. Fossils of extinct armor-plated fish and primitive lungfish have also been found. About 300 to 250 million years ago, the Alleghenian Orogeny uplifted the area of the Allegheny Plateau, especially the Catskills. This area eroded down to a relatively flat plain until the middle of the Cenozoic era, 30 to 40 million years ago, when the plateau was again uplifted. Streams and later glaciers eroded the rocks of the plateau, eventually carving the steep valleys and mountainlike features we see today.

THE NEWARK LOWLANDS

Due to an extended period of erosion, millions of years of the rock record are missing from the Hudson region between the Devonian period and the Mesozoic era. During the Late Triassic period, more than 200 million years ago, separation of the continents caused basins to be formed up and down the East Coast of North America. The Newark Basin, the largest of these, borders the west side of the Hudson from West Haverstraw south to Staten Island and includes much of northern and central New Jersey. Streams eroding the newly uplifted Hudson Highlands deposited silt and sand in the basin, which accumulated until they were thousands of feet thick, then hardened into orange and reddish sandstones and gray and black shales. Because of the presence of the mineral hematite, the sandstones usually weather to a brownish color. They were quarried extensively during the nineteenth century and used to construct the famous brownstones of New York City.

The climate during the Triassic period was tropical, with alternating dry and wet spells. In the lakes and streams swam such fish as the coelacanth. (Long thought to be extinct, a number of individuals of this "living fossil" have been discovered off the coast of Africa.) Dinosaurs, like the agile ten-foot predator Coelophysis and other extinct reptiles and amphibians, waded in the shallow water and walked on the beaches, leaving behind their footprints. Remnants of these footprints have been found in a number of places, including along the Hudson south of Nyack. Fossil bones have been collected, too, including the remains of the crocodilelike phytosaur and of the oldest known gliding reptile.

There was also considerable volcanic activity in the basin during this time, and the most prominent feature of this formation is the Palisades, which extend for nearly forty miles from Staten Island, north to west of High Tor. The Palisades are a sill, a horizontal intrusion of magma 195 million years old. The magma cooled and formed diabase, or "trap," as it is often called. A tough, fine-grained crystalline igneous rock, it forms the imposing three-hundred-foot cliffs that face the Hudson.

GLACIAL HISTORY

Much of what we see around the Hudson region today has been shaped by glaciation. During the Pleistocene period, approximately 2 million years ago, worldwide temperatures were much colder, and at least four separate ice sheets invaded the region in succession. Only traces of the last, the Wisconsin Ice Sheet, have survived.

The Wisconsin Ice Sheet began about 75,000 years ago, advancing at approximately a foot a day. About 21,750 years ago it reached its farthest southern extent. During this time most of eastern North America and all of the Hudson region was covered by a huge sheet of ice thousands of feet thick. The ice sheet carried enormous amounts of rocky debris, and that debris, as well as the ice, scraped the land, softening many of its more rugged features. In the Hudson Highlands Gorge, the ice sheet scooped out a channel 787 feet below sea level. Remnants of the glacier can be seen in glacial erratics (boulders transported by the glacier, sometimes many miles) and in exposed bedrock that bares grooves and scratches, called striations, which the ice sheet carved as it polished and scraped the rocks. The weight of the glacier also depressed the land: The ocean level was hundreds of feet lower than it is today, and the shoreline extended much farther out to sea. Through this now-submerged coastal plain, the meltwaters of the glacier dug a channel extending 120 miles beyond New York Harbor. Eventually this channel was blocked by a vast terminal moraine, a pile of sediment pushed by the advancing ice sheet, forming a long continuous ridge covering much of Staten Island and Long Island. This, many scientists believe, diverted the course of the ancestral Hudson River west through the Sparkill Gap, emptying into the Atlantic south of Staten Island.

As the earth gradually warmed, the glacier melted and began a slow retreat to the north, depositing debris along the way. Much of the Hudson Valley was submerged by meltwaters from the retreating glacier. Lake Albany, about 30 miles wide at its widest spot, was formed where the present-day Hudson and Mohawk Rivers converge. Remains of ancient shorelines and beaches at least a hundred feet above the present shore can still be seen in a number of places along the Hudson. Meltwater streams transported clay from the surrounding uplands and deposited it in Lake Albany. These clay deposits supported the Hudson's once-thriving brick industry. Lake Albany lasted approximately four to five thousand years.

As the glacier retreated, the ocean gradually rose 328 feet, drowning the coastal plain and the Hudson's channel. Debris from the retreating glacier may have cut off the Hudson's channel near the Sparkill Gap, diverting the river southward till it eventually pierced the terminal moraine at the Verrazano Narrows. Or the rising sea may have pierced the moraine, eventually pushing northward until it met the Hudson and provided an easier drainage channel.

During the period when the Wisconsin Ice Sheet was retreating, the climate was still much cooler and damper than it is today. The area just south of the glacier probably supported the kinds of tiny plants, shrubs, and flowers that today inhabit tundra regions. Farther south, coniferous boreal forests of spruce, birch, and willows grew. Plants that retreated south during the advance of the ice sheet returned as the glaciers withdrew. During the postglacial period, twenty to ten thousand years ago, now-extinct mastodons and mammoths, woolly members of the elephant family, roamed the region. Some of the very best specimens were excavated in the vicinity of the Hudson, including a complete fossil skeleton of a mastodon from Newburgh on display at the American Museum of Natural History in New York City. Remains of caribou and horses, animals that no longer inhabit this area, have also been found.

Natural Communities and Habitats

The Hudson region supports diverse habitats, also called natural communities, which are the different types of places where animals and plants occur. These can be large areas of several square miles or tiny ones of just a few square feet. Conditions in natural communities tend to be relatively uniform, and specific habitats usually support certain characteristic species of plants or animals. Natural communities are rarely exclusive, however. Plant and animal species may be present in more than one habitat. In fact, they may depend on a number of different habitats to survive. The favorableness of the conditions effects the relative abundance of plants and animals as well as the number of species present.

THE RIVER CHANNEL

While walkers and bikers won't experience this area firsthand, it's important to know that the Hudson River Channel provides a habitat for a number of creatures adapted to life in deep water. The large amount of sediment and organic matter in the river means that there is less light penetration. In more than six feet of water, the lack of light means these areas are unable to support rooted plants, which depend on light for photosynthesis. Plants and animals that float in the water comprise the planktonic community. Rootless, single-celled microscopic plants, referred to as phytoplankton, exist close to the surface of the river where there is some light penetration. These include diatoms, green algae, blue-green algae (actually a cyanobacteria), and dinoflagellates.

In the Hudson River microscopic planktonic animals, referred to as zooplankton, are primarily crustaceans. Copepods, which resemble minuscule shrimp, are the most common. The river channel provides a habitat for numerous fish. Before we go any further, it should be noted, there are more than two hundred species of fish in the Hudson and its tributaries.

Resident estuarine species of fish spend their entire life in the brackish waters of the lower estuary. These include the bay anchovy, a small delicate fish that travels in schools. Another resident of the lower estuary is the hogchocker, or American sole, a small brownish flatfish with tiny eyes that lives on the bottom of the river.

The Atlantic tomcod is an anadromous member of the cod family. Anadromous fish spend their juvenile years in the estuary, their adulthood at sea, and return to the estuary to spawn. Another anadromous fish is the primitive Atlantic sturgeon, which can grow up to seven feet. Its head is covered with bony plates; it is toothless and scavenges in the mud for arthropods and detritus. Sturgeon were once so plentiful in the Hudson that they were referred to as "Albany Beef." Male sturgeon return to the river to spawn at the age of twelve years; females may be even older. A pregnant female may carry one to three million eggs. Alewives and blueback herring, called river herring, are small fish that are commercially harvested.

Shad are the largest members of the herring family. They are the chief commercial fish of the Hudson, which is one of the leading shad rivers in North America. The flesh and eggs (roe), are considered to be a great delicacy. In spring three-to-five-year-old shad return to the Hudson to spawn, primarily in the area between Kingston and Coxsackie. After hatching, the juveniles overwinter in the broad shallow areas of Haverstraw Bay and the Tappan Zee, which afford them protection from striped bass and other predators. These areas are among the most productive fish nurseries on the east coast between Chesapeake Bay and the Saint Lawrence. In summer they migrate upstream. In the fall young shad, three to five inches long, swim downriver to the Atlantic.

Striped bass are also anadromous. They usually spawn in the deep waters between Bear Mountain and Storm King. Depending on size, females produce millions of eggs, which are fertilized by a number of males. After Chesapeake Bay, the Hudson is probably the second most important propagating area on the East Coast for striped bass. (In 1985 commercial striped bass fishing was outlawed in all New York State waters due to PCB contamination.)

Catadromous fish live in freshwater and return to the ocean to spawn. The American eel is the region's only catadromous fish. It lives in the Hudson and its tributaries for twelve to fifteen years, then journeys all the way to the Sargasso Sea (part of the Caribbean), a trip that takes up to two years. Eels appear to be less affected by poor water quality than are most other fish. They can also slither around human-created barriers in order to travel upstream. Adult eels in the Hudson River are likely to be contaminated with PCBs and are therefore unavailable to commercial markets.

A number of birds feed on fish from the river's channel, snatching them from the surface in the case of ospreys, or diving underwater as cormorants and certain duck species do. Rare inhabitants of the river channel—whose numbers were greater in the past—include such marine mammals as porpoises, whales, and seals. As the Hudson has gotten cleaner, sightings of harbor seals have been reported on the rise.

Bottom-dwelling (benthic) creatures subsist on the river's deep bed. Many species are microscopic, including hydras, which are the polyp phases of small jellyfish. Others include amoebas, foraminifera, and bacteria. They feed on organic detritus and other tiny animals. Though small, they provide a necessary step in the food chain, converting decaying plant and animal material into tissue, which in turn feeds larger animals.

The river's bottom is also populated by sponges, numerous worms and wormlike animals that burrow in the mud, and sea anemones, which inhabit the more saline waters of the Hudson's lower estuary. Clams, mussels, and snails bury themselves in the mud or cling to rocks or human-made objects. Oysters, once extremely abundant in the brackish waters of the lower estuary, were a primary food source for Native Americans, who left piles of empty shells along the shoreline. They were similarly popular with Europeans, who consumed great quantities as cheap "fast food." However, during the nineteenth century, pollution destroyed these once-prolific beds.

Benthic arthropods include amphipods, tiny shrimplike crustaceans (scuds, sideswimmers); barnacles, primarily marine creatures though they are found in the Hudson Estuary as far north as Newburgh Bay; and water mites, which are arachnids and resemble midget spiders.

Most bottom-dwelling creatures in deep water are tiny, but a few, like crabs, can be sizable. Large adult blue crabs can be up to six inches across. They are found primarily in brackish waters, but range as far north as Albany. Omnivorous and active predators, feeding on a variety of benthic organisms, small fish, vegetation, and dead organisms, they are caught commercially.

SHALLOWS, MUDFLATS, AND SHORE AREAS

Subtidal zones, or shallows, occur at depths of a few inches at low tide, up to six feet. They can be found along the Hudson's shores, but also sometimes in the middle of the river. These areas are affected by tidal actions, summer heat, and scouring ice in winter. Phytoplankton inhabit the shallows, appearing as broad mats on the surface of the water. Microscopic crustaceans are other denizens of the shallows.

The shallows also support sparse-to-dense growth of limp-stemmed buoyant aquatic vegetation, such as the tapelike water celery, waterweeds, pondweeds, duckweeds, and exotic (nonnative) species such as the bushy water milfoil and the water chestnut. Shallow brackish waters support water celery, sago pondweed, and widgeon grass. These plants are rooted to the bottom and are exposed to the air only at low tide or not at all. Some, like the water chestnut, float on the surface and are exposed all the time.

Submerged aquatic plants provide an important habitat for many small invertebrates, including such insect larvae as dragonfly and caddisfly nymphs. Crustaceans and snails cling to the vegetation and feed on plankton and detritus. Larger invertebrates of the shallows include crabs and crayfish.

Resident freshwater fish of the shallows include shiners, bass, carp, catfish, and suckers. Anadromous fish often use the shallows for spawning, and the shallows serve as a nursery for juvenile fish like striped bass, which subsist on the abundant food supply while utilizing the cover of vegetation to hide from predators, especially larger adult fish. Various aquatic birds, such as ducks, geese, gulls, grebes, coots, and cormorants, hunt the shallows for small fish and invertebrates. Herons, egrets, and bitterns (a smaller variety of heron) wade in the shallows, capturing prey with lightninglike thrusts of their long beaks. Water snakes, snapping turtles, muskrat, beaver, and river otter also utilize the shallows for feeding.

Mudflats are large open areas of thick mud or sand that lie outside the main channel of the river, where the current is slower and more deposits of sediment take place. Submerged most of the time, these areas are fully exposed at low tide. Plants must be adapted to these changes. Mudflats support periphyton (attached algae) and bacteria, which break down plant matter. Aquatic plants include strap-leaf arrowhead, grass-leaf arrowhead, mudplantain, and golden club. Mudflats in the more brackish parts of the lower estuary support spongy arrowhead, mudwort, and tape grass. Like the shallows, mudflats are important feeding grounds for a number of fish species. They are utilized for breeding and as nursery areas for juvenile fish. Mudflats are also breeding grounds for insects such as dragonflies, caddisflies, mosquitos, flies, and beetles. A number of bird species, such as rails, sandpipers, and plovers, hunt in the mudflats at low tide for suitable plants to eat, as well as fish and small animals.

Shore areas are narrow, rocky, or sandy beaches, gravelly banks between high- and low-tide marks, or ledges and cliffs. Shore areas occur at the feet of relatively steep embankments adjacent to uplands. Mudflats and marshes have not been able to form in such areas. Exposed to frequent wave action, ice scour, and erosion from neighboring uplands, shore areas tend to be relatively harsh environments for most plants and animals. Vegetation tends to be sparse, often rooted in rock crevices above the high-tide level.

TIDAL MARSHES

Tidal marshes represent a transition stage between open water and forest. Found at the mouths of tributaries or in protected backwaters and coves where sedimentation rates are high, they are among the most productive habitats in the world in terms of the amount of organic matter produced. Beneath the marsh is a rich, dark, oozy muck composed of silt, clay, and organic detritus (decaying organic matter). Many fish, including killifish, darters, sunfish, and carp, depend on marshes as feeding areas. Snapping turtles, which can grow up to thirty-five pounds, are relatively common marsh inhabitants. They can be aggressive, especially when encountered on the land. Except for snapping turtles and water snakes, however, reptiles and amphibians are relatively scarce in the Hudson's tidal marshes.

Twenty-two species of birds nest in Hudson River tidal marshes. The most common are marsh wrens, though they are small and difficult to spot. They prefer dense stands of cattails, and their nests are round balls of cattail leaves. Male redwing blackbirds have the distinctive reddish-orange patch on their wings. They tend to be very territorial and can be seen guarding their section of marsh against intruders. Virginia rails are another common inhabitant of tidal marshlands. Their large feet enable them to walk on soft mud surfaces, where they use their long bills to extract insects and other invertebrates from mud and shallow water, also feeding on the seeds of marsh plants. Sparrows, flycatchers, least bitterns, goldfinches, and a number of duck species also nest in tidal marshes.

Muskrat are one of the most important marsh inhabitants. They are active year round and breed from spring through summer. Muskrat burrow in embankments or build lodges of plant material and sediment. These shelters may support one to six muskrat and may last from six months to several years. Cattails, bulrushes, arrowheads, wild rice, wild celery, and sweetflag are favored muskrat foods, but they will subsist on a wide variety of plant material and freshwater mussels. Muskrat harvest two to three times as much as they eat, storing their food in the lodges as well as smaller feeding stations. These piles of decaying vegetation are like compost heaps and are a rich source of nutrients that benefit the entire marsh. Muskrat aid in the dispersal of certain plant rhizomes and tubers, and their clearings provide openings in which a wide variety of marsh plants can flourish. Muskrat shelters are utilized by birds as nesting sites. Muskrat are preyed on by snapping turtles, snakes, birds of prey, and other predators. Other denizens of the marsh include mink, a nocturnal carnivore that feeds on muskrat and other small mammals, fish, amphibians, and invertebrates and is active throughout the year, and river otter, which are fairly widespread, though not often seen.

Left undisturbed, marshes eventually fill with sediment and organic detritus and become dry land. Three main types of marsh habitats may be distinguished; lower, or younger, marsh; upper, or mature, marsh; and between the two an area of transition marsh.

Plants of the lower marshes have to endure wide daily fluctuations of water level and complete submersions twice a day. Most have broad leaves rising on long stalks. Pure stands of spatterdock or mixed stands of spatterdock and pickerelweed occur in this environment. Yellow pond lily and bulrush are some of the other common plants. Spatterdock has large heart-shaped leaves up to a foot long and a single yellow blossom. It is an extremely aggressive landbuilder and pioneer on sediments that are exposed at low tide. The leaves of pickerelweed are similar to spatterdock's but smaller, and the plant has a spike of purple flowers.

Transition marshes occur in well-developed marshes and along the banks of tidal creeks that muskrats have disturbed. These areas exhibit the greatest diversity of plant species in the estuary system. Many of the plants have tissues rich in cellulose and silica, which contribute heavily to the food chain. Arrow arum, broad-leaved arrowhead, pickerelweed, rice cut-grass, smartweed, cattails, wild rice, jewelweed, bulrush, and water hemp may be observed in freshwater areas. Purple loosestrife, an exotic plant, also inhabits freshwater transition marshes. In brackish marshes from Iona Island south, swamp rose mallow, cordgrass, and cattails may be common.

Upper, or mature, marsh lies above the mean tidal level but is subject to periodic flooding. At high tide mature marsh will be infiltrated by small pools and lines of water. Plants that inhabit these areas undergo only partial submersion. Narrow-leaved cattail is the dominant native plant and can be found in every mature marsh habitat along the Hudson. Cattails have erect swordlike leaves averaging six feet in height. Cattail stands, which provide nesting cover for many birds and shelter for birds and mammals in winter, contribute heavily to the detritus supply because of their resistance to decay. They absorb nutrients and transform them into plant matter, which is then consumed by many marsh inhabitants, especially muskrat. Cattails have to compete, however, with purple loosestrife and common reed (Phragmites). Both are usually considered pests since they can overrun marsh habitats, crowding out more desirable species.

TIDAL SWAMPS

Tidal swamps endure brief periods of regular flooding. Some sections see only occasional flooding from severe storms and during high-water years. Flooding undercuts soil and can damage plants; however, it also deposits silt, which plants depend on, and those that inhabit tidal swamps are adapted to survive periodic flooding. Freshwater tidal swamps are a unique environment. Only five sizable freshwater tidal swamps occur in New York State, all of them located along the Hudson. Rogers Island, opposite Catskill; Mill Creek, north of Stuyvesant; Esopus Estuary, near Saugerties; Ramshorn Creek, south of Catskill; and Stockport Creek, north of Hudson, are freshwater tidal swamps.

Because of their moist black soils, tidal swamps are very rich in plant life. Trees and woody shrubs, which sit atop peaty hammocks on elevated root bases, are the dominant plants. Between the hammocks are pools of water. Red maple, red and black ash, willows, white cedar, button bush, spicebush, smooth alder, dogwood, many varieties of ferns, jewelweed, Virginia creeper, common monkey flower, and skunk cabbage are some of the more typical plants. Such bryophytes as mosses and liverworts are also fairly common. The tidal swamp is also home to ruffed grouse, woodpeckers, pheasants, songbirds, rabbit, squirrels, chipmunks, woodchucks, muskrat, beaver, deer, foxes, raccoon, weasels, moles, shrews, mink, turtles, snakes, salamanders, frogs, and toads. Killifish (banded and mummichog) and bass swim in the streams that penetrate tidal swamps, and great blue herons build nests in trees in tidal swamp areas. Because of their dense vegetation, mud, and inaccessibility, tidal swamps tend to see the least amount of human disturbance.

ISLANDS

A number of islands in the river range in size from tiny rock surfaces barely above the river level at high tide to 282-acre Constitution Island. Rocky islands, mostly located between Peekskill and Saugerties, have foundations of solid bedrock, which vary in composition depending on location. Despite the fact that they are islands, however, water is frequently in short supply. Soils tend to be thin, nutrient-poor, or nonexistent in places. In many ways they resemble the habitats of bare summits and ridges. Their isolation makes them attractive habitats for such rare species as map turtles; a number of bird species use them for nesting and roosting; and harbor seals use them to leave the water. Many of them, such as Constitution, Cruger, Iona, Oscawana, and Georges Islands, have been connected to the mainland by causeways, railroad development, and landfill. Nonetheless, rocky islands tend to be fragile environments and may be deeply affected by any human use that involves trampling, disturbance of sensitive species, or littering.

Just south of Albany are floodplain "islands," including Papscannee, Campbell, Schodack, and Houghtaling, which have been connected to the mainland by landfill and rail lines. Their shorelines have been altered with bulkheads (concrete or rock walls) to prevent erosion and silting of the river's main channel. Marshes and swamps are often found in close proximity to these low-lying areas. The rich alluvial soils of these former islands are the best in the Hudson Region; they support young forests dominated by cottonwoods, elms, birches, oaks, willows, maples, and diverse animal life, but they have also seen a large amount of human disturbance. Some have been farmed for hundreds of years by Native Americans and European settlers.

Found north of Hudson and south of Castleton, dredge-spoil islands are not natural islands. Created from excess dredge spoils—sediments excavated from the river channel to ensure adequate depth for ships—they have a very sandy base. A good example is Stockport Middle Ground. Dense young forests of eastern cottonwood, black locust, black cherry, willows, sassafras, silver maples, elm, and poison ivy flourish in these human-created environments. Birds find them useful for nesting and roosting. Snapping turtles and aquatic mammals like muskrat may be seen on these islands too.

STREAMS, PONDS, LAKES, AND INTERIOR WETLANDS

Tributaries of the Hudson represent another distinct aquatic habitat. The lower reaches of many of these streams exhibit the same tidal characteristics that the main channel of the river does. Many streams have been dammed or diverted, which results in decreased water flow and may block the migration of spawning fish. Streams provide a source of moisture necessary to support a variety of life. Stream water may be rich in oxygen, especially when the current is swift and the stream tumbles over rocks. The current also removes wastes. Organic matter in the form of leaves and other debris falls into the stream, often accumulating in pools and providing a food source for various animals as well as a surface on which one-celled diatoms (tiny microscopic plants) and protozoans can colonize. Planaria (flatworms) can be found under stones on the edges of streams and ponds. Other stream inhabitants include freshwater snails, crayfish, aquatic insects like backswimmers and waterstriders, and fish. Certain species, called potamodromous, require the cold water and high oxygen content of streams to survive. Among these are such resident river fish as perch, catfish, shiners, sunfish, and bass, which utilize tributaries for spawning. Some anadromous fish, like alewives and blueback herring, whose eggs and young require swift-moving, well-oxygenated, sediment-free colder water for spawning, also utilize tributaries.

The aquatic water snake and the distinctive black-and-yellow-striped eastern garter snake prowl the banks of streams for amphibians, fish, and other prey. A number of species of turtles, including the brightly colored painted turtle, are common along streams. Muskrat, mink, and river otter can also be found along streams.

Ponds are more or less permanent bodies of water, seldom more than twelve to fifteen feet deep, and shallow enough to permit the growth of rooted vegetation on their bottoms. Ponds may form in floodplains or natural depressions, or they may be humanmade or the result of human disturbance. They are habitats for a variety of aquatic insects, crayfish, freshwater fish, salamanders, and larger frogs like green frogs and bullfrogs, whose tadpoles take up to two years to reach maturity. Beaver, turtles, water snakes, muskrat, mink, and river otter are also denizens of ponds. If left undisturbed, ponds will grow in terms of species richness, reach maturity, and then become old, filling with sediment and organic detritus (mostly dead leaves), and shrinking from encroaching plants, eventually changing into wetlands.

Lakes and reservoirs are generally bigger and deeper than ponds. Due to the lack of light, their bottoms are free of vegetation. Because of their size, lakes tend to last much longer than ponds and, where conditions are favorable, they tend to support more fish species.

Interior wetlands are usually the product of pond succession, but humanmade excavations—roads and railroads and other developments that block drainage—can also create wetlands. Unlike their tidal counterparts, interior wetlands are relatively short-lived phenomena. As these areas fill with more sediment and organic matter, they eventually become swamps. Like their tidal counterparts, inland swamps are primarily characterized by a variety of trees and shrubs that thrive in moist conditions, some supported by elevated root pedestals. The diversity of trees is greatest in this type of environment. Red maple is especially common; sycamore, black tupelo, pin oak, American elm, hickories, red mulberry, ashes, and yellow birch also occur. Common shrubs include spicebush, buttonbush, maleberry, arrowwood, American hazelnut, swamp azalea, and elderberry.

Small depressions in which water temporarily gathers may support sphagnum moss, duckweed, and mats of filamentous algae floating on the surface. The absence of fish makes these pools attractive breeding grounds for a variety of amphibians and aquatic insects. Predators, including ducks, herons, raccoon, fishing spiders, turtles, and water snakes, visit these pools to feed on the tadpoles and insect larvae.

FORESTS

Forests are the dominant natural terrestrial communities in the Hudson region. Because of the relatively moist climate and well-developed soils, natural nonforest communities tend to be displaced by forests in time. Though not rain forests, forests of the region are often dense and lush, supporting a wide variety of plant and animal species. Forest areas range in size from tiny stands of a few acres or less, surrounded by human development, to large forested tracts such as in the Catskills and Harriman State Park. The number of species (biodiversity) is greater in the larger tracts.

In the Hudson region a mature forest is dominated by large, wide-circumference trees. In a mature forest, different layers of forest are discernible. The crowns of the tallest trees form the canopy. During summer, when trees have their full complement of leaves, the canopy of a mature forest captures up to 99 percent of the sunlight, leaving the rest of the forest dark and shaded.

Trees are habitats for squirrels and birds. Birds' nests in the canopy are often placed away from the trunk, on branches that are too thin to support the weight of potential predators. Birds like woodpeckers, purple martins, and eastern bluebirds utilize cavities in trees. The black rat snake, sometimes more than six feet long, is the largest snake in the region. An excellent tree climber, it can crawl right up the side of thick tree trunks. It feeds on rodents, chipmunks, squirrels, and birds, killing them by coiling its body around the victim and suffocating it.

In many cases there is an understory of smaller or immature trees. Below that is the shrub layer, and beneath that a layer of ferns and wildflowers. Atop the soil itself is a litter of decomposing leaves, wood, and occasionally animal carcasses. The litter provides habitat for bacteria, fungi, land snails, and slugs. (Slugs are shell-less gastropods.) It is also home to numerous arachnids, such as spiders (no spider species in the region is harmful to humans), mites, daddy longlegs, millipedes, and centipedes. Isopods (also called pill bugs, they are a form of land crustacean), beetles, ants, termites, and other insects, and earthworms are other inhabitants of the forest floor. Bacteria and fungi consume up to 90 percent of the decaying matter on the forest floor. In turn they provide food for insects, roundworms, and protozoans. Slimy salamanders and red-backed salamanders live in damp areas under rocks or logs or in leaf litter. Lungless, they breathe entirely through their skin and throat and must keep their body moist or suffocate. Diminutive northern ring-necked snakes and brown (DeKay's) snakes hide under rocks and logs. The colorful box turtle is the region's only entirely terrestrial turtle. Nocturnal mammals, primarily mice and voles, prowl the forest floor at night. They are preyed on by owls, who use their excellent vision to swoop down on them silently.

Though wild turkeys can fly, they prefer the forest floor, building nests on the ground and using different strategies to protect their nests and young, sometimes acting as decoys to ward off predators. During the day wild turkeys forage on the ground for seeds, nuts, acorns, and insects, roosting in trees at night. Woodcock, ruffed grouse, and many species of warblers are among the other varieties of birds that nest on the ground.

Deer are the most common large mammals in Hudson region forests. Weasels, foxes, and coyotes are forest predators, which feed primarily on small mammals. In the Catskills and more remote areas, bobcats and bears are occasionally seen. It appears that bears are returning to areas formerly vacated due to loss of habitat; young males are regularly seen wandering in populated areas.

Much of the forest in the region is young: second-, third-, or fourth-generation growth. Young forests have a higher diversity of trees of varying heights, their trunks usually averaging less than a foot in diameter. There are thick layers of shrubs and herbaceous plants, because sunlight is more plentiful, and the litter layer tends to be thinner than it is in mature forests.

In the Hudson region, which is part of the Atlantic Coastal Plain, northern-ranging species from southern forests inhabit the southern parts of the region as well as warmer lowlands, which have longer growing seasons. In this type of mixed deciduous forest—the most prevalent in the eastern United States—oaks and hickories are dominant. Oaks recover quickly from cutting and fire damage, sprouting from stumps and even burned logs; and oak seedlings can get along with little sunlight. Oaks and hickories are nut producing, moreover, and by burying and sometimes forgetting about the acorns and nuts, squirrels play a primary role as dispersal agents of these trees. For all these reasons, young forests tend to be mainly oak and hickory.

Chestnut trees were once among the dominant canopy trees in oak-hickory forests. However, in 1906 a chestnut blight invasion practically wiped out the entire population. Some roots survived, and these still send up shoots that eventually succumb to the blight before reaching maturity. Other trees of the mixed deciduous forest include maples, black birch, and ash. Chestnut and flowering dogwood are primary understory trees, and maple-leaf viburnum is the primary shrub. Laurels and blueberries may also be present. Generally the farther south you go, the more southern species—sassafras, tupelo—you are likely to encounter. Sugar maples are very tolerant of shade but extremely vulnerable to fire. In many places where fire has been suppressed, they are replacing oaks and hickories.

Many of the region's forests are characterized by mixed coniferous and broad-leaved hardwoods. These are northernmost forests of mostly deciduous trees, and they have many species in common with boreal forests to the north and oak-hickory forests to the south. They support Appalachian tulip trees, Canadian hemlocks, white pine, and such northern hardwoods as maples, American beech, and yellow birch. Striped maple is a typical understory tree. The more acidic soils of the Hudson Highlands also harbor huge stands of mountain laurel and wild azaleas. Coniferous/hardwood forests have the most prolific wildflowers. Hemlocks thrive on cooler north-facing slopes, by large bodies of water such as the Hudson, and in sheltered ravines. Their dark shade and extensive root systems make it difficult for other types of trees to establish themselves nearby. Hemlock seedlings can tolerate deep shade, however; they grow very slowly and have been known to survive for hundreds of years. Great horned owls and American crows nest in these areas.

RIDGES, SUMMITS, AND TALUS SLOPES

Rocky ridges and summits in the Palisades and Hudson Highlands, from hundreds to more than a thousand feet in elevation, are generally inhospitable to plants due to the colder temperatures, shorter growing seasons, strong winds, and nutrient-poor or nonexistent soil. There may be rain frequently, but the bare rock and steep slopes causes most of it to run off. Direct exposure to sun in these treeless areas causes most of the remaining moisture to evaporate. These are the region's driest areas, and those most susceptible to forest fires—another factor preventing trees from growing to maturity. Evidence of recent fires is widespread in the Hudson Highlands.

Lichens are usually the first plants to colonize bare rock. In time lichens tend to soften the rock with their acid secretions, and mosses can then establish themselves. Plants in high, rocky, exposed areas tend to be small. In rocky places rootholds are often scarce and plants have expansive root systems to suck nutrients from the nutrient-poor soils. Shrubs like scrub oak, chokecherry, prickly ash, and prickly pear cactus can be seen. Small shrublike trees, such as red cedar, American hackberry, and pitch pine, grow through the cracks. Pitch pine, distinguished by their often stunted, gnarled trunks, depend on forest fires for reproduction. They have tough, fire-resistant bark and specially adapted cones that open only when exposed to heat from fire. Fire removes competition from other seedlings, allowing pitch pine seedlings to establish themselves and grow. Some are among the region's oldest trees. Exposed rocky areas are often frequented by reptiles like snakes and the colorful five-lined skink (a lizard). Being cold-blooded, they cannot produce sufficient body heat to maintain a high enough body temperature, so they often sun themselves on rocks to gain warmth.

At the base of cliffs like the Palisades, and in the Hudson Highlands, there are often talus slopes: piles of boulders, some of them giants, either eroded from the cliffs above or blasted in quarry operations. These rocky environments with little or no soil base are habitats for plants like red elderberry, purple-flowering raspberry, Virginia creeper, poison ivy, dogwoods, Allegheny vine, and witch hazels. Skinks and millipedes can be found there. Foxes, raccoon, and various snakes, including the region's two venomous species, copperheads and timber rattlers, use these areas for shelter, hibernation, or nesting.

OPENINGS IN THE FOREST

Around large bodies of water, such as ponds, lakes, and rivers like the Hudson, there are openings with plentiful sunlight and abundant moisture, ideal growing conditions for a wide variety of plants. Chances are that these areas have seen a fair share of human disturbance and are therefore likely habitats for exotic plants. Red maples, sycamores, hackberries, black locusts, and box elders are typical of such environments. Sun-loving weeds and vines such as Japanese honeysuckle, bitter nightshade, poison ivy, Canada mooseseed, Virginia creeper, Asiatic bittersweet, and thorny brambles (blackberry, prickly dewberry, raspberry, greenbrier) also thrive in these conditions.

Other types of openings are always the result of a disturbance. Some of these disturbances are natural: Forest fires, floods, catastrophic storms, wind, insects, and disease can all create openings in the forest, a heavy wet snowfall or ice storm can break branches and even topple trees, creating openings in the canopy. Other openings, the result of human activity, may be tiny or larger, up to an acre. The presence of sunlight provides an excellent growth opportunity for subcanopy species. It also provides an opportunity for colonizing species to gain a foothold in the forest. Seeds of colonizing plants have to be widely dispersed. They may sit dormant in the soil for years waiting for conditions suitable for germination. Thus, colonizing species have to be fast growing and fast reproducing.

Larger openings, called old fields, may be the result of natural causes such as fire, but most are the result of human disturbance. Most old fields were lands formerly cleared for cultivation or timber, or for pasture, or even for aesthetic reasons, as in the case of old estates. No longer in use, they are returning to a "wild" state. Through a process called succession, cleared areas, if left alone, slowly over a period of decades gradually return to forest.

Many of the first plants to populate old fields are broad-leaved herbs, such as ragweeds, asters, and goldenrods, as well as grasses. Exotic species tend to thrive in these conditions. Many of the herbs are annuals, which complete their entire life cycle in a single season, sprouting in the spring, growing to maturity, flowering by late summer, and dropping seeds in the fall. Annuals can tolerate conditions of strong direct sunlight. However, they do not compete well with biennials and perennials, plants whose life cycles are longer. Grasses and herbs are followed by vines and brambles like Virginia creeper, wild grapes, bittersweet, greenbrier, and poison ivy. Some vines, like cow vetch and bindweed, utilize the stalks of taller upright plants. Lacking their own strong supporting trunks, vines need fewer nutrients and mineral resources, and most of their energy is devoted to leaf production and rapid growth. Vines and brambles are succeeded by shrubs like hybrid honeysuckle, multiflora rose, shadbush, sumacs (relatives of poison ivy), northern bayberry, and members of the heath family: blueberries and huckleberries.

The shrubs are followed by small, fast-growing, sun-loving "pioneer" trees like aspen, black cherry, red cedar, black locust, ash, and gray birch. Red cedars depend on birds, which eat their seeds and defecate them, thus dispersing them. Other pioneer trees depend on wind for seed dispersal. As the trees grow larger and produce more shade, only shade-tolerant seedlings of oaks, birches, and maples survive. These eventually replace the species that require sun to reproduce. The old field may be characterized by patches of trees and shrubs interrupted by fields of grass. Eventually it may be transformed into a young forest and, later, a mature forest. The process of succession rarely follows a precise course: All sorts of new disturbances, both natural and humanmade, can change the pattern.

It is in the early stages of succession that species diversity is greatest, and many of the herbs and shrubs are excellent food sources for deer and other animals. Insects are attracted to the beautiful flowers that decorate old fields. Transition areas between forests and old fields include species from both habitats, and thus may support a greater diversity of species than either one. Such snakes as milk snakes and black racers as well as box turtles, deer, foxes, woodchucks, and rabbits are especially prevalent in these areas.

In addition to old fields, there are areas lacking topsoil, recently stripped of vegetation, or subjected to continual stress from human development. Sun-loving herbs thrive in these conditions: Those that are highly successful but undesirable are called weeds. These areas may be very transient and subject to rapid changes, and so plant colonizers invest more in reproduction, producing large numbers of colorful flowers to attract insect pollinators. They also provide food for woodchucks, rabbits, rodents, and deer. Weeds serve a useful purpose, increasing the organic content and the stability of the soil, making it more suitable for later inhabitants. Roadway and power-line corridors are usually characterized by thick growth of low-spreading shrubs maintained through cutting and the use of herbicides.

THE SKY ABOVE

A number of animal species use flight as a means of locomotion and for food searches. These include numerous insects, birds, and bats (primarily nocturnal, bats comb the night sky for insects). Some of the most impressive bird displays occur during migrations, when birds often flock, which helps them avoid individual predation. Flocking also provides young birds with guidance to preferred habitats, food sources, and nesting sites. The region has a number of raptors (birds of prey). Many, including owls, hawks, falcons, eagles, and vultures, are large and conspicuous. Raptors are primarily carnivores and have sharp beaks and talons for seizing prey and tearing flesh.

Hawks circle high in the air, using their keen eyesight to spot prey (mice, rabbits, and snakes). Like other raptors with large wings, turkey vultures depend primarily on soaring as a means of long-distance travel. Launching themselves from cliffs in the Palisades and the Hudson Highlands, they can literally ride the air currents for hours, seldom flapping their wings, circling and hunting for food. These scavengers, equipped with nature's keenest sense of smell, can sense a carcass miles away.

ENDANGERED AND THREATENED SPECIES

The Hudson region is home to a number of threatened and endangered species of animals and plants, many of them protected by such laws as the 1973 Federal Endangered Species Act. Endangered species are those faced with imminent extinction; threatened species require special protection or they will become endangered. Preservation of habitats in which endangered or threatened species of animals and plants live is crucial to their protection. The New York Heritage Program was established with funding provided by the Nature Conservancy and the New York State Department of Environmental Conservation to inventory threatened and endangered species and their significant habitats.

The bald eagle, a former endangered species, is well known, and has a very distinctive and familiar appearance (though in fact few residents have ever seen one locally). The Hudson is one of only four New York State overwintering sites for bald eagles, which in winter depend on large bodies of unfrozen water, like the Hudson, as food sources. Bald eagles have only recently begun nesting near Stockport Flats, the first time they have done so in the region in many decades. Bald eagles feed primarily on dead fish, though other forms of carrion, as well as live fish and water birds, are also found in their diets. Eagles are very sensitive to pollutants such as pesticides and PCBs, which accumulate in the fat of fish they eat. Eagles were once very common along the Hudson, and only recently have their numbers increased due to protection.

The peregrine falcon is a federally recognized endangered species. Known as the world's fastest bird, it can dive at more than 150 miles per hour. It feeds almost exclusively on birds, which it strikes from the air. The peregrine is favored for the sport of falconry. Like other raptors, peregrine falcons were profoundly effected by the use of pesticides, and their numbers severely declined. Restrictions on the use of pesticides and a successful program to reintroduce them have resulted in their return to the area. Ironically, however, peregrines have, in most cases, chosen urban environments, such as Manhattan, and tall buildings and bridges as nesting sites.

The shortnose sturgeon is a federally recognized endangered species; its largest concentration is in the Hudson River. Unlike the Atlantic sturgeon, it spends most of its life in the estuary. Shortnose sturgeon range up and down the river according to the season, overwintering in the lower portion of the estuary in deeper water. At the beginning of spring they congregate at Esopus Meadows, then migrate to the spawning area just north of Coxsackie. Shortnose sturgeon appear to be very sensitive to pollution, particularly PCBs when they occur in sediments where the fish feed.

The timber rattlesnake—one of only two poisonous snakes native to the region—is a state-recognized threatened species. Timber rattlesnakes have an unfortunate reputation for being dangerous, and many have been hunted and killed; loss of habitat is another major reason for their decline. They are actually nonaggressive and generally pose little threat to human beings: they are predators of rodents and other small mammals.

The osprey, or fish hawk, is another state-recognized threatened species. It feeds exclusively on live fish and hovers over the water, plunging talons-first into the water to seize the fish at or near the surface. It, too, was once more common here, nesting along the river. Destruction of habitats and use of pesticides caused a serious decline in the numbers of ospreys, which only recently have begun to turn around. Today they utilize the Hudson primarily as a feeding ground, preferring to hunt from islands and at the mouths of streams. Efforts have been made to encourage ospreys to nest here once again.

The marsh hawk is another state-recognized threatened species, and the diamondback terrapin is a state-recognized species of special concern, while the bog turtle and Indian bat are other federally recognized endangered species.

Heartleaf plantain, golden club, and estuary beggar-tick are state-recognized threatened species of plants. The area is home to a number of other rare species of plants as well.

The Historical Landscape

PART ONE

Native Land

For thousands of years before the arrival of the first European explorers, the Hudson region was home to native people. The temperate climate, presence of plentiful game, edible plants, and a great river—useful as a source of fish and oysters and for transport and trade—made this an attractive area for the region's oldest settlers. Unlike their counterparts in other regions of the Americas, the indigenous people of the Hudson region did not build monuments or permanent dwellings. Except for some shell middens (refuse piles) and stone formations, possibly of native origin, the legacy of those thousands of years of human habitation has largely been erased. The intense agricultural, industrial, urban, and suburban development of the past 350 years has destroyed most remnants of prehistoric native cultures. Despite this, a number of sites have been excavated using scientific methods and much has been learned.

Archaeologists have divided the span of pre-European native habitation into three basic periods: the Paleo-Indian stage, the Archaic stage, and the Woodland stage. At many sites the artifacts of different stages and cultures are present, attesting to the use of such localities over long periods of time and by a number of peoples.

PALEO-INDIAN STAGE

The native peoples of the Hudson Region were descendants of emigrants from Asia who crossed the Bering Strait on a temporary land bridge more than twenty thousand years ago. Arriving in the Hudson Valley probably as the Wisconsin Ice Sheet retreated, between fifteen

thousand and twelve thousand years ago, these were small bands of no-
mads in pursuit of large migratory game—primarily caribou and mammoths and mastodons—which inhabited the open tundra that then
characterized the area's postglacial topography.

The region's oldest carbon-dated evidence of these Paleo-Indian
hunters is from a rock shelter near Goshen, in Orange County. There archaeologists uncovered caribou bones that had been broken for their
marrow, and a single fluted spearpoint, estimated to be twelve thousand
years old. Paleo-Indians used fluted spearheads known as Clovis points,
similar to ones used throughout North America at the time. Evidence
elsewhere indicates that they already had the use of fire and could fashion clothing made of skins to protect themselves from the harsh, cold climate. They probably lived in simple shelters made from willow branches
draped with animal skins and moss. Very small in number, they ranged
widely, following main river systems such as the Hudson.

On what was once a bare hill near the present-day village of Athens,
just two miles west of the Hudson, Paleo-Indian hunters found an excellent vantage point for observing migratory game as well as a source of
high-grade flint they quarried to make spearpoints. This and a neighboring site have yielded nearly two thousand artifacts, making it one of
the largest and most significant Paleo-Indian sites in eastern North America. While most of the artifacts were of local origin, a few showed that at
least some of the hunters had traveled from Pennsylvania, western New
York State, and Ohio. This site is marvelously re-created in a realistic
diorama in the New York State Museum in Albany, showing some members of a Paleo-Indian family manufacturing flint spearpoints, while others butcher a caribou carcass for a multitude of uses. By 8000 B.C.E.,
Paleo-Indians had vacated the area, probably because of climatic changes
and the departure or extinction of their principal food sources.

ARCHAIC STAGE

This stage lasted from 6500 to 1300 B.C.E. People of the Archaic
stage were less nomadic than their Paleo-Indian ancestors. By now deciduous forests had replaced the postglacial tundra and boreal forests of
Paleo-Indian times, and the climate and conditions were probably similar to those of the present. Archaic people had not yet developed the use
of pottery or agriculture; they were primarily forest dwellers who also
made greater use of a wide variety of resources. They used tools of copper and bone, ground and polished stones, and felled trees, shaping the
wood into useful objects such as dugout canoes, which they used for
hunting, fishing, communication, and trade. Their primary weapon was
the *atlatl*, a two-foot-long flat piece of wood used as a spear thrower. Dogs

were used to assist them in the hunt, but its likely they consumed them as well. Acorns, which they pounded into a coarse flour, made up a significant part of their diet.

Dwellings were constructed primarily of bark. During the warmer months, Archaic people settled along the Hudson and larger tributaries to fish, hunt waterfowl, and gather shellfish, which also made up a large part of their diet. The onset of winter led to a general dispersal of the population into smaller bands in the back country. There they lived in temporary camps, such as rock shelters, and hunted for bigger game, such as deer and bear.

WOODLAND STAGE

The period from 1300 B.C.E. until the arrival of the first Europeans is referred to as the Woodland stage. During the beginning of this stage, stone pots were introduced into the Northeast, later to be replaced by ceramic ones. As time passed, styles of pottery and decoration became more ornate and varied. Other technological developments during this period include the use of the bow and arrow for hunting. Later in this stage, agriculture was developed and the natives settled in more stable communities located near crop fields.

NATIVE LIFE AT THE TIME OF THE
FIRST EUROPEAN EXPLORERS

What we know about Native Americans during this period is largely the product of observations by the European explorers and colonists, and some by the indigenous people themselves. In the area along the Hudson, the people were Algonquin, part of the widely distributed Algonquian linguistic family. Within the Hudson region, the Algonquin formed three loose confederacies: the Mahican, or Mohican, who occupied both sides of the river south of Albany and were called the River People by the Dutch; the Lenape, or Delaware, on the western shore from present-day Catskill into New Jersey and south and west into Pennsylvania and Maryland; and the Wappinger, who inhabited the east side of the river from the mid-Hudson area south to Westchester. The boundaries of each confederacy were fluid and constantly shifted.

The same is true of the numerous tribes that lived within each confederation, such as the Esopus, who lived in the area along the west side of the Hudson south of Mahican territory, near present-day Kingston, and the Wiechquaesgecks who inhabited Manhattan, the Bronx, and southern Westchester. Tribes were not well-defined units. They consisted of many independent clans, based on matrilineal descent. Tribes were led by sachems, who were responsible for promoting the welfare of their members and maintaining friendly relationships and alliances with other tribes. Though the tribes and confederacies of the Hudson region frequently interacted with one another, for the most part they were independent. Sometimes, however, the sachems would convene a general council and make collective decisions; sometimes, too, they joined in cooperative alliances.

West of the Hudson region, in the valley of the Mohawk River and in central and western New York State, lived the Five Nations of the Iroquois. The Mohawk, one of the five nations, occupied the Mohawk Valley and were known for their longhouses and their light bark canoes, which they could effectively portage, thus enhancing their mobility. While the Mohawk did not inhabit the area along the Hudson at the time of the first European explorers, they often exerted a significant impact on the tribes that did, as well as on the Europeans with whom they traded.

According to historical accounts the native people camped mainly along the mouths of streams that emptied into the Hudson, or along bays or coves. There was an abundance of fish, shellfish, crabs, game, waterfowl, eggs, and plant food at these sites. The river's floodplains, as well as its tributaries, were cultivated for an assortment of corn, beans, squash, and tobacco. The land was cleared by burning it: Fire releases minerals in the soil, which act as fertilizers and decrease the acidity of the soil, thus creating rich farmland. The Native Americans also made wide use of the technology of fire to remove shrubbery and thin the forests, creating open, parklike conditions with widely spaced trees and forest floors that were favorable for herbs, grasses, and berries. It also made for easier hunting and trail building. Openings in the forest, created by fire, allowed sun-loving plants to thrive, which in turn provided food for deer and other game.

Native fields supported a mixture of various crops. Mixing crops helped preserve the fertility of the soil, reduced weed growth and maintenance, sustained the soil's moisture, and produced higher yields. Corn was harvested, dried, pounded, and mixed with water to make *sapaen,* a mush dish that accompanied most meals. While hunting, fishing, and gathering were important activities, agricultural produce comprised the bulk of their diet. Corn and beans were buried in caches in the ground or stored in their dwellings to provide food throughout the winter. Having a dependable food source like agriculture enabled the native population to grow.

Wigwams were a widely used housing structure. These were constructed from a frame of hickory poles set into the ground and bent over, tied together at their meeting place at the top, then covered with tree bark. A hole in the center of the roof allowed smoke from the fireplace to escape. Some of these communities were surrounded by palisades of upright sharpened timbers for defense. In the winter, villagers dispersed into smaller family units that traveled into the backcountry and hunted larger game by following their tracks in the snow.

Every few years depletion of local resources such as firewood, soil fertility, and game, plus an accumulation of garbage, caused the Native Americans to abandon village sites and move to new locales. Wigwams were built so that they could be quickly dismantled, moved, and reassembled. Similarly, tools, weapons, and supplies had to be light and easily transportable. Moving allowed old village sites and fields to replenish themselves and permit future exploitation.

For the Native Americans along the river, the Hudson was a major corridor of trade. They used dugout canoes for hunting waterfowl, fishing, communication, travel, and trade. Trade was a big part of their lives. They traded for a wide assortment of goods and materials, including some objects like shells and precious stones that found their way there from across the continent.

In general, Native Americans practiced a subsistence lifestyle, producing only enough for immediate needs and to guarantee survival. Their transient lifestyle discouraged the accumulation of personal possessions. What they had they tended to share; gift giving was a crucial means of sustaining power relationships. In this class society, status was communicated through decorative clothing and ornamentation, and through wampum, long strings of purple and white shell beads, sewn together in belts.

Native men often left the village and went on extended hunting and fishing trips. The women, on the other hand, did the farming, an activity that could be performed simultaneously with child care. They gathered berries, acorns, and chestnuts and made clothing, tools, bowls, and other useful objects.

The Native Americans were very aware of their dependence on the land and nature for what they needed—an awareness that was reflected in their beliefs and spiritual practices. For them there was little separation between the activities of daily living and the rituals of the spirit. Fishing, farming, and hunting were, in part, spiritual enterprises. The size of the harvest or the bounty of the hunt was seen to be as much a reflection of their relationship to the higher powers as it was a measure of skill or effort. Like other agrarian societies, they took a special interest in the sun, the moon, and stars, and their worship focused on the change of seasons. Planting and harvesting were celebrated with music and dancing. The tribes also believed in the literal interpretation of dreams. Shamans had special knowledge of the spirit world, could heal the sick, and—using dreams and visions—foretell the future. Since they did not have a written language, their folklore and traditions were passed on through storytelling.

Those interested in archaeology and the history of Native Americans along the Hudson should visit the small but fascinating Trailside Museum at Bear Mountain, and the New York State Museum in Albany. Constitution Marsh Sanctuary has a native rock shelter on display. The American Museum of Natural History has a hall devoted to natives of the Eastern Woodlands. The Smithsonian Institution's National Museum of the American Indian, while not specific to Hudson region, has wonderful exhibits on the cultural heritage of Native Americans as a whole.

Early European Exploration and Dutch Rule

A CUL-DE-SAC

Following Columbus's discovery of the Americas, many viewed this new landmass as an unfortunate barrier blocking ships from trading with the Far East, the original goal of Columbus's voyage. Rather than sail around this huge obstacle, European explorers hoped to find a waterway, a Northwest Passage, which would serve as a shortcut to Asia. One such explorer was Henry Hudson, a renowned English navigator. Dedicated to finding the Northwest Passage, he had already led two expeditions to locate it when, in 1609, the Dutch East India Company hired him to lead a third expedition to discover the mysterious waterway. He left Amsterdam on April 6 of that year aboard the *Half Moon,* an eighty-ton, three-masted, sixty-three-foot-long ship, carrying an English and Dutch crew of twenty. Following a tip from his friend Capt. John Smith, Hudson sailed for the east coast of North America, believing the sought-after passageway might be located there.

Hudson explored the Atlantic coast from Nova Scotia south, finally dropping anchor at Staten Island on September 4. He wasn't the first European to get this far: Eighty-five years earlier the Florentine Giovanni da Verrazzano had sailed into the narrows that would later bear his name and explored New York Harbor, "the mouth of a very great river." A flotilla of curious Native Americans in canoes approached his ship, presumably to welcome him, but a sudden storm forced Verrazzano to vacate before he could make contact with them. A year later, in 1525, Esteban Gomez, a black Portuguese mariner, had reportedly reached New York Harbor. In addition French traders may have traveled down from Canada and visited the Hudson, and—who knows—maybe centuries earlier the Norse also visited here.

Almost all of Hudson's original diaries have been lost, and what is known of these events comes from Robert Juet, one of his officers, who kept a detailed record of the voyage. The *Half Moon* anchored off Staten Island for seven days and traded with the natives. On the fifth day, for unknown reasons, a small exploration party was attacked by a band of natives, and the leader of the crew was killed. On September 11 Hudson hoisted anchor, and the *Half Moon* proceeded north into what he thought might be the fabled Northwest Passage. Stopping at the north end of Manhattan, the ship was greeted by two canoes of armed warriors. Fearing another attack, the crew took two natives hostage. (Later the captives managed to escape.)

For the next few days the *Half Moon* sailed north. Hudson described the river as "clear blue and wonderful to taste" and the country as "pleasant with grass and flowers and goodly trees" and "very sweet smells."

On September 17, they arrived at present-day Castleton—here the river channel was narrow, shallow in places, and difficult to navigate. Presumably by this time Hudson had concluded that this was not the elusive Northwest Passage he sought. They continued north, however, stopping on the nineteenth just below the site of present-day Albany. Juet, in a small boat with a small crew, rowed another twenty or thirty miles north and returned. Meanwhile Mahican natives flocked to the ship in droves, bringing grapes, pumpkins, roasted venison, tobacco, and beaver and otter pelts, all in exchange for beads, knives, and hatchets. A few of their leaders were invited on board, where they first tasted European alcohol.

According to native accounts, some thought the *Half Moon* was a big canoe with white wings, and they were fascinated by the pale skin of the explorers. The Mahican, whom Juet described as "loving people," regarded Hudson and his crew as special guests, entitled to protection and assistance. Hudson's crew must have shared Juet's view, since security was lax and sometimes they ventured well beyond the safety of the ship.

On September 23 the *Half Moon* weighed anchor and headed back downriver. The next day, near Castleton again, it ran aground on a sandbar in the middle of the river but was rescued by the tide. The trip south was uneventful until they arrived at Stony Point, where two Native Americans sneaked on board. One was shot to death after he was caught ransacking Juet's cabin, and another drowned. The next day the crew was attacked by two canoes full of warriors avenging the earlier hostage taking on Hudson's upriver trip three weeks before. Arrows and volleys of musket balls and cannon were exchanged, and a number of Native Americans were killed. The *Half Moon* departed New York Harbor two days later.*

EARLY SETTLEMENT

At the time of the first European explorers, the Hudson region appeared quite different from how it does today. The land comprised mostly forests, but the Native Americans had cleared meadows by using controlled burning. Game was plentiful: wolves, mountain lions, elk, and bears roamed the land. Whales, porpoises, and seals inhabited New York Harbor and were found upriver as far as present-day Peekskill. The water in the streams was drinkable, the air was fresh and unpolluted, and the river itself was a great source of fish and oysters. To the early European explorers and settlers, the region appeared to be a vast wilderness of endless untapped resources. The Dutch claimed the land between the Delaware and the Connecticut Rivers. The Hudson was named the North River, and they referred to their territory as New Netherland.

A year after Hudson's voyage, Dutch merchants returned to trade with the natives for beaver pelts. Hats made from beaver fur were very fashionable in Europe, and they were in great demand. By 1614 the Dutch East India Company built Fort Nassau, on an island south of present-day Albany. The establishment of a fort permitted trade with the natives on a year-round basis and discouraged competition from other trading companies.

In the beginning various Dutch companies had competed for the fur trade. In 1615, however, the Dutch government, fearing that trading rivalry would drive up the price of furs and decrease profits, granted a fur-trade monopoly to the New Netherland Company, a subsidiary of the Dutch East India Company. Besides having a monopoly over the fur trade, the company had its own military, power to set up governments, and control of the economic life of the colony. In 1621, control of the fur trade was transferred to the newly formed Dutch West India Company, which, in 1624, established Fort Orange, where Albany now stands. (Fort Nassau had been abandoned because it was regularly damaged by floods.) The first settlers at Fort Orange were mostly Walloons, French-speaking Protestant farmers from Belgium, refugees forced to emigrate because of

---

*Short on supplies, they stopped in Dartmouth, England, on November 7, where Hudson was detained. The following spring, sailing under the English flag, Hudson set out on his fourth and final voyage to discover the Northwest Passage. In the frozen wastes of the huge bay now named after him, his crew mutinied and set him, his young son, and seven others adrift in a small boat. They were never seen again.

pressure from Roman Catholic Spain. These included women and children. The Mahican donated the land for the settlement, believing that establishment of a trading post would benefit both parties.

In 1625 the director general of New Netherland made Fort Amsterdam, another trading post located at the southern tip of Manhattan, the capital of the new province, changing its name to New Amsterdam. New Amsterdam quickly became a thriving port and the largest, most important town in the colony.

TRADE

Contact between the Dutch and the indigenous people of the Hudson region focused primarily on the fur trade. Beaver pelts were traded for wool cloth, tools, kitchenware, clothes, liquor, and weapons. Wampum was also desired by the Native Americans, and the Dutch soon began purchasing or extorting large quantities from Algonquin who lived along Long Island Sound. Cloth was particularly desirable because it did not require lengthy treatment before wearing, did not harbor fleas as furs did, and was a sign of direct contact with Europeans, which was a symbol of status. As these materials replaced leather and furs as the primary sources of clothing, the natives became more dependent on trade with the Dutch to supply them.

Trade with the Dutch obviously had a major impact on the Native Americans. Many were impressed with the new technologies they saw. Trading took up a greater portion of their lives, as they spent more time hunting furs and game for the Dutch and growing food for them. (It was the first time they had produced more than for their own needs, some native settlements even moving closer to the trading posts.)

The Native Americans were also exposed to the diseases of the Europeans as well as their liquor and other vices. They had little resistance to European diseases, whose impact was often devastating. Dutch fur traders were notorious abusers of alcohol, a practice many natives were also quick to adopt. (The sale of liquor and weapons to the natives was prohibited by law but rarely enforced, and punishments were usually light.) Native drunkenness became a common problem, leading fearful Europeans to characterize them as drunken savages. Nonetheless, the natives also respected the power of the Dutch authorities and their army.

The Dutch clearly viewed the Native Americans as heathens and inferior, but tried to maintain friendly relations to help facilitate trade. Because of the New Netherland fur trade, natives were not driven away as they were in some of the other colonies. Dutch courts tried to maintain the peace by dealing leniently with native violators of the law. Dutchmen slept with native women and fathered mixed-heritage children.

Despite the monopoly of the Dutch West India Company, a certain amount of fur smuggling went on, particularly with the English in New England, where better prices could be gotten. In just a few short years, the supply of furs in the Hudson Valley had been exhausted and the Dutch traded with natives who obtained their furs elsewhere. This engendered new rivalries between the tribes that populated the area along the river, and those like the Mohawk, who lived farther west. At the time of the *Half Moon*'s visit, these confederacies were at peace. When the Mohawk learned that the Mahican were trading with the Dutch, they requested and were granted permission to cross Mahican land so that they could trade with them as well. The presence of their former enemies was at first tolerated by the Mahican, who must have been protective of their special relationship with the Dutch. However, tensions grew, eventually leading to violence. Between 1625 and 1629 the Mahican and Mohawk fought a series of engagements in which the Mahican were eventually defeated and driven from the area around Fort Orange.

LAND PURCHASES

The Dutch pursued a policy of purchasing land from the native peoples. Though those of the Hudson region had no concept of land ownership per se, due to a decrease in the availability of furs, they were often eager to sell land in order to acquire desirable trade goods from the Dutch. Decimated by disease, the natives also had more difficulty sustaining their hunting, gathering, and farming lifestyle and became more dependent on selling land to obtain basic necessities. As more of the best land was sold, and European settlers moved in to farm it, the natives discovered that there was less land left to support their hunting and agriculture. This drove them to sell even more of their land and move away.

Before a patent, or grant, could be obtained from the director general, the Dutch West India Company compelled buyers of land to provide written assurance that Native American owners were satisfied with the arrangements made. Certainly there were cases in which natives were cheated by unscrupulous buyers, often by getting them drunk.

The natives, who did not have the same concepts of land ownership that Europeans had, at first did not grasp the true implications of land sales. In time it became apparent that land sold meant a permanent loss of rights to the land. In order to placate them the Dutch frequently offered hunting, fishing, and planting rights, but sometimes natives returned demanding further payments for lands they had already sold. Moreover, the Dutch were often unsure whom they could purchase land from, since many would claim ownership if they saw an opportunity to obtain trade goods.

PATROONSHIPS

As a navigable body of water, the Hudson provided an avenue of inland penetration few other colonies possessed. However, settlement of the new colony proceeded slowly. Harsh winters, the threat of "savages," wild beasts, and the hardships of life on the frontier deterred most Dutch, who did not wish to leave comfortable lives in the relatively prosperous Netherlands, and most who came did so for the fur trade. Most of the land between New Amsterdam and Fort Orange remained unsettled frontier. In 1629, in a misguided effort to encourage agricultural settlement, the Dutch West India Company drew up a charter, whereby any large shareholder could buy enormous tracts of land that would be free of taxes, customs, and other obligations for a period of ten years. The only requirement was that the purchaser, referred to as a patroon, should establish on his land a colony of at least fifty persons, called a patroonship.

A patroon had considerable powers. He could appoint local officers and magistrates, establish courts, and carry out punishments, including capital punishment. A patroon had the right to trade in anything except furs, which was retained by the company.

Several patroonships were established along the Hudson. The largest was Rensselaerwyck, located in the area around Fort Orange. It was the only one successful at attracting enough settlers to keep its charter. In terms of generating settlement, patroonships were a dismal failure. Patroons were aristocrats, proponents of Europe's strict social and economic class system. Tenants were bound by an almost feudal system of permanent leases, had to pay exorbitant rents as well as provide goods and services, and were treated harshly. It is easy to see that this was not an appealing arrangement. Both patroons and the Dutch West India Company discouraged settlers from buying land independently.

LATER SETTLEMENT

By the 1640s it had become apparent that the colony of New Netherland was not succeeding economically. Trade in beaver pelts and timber was not profitable enough to offset the huge costs of maintaining the colony. As a result, policies were loosened. The Dutch West India Company forfeited its monopoly on the fur trade, figuring it could generate greater profits through free enterprise, taxation, and regulation. A greater emphasis was placed on colonization, with the hope that someday the colony would be self-sufficient and even export food. Thus the purchase of land became easier and cheaper. Areas that were not under the control of the patroons were settled more quickly; these settlers were anxious to own their own land and did not wish to rent from the patroons.

In 1650 Catskill was founded, followed by Wiltwyck (Kingston) three years later. By 1664 the population of the colony was nearly ten thousand. The new settlers planted crops on land the Native Americans had already cleared, or they cleared new lands using the same slash-and-burn techniques to clear the forest.

Once the land was cleared, they grew potatoes, corn, barley, oats, wheat, rye, and flax. The settlers also planted fruit trees they had brought with them from Europe. Sheep and pigs were raised; cattle were a source of meat, dairy products, and labor. Using ox muscle, Dutch farmers could plow larger fields and produce more surpluses. Oxen pulled carts to transport produce to docks along the river, where it could be shipped to market.

Like the Native Americans, European farmers also hunted game, fished, and gathered shellfish and wild fruits from the forest. They also shot large predators like bears, mountain lions, and wolves that threatened humans and livestock. Most farms were self-sufficient, but the total agricultural output failed to meet the demands of the colony, which still depended on the old country and the natives to keep them supplied with food.

Sawmills and gristmills sprang up along the Hudson's tributary streams, or "kills," as the Dutch called them. Processing these raw materials became a central focus of commercial activity in the colony. Once fully settled, the Dutch constructed sturdy houses of stone with sloping, overhanging roofs and porches that extended over the entire side of the house. The Dutch homes had low ceilings to conserve heat and used very large timbers to support attic floors that were utilized for storage and as slave or servants' quarters. Split ("Dutch") doors kept farm animals and wildlife outside, kept toddlers inside, and allowed fresh air and sunshine inside when the weather was good.

In urban communities like Beverwyck (the community outside Fort Orange) and New Amsterdam, there were tall narrow wooden structures with high stoops and brick sides facing the streets. Roofs were gabled and steeply slanted to shed snow easily. The Dutch often used curved roof tiles, which they imported from Holland. Windows were tiny, since glass was also imported and large windows allowed too much heat to escape. Wealthier residents could afford to import fine furnishings and decorations from Europe. Travel back and forth to Holland took anywhere from six to twelve weeks, depending on the season and weather.

The population of New Netherland was from the beginning very diverse and included many nationalities. Anxious to populate the colony, the Dutch West India Company was not too particular about who came. The Dutch Reformed Church was the only officially recognized religion in New Netherland and the only one that could hold public ceremonies; however, other religions could be practiced in private. Most Dutch colonists were more concerned with the secular practice of business and trade, and the Dutch West India Company did little to promote religion.

Jews arrived in the colony in 1654. A large group, originally from Portugal, were bound for Holland from Brazil, captured by pirates, and freed by a French vessel whose captain nonetheless demanded payment. The Jews disembarked in New Amsterdam destitute. However, many became merchants, and prospered. To make up for the acute labor shortage, the Dutch West India Company imported African slaves from the Caribbean. Many businesses and Dutch settlers owned slaves, though rarely did anyone own more than a few. The costs of maintaining them were prohibitive, and so a policy of leasing slaves out to other owners developed, under which owners would often pay their slaves, thereby enabling some to purchase their freedom. Thus there existed in New Netherland a small population of free blacks who had almost the same rights as the white citizens. However, liberated blacks were often required to pay tribute and forced to live on the outskirts of New Amsterdam as an "early warning system" against raids by Native Americans.

Women in New Netherland had more rights than did women in the other colonies. Women could own land, run businesses, vote, and participate in government. However, most were housewives and performed traditional domestic duties as well as working in the fields alongside their husbands.

Favorite recreational pursuits of the colonists included such sports as bowling and ice skating, which was a national pastime in Holland. Gambling and drinking alcohol were other major pursuits. Nearly one-quarter of the buildings in New Amsterdam were taverns. Brewing beer was also a favorite hobby. Drunk driving (of carts and wagons) presented a serious hazard to pedestrians. Strict ordinances were issued against such offenses, as well as disorderly conduct and disturbing the peace. Curfews were established but rarely obeyed.

Roads along the Hudson were nonexistent in most places and very poor in others. Both passengers and cargo were transported up and down the river—the colony's main highway—in so-called Hudson River sloops, patterned after similar flat-bottomed canal craft used in Holland. A typical river sloop was sixty to a hundred feet long and twenty to twenty-five feet wide, and could carry a fifty- to two-hundred-ton load. The single mast was eighty to a hundred feet high, placed well forward, and rigged with a large mainsail, a small jib, and sometimes a topsail. Usually manned by a crew of ten, including a captain, a cabin boy, and a cook, sloops were often painted in bright colors. Sloops such as these were the primary means of transport on the Hudson River for the next 250 years.

DUTCH/NATIVE RELATIONS

Following a pattern that appears to have been set during Henry Hudson's voyage, relations between the Dutch and the Mahican who lived along the Upper Hudson remained strained but relatively peaceful. Meanwhile the Dutch did strive in their own self-serving way to placate their hosts and avoid conflicts that would increase their insecurity and disrupt the fur trade. Conflict was also destructive to the interests of the Native Americans, who relied on the fur trade and, therefore, good relations with the Dutch. The absence of major clashes in the area is notable.

In the area along the Lower Hudson, conflict was often the rule. There was deep resentment toward the Dutch because of incursions on native land and a tax on corn to pay for fortifications and a security force whose purpose was to protect Dutch settlers from them. There was a rising level of tension, in which minor provocations were met by severe reprisals. Violent conflicts led to massacres of both natives and Dutch settlers, seizures of hostages, burning of settlements, and the consolidation of Dutch inhabitants in fortified communities like New Amsterdam, Fort Orange, and Wiltwyck. Sachems from other tribes were frequently called in to help settle these conflicts.

AN EXPENDABLE COLONY

The years of Dutch rule along the Hudson were often characterized by strife and disunity. Conflicts with the natives added to the insecurity, hampered settlements, and drained the colony of needed military resources. The Dutch were unable to defend the borders of their colony and prevent incursions by the Swedes and English into New Netherland's mostly vacant territory. As a source of fur and timber, New Netherland was never as high a priority as some other Dutch colonies, which supplied valuable minerals and spices, and the Dutch government invested little in the colony's development and even less in its defense.

The colony's population remained small and most of its land unsettled and undeveloped. Bickering and squabbles between individuals, the Dutch West India Company, and the Dutch government contributed to the atmosphere of suspicion, competition, dissatisfaction, and narrow self-interest that prevailed.

Those interested in the period of early exploration and Dutch rule should visit the New York State Museum, the Albany Urban Cultural Park Visitors Center, and Fort Crailo. The Bronck House near Coxsackie and Philipsburg Manor near Tarrytown provide vivid portraits of Dutch settlements in the seventeenth and eighteenth centuries.

A British Colony

THE DUTCH COLONY FALLS AND THE
HUDSON RIVER GETS ITS NAME

Dutch claims to New Netherland were never accepted by the English, who also claimed the land based on earlier sixteenth-century expeditions of the explorer John Cabot. Capturing New Netherland would remove the barrier between New England and the southern English colonies. It would also provide a base against their rivals, the French in Canada. On March 22, 1664, King Charles II of England granted his brother, James, duke of York, title to all of the mainland between the Connecticut and Delaware Rivers, with authority to expel anyone who resided there. In late summer of that year, heavily armed British vessels sailed into the harbor at New Amsterdam and demanded that the Dutch surrender the colony. They also promised easy terms and relief from the exorbitant taxes of the Dutch West India Company. Without a shot being fired, the colony capitulated.

Under British rule the name of the colony was changed to New York. The Hudson River acquired its modern name, as did Albany, New York City, and Kingston. British authorities did not interfere much in the economic and political structure the Dutch had created. For most, life went on as it had before. Some Dutch citizens continued to hold positions of power under British authority.

NATIVE AMERICANS AND DUTCH UNDER BRITISH RULE

Under the English, European settlement continued to spread, and more native land was lost for hunting and planting, forcing many to migrate from the area. Throughout the seventeenth century, the native population of the Hudson region declined. Warfare, alcoholism, and European-introduced diseases like smallpox led to the destruction of native cultures. By the beginning of the eighteenth century, few Native Americans were left in the Hudson Valley. Along with escaped slaves and other outsiders, surviving natives retreated to the hills, where they managed to eke out an existence beyond the margins of society.

Using arms obtained from the English, the Mohawk continued to exercise their dominance over other neighboring tribes. The English sought to extend their influence into western New York, the Great Lakes, and the Ohio Valley. As their rivalry with the French grew more intense, they actively pursued an alliance with the Mohawk and other Iroquois tribes. The Mohawk, while more than willing to accept British gifts and support, particularly in the form of guns, preferred to remain neutral and trade with both sides.

Dutch settlers generally accepted British rule, though tensions between them and English military garrisons sometimes led to violence. Dutch merchants became jealous of their English rivals, who could employ their connections with the English government to gain an advantage when conducting business, as well as their own brethren who ingratiated themselves to the English to attain status and privileges.

The Dutch population grew and continued to constitute a major part of the colony's residents. In many places Dutch language and culture were overwhelmed by English. However, in other places, particularly in the Albany area, they remained intact, and Dutch language, culture, religion, and architectural styles prevailed, even into the nineteenth century.

BREADBASKET

Due to a change in fashion and the rapid depletion of fur-bearing animals, the fur trade along the Hudson declined in the latter part of the seventeenth century. The area's economy gradually shifted to the cutting and shipping of timber and the production and exportation of grain and livestock primarily to the British West Indies, which needed such products to feed and supply their sugar plantations. The Hudson Valley became one of the leading grain-producing regions in the American colonies. Mills were constructed along the Hudson's tributaries to harness waterpower for cutting wood and processing grain into flour. Farmers along the river were well situated for shipping their produce to market, and sloops loaded with grain, flour, and other goods were numerous. In 1698 the British rulers William and Mary granted Frederick Philipse permission to build a bridge across the Spuyten Duyvil Creek, a tributary of the Hudson at the north end of Manhattan. This became known as Kingsbridge, and the road that crossed it was referred to as the King's Highway. Eventually it extended from New York City up the east side of the Hudson to just opposite Albany. The journey by stage from New York to Albany would take two to three days in good conditions, longer when it was rainy or wet. Later other roads were built, which helped augment the river traffic, especially in winter when the river was choked with ice.

MANOR LORDS

To the English, land ownership defined status. They expanded the feudal patroonship system that was in practice in many parts of the Hudson region, granting additional land patents in exchange for political favors and/or rent. With conditions in England at the time far worse than they were in Holland, many desperately poor individuals, lured by the hope of someday owning a piece of land, willingly accepted the arrangements of the tenant–manor lord system. The manor lords of the Hudson region included the Dutch Rensselaers, whose manor, Rensselaerwyck, continued to expand and prosper under English rule. Other manor lord families included the Livingstons, the Philipses, and the Van Cortlandts.

The manor lords wielded great political and economic power in the region. Copying the lifestyle and refinement of English nobility, they lived on large country estates in elaborate brick mansions built in the Georgian style and lavishly decorated with imported furniture and works of art. It took incredible amounts of wood to heat these mansions, with their large rooms, wide hallways, high ceilings, and big windows and doors, but wood was plentiful in the Hudson region. Besides, manor lords could afford such extravagances. They sent their sons to be educated in the finest schools in Europe. They also had servants and could usually afford a number of slaves. They managed to acquire most of the best farmland in the region: Farmers seeking to own land in the Hudson region found that little was available. Tenant farmers, meanwhile, had virtually no political rights, paid exorbitant rent, and were often forced to live in impoverished conditions.

A DIVERSE POPULATION

The English colony of New York contained a very diverse population. The Dutch continued to constitute a large segment. Farmers from New England, having exhausted the thin, rocky soils of that region, migrated to the Hudson Valley in search of new, richer cropland, many becoming tenant farmers on the large estates. Other immigrants included English, Scots, Irish, French Huguenots, and Germans. Many came as indentured servants, required to work a number of years as servants or laborers for whoever financed their passage. The Anglican Church was the official religion of the colony and the only one that received public financial support. However, a number of other religions were openly practiced, and religious tolerance was usually the norm. It seemed that religion played a smaller role than it did in some of the other English colonies, such as Massachusetts.

THE FRENCH AND INDIAN WARS

In 1689 the struggle between the French and the English for worldwide dominance broke out into full-scale war. A series of wars ensued, interrupted by extended periods of peace, with the most severe fighting taking place between 1755 and 1759. Both nations had large colonies in North America, and the native land that bordered these colonies, primarily the area south of New France (Quebec) and north of Albany, became a major focus in this conflict. During this seventy-year period, the threat of raids by the French and their native allies was a great deterrent to settlement of this thinly populated region.

The native tribes tried to maintain their neutrality and often played one side against the other, trying to secure more favorable trade arrangements. They provided a buffer between French and English frontier settlements. The Iroquois, particularly the Mohawk, generally sided with the English, who in turn supplied them with weapons. Whether neutral or allied with one side or the other, Native Americans were frequently targets of much violence.

By 1759 Quebec, the capital of New France, had fallen to the British. Many men of the Hudson region had served in the war as officers and troops. A number of merchants had profited from outfitting and supplying the British army or from smuggling goods. Others suffered from the inflation resulting from the war effort, and many resented having to billet British troops.

CLEARING THE LAND

Following the conclusion of the conflict and the end of the threat from the French and their native allies, the population of the region rapidly expanded. Many soldiers who had fought in the war decided to remain. Immigrants from Europe also arrived in large numbers. As new settlers moved into the region, previously forested land was cleared for farmland. Since many colonial farmers grazed livestock, which used more land than did other agricultural activities, more forest needed to be cleared. Clearing forest with an ax was one method that required tremendous effort. Many colonists practiced girdling—cutting a swath of bark around the trunk to prevent moisture from reaching the branches and leaves. This eventually kills the tree, and after a few years a forest of girdled trees becomes a field. Girdling was the most time-consuming way of clearing a forest, but it required the least amount of manpower, which was in short supply in the colony. Also, the rotting tree trunks were a source of nutrients for the field.

As population and economic activity expanded, more timber was needed for building new homes, buildings, and ships. The tall white pines of the region were favored for making ships' masts. Colonial fireplaces burned very inefficiently and needed huge quantities of wood for cooking and to keep homes warm. Tending to view the resources of the continent as unlimited, colonists were as a result very wasteful in their use. As the region's farms grew more prosperous, the settlers built larger clapboard homes. Besides using more timber in their construction, these also required more wood to heat. The use of brick for construction similarly meant the consumption of large amounts of wood to fire the bricks. By the beginning of the American Revolution, the once vast, endless forests of the Hudson region were rapidly disappearing.

Pioneers in the Hudson region who were dependent on nature for their survival and livelihood, and who suffered numerous hardships in the process of subduing it, were not especially inclined to view nature favorably. They held the utilitarian view that the land existed primarily for humans to exploit for economic gain. Many also perceived nature as unruly, dangerous, and profane. For many Europeans, therefore, the challenge of taming and transplanting their refined vision of civilization to the wild landscape here was seen as a noble mission, a moral crusade.

The loss of forest had a profound effect on the ecology of the region. Hunting and loss of forest habitat caused wolves, mountain lions, elk, and beaver (victims of the fur trade) to vanish from the area. Other creatures like deer, bears, and wild turkeys were greatly reduced in numbers. Loss of the forest canopy, which shaded the soil from direct sunlight, resulted in an increase in evaporation, which dried the soil, decomposing the organic matter in it and reducing its capacity to hold water. Thus, the amount of precipitation runoff multiplied, washing away dissolved nutrients, and soil erosion and flooding became more widespread.

The reduction in forest and the decline or elimination of certain predators created an ideal habitat for certain very adaptable native and nonnative species to thrive. As well as domestic animals and plants, numerous nonnative species of wild plants and animals were introduced by accident or on purpose. These took up a sizable niche in the region's altered human environment.

SLAVERY

A very large portion of the residents of the New York colony—the largest number of any colony north of Chesapeake Bay, between 10 and 15 percent of the total population—were slaves, primarily Africans. Because of the chronic shortage of labor, a large percentage of the population owned slaves. At one point half of New York City's households owned at least one slave. Since homesteads in the region were generally small, the number of slaves any individual or family owned was also generally small, usually less than three, though a few of the large landowners might own up to thirty or sixty. This differed from the situation in the South, where numerous large plantations with many slaves were prevalent. Like the rest of the population, slaves in the Hudson region were primarily employed in agriculture and domestic duties. However, a large number, such as blacksmiths, bricklayers, and carpenters, performed skilled labor. Slaves were extensively employed in the milling of grain and in the production of lumber and other building materials. In Hudson River ports, many slaves, as well as free blacks, worked on the docks and crewed the ships and sloops that sailed up and down the river. White artisans and laborers naturally resented the use of slaves, whom they regarded as competition.

The white population was very fearful of the possibility of a slave revolt. A rebellion in 1712, in which several whites were killed, resulted in the passage of harsh slave codes further restricting their rights, making it impossible for slaves to purchase their freedom, imposing strict curfews, outlawing any type of gathering and the sale of alcohol to slaves. Severe penalties were inflicted for any infractions of these laws. In 1741 some thefts and arson in New York City led to allegations of a Negro plot to burn the city and kill all the white inhabitants, a fear that resulted in the arrest and execution of more than thirty innocent blacks and the deportation of many others.

In 1991 the construction of a Federal Office Tower in Lower Manhattan uncovered a long-forgotten eighteenth-century African burial ground. It is assumed that most of the remains there belong to slaves. Scientific study of the site and the remains may add considerably to what is known about the institution of slavery in the New York colony and about the lives of the slaves themselves. The New York City Landmark Preservation Committee has created the African Burial Ground and Commons Historic District, encompassing the site and focusing on its study and preservation, as well as the placement nearby of a commemorative plaque.

THE COMING OF THE REVOLUTION

Like the rest of the American colonies, the area along the Hudson saw growing dissatisfaction with British rule. The idea of taxation without representation, inherent in the rule of colonies by the motherland, enraged merchants and made such landowners as the Livingstons fearful that the English would tax their large landholdings. Tenant farmers meanwhile, frustrated with the manor lord/tenant system, hoped a revolution would open up new land for settlement. Merchants in New York City and other ports along the river were unhappy with the repressive mercantile policies of the British government, which inhibited free trade and limited their profits.

Besides strictly economic motives, there was an increasing sense of separation between the colony and the mother country. Of course the great physical distance was a major factor, but there were also cultural differences. The Hudson region was populated by citizens of diverse, often non-English backgrounds, and there was a growing identity that was distinct from that of England. This was also the period of the Enlightenment and the concomitant spread of beliefs in individual freedom, natural rights, and democracy. These ideas comprised much of the thinking and discussion around independence and characterized much of the protest leaders' rhetoric.

Gratitude toward Britain for successfully defending the New York colony from the French proved short-lived. The British government believed that the colonies should have to pay for their own defense, and so a series of taxes was implemented to cover the cost of the French and Indian War. Resentment intensified when, after the war's end, the colonial economy crashed. In 1765 a Stamp Act Congress met in New York City, hoping that economic pressure, boycotts, and the development of local manufacturing would reduce the colonies' dependence on Great Britain. There were also Stamp Act Riots in the city, and effigies of British officials were hung. In 1770, a contingent of British soldiers stationed in New York was harassed by members of a radical proindependence group called the "Sons of Liberty." British troops responded, charging the crowd with sabers drawn, and some in the crowd were injured—and at least one killed. In 1774, incited by Paul Revere of New England, a mob opposing a tax on tea dumped a shipload of tea in New York Harbor, in an action similar to the more famous protest in Boston.

Hudson Valley landowner Robert R. Livingston was one of the Committee of Five—the others were Thomas Jefferson, Ben Franklin, John Adams, and Roger Sherman—which drafted the Declaration of Independence, signed in July 1776 at Independence Hall in Philadelphia. However, many residents along the Hudson hoped that differences with the British government could still be resolved peacefully, without secession. As a result, the New York colony was the last to ratify the Declaration.

Those interested in the period of British colonial rule should visit the Van Cortlandt Manor in Croton, Philipse Manor Hall in Yonkers, and the Schuyler Mansion in Albany. All are fine representations of Georgian-style architecture. Philipsburg Manor north of Tarrytown is an excellent example of an eighteenth-century working farm and mill. There are many other superb examples of eighteenth-century stone and clapboard homes throughout the region, many of them private residences.

The War of Independence

TAKING SIDES

As news of the Revolution circulated, there was widespread rejoicing throughout the colonies. In New York City a statue of King George III was toppled during a celebration, and huge bonfires were lit. Not everyone was celebrating, however. Many residents of the Hudson region, though opposed to the British government and its policies, did not desire independence and tried to remain neutral in the conflict. Others, because of loyalty to the Crown or an aversion to change, maintained their allegiance to the British government; these included tenant farmers, promised free land by the British if they revolted against their landlords who had joined the patriot side. It is estimated that those who actively sided with the English, referred to as Tories, comprised nearly 25 percent of the population in the New York colony, and they played a large role in disrupting efforts by the patriots fighting for independence, as well as assisting and supporting the British in their attempts to regain control. In addition, there were others whose loyalty shifted depending on which side appeared to be winning.

As one of the most important transportation corridors in the thirteen colonies, control of the Hudson River and the city and harbor at its mouth was considered vital by both the American and British sides. By controlling the river, the Americans could maintain essential communication links between New England and the rest of the colonies and protect the Hudson Valley, which was an important source of grain and other foodstuffs, necessary to feed an army as well as an embattled population. The Hudson Highlands, particularly the area in what is now Harriman State Park, were rich in iron deposits that were used to produce ammunition for the patriot side. The British realized that by commanding the river, all communication and supply links between New England and the rest of the colonies would be severed, thereby dividing the colonies in half. Control of New York Harbor would provide an excellent staging area from which the rest of the colonies could be pacified.

THE FALL OF NEW YORK CITY

On June 30, 1776, a large British force under the command of Gen. Sir William Howe landed on Staten Island. For the next two months that force grew to nearly thirty thousand men, the largest British fighting force ever assembled up to that time. It included eight thousand Hessian mercenaries from Germany who had been hired to fight for the British. Following the defeat of American troops under the command of Gen. George Washington, guarding Brooklyn Heights, New York City fell to the British on September 15. Two weeks later British troops landed at Dobbs Ferry and battled American forces near White Plains. The British then marched south and, on November 16, captured Fort Washington, the Americans' last stronghold on Manhattan. Four days later Washington and his troops were forced to abandon Fort Lee atop the Palisades.

THE BRITISH PLAN TO DIVIDE THE COLONIES

Having secured New York Harbor, the British were now ready to embark on a plan to divide the thirteen colonies. Three British armies were to set out from various strategic outposts: One, led by Gen. John Burgoyne, was to embark at Montreal and head south along Lake Champlain. A second, under the command of Lt. Col. Barry St. Leger, would march east from the Great Lakes and down the valley of the Mohawk River; and a third, under the command of General Howe, would sail up the Hudson from New York City. All three would converge at Albany in October 1777.

Due to a bureaucratic slipup, Howe never received the orders to proceed north and meet General Burgoyne. Instead, with the majority of his troops, he captured the patriot capital of Philadelphia, leaving the rest of his army under the command of one of his generals, Sir Henry Clinton. In October 1777, Clinton was informed that Burgoyne was trapped in Saratoga and required immediate assistance. Clinton knew his forces could never reach Burgoyne in time, but that he might create a diversion by threatening the Hudson from the south—enough so the Americans might call off their attack on Burgoyne's army to meet this southern threat.

On October 6, 1777, a British force surprise-attacked and captured the twin American forts, Fort Clinton and Fort Montgomery, that guarded the Hudson near the present-day Bear Mountain Bridge. The British broke the iron chain the patriots had used to block the channel there. The British warship *Friendship*, with troops under the command of Gen. John Vaughn, sailed upriver easily passing batteries on Constitution Island and at Plum Point. The British continued on to the provincial capital at Kingston and on October 16, burned it. The next day, they burned Clermont, the home of Robert Livingston.

These battles were not decisive. Burgoyne's army surrendered while St. Leger was stopped at Oriskany. The British plan to unite their forces in Albany was foiled. Deep in patriot territory, the British withdrew from the Hudson Valley to help defend New York City. As the British sailed south, Americans stationed at Plum Point raked their flotilla with cannon fire, doing little damage but symbolically declaring that the Hudson would remain forever in American hands.

STALEMATE

Through the remainder of the war, the Americans firmly held the highlands and the north country, while the British occupied New York City. Peaks in the Hudson Highlands served as signal beacons, part of an elaborate communication network that connected patriot forces between Boston and Philadelphia. To guard the river, the Americans built what was considered to be an impregnable fortress at West Point, again installing an iron chain to block British ships from sailing north.

The area between the British and American forces changed hands frequently and was not afforded the protection of either army. Looting, vandalism, and other crimes proliferated in the guerrilla war between Tory sympathizers and those alleged to favor the patriot side; noncombatants had much to fear since both sides preyed on them.

On the night of July 16, 1779, in a daring surprise raid, the patriots under Gen. "Mad" Anthony Wayne captured a British force defending Stony Point, a fortress that had changed hands several times. However, the Americans decided to abandon it two days later.

Benedict Arnold, the infamous commander of West Point, treacherously planned to turn America's strongest fortress over to the British. However, on September 23, 1780, his contact, Maj. John André, a British officer, was captured by patriot militia near Tarrytown with the plans he had received from Arnold. The plot to turn over West Point was uncovered, and Arnold was forced to flee. He made it safely to British lines, but André was executed as a spy.

NATIVE AMERICANS IN THE CONFLICT

Native tribes of the Hudson region were divided in their support during the American Revolution. Some remained neutral, but others like the Wappinger and Mahican, as well as the Iroquois nation of the Oneida, actively supported the patriot side, though three other nations of the Iroquois—the Seneca, Onondaga, and Cayuga—sided with the British. Following a tradition of loyalty to the Crown, and threatened by incursions of settlers in their territory, these tribes marched with Burgoyne and St. Leger in their unsuccessful campaign to divide the New York colony. With Tory help they also participated in a series of brutal raids on frontier settlements. Settlers were urged to withdraw from these scattered frontier communities and resettle temporarily in the security of the Hudson Valley. Forts were built, guarding some of the key trails through the Catskill Mountains, in order to protect the Hudson from the west.

Following General Washington's orders, Gen. John Sullivan and Gen. James Clinton led patriot forces in the summer of 1779 into the heart of Iroquois territory in central New York, ravaging native villages and destroying crops. Many Iroquois later perished from disease and starvation. This prompted reprisals, and native warriors, with their Tory allies, staged a series of even more ferocious raids on colonial settlements. The peace treaty between the Americans and British resulted in the permanent division of the Iroquois nation. The Cayuga, Onondaga, and Seneca were all expelled from their territory, which became part of the new United States, but even the neutral tribes and those that had sided with the Americans were forced onto shrinking reservations, and many opted to leave the area altogether.

THE END OF THE CONFLICT

Following the decisive American victory at Yorktown, Virginia, in 1782, Washington moved his headquarters to the Hasbrouck House in Newburgh, where he stayed for the remainder of the war, awaiting the results of peace negotiations, which were then taking place in Paris. The cessation of hostilities was announced and ratified by Congress in 1783. On November 25, as the British under Gen. Sir Guy Carleton evacuated New York to ships waiting in the harbor, the triumphant Continental Army, led by Gen. Henry Knox, marched victorious into the city.

Those interested in the Revolutionary War period have a multitude of sites worth visiting in the region. The Fort Lee Historic Park, Stony Point, Bear Mountain's historic trails and the Trailside Museum, West Point—especially the museum—and Fort Putnam, the Hasbrouck House in Newburgh, the New Windsor Cantonment, Knox Headquarters, the Senate House in Kingston, and Clermont are just a few of the major sites.

The Historical Landscape

PART TWO

The Age of Development

A NEW NATION

Almost from the beginning the Hudson region played a significant role in the new nation's future. New York City served as temporary capital of the Republic from 1785 to 1790. The region produced many of the country's top political leaders: Alexander Hamilton, a leading Federalist and supporter of a strong centralized government, served as secretary of the treasury for the new nation, but in 1804 was killed in a duel with Aaron Burr in Weehawken, New Jersey, overlooking the Hudson. John Jay helped negotiate the Treaty of Paris in 1783, which ended the War of Independence, and was the nation's first chief justice. He later served ably as governor of New York from 1792 to 1800. George Clinton, a militia leader during the war, then served seven terms as New York's first governor, and two as the country's vice president. He was a strong defender of individual and states' rights and a prime supporter of the Bill of Rights. Robert Livingston served as the nation's first secretary of state and ambassador to France and helped negotiate the Louisiana Purchase.

Following the war the number of free blacks grew dramatically. Many had escaped their masters during the war. Also, the availability of cheap immigrant labor made the employment of slaves in most occupations uneconomical; thus many were sold or freed. Those who remained slaves became increasingly restless, and New York City was a haven for runaway slaves. The popularity of the principle of individual rights resulted in laws that restricted and eventually abolished the practice of slavery in New York State. However, New York was the last of the northern states to free its slave population.

Freed slaves in the Hudson region remained second-class citizens. Racial prejudice was widespread and violence against blacks commonplace. Blacks were rarely permitted the right to vote and were banned from many public places. On Hudson River steamers, blacks were not allowed inside the cabins and were restricted to the outside decks, regardless of weather conditions. They were also barred from many jobs. Many became domestics or low-paid laborers. Black males were employed as hands on ships. Blacks were usually segregated to poor neighborhoods where the worst conditions prevailed. Later, middle-class blacks and whites joined together in the crusade to abolish slavery in the South. Some helped runaway slaves in the Underground Railroad.

The population of the Hudson region grew tremendously in the years following the end of the war. Much of that growth was due to the high birthrate: The average family had more than seven children, and the majority of the population was under sixteen.

CHANGES IN AGRICULTURE

Despite the Hudson's importance as a commercial waterway, the area along it remained predominately rural, with a primarily agrarian economy. By 1820 only 15 percent of the population of the Hudson region lived in communities of more than three thousand residents, and these included New York and Albany. The rest of the nation had similar patterns of rural development.

One big change was the breakup of the large agricultural estates. The Revolutionary War divided the ranks of the landowning aristocracy. Those who supported the British had their lands confiscated, and many were forced to flee. Some, like the Rensselaers and Livingstons, who supported the patriot side, did so hoping the new government would protect their property rights. However, the strong egalitarian and democratic ideas that led to the abolition of slavery in the Hudson region were a central feature of the new Republic. The concept of the independent self-sufficient yeoman farmer working his own small plot of land was idealized by Thomas Jefferson and many of the nation's other political leaders. Much of the pressure for reform came from tenant farmers themselves. In what is popularly referred to as the Tin Horn Rebellion (tin horns were used to celebrate at gatherings, and as signals), tenant farmers dressed as American Indians refused to pay rent. Some of these strikes, which led to violent clashes that local militia were called in to squelch, contributed to the public perception that the large estates represented a continuation of the exploitive tenant/manor lord system, which the 1846 state constitution finally abolished.

Grain production along the Hudson continued to increase through the beginning of the nineteenth century but then began to wane, as years of wheat production depleted the fertility of the soil, which in many places in the Hudson Valley was thin and not really suited for intensive cultivation. Erosion was another factor, and new (introduced) diseases and pests, such as wheat midge, rust, and Hessian fly, also hurt productivity. One of the biggest factors, though, was the increased competition from farmers settling in the fertile areas to the west, farmers from the Hudson region among them.

As wheat production declined, farmers turned to other crops. Corn and oats, grown primarily as feed, increased in importance, as did barley, which was used to brew beer, in distilleries. Potatoes also became a major food crop.

By 1800 the decline of such predators as mountain lions and wolves, and the presence of newly vacant former wheatfields, encouraged the growth of cattle and dairy farming in the region. The spread of grazing land crowded out smaller farms. Harsh winters, diseases, and predation had limited the production of wool in the Hudson region, but in 1807, Robert Livingston introduced merino sheep from Spain, enabling farmers to produce wool as a cash crop.

Horticultural experimentation was often practiced by the landed aristocrats, and societies were formed to promote the use of scientific farming methods. Farmers began to employ crop rotation, better fertilizers, and methods of planting and harvesting that helped to retain the fertility of the soil, decreased erosion, and increased production. The introduction of new technologies such as the cast-iron plow, the mowing machine, and the reaper all made farming more efficient and productive while decreasing the need for manpower.

THE ADVENT OF STEAM

After 1800 traffic on the Hudson continued to grow. Most river vessels were sloops, and these proved extremely useful for carrying heavy cargo and bulk goods, but they were too slow to carry passengers. Trips between New York and Albany could take between three to nine days, depending on conditions.

Robert R. Livingston and Robert Fulton, an engineer and designer, developed the Hudson's first steam-powered vessel, the *North River* (later popularly referred to as the *Clermont*, after Livingston's estate on the Hudson). The *North River*'s departure from New York City in 1807 drew a large crowd, many hoping to witness history, though others derisively called it "Fulton's Folly." Averaging five miles per hour, the *North River* steamed up the Hudson in thirty-two hours, spending the night at Clermont and arriving in Albany the next day.

Fulton and Livingston secured a monopoly on steamship travel on the Hudson and other bodies of water in New York State. The monopoly—which stifled competition, kept fares high, and actually limited steamboat development on the Hudson River—was ruled unconstitutional in the landmark *Gibbons v. Ogden* case (1824), opening the Hudson up to competition, lower fares, and more steamboat development.

By 1840 steamboat speeds had increased enough to enable travel between New York and Albany in just eight hours. Steamships raced to arrive at wharves first and pick up waiting passengers. Competition between the steamboats was so fierce that ships would sometimes force their competitors to run aground: Accidents were frequent; boilers would sometimes explode, causing fires; boats would collide.

Paddlewheelers were popular because they were well suited to the river's often shallow draft and caused a minimum of turbulence. Some were lavishly furnished and decorated like floating palaces—the most famous being the *Mary Powell*, which provided regular service between Rondout and New York City.

ROADS AND CANALS

Until the nineteenth century most roads in the region were poorly maintained, subject to flooding, mud, and vegetation and in many places little more than barely cleared paths. They were so miserable that many farmers preferred to wait until winter and ship their grain by sleigh. The high cost of transporting agricultural produce was a serious impediment to its profitability, and farmers who were not situated close enough to the river suffered. Communities along the Hudson, anxious to secure a share of the growing market in the transport of agricultural goods, actively promoted the establishment of toll roads, and between 1797 and 1827, a number of private companies were chartered to build roads. Towns like Newburgh, Catskill, Hudson, and Poughkeepsie had toll roads connecting them to rich agricultural areas and prompting their development as busy shipping ports.

The Appalachian Mountains formed a natural barrier to westward expansion of the new nation. However, the Hudson River and the Mohawk River Valley provided the best passageway through the mountains. As early as 1783 George Washington had urged the construction of a canal between the Hudson and the Great Lakes. Canals had long been a common means of transportation in Europe. In 1810 a committee was formed that included Fulton, Livingston, and Governor Dewitt Clinton

(George's son), which advocated the construction of a canal. Governor Clinton became the primary supporter of the canal and in 1817 was able to get the New York state legislature to approve the project. Many of the project's detractors called it "Dewitt's Ditch." It took only eight years and seven million dollars to complete the 350-mile long canal from Albany to Buffalo on Lake Erie, America's first great engineering achievement. On October 26, 1825, the Erie Canal officially opened amid large-scale celebrations, and water transported all the way from Lake Erie was symbolically poured into New York Harbor. The canal was an immediate success: The entire journey from Buffalo to New York City now took only nine days; shipping rates between the Great Lakes and New York City plummeted; and New York City and Albany became major centers of commerce and trade.

One unforeseen side effect of the canal was the introduction of Great Lakes fish, such as small- and large-mouthed bass, into the Hudson. The canal helped establish the Hudson as the nation's primary transportation corridor, leading to a rapid increase in population and economic activity. The growing population depended on locally produced food, fuel, and building supplies, a fact that certainly benefited the region's agriculture but also led to the wholesale destruction of the area's remaining forests, primarily for fuel to heat homes and power steamboats and local industries. By the middle of the century even the Catskills and Hudson Highlands had been largely denuded of any old-growth forest. In some cleared areas the forest grew back only to be cut again and again. Mountains and hillsides stripped of forests created serious erosion problems, which often led to flooding and contamination of water supplies. Runoff from logged slopes altered circulation and sedimentation patterns, slowing circulation so the river and its tributaries deposited more sediment. This, along with the construction of railroads along the river, speeded the development of tidal wetlands.

The financial success of the Erie Canal prompted the construction of other canals. One of them, the Delaware and Hudson, completed in 1828, was 108 miles long and stretched from Pennsylvania to the Hudson. Its primary purpose was to transport anthracite coal—touted as a more efficient, cleaner-burning fuel—from the mines of northeastern Pennsylvania to New York City. Gravity railroads were used to carry the coal from the mines to Honesdale, Pennsylvania, where it was loaded on canal boats and then towed by mules to Rondout (Kingston). At Rondout, the coal was transferred to bigger barges and then shipped down the Hudson to New York City. In addition to coal, cement and other building materials and agricultural products were shipped on the canal.

RAILROADS

In 1825 John Stevens, one of the country's primary proponents of railroad technology, constructed America's first experimental stretch of circular track along the Hudson in Hoboken, New Jersey, and upon it, a vehicle with a steam-powered engine that could propel passengers around the track at six miles an hour. In 1831 the first rail line in New York State began operating, between Albany and Schenectady, at thirty miles per hour. The locomotive, which was named the *Dewitt Clinton,* was constructed at the West Point Foundry near Cold Spring. The rail line was extended westward in sections and by 1840 stretched all the way to Buffalo, paralleling the Erie Canal. In 1853 Erastus Corning consolidated the different lines into the New York Central.

Despite its position as America's largest city, most important port, and commercial center, New York's rail development lagged behind that of other metropolises. The fact that Manhattan was an island surrounded by wide bodies of water such as the Hudson was a serious barrier to rail development. Natural features like the Palisades and the Hudson Highlands to the north presented formidable obstacles to construction, as did a thriving steamship industry, which had enough political clout to stop or delay such a project. Wealthy landowners along the Hudson, jealous of their privacy and concerned about the impact a rail line would have on their property, also opposed construction of a railway along the river. Engineer John B. Jervis did the preliminary survey of the proposed route as well as the market analysis to prove its viability as an economic venture. The railroad, finally built between 1847 and 1851, proved to be the most difficult and expensive one to construct up to that time. In order to shortcut through the bays and inlets, much of the track was laid on rock fill in the river. Where the river was deep, a bench of rock had to be cut from the steep shore. At Breakneck and Anthony's Nose, tunnels were drilled through solid rock.

The construction of a rail line along the Hudson had a greater visual and environmental impact on the river than did any other single project. It effectively changed the shoreline and cut off access to the river for most residents on the eastern shore. The railroad also created sheltered coves that collected sediment eroding from nearby bluffs and from silt-laden tidal waters. These became the marshlands we see today along the Hudson's east bank. In 1884 another rail line was constructed along the Hudson's western shore, which had a similar impact.

NATURE, ART, AND CULTURE

Following the Revolution the Georgian style of architecture was renamed the Federal style, and it continued in eminence into the early nineteenth century. Influenced by the ideals and culture of classical Greece and Rome, architects like Thomas Jefferson promoted a new, highly decorative style of architecture, later called Greek Revival. (Sympathy for the Greeks, who were fighting for their independence, was another reason for its popularity.) Features such as columns, pediments, and cornices were constructed of affordable wood. It reached its peak in prominence in the 1830s. Many fine examples of Greek Revival homes and buildings still survive today in Athens, Rhinebeck, and other places along the river.

Alexander Jackson Davis, one of the area's leading architects, designed Greek Revival homes and buildings like the Dutch Reformed Church in Newburgh and the Customs House on Wall Street in Manhattan. Later he became a prominent proponent of the romantic Gothic Revival style of architecture, which became popular in the 1840s, and designed Lyndhurst in Tarrytown.

The nineteenth century saw changes in Americans' attitude toward nature. The romantic movement, which had begun in Europe in the eighteenth century, spread to America's shores. Romantics viewed nature as innocent, pure, mysterious, and sublime. For writers and intellectuals such as William Cullen Bryant, the presence of large relatively unspoiled natural areas in the United States distinguished it from its more staid counterparts in Europe, where wilderness had long been tamed. He urged Americans to rediscover the wild splendors of their own nation.

In the early 1800s New York–based Knickerbocker writers like Bryant, Washington Irving, and James Fenimore Cooper became internationally famous, producing works celebrating and describing American life and the frontier experience. The Hudson River was the setting for many of their stories, such as Irving's *Legend of Sleepy Hollow* and *Rip Van Winkle* and Cooper's *The Spy* and *Last of the Mohicans*, and they helped to establish New York City as the cultural capital of the new republic.

Nineteenth-century artists who glorified America's natural landscape in their work became known as the Hudson River School. It was centered in New York City, whose wealthy merchants and entrepreneurs would be its primary financial supporters.

Detailed and romantic representations of natural landforms became the focus of Hudson River School compositions. Thomas Doughty's subdued and moody landscapes were among the earliest examples. Thomas Cole expanded their romantic vision and broke with tradition by often omitting any sign of human beings or relegating human developments to the background and reducing human figures to tiny antlike proportions, dwarfed by nature's grandeur. Like other Hudson River painters, he used rich colors, dark shadows, and golden light to enhance and exaggerate such natural features as gnarled tree trunks, deep chasms, and lofty peaks for dramatic effect. William Cullen Bryant, an admirer of Cole, called his paintings "acts of religion."

The majestic Hudson, with its towering mountains, steep precipices, and primeval forests, provided the perfect subject Cole and other Hudson River painters needed for their aesthetic and spiritual inspiration. However, later Hudson River artists, such as Asher B. Durand, Frederick Church, John Kensett, and Jasper F. Cropsey, did not limit themselves to painting only Hudson River scenes, and Albert Bierstadt and Thomas Moran focused on the spectacular landscapes of the American West.

Those interested in this period should visit Boscobel in Cold Spring and the Ten Broeck House in Albany, both superb examples of Federal-style architecture. The Crawford House in Newburgh and the chapel of Our Lady of Cold Spring are among the many fine examples of Greek Revival architecture in the region. The Maritime Museum in Kingston often has exhibitions covering the steamboat legacy of the river. Visits to Washington Irving's Sunnyside, near Tarrytown, and Frederick Church's Olana, near Hudson, will expand one's appreciation of the intellectual and artistic movements of the period. The Albany Institute of Art, the Frances Lehman Loeb Art Center on the campus of Vassar College in Poughkeepsie, and the Metropolitan Museum of Art in New York City have marvelous collections of Hudson River School paintings.

The Industrial and Postindustrial Age

THE MEANS OF PRODUCTION

Manufacturing in colonial times consisted mostly of the use of waterpower in the processing of raw materials, primarily lumber and grain. This continued into the early part of the nineteenth century, until the production of grain declined and the timber supply dwindled.

During colonial times in the Hudson region, households were primarily self-sufficient, manufacturing their own goods. As the population of the Hudson region grew and communities developed, village shops manned by artisans, millers, shoemakers, blacksmiths, coopers, weavers, and tanners produced goods that were used locally.

Large-scale manufacturing as we know it took a long time to develop in the Hudson region. A lack of capital, most of which was already invested in land and commerce; competition from well-established British manufacturers; a lack of expertise in how to build, operate, and repair the equipment; and the fact that many Americans idealized agriculture or commerce and were suspicious of and/or hostile to the idea of manufacturing were all serious impediments to the growth of industry along the Hudson. Between 1798 and 1814 the Napoleonic Wars, which involved most of Europe, drastically reduced the importation of manufactured goods. There was also a surge in patriotism, and the idea of American self-sufficiency was promoted. During this period the federal government fostered the development of industry through protectionist policies, allowing some industries tax-free status and creating tariffs to block the importation of foreign manufactured goods.

In the United States, industrial development first took place in New England, but eventually manufacturers were attracted to the Hudson region by its abundance of cheap unskilled immigrant labor and the Hudson itself, which provided an inexpensive means for transporting goods and materials.

Factories were often located close to the river's edge to take advantage of it for transportation and as a convenient place to dump their waste. Riverfront towns were where the population was centered, and factories were located so workers, in those preautomobile days, could walk to work. Factories often hired women and children and poor immigrant labor, who would work in spite of low pay and disagreeable conditions.

A large number of diverse industries flourished in the towns and cities along the Hudson's banks. Dutchess and Columbia Counties were early leaders in the textile industry. Shipbuilding was also prominent in ports along the river. New York City was growing rapidly, and building materials were needed for construction. The presence of good-quality clay and cheap transportation via the river fostered brickmaking as a major industry in the area. Another important industry was the production of ice, which was cut directly from the Hudson, packed, and shipped downriver to New York City in the days before refrigeration.

In many places the Hudson's shores were lined with factories and smokestacks, spewing pollution into the atmosphere or directly into the river. The rising demand for riverfront space for industry resulted in the creation of new land along the river, greatly altering the shoreline in many places. The Hudson's industrial theater was frequently viewed as a proud sign of economic prosperity, American industrial might, technological achievement, and progress.

Industrialization led to the rapid growth of urban centers along the river as displaced farmers and immigrants were attracted by the prospect of factory jobs. Growing population put additional stresses on the environment, as bacteria-laden untreated sewage was dumped directly into the Hudson or its tributaries. Raw sewage, as one might well imagine, is extremely unhealthy for the environment for a number of reasons: The bacteria can infect fish and animal life. Sewage also contains nitrates, which promote algae growth and microbes; if unchecked, algae and microbes will use up all of the available oxygen in a river, thus depriving other organisms. During the nineteenth century, overfishing and pollution caused certain fish populations, such as sturgeon, to decline and for the river's once-extensive oyster beds to disappear.

THE PLEASURE HIGHWAY

In the early nineteenth century, as the United States expanded in area and population, there was a growth of patriotic feelings, interest in historic sites connected to the nation's birth, as well as an awakening appreciation of its stunning natural beauty. Travelers from Europe were attracted to America's spectacular wilderness scenery. True wilderness had by then ceased to exist in Europe, and there were areas along the Hudson that were still relatively pristine compared to anything in Europe. Because of its proximity to New York City, a major point of entry for European tourists, the development of steamship travel on the river, and the presence of beautiful scenery and historic sites associated with the American Revolution, the Hudson became part of the "Pleasure Highway," leading to other important tourist destinations such as Saratoga Springs and Niagara Falls. But most took their time admiring the Hudson and surrounding countryside, stopping at various points along the way.

One of the favorite stops was West Point. Located in the heart of the majestic Hudson Highlands, the military academy, with its fortress ruins, became one of the nation's first big tourist attractions. Opulent hotels and resorts were built along the river to provide luxurious accommodations for wealthy visitors, many of which became attractions themselves. The Catskill Mountain House, because of its magnificent location, was the most famous of these. In addition to the luxury resorts, a number of hotels sprang up along the river that catered to middle-class vacationers.

New York City, like other American cities in the nineteenth century, was a crowded, dirty, unhealthy place. Streets were often unpaved, either dusty or muddy, and always covered with human and animal dung. There were open sewers and no sanitation. The air was polluted by wood-burning and, later, coal fires. Diseases such as smallpox, typhoid, tuberculosis, cholera, and malaria were rampant, epidemics frequent, and the death toll high.

Fresh air and exposure to country living was greatly desired by the masses of urban dwellers. Ever since the time of Dutch rule, the city's wealthy residents had built comfortable villas in the country. In the nineteenth century the Hudson Highlands became a popular health resort area, where patients suffering a variety of maladies came for treatment, to eat healthy locally produced fresh food, to exercise, and to breathe unpolluted air.

THE ARISTOCRATIC LANDSCAPE

The large estates of the Hudson's old landowning families were divided among numerous heirs who built elaborate homes overlooking the river and continued to enjoy a life of privilege and luxury. Large areas of these estates were landscaped to improve their aesthetic qualities, many based on the principles of Andrew Jackson Downing. Downing, a native of Newburgh, promoted the use of natural landscape design to take advantage of the area's scenic beauty, but also to enhance it in the romantic style. He began an architectural firm with English architects Calvert Vaux and Frederick Withers. He also published popular guides on landscape architectural design. In the design of cottages, he promoted the use of such decorative features as pointed arches, bay windows, verandas, decorative trims, gables, turrets, buttresses, and thick planking. In landscape design he advocated the use of native species of trees and shrubs as well as ornamental nonnatives, and setting aside natural areas to contrast with landscaped sections. Paths and carriage trails were designed to feature certain cherished views, especially of the Hudson and distant mountains. Following his tragic death in a steamboat accident, Calvert Vaux and Frederick Law Olmsted applied his principles to designing public parks.

By the end of the Civil War, the Hudson's old landowning aristocracy faced competition from those who made their wealth in the fields of business and commerce. It became fashionable for wealthy financiers and owners of the railroad monopolies to build magnificent country retreats along the river, many of them seeking conspicuously to display their wealth. They employed the nation's best architects, like the prestigious firm of McKim, Mead & and White, founded in 1879, which designed homes and buildings in the eclectic beaux-arts style, often copying the style of European palaces. Some of the older villas were expanded and remodeled or replaced by larger, more extravagant ones. These homes were lavishly decorated with imported furnishings and art. Some, like Lyndhurst, Castle Rock, and Bannerman's, intentionally resembled medieval fortresses in the romantic tradition, and their owners fancied themselves as barons who dwelled in castles overlooking the Rhine.

These new wealthy residents of the Hudson wanted to live in the same style as the Hudson's older aristocracy. They also appreciated nature, the outdoors, and country living, and believed in the health benefits, both physical and spiritual, of this lifestyle. This was also the Gilded Age, and the most status-conscious individuals had to observe strict codes of etiquette and dress, belong to the right clubs, associate with the right people, and participate in certain favored activities in order to gain admittance to the Hudson region's highest, most exclusive social circles. For many the luxurious estates were merely seasonal residences, their owners maintaining other homes in New York City; Newport, Rhode Island; and similar fashionable locales.

ROMANCE WITH NATURE

Not everyone viewed the technological "progress" of the nineteenth century with favor, however. Some intellectuals felt that America was becoming overcivilized. They were concerned about the artificiality and materialism of modern industrial society. They were also distressed by the wanton destruction of the nation's forests and wilderness areas. Writer-philosopher Henry David Thoreau advocated balancing the needs of civilization and nature. For him the freedom and solitude of nature offered a respite from the stress and demands of society and an opportunity for self-exploration, to discover one's natural self. Thoreau believed that nature was a rich source of intellectual and spiritual nourishment. By living a simple, more natural life, one might harness a creative spirit and vigor that was often missing from civilized life.

John Muir, an environmentalist, explorer, and writer, felt that human beings should have a strong maternal bond with nature, a sense of connection often thwarted by civilization. His writings and works helped promote the idea of protecting unspoiled natural areas from development, as refuges where people could experience nature firsthand.

By the late nineteenth century, hiking, bird watching, and other forms of outdoor activity and nature study were becoming popular. The Appalachian Mountain Club was founded in 1876, and in 1892, John Muir founded the Sierra Club. These two clubs promoted preservation of natural areas as well as outdoor activities that increased the public's knowledge of them. Avid sportsmen like Theodore Roosevelt and other wealthy outdoor enthusiasts organized exclusive clubs that promoted conservation to protect game and establish refuges and reserves for their own private use. The nature writing of the popular Hudson Valley poet and naturalist John Burroughs also increased the public's appreciation of nature and the environment.

Frederick Law Olmsted and Calvert Vaux recognized the need for city dwellers to commune with nature and helped design and create large public parks such as Central Park and Riverside Park, in New York City, where citizens of different backgrounds, social classes, and races, could intermingle freely in a pleasant, tranquil atmosphere—a refuge from urban stress. Olmsted also advocated linking parks through parkways and creating park systems.

Much of the early impetus behind wilderness preservation was based on the need to protect watersheds and municipal water supplies. Nature enthusiasts used the issue of watershed protection as a rationale to promote creation of the Adirondack Forest Preserve in 1885 and, as an afterthought, the Catskill Forest Preserve. Use of these preserves for such outdoor activities as hunting, fishing, hiking, canoeing, and camping was at first mostly restricted to the wealthy—the only ones who had the time and money for travel and recreation. Only later, with the growth of the middle class and the use of cars, would the land preserves become accessible to more of the general public.

The growing commercial and industrial centers of the Hudson region required vast quantities of stone for constructing roads and buildings. Granite and gneiss were blasted and quarried from some of the Hudson Highlands' most prominent natural features, such as Breakneck. Trap rock was quarried from the cliffs of the Palisades. Destruction of these scenic wonders galvanized public support for their protection, and thanks largely to the New Jersey Federation of Women's Clubs, the Palisades Interstate Park Commission was established in 1899. This largely independent body was able to acquire the Palisades and end quarry operations there, later expanding its jurisdiction north to Hook Mountain, Stony Point, and the Hudson Highlands.

THE GATEWAY

Throughout the nineteenth century, the population of the Hudson region expanded. New York City's population multiplied, but other cities along the Hudson saw more modest growth, and some rural areas actually lost population during this period, as farmers migrated to the new lands outside the region or to urban centers to work in the factories. Much of the population growth was the result of lower mortality, which came about through improvements in health care and living conditions.

Population growth in the region was also due to immigration. In the late eighteenth and early nineteenth centuries, most of the immigrants were transplants from New England. Many were farmers in search of better soil, but also whalers and merchants seeking new business opportunities. Prior to 1880 most of the new immigrants to America were from the British Isles. Irish, driven from their homeland by a rising population, scarcity of land, and the potato famine of 1847, and lured by the prospect of jobs in the New World, also made up a considerable portion. Germans, many of them farmers suffering from their own potato blight, and weavers unable to compete with British textile manufacturers, came seeking economic opportunity. In the wake of the failed revolutions of 1848, multitudes of political refugees came seeking freedom. Many of the immigrants, especially those like the Irish and Germans, who had a distinct culture, religion, or language, faced prejudice and discrimination from the resident population. Often they had to take the worst, most difficult, or most dangerous jobs for the lowest pay. Many were exploited by unscrupulous entrepreneurs, and most were forced to live in slums that were by then part of just about every Hudson River town and city, especially New York.

Between 1880 and 1914, hundreds of thousands of Italian immigrants settled in the Hudson region, primarily in New York City. Persecution in their homeland and changing economic conditions drove thousands of Russian Jews and other Eastern Europeans to the New World and many stayed in New York City or migrated to other towns along the river. New York City's Castle Clinton and, later, Ellis Island became the major debarkation points for immigrants to this country, many of whom remained in the Hudson region. New immigrants to the United States encountered a culture radically different from the one they had left. Language was often a barrier, as few were already fluent in English. Many gravitated toward ghettos where other recent arrivals from the "old country" tended to congregate. Despite usually overcrowded and unhealthy conditions, ghettos also provided a haven where the immigrants' language was spoken and their customs practiced.

Many Americans were resentful or felt threatened by the huge influx of foreigners, who they felt depressed wages, competed for jobs, and posed a threat to American culture and values. However, most immigrants assimilated rapidly into American society and made lasting contributions. Nonetheless, by 1924 Congress had enacted laws that greatly decreased the numbers of new immigrants permitted to come to this country.

In the early and middle parts of the twentieth century, there was a mass migration of blacks from the rural south. Changes in agricultural production there and the prospect of jobs and greater freedom in the north were the main impetus. Like other immigrants before them, blacks encountered prejudice and discrimination and, for the most part, were forced into segregated neighborhoods such as Harlem. However, unlike other immigrant groups that preceded them, blacks remained a very visible minority and thus subject to continuing discrimination.

In the fifties and sixties, rapid population growth in Puerto Rico and a lack of job opportunities there, as well as easy access to the mainland, encouraged hundreds of thousands to migrate to New York. With a primarily rural background, different language, and distinct culture, Puerto Rican immigrants faced many of the same challenges as had earlier immigrant groups. Today the region's newest immigrants are primarily from the Caribbean, Latin America, Asia, and Eastern Europe. While the Hudson region's heterogeneous character—one of the most ethnically diverse in the world—continues to be a source of stress and strife, it also makes it an interesting and colorful place to live and visit.

THE AGRARIAN VIEW

By the 1870s cleared land in the Hudson region reached its greatest extent. Most Hudson Valley farms were specialized in the production of cash crops. Hudson Valley agriculture benefited from the growth of the New York metropolitan area, which provided a ready market for fresh farm produce. Technological improvements such as tractors and milking machines decreased the need for additional labor; improvements in transportation enabled farmers to get their produce to market sooner; experimentation and the use of hybrids and chemical fertilizers resulted in higher crop yields.

Agrarian life at the beginning of the twentieth century was still characterized by long, hard hours and homes that in most cases lacked running water, were still heated by wood stoves, and lacked indoor plumbing facilities. Country roads were poor and discouraged travel. Except for farms immediately adjacent to the Hudson or other main transportation links, farm life tended to be isolating. Public education was provided in tiny one-room schools. Church-related activities provided the primary social and cultural life; so did the country general store, which in those days often purchased farmers' produce for cash or barter and sold a wide assortment of essential tools and other goods as well as luxury items.

A REVOLUTION IN TRANSPORTATION

Sloops and paddle wheel steamers were eventually replaced by diesel-powered tugboats and barges. Slower than trains or trucks, boats and ships often could not compete with the faster means of transport and traffic, and shipping on the river declined. Many of the canals were abandoned, including the Delaware and Hudson in 1899. The Erie Canal was upgraded and in 1918 became the New York State Barge Canal. Between 1926 and 1930 the Hudson channel was dredged by the Army Corps of Engineers to a depth of twenty-seven feet for larger oceangoing vessels bound for the Port of Albany. The channel was deepened again, between 1954 and 1966, to its present depth of thirty-two feet. Maintenance dredging—most of it has taken place between Nyack and Peekskill and between Kingston and Albany—is required to remove new accumulations of sediment. Dredging destroys aquatic habitats, and dredge spoils have greatly altered the Hudson shoreline between Catskill and Albany. When not done through special suction methods, which are being proposed for PCB cleanup, dredging can stir up and spread around toxic chemicals in the sediment. The drafts of large ships and barges can affect the plants and animals along the shore. Icebreakers are employed by the Coast Guard to keep the river channel open through the winter.

Today the Hudson still plays an important role as a means of commercial transportation in the region. Large, heavy, relatively cheap bulk items, like fuel, building materials, and grain, can be carried on the river in a cost-effective way, if speed of delivery is not the primary consideration.

The railroads suffered from an overextended system, fierce rivalry between the various lines, and, later, competition from the automobile. By the twentieth century many rail lines had ceased operating. Today railroads still serve a vital role in the transport of people, bulk goods, industrial equipment, and vehicles and are a low-cost, energy-efficient alternative to automobiles or truck transport. The primary freight line in the region is the West Shore Rail Line, operated by Conrail, which serves the west side of the Hudson from New Jersey north to Albany. In the late 1880s, electric trolleys were introduced and flourished briefly in the Hudson region. Practically every town and city along the Hudson had trolley service. But after World War I, trolleys also fell victim to competition from the automobile.

The advent of the automobile had a bigger impact on the economic and social landscape of the Hudson region than did all rival technologies combined. Soon it became the primary mover of both people and goods, forcing other means of transport into a diminished role. The older infrastructure of country roads and ferries was inadequate to meet the demands of growing automobile traffic, and a huge new network of roads, highways, bridges, and tunnels was constructed to accommodate the new technology. These in turn had a huge impact on the landscape as well as a dramatic effect on the population, which was now increasingly mobile.

THE MODERN INDUSTRIAL AND POSTINDUSTRIAL LANDSCAPE

By the late nineteenth century the Hudson region was one of the leading industrial centers of the world. There was a great diversity in manufacturing enterprises, much of it centered in New York City, though other cities along the Hudson, including Newburgh, Poughkeepsie, and Kingston, were also manufacturing centers.

The industrial age spawned a new class of technocrats: engineers, technicians, plant managers, and other professionals, who constituted a small but growing middle class. These professionals could afford to live comfortably in Victorian-style homes and row houses, emulating the wealthy, but on a smaller scale. Through their writings and work, such architects as A. J. Downing and Calvert Vaux promoted tasteful design for middle-class homes and properties.

While manufacturing remained important, its role in the region's economy declined through most of the latter part of the twentieth century. Labor and building costs in the Hudson region have increased, while cheaper rates in other parts of the country and abroad enticed industries to relocate outside the region. Competition from these new industrial centers hurt the region's manufacturers, and the growth of other sectors of the economy eventually eclipsed manufacturing's leading role.

Today most of the industries in the region are so-called light industries, such as the manufacture of computer chips, which produce fewer pollutants than did the older industrial enterprises. The presence of excellent transportation systems; large numbers of skilled workers and services; and the region's location near population centers and markets are some of the reasons why industries have chosen to locate here.

While much business and industrial activity remains centered in New York City, a great deal has transferred to the suburbs to take advantage of lower costs and the presence of a skilled workforce. Westchester County is now home to many corporate headquarters as well as other business- and research-related activity. The computer giant IBM established major manufacturing facilities in Poughkeepsie, East Fishkill, and Kingston in the 1950s and 1960s, which at their height employed more than twenty thousand people. Despite downsizing in the 1990s, IBM remains a significant presence in the region. However, most new business growth in the area is by relatively small companies.

In the past most industry was located in a narrow corridor close to the river and major rail lines. The introduction of the automobile, the growth of the trucking industry, and decreasing dependence on raw materials encouraged the majority of businesses to locate away from the riverfront. Today most have established themselves in industrial/business parks that are diffused throughout the region, often in close proximity to highways, airports, and other modern-day transportation hubs. Sprawling complexes like these need space, so most have located outside central cities—a pattern of development that has contributed to the steady erosion of jobs and economic activity away from the cities and into the countryside: Hudson River cities and towns have wasted away, and riverfront areas have been transformed into scenes of dilapidated, abandoned buildings, vacant lots, and trash dumps.

The Industrial Revolution created a more urbanized population, with specialized jobs. As people became less self-sufficient they were increasingly dependent on services, such as retailing and education, to provide their basic needs. In the expanding twentieth-century economy the demand for better services has also resulted in an expanded role for government, which became another major employer in the Hudson region.

Tourism played an even bigger role in the region's economy, as transportation improved and more people could afford to travel. Today, in the area north of Westchester and Rockland, it is the primary industry, generating more than two billion dollars a year in revenue and employing more than ninety thousand. New York City is the region's leading tourist destination. Areas along the Hudson, with their rural ambience and charm, historic and cultural sites, recreational opportunities, and easy access from population centers (twenty-six million are within a day's drive), are attractive destinations for city refugees and vacationers. This is especially true now with time constraints that limit many people's ability to travel far. However, not enough is done to promote the region as a tourist destination, or to protect those qualities of scenery and lifestyle that attract tourists.

THE POWER ISSUE

The region's expanding population and growing economy required new sources of energy. Seven large power plants were built along the river to address that need. Most operate on coal or other fuel, but one of them, the controversial Indian Point Plant, is nuclear powered. Among the largest structures ever built along the river, these plants had a very dramatic visual impact on the topography. New power lines stretched across the landscape, crossing mountains and other features. The Hudson's power plants require huge volumes of water for cooling, hence their siting near the river. The force of water rushing into the cooling systems can suck up fish larvae, eggs, and microorganisms. Removing large quantities of water might also affect the position of the saltline. It is feared that the heated water that is discharged from these plants might raise the Hudson's temperature and oxygen levels, which in turn could have a negative impact on the river's delicate ecology. Fish are cold-blooded. Sudden temperature changes can kill them or reduce their spawning activity. Public concern over the safety of nuclear plants has increased since the Three-Mile Island and Chernobyl accidents.

The single most important environmental controversy to arise along the river was Consolidated Edison (Con Ed)'s plan to build a giant pump-storage facility at Storm King Mountain south of Cornwall (see chap. 9). The Storm King controversy did more than any other issue to raise public awareness of the Hudson's value as a scenic resource and the need to protect it. The region's major environmental groups, which all took shape at this time, continue their preservation efforts today.

THE CLEAN WATER ACT

In 1972 Congress passed the Clean Water Act, which incorporated earlier measures to address the nationwide problem of water pollution that effected the Hudson as well as many of the other major U.S. water bodies. The Clean Water Act required municipalities to provide secondary treatment of their sewage and provided federal funds for the construction of sewage treatment plants. By the mid-1980s the Hudson's shores were lined with sewage treatment plants. The Clean Water Act's National Pollution Discharge Elimination System limited the amount of pollutants that industry could dump into the river. The river's water quality immediately improved, even in its worst sections.

HOUSES IN MOTION

By the beginning of the twentieth century the population of the Hudson region was overwhelmingly urban, centered in and around New York City, Albany, and a few smaller cities and towns along the river. However, much of the region remained rural and thinly populated. With rapidly growing urban centers and improvements in transportation, urban dwellers began to exit the cities in greater numbers. New York and other cities had completely developed within their boundaries, and population spilled over into the surrounding countryside. Increasing numbers of city dwellers purchased or rented homes in the country to use as weekend getaways or summer retreats. Retail establishments migrated to the new suburbs in search of new markets.

Westchester County, north of the city, and Bergen County, across the river in New Jersey, were the first to feel this expansive growth and were the most rapidly growing areas in the Hudson region throughout much of the twentieth century. The completion of the Tappan Zee Bridge in 1955 opened up Rockland County to this kind of development. By the 1980s other parts of the New York metropolitan area had become fully developed. The fringe of the metropolitan area—northern Westchester, Putnam, Orange, Dutchess, and even Ulster Counties—began to feel the effects of rapid suburbanization. The last three counties comprising the Mid-Hudson region became the fastest-growing area in New York State. With the downsizing of IBM, that growth has slowed in the nineties, but will likely be subject to future pressures.

Migration to the area's suburbs has not been without problems. Parts of the region began to suffer from overcrowding, pollution, and crime—

the same conditions city dwellers had moved to avoid. The rural infrastructure of roads has often been ill equipped to handle the massive increases in traffic. Businesses and retail abandoned the downtown areas of the region's cities and towns to relocate in malls that became the new activity centers. Meanwhile the core cities withered, became magnets for the disadvantaged, and in some cases were demolished in the name of urban renewal.

Decentralization of population has meant that residents of the region are often forced to commute long distances to work, not always from suburb to city, as was the usual pattern, but more likely from rural area to suburb or from suburb to suburb. This is also true for residents trying to access shopping, entertainment, and professional services that often are not located in population centers. The haphazard patterns of development in the region are frequently at odds with the use of a public transport system that has traditionally depended on transportation corridors and concentrations of population to make it viable. The lack of public transport means that the majority of residents are dependent on the automobile for long and even short trips. To counter this, efforts have been made to encourage carpooling or commuter-van use, often facilitated though park-and-ride centers.

THE WORKING LANDSCAPE

Agriculture remains an important component of the region's economy. In the Hudson Valley it is the second largest industry, generating one billion dollars annually. Dairy products, beef, hay, alfalfa, oats, corn, fruit, berries, and vegetables are the primary crops. The Hudson Valley is one of the leading apple-producing regions in the world. Peaches, plums, pears, table grapes, and cherries are also significant. Twenty vineyards occupy one thousand acres of Hudson Valley land, making this one of the four leading viticulture regions in New York State, the second largest wine producer in the nation. Picking fruit is still a labor-intensive activity, primarily performed by migrant farm laborers who follow the harvest from state to state.

While agriculture is a significant part of the economy, labor-saving technological improvements have limited the number of people involved in farm production. Today less than 1 percent of the region's population works on farms. Twentieth-century improvements in communication and transportation, the advent of centralized schools, and a large influx of people not involved in agriculture have dramatically transformed rural life in the Hudson region. While these areas may still appear rural to the casual visitor or weekend or summer guest, they are no longer distinguishable culturally or economically from their suburban counterparts.

Now farmers throughout the region are likely to shop in malls and chain stores, rent videos, listen to CDs, browse the Web, and microwave their leftovers. Many, in fact, are forced to work second jobs in order to keep their farms operating.

Agricultural land requires much less in the way of services than other land uses and thus is less of a burden on taxpayers. Pastoral land can also serve as a barrier to sprawl development. Aesthetically it maintains the beauty of the countryside and also provides a connection to our agrarian heritage. Agriculture compliments the region's largest industry, which is tourism. Many local farms are small family-run operations that have been passed down from generation to generation.

However, today agriculture in the Hudson region, particularly the family-run farm, is under siege. Of the approximately 700,000 acres of farmland that existed in the Hudson Valley in 1989, an estimated 18,600 are lost each year, half to residential or commercial development. The American Farmland Trust, a national nonprofit organization promoting farmland preservation, has ranked the Hudson Valley among the nation's ten most threatened farming regions. Local agriculture, which is usually small-scale, has to compete against large-scale corporate agribusiness, which is prevalent outside the region and has superior resources for distributing and marketing goods. Farmers have traditionally been encouraged by government policy and their creditors to take on more debt and incur greater production expenses in an effort to boost crop yields. This has gotten many small farms into financial trouble, especially when commodity prices have fallen or during years when crop yields were low.

Another major factor in the decline of farming is suburban sprawl, which has reduced the amount of land available for agriculture while raising land prices and taxes. Zoning laws are frequently amended to accommodate developers.

In a densely populated area like the Hudson region, the use of chemical fertilizers and pesticides often puts farmers at odds with their neighbors, who justly feel threatened by these products. Many farmers believe that there is too much regulation and public pressure, which interferes with their ability to be productive.

The high capital costs of getting into farming deter young people from starting out. More can be done to encourage small-scale farming, specialty crops, farm cooperatives, and organic sustainable farming, which recycles nutrients and has little negative impact on the environment and a ready market for its chemical-free products. Farmers' markets, pick-your-own operations, county fairs, and harvest festivals provide consumers with direct links to the area's agrarian economy. The establishment of agricultural districts encourages the maintenance of farms through favorable property assessments and lower tax rates.

THE FOREST STRIKES BACK

One of the most dramatic changes in the twentieth-century landscape of the Hudson region is the return of the forests. The regional decline of agriculture and the timber industry are two of the primary reasons for this phenomenon. Also, by the early twentieth century, the Hudson fell out of fashion as a retreat for the wealthy. Many large estates were sold or donated to the public, and in many cases areas that had been landscaped or farmed have returned to forest. Forest fires, a natural phenomenon, but one actively used by the Native Americans and early European settlers, have been suppressed now for at least two hundred years, allowing new forests to grow unchecked, and fire-sensitive species like maple, beech, and hemlock to proliferate.

This trend has also been observable throughout much of the eastern United States between the Atlantic coast and the Appalachians. In addition to the return of the forests, once nearly extinct species such as deer, wild turkey, beaver, and bear have reappeared in large numbers. However, with the many changes that have taken place, the introduction of nonnative species, and the absence of certain native ones like the wolf, mountain lion, and the extinct passenger pigeon, the current forest will never be the same as the wilderness forest that existed before. It has been greatly affected by the recent proliferation of deer, favoring species of trees and shrubs unpalatable to them. The present-day forest also shows the evidence of past human activity in the form of stone walls, foundations, and old roads, now trails. Largely fragmented, separated by developed areas and crisscrossed by roads and powerlines, it exists in close proximity to centers of human population. Water and air carry the effects of human activity in the form of pollution. Of particular concern is the impact acid rain has on forests: Pollution generated far from the region can still affect the health of the area's forests.

4 The Dynamic Landscape

Environmental Problems

NONNATIVE SPECIES

Ever since advent of the first European settlers, exotic species of plants and animals have been introduced to the region, sometimes on purpose and sometimes by accident, and the process continues to occur today. Lacking competition or threats from their normal predators or disease, and finding the human-disturbed landscape ideal for establishing themselves, many species of foreign plants and animals have thrived. These include attractive species of birds like swans and ring-necked pheasants, and ornamental trees, shrubs, and flowers that brighten forests and fields. Many have done so well that most people scarcely realize they are nonnatives. It is estimated that roughly 18 percent of the plant species in the region are exotics. In many cases exotics are considered pests, some of them threatening to crowd out native species, which are more specialized, less adaptable to changes, and less suited to human-disturbed environments. The introduction of English sparrows and starlings, for example, increased pressure on eastern bluebirds, a native species, to find suitable tree cavities for nest sites. Only the use of humanmade nests has led to a resurgence in their population. Nonnative species of plants are often not as nutritious to the animals that feed on them as their native counterparts. When the native plants are eliminated, the animals that depend on them also suffer. Some of the more harmful exotic species are listed below:

Water chestnuts, originally from southern Europe and Asia, arrived in Massachusetts in 1875 for use as an ornamental plant. An annual that inhabits freshwater sections of the Hudson, from Garrison north, it floats in shallow water rooted to the bottom and produces hard spiny nuts that are prevalent in many places along the Hudson shoreline. The water chestnut thrives in nutrient-rich, still waters and is extremely prolific, able to spread over large surfaces in a relatively short time, crowding out more desirable plants and limiting such human activities as swimming and boating. It has been reported that dissolved-oxygen levels are low where water chestnuts are concentrated, and this may inhibit the use of such habitats by fish (those that do are primarily exotics like the European carp). Water chestnuts rot quickly when dead and are not valuable as a food supply for marsh animals.

Purple loosestrife, a perennial herb introduced from Europe in the 1800s, produces tall spikes of bright purple flowers that are extremely attractive from a distance. It thrives in a variety of sunny wet habitats, especially mature marshes, where it competes with cattails and other native plants. There is no best way of controlling the population. The most that can be done is closely monitor areas that have not been invaded yet and remove any new exotic plants before they can establish themselves.

Eurasian water milfoil form large, exclusive patches in some shallow-water areas. Water milfoil stands are not attractive to feeding waterfowl. Like the water chestnut, the water milfoil is fast-decaying and therefore a poor source of nutrition for animals.

Common reeds are a perennial grass, also referred to as Phragmites, the scientific name. These are actually native to the region, but their numbers have proliferated and they thrive in human-disturbed environments from drainage ditches to marshlands. Like purple loosestrife, they compete with cattails and other native marsh plants and are considered pests.

Gypsy moths were accidentally released in Massachusetts around the turn of the century. Within forty years they had spread throughout the Northeast and Midwest, devouring the leaves of oaks and other trees, sometimes defoliating whole sections of forest. They are particularly destructive in oak-hickory forests. Gypsy moth outbreaks occur in cyclical patterns, with population explosions followed by years of population declines, the result of predation and disease. Fortunately forests have shown an amazing capacity for recovery and renewal following these destructive outbreaks. After a few years forests have regenerated themselves and most traces of the gypsy moth destruction have vanished.

A more recent arrival in the area is the zebra mussel. This small, one- to two-inch long freshwater bivalve came to the United States in the ballast water of ships from Europe, quickly infested the ports of the Great Lakes, and traveled via the New York State Barge Canal to the Hudson.

The population now numbers in the billions. Zebra mussels are especially pernicious to humankind, clogging water-intake pipes and valves. They are expensive to remove and nearly impossible to prevent.

AIR POLLUTION

In 1970 passage by Congress of the Clean Air Act established a series of deadlines for all areas of the country to meet the standards detailed in the act, or face sanctions. The Environmental Protection Agency (EPA) has set standards for seven prominent pollutants including nitrogen, ozone, carbon monoxide, lead, and sulfur dioxide. Studies show that these contribute to a vast range of health-related problems, including damage to the immune system, eye irritation, lung damage, asthma, bronchitis, emphysema, and heart disease. In addition they have a negative impact on the environment, adversely affecting plants and animals, producing acid rain, damaging forests and crops, polluting water bodies like the Hudson River, and corroding materials such as rubber, stone, and paint. Other highly toxic pollutants, not measured or regulated by the EPA, include dioxins, which are known carcinogens and cause birth defects and liver and endocrine damage. Dioxins are formed when certain products are combined with chlorine in the combustion process that is usually associated with incineration.

In the nineteenth century coal and wood stoves and industry were the main source of air pollution in the region's urban areas. Fortunately coal and wood stoves are no longer so prevalent, and newer models have been designed to emit fewer pollutants. In the Hudson region most of the worst industrial sources of air pollution have either closed or moved away. However, automobiles and trucks are now the major source of air pollutants, and suburban sprawl is the primary factor in spreading pollution throughout the region. Better planning and use of open space to keep population concentrated reduces sprawl. The major car manufacturers are also under pressure to produce vehicles that emit fewer pollutants, though it is unlikely an affordable pollution-free automobile will be available anytime in the near future.

WATER POLLUTION

While the Clean Water Act has immensely improved the quality of the Hudson River's water, there are still outstanding issues. For example, the problem of sewage is complicated by the use of combined sanitary sewers and storm drains in a number of urban centers. After large rainstorms, the overflow may flush the system, sending untreated sewage directly into the Hudson or one of its tributaries. Upgrading systems so that sanitary sewers and storm water pipes are separated or building storage tanks to collect the overflows for later treatment are expensive options. New York State's Pure Waters Program subsidizes the construction of new waste-water facilities. Meanwhile new commercial and residential developments tax existing sewage systems, which may be unable to keep up with the demands. Water conservation measures can reduce the demands on existing systems and delay or eliminate the need for expanding facilities.

Another major source of pollution is the industrial discharge of chemicals and heavy metals, such as cadmium, lead, and mercury, directly into the river and its tributaries. These are acutely toxic to both wildlife and human beings. They are not water soluble. They accumulate in sediments, are consumed by living things, and their concentration grows with each consumption. As mentioned in chapter 3, one key program of the Clean Water Act is the National Pollution Discharge Elimination System, or the State Pollution Discharge Elimination System (SPDES) when administered by the states, as it is in New York and New Jersey. It required the states to establish water-quality programs at least as stringent as the EPA and created standards for ninety-five hazardous substances and guidelines for one hundred additional substances. Based on this system of classification and water-quality standards for each classification, the SPDES can issue permits to facilities discharging wastes as long as they fall within the guidelines. By controlling what is discharged, and the amount, the SPDES has certainly limited polluting discharges into the river, but it is not designed to eliminate them. Also, because of limited staff and resources, enforcement is insufficient, primarily dependent on self-monitoring with only occasional inspections. Without a doubt, numerous illegal discharges take place.

Runoff from the land is another major problem affecting water quality in the river and its tributaries. Fertilizers, which include nitrogen and phosphates, and pesticides (used in lawn maintenance and landscaping) associated with suburban developments and agriculture, and the use of herbicides and rock salts along roadways and railroads, send potentially harmful chemicals and other toxic substances into streams and, eventually, the river. Pesticides and herbicides often kill animals and plants that were not their intended victims. Rachel Carson's famous book *Silent Spring* (1962) helped publicize the problem that DDT use was having on a number of bird species whose reproductive systems were impacted by the pesticide, leading to their decline. Some pesticides and other chemicals have been known to have harmful effects on human populations as well. Only since the use of certain pesticides, including DDT, has been banned have many bird species, such as the osprey, begun to make a comeback. Better land-use planning may prevent some of this runoff.

Protection of watersheds is a key element in such measures. Also, reductions in the use of potentially harmful chemicals will ultimately reduce their presence in the environment. In most cases nontoxic or less toxic alternatives exist and can be successfully employed.

Barges and ships sometimes collide or run aground and spill their contents into the river or its tributaries. Despite safety measures such accidents occur too frequently. In 1977 the barge *Ethel H* ran aground at Con Hook, just north of the Bear Mountain Bridge, and released four hundred thousand gallons of oil into the river, creating an oil slick that extended as far as Long Island. Oil and other chemicals have properties that make them difficult to remove from the water, making cleanup efforts problematic if not impossible. While much of the impact is immediate—blackened shorelines and beaches, oil-soaked birds—much of it is also long term. Oil floats on water and is destructive to plant life, fish larvae, and invertebrates such as insect larvae and zooplankton, which utilize the water surface and form a vital part of the food chain larger animals depend on.

Efforts to reduce the risk of spills take the form of more rigorous standards and more frequent and thorough inspections of facilities and vessels. Improved training for operators and better equipment may also reduce the risk of spills. Better contingency plans and implementation may help reduce the negative impact of spills should they occur. All these measures are costly, but so is cleaning up spills.

PCBs

One hundred and fifty years of industrial activity along the Hudson have left an unfortunate legacy of toxic chemical residues in many places, long after the offending industries have closed or departed. Trying to clean up that residue is one of the greatest challenges faced by environmental advocates in improving the quality of the river's water. For more than thirty years the General Electric Company (GE) dumped 1.3 million pounds of PCBs into the Hudson River from two of its manufacturing plants, located in Fort Edward and Glens Falls. Manufactured since 1929, PCBs (polychlorinated biphenyls) are odorless, colorless chemical compounds that range in consistency from heavy, oily liquids to waxy solids. They are relatively stable, conduct heat but not electricity, and are not water soluble and therefore have many industrial applications, including electrical insulation, fillers in adhesives, plastics, fabric dyes, paint, and carbonless copy paper. Environmental and health problems associated with exposure to PCBs include cancer and birth defects and damage to the reproductive, nervous, and immune systems. Despite knowing that PCBs were potentially toxic, GE continued to produce and dump them into the river until they were finally banned in 1977. (Some foreign countries still produce them.)

Though more than twenty years have passed since GE stopped dumping PCBs into the Hudson, the damage has yet to be cleaned up. Settling on the river bottom near the GE plants, PCBs have continued to spread throughout the river and the organisms that inhabit it. Since PCBs are fat soluble, they accumulate as they move up the food chain. Many species of fish and turtles now contain PCBs, and top-of-the-food-chain predators, such as mink and osprey, have also suffered from PCB contamination. Human exposure to PCBs comes primarily through the consumption of fish that feed in contaminated sediments. As a result many fish caught in the Hudson, including striped bass, are considered unsafe to eat. Though the Department of Health and the Department of Environmental Conservation have issued advisories against eating certain species of Hudson River fish, many fishermen are unfortunately unaware of the warnings or choose to ignore them. While PCB levels in fish have declined since the 1970s, the more chlorinated, more toxic PCB compounds have not declined as much as the less chlorinated ones. The danger still persists, and PCBs are the primary contaminant in the Hudson, preventing full use and enjoyment of the river.

Suction-dredging of contaminated sediments, using the most up-to-date technologies, and then treating them before depositing them in a landfill, is the method of cleanup favored by most environmental groups. This is the one the EPA has recommended for other contaminated waterways.

The EPA has gotten involved through the 1980 Federal Superfund Program, which requires that known polluters pay the full costs of cleanups (hundreds of millions of dollars in this case) and can even go after GE to pay compensation for damage its PCBs have caused. In 1983 the Hudson south of Hudson Falls all the way to the Battery was designated by the EPA on its Superfund Priority List, making it one of the largest Superfund sites in the nation. However, to this day, only limited remedial action has taken place. In 1991 and 1992 it was discovered that PCBs were continuing to leak from GE's old plant sites directly into the Hudson. GE has continued to resist pressure to remove the contaminated sediment from the river, claiming that it is safer to leave it alone and that it will eventually biodegrade.

THE PROBLEMS OF RECREATION

As the Hudson's waters became cleaner, multitudes found that the river and its vicinity were desirable again for recreational activity. What was once a major avenue of commerce is today also a recreational river.

While recreational boating activity has been one of the primary positive forces behind efforts to improve and redevelop the Hudson's waterfront, it has also created new stresses for the environment. There has been a proliferation in the use of powerboats and jet skis. Besides being noisy and disturbing users of such nonmotorized craft as canoes, kayaks, and sailboats, motorized craft create large wakes that sometimes damage shallow bottoms, churning up sediments and harming aquatic plants and other life. The noise also frightens wildlife, which needs a relatively tranquil environment, especially for breeding and nesting. Since their motors often use leaded fuel, accidental spills or deliberate dumping can be a source of toxic pollutants in the river. Unfortunately some users of motorized craft are also a source of sewage and litter. Facilities for motorized craft are limited and unable to meet the growing demand, thereby increasing the pressure to build new facilities in environmentally sensitive areas.

On trails, motorized vehicles, called all-terrain vehicles (ATVs), crush vegetation and small animals, and the noise frightens wildlife as well as humans who have come to enjoy peace and tranquility in the woods. The wide tires of ATVs carve deep ruts in the ground, which fill with water and become muddy, making the trails unpleasant for walkers and causing them to detour around the muddy sites, thus trampling more vegetation in the process. ATVs have done a considerable amount of damage in places like Mount Beacon, which is only beginning to recover. Though ATVs are banned from most open-space land, their owners risking arrest and fines should they get caught, a number of ATV users trespass despite the deterrent.

Not all problems are the result of motorized use, however. Hunters and fishermen trample vegetation and sometimes leave litter behind. In the case of marshland, trampled vegetation creates niches where undesirable nonnative vegetation can gain a foothold and eventually crowd out the native species. Mountain bikes, though not as damaging as motorized vehicles, in large numbers can seriously degrade trails, cause erosion, and create hazzards for wildlife and pedestrians; they are banned from most hiking trails in the region. Even hikers and walkers can degrade an area through overuse. Some well-traveled hiking trails have experienced a significant amount of soil erosion. Trampling vegetation and disturbing wildlife are other problems caused by recreational pedestrian use. Any place that supports recreation is prone to graffiti and other forms of vandalism, and litter. To decrease erosion, trails on slopes shouldn't be built at too-steep angles. Instead they should be located on the crest of the slope or, in some cases, the bottom, avoiding sensitive habitats whenever possible. The amount of use a sensitive terrain can tolerate before it is seriously degraded is called its carrying capacity. The effect such use might have on animal and plant life has to be carefully calculated before new areas are opened to the public.

Programs, Organizations, and Solutions

PRESERVING OPEN SPACE

Open space is necessary to preserve habitats for native plants and wildlife as well as historical, archaeological, and cultural resources. Developed areas where vegetation has been stripped and soils compacted, such as lawns, streets, and parking lots, do not retain water nearly as well as land that is naturally forested. Open-space preservation protects watersheds, thus reducing runoff, which prevents soil erosion and flooding, ensuring better water quality as well as an adequate supply. Many feel that the presence of open space is necessary for our mental, spiritual, and even physical health by providing refuge from urban crowding and the stresses of modern life. Open space offers opportunities for privacy, solitude, and contemplation outside the confinement of our abodes. It also affords a place for such recreational activities as hiking, biking, bird-watching, hunting, fishing, canoeing, kayaking, sailing, cross-country skiing, picnicking, and snowmobiling, to name only a few. Open-space protection provides a buffer from development while preserving an area's scenic character. This may help to promote tourism, but it also ensures a higher quality of life outside the buffer, and this in turn may encourage new residents, as well as new businesses and services, to migrate there. It also forces developers to make more efficient use of the land that is available. Preservation of open space may actually improve the economic, social, and environmental health of neighboring communities. A scenic resource like the Hudson River in the center of a populated region can provide a key focal point for open-space preservation efforts.

The idea of preserving open space through planning is not new. In the nineteenth century Frederick Law Olmsted was among those who advocated setting aside undeveloped land in its natural state for the public. Unlike those who focused solely on wilderness areas, he felt that easily accessible open space close to urban areas was desirable.

In the past most open space was preserved through acquisition of land by the state. Land acquisition programs were generally well funded, and where owners of land refused to sell, the state could exercise its right to eminent domain—to condemn the property for the best interests of the state's residents—in which case the owners would be forced to sell. New York State–owned open-space land is managed by the Department of Environmental Conservation (DEC), the Office of Parks, Recreation, and

Historic Preservation (OPRHP), and the Palisades Interstate Park Commission (PIPC), a semiautonomous body that owns and manages parklands on the west side of the Hudson, in New York and New Jersey. In the twentieth century most funding for open-space acquisitions in New York State were through special appropriations or through the issuing of bonds approved by the voters in a referendum. Bond funding spreads the costs over a number of years, but results in higher interest rates.

More recently state funding for land acquisition has been significantly cut back. Property rights advocates have grown stronger, and antipathy toward government authority is more widespread. The practice of eminent domain has become very unpopular and now is rarely used for open-space protection. Also, land has become more expensive, something that is particularly true along the Hudson River. Recent improvements in the river's water quality and the environment along its banks has made it more desirable and enticing to developers. Suburban sprawl and the desire of many urban dwellers to purchase second homes in the Hudson Valley have also increased these pressures. Rising land values and taxes have made it difficult for owners of large tracts of land, especially farmers and owners of forest land, to not succumb to the pressure to subdivide and sell their property. The loss of individual tracts of land to development may be relatively small, but the cumulative impact of many such losses is huge, as areas of open space disappear.

TOWN PLANNING BOARDS

Most land-use planning decisions are made at the local level by town planning boards—elected bodies that develop zoning ordinances to regulate the types of permissible land use in each zone. Planning boards also consider proposed development projects, providing a public forum where citizens can comment on a proposed project's desirability, raising aesthetic and environmental concerns. Boards may require that an environmental impact statement (EIS) be completed, per the New York State Environmental Quality Review Act (SEQRA). SEQRA requires that any potential environmental impacts be investigated and that there be full public disclosure of the results. EIS statements can be challenged in the courts. Certain projects may also require a variance of local zoning laws, which means that environmental and other impacts have to be considered before a variance will be granted.

Unfortunately planning board members often have little expertise in environmental issues and are subject to pressures from developers to approve their proposed projects. Because of elections and turnover, planning boards are always subject to change. And what one community rejects another may embrace with open arms. More effective permanent ways need to be found to ensure the protection of significant lands.

LAND TRUSTS

Today most open-space land preservation is done by private agencies purchasing the land, often with the support and cooperation of the state. Nonprofit private land agencies, frequently called land trusts, may be national organizations like the Nature Conservancy, the National Audubon Society, and the Open Space Institute, or more regional organizations, such as Scenic Hudson. Columbia, Dutchess, and Westchester Counties have their own land conservancies. These have greater flexibility than state agencies when it comes to purchasing land. Land often becomes available and is sold faster than a state agency, with its cumbersome bureaucracy and policy of review, can act. Land trusts can react more quickly and can utilize a greater range of funding options, and land ownership can later be transferred to the state or a local community at a more convenient time. Today, however, many land trusts are maintaining ownership and managing their own properties. Land trusts can also act as facilitators, helping broker deals between landowners and state agencies.

CONSERVATION EASEMENTS

By far most open-space land is privately owned. Purchasing open space is not the only option for protection, nor is it always the best option. A conservation easement is a legal agreement a property owner makes voluntarily to restrict some or all of the development rights on a designated property he or she owns. The land remains in his or her possession, but future development of the land is restricted by the terms of the easement. The donation of an easement for conservation purposes to a qualified conservation organization or public agency is considered a tax-deductible charitable gift.

THE NATIONAL PARK SERVICE: RIVERS, TRAILS, AND CONSERVATION ASSISTANCE PROGRAM

The National Park Service operates a series of programs to help state agencies, communities, and nonprofit organizations cooperatively plan and develop projects to preserve open space, to create greenway corridors and trail systems, revitalize urban areas, convert abandoned rail lines to trails, and improve access for recreational purposes. These programs rely on partnerships to accomplish their objectives. The National Park Service role is catalytic and limited to two or three years. To win program support, projects must demonstrate need, the quality of the resource to be developed or protected, tangible results from the project, and community backing. The Rivers and Trails Program provides technical assistance through its planners, engineers, and landscape architects, who help with assessments, planning, seeking funding sources, and project implementation. The National Park Service also helps publicize and promote these projects.

WETLANDS PROTECTION

The Hudson River Estuary is an area of immense value both as open space and as vital habitat for numerous fish, birds, and other wildlife (many of which are endangered or threatened), as a feeding, nesting, or spawning ground. The estuary includes thirty-four sites designated as Significant Coastal Fish and Wildlife Habitats. Unfortunately five thousand acres of Hudson Valley wetlands have already been developed. The 1975 Freshwater Wetlands Act, administered by state and local governments, regulates activities potentially harmful to wetlands but only covers wetlands more than 12.4 acres in size. The DEC and the EPA have helped various entities work cooperatively to develop a comprehensive long-range management plan for the Hudson River estuary to balance sustainable use with the needs to protect this valuable resource.

THE COASTAL ZONE MANAGEMENT PROGRAM

In 1972 Congress passed the Federal Coastal Zone Management Act, which encourages states to preserve or restore their coastlines. The Hudson estuary as far north as Troy is considered part of New York State's coastline. Authorized by the Coastal Zone Management Act, the DEC in cooperation with PIPC, the OPRHP, and the Department of State manages four of the Hudson River's largest wetlands—Piermont, Iona Island, Tivoli, and Stockport—as part of the 4,130-acre National Hudson River Estuarine Research Reserve. New York State's Coastal Zone Management Program also stimulates communities to develop local waterfront revitalization plans to set guidelines for development. The state provides technical assistance and some funding to develop these plans. So far, more than half the communities along the Hudson have participated in this process, and thirteen have state-approved local waterfront plans.

URBAN CULTURAL PARKS

In 1982, New York State established the Urban Cultural Park System, administered by the OPRHP. Urban cultural parks are living communities in restored historic urban neighborhoods. The purpose of the program is to promote preservation, education, recreation, and economic development through a host of activities including walking tours, festivals, shopping, and dining. Each urban cultural park has a visitors' center with exhibits and information on ways to better experience the park. Communities in the process of revitalizing their historic neighborhoods can apply for state designation as urban cultural parks.

Kingston has two urban cultural parks: the Stockade District and the Rondout. Albany and Ossining also have urban cultural parks.

ENVIRONMENTAL GROUPS

A large number of not-for-profit environmental groups are striving to improve the environment in the region. Some are nationally based, such as the Sierra Club, the National Audubon Society, and the Nature Conservancy. Others are more community based or issue focused. Three of the most prominent ones that focus primarily on the Hudson River are the Riverkeeper, the Hudson River Sloop Clearwater, Inc., and Scenic Hudson. The Riverkeeper, a program of the Hudson River Fishermen's Association, which was founded in 1966, represents the Hudson's commercial fishermen and is dedicated to protecting the river from polluters. Historically fishing has been an important activity along the river. However, in the nineteenth and twentieth centuries, commercial fishing in the Hudson steadily declined because of pollution, habitat loss, and stock depletion. The number of commercial fishermen in the Hudson decreased from seventy-one in 1933 to only thirty-one in 1974. PCB contamination has halted practically all commercial fishing in the river. Only sturgeon and shad can be safely fished because they feed primarily in the ocean, returning to the river only to spawn.

In 1983, using moneys won in its suit against Con Ed, preventing it from building the pump-storage facility at Storm King, HFRA established the Riverkeeper program and hired John Cronin, a longtime environmental advocate, to patrol the Hudson by boat and catch polluters in the act of dumping waste illegally. In his first assignment Cronin was alerted by local residents in the Hyde Park area that Exxon tankers were discharging seawater into the Hudson and refilling the tanks with water from the river. They would then transport the water to Aruba, in the Caribbean, where fresh water is at a premium, and sell it for a high price or use it in the refinery there. Caught in the act by Cronin, with the media present, Exxon was sued by the Riverkeeper and the state. The company agreed to halt the practice and pay the Riverkeeper half a million dollars, used to establish the Riverkeeper Fund.

In 1984 Robert F. Kennedy Jr. was hired by the Riverkeeper as an attorney to pursue lawsuits against polluters, and in 1987 he established the Pace University Law School Environmental Law Clinic. Since 1983

Cronin and Kennedy have successfully settled 150 suits against major Hudson polluters. Due to the effectiveness of this program, a number of riverkeepers have been established on other major water bodies in the country. Their address is Riverkeeper, 25 Wing & Wing, Garrison, NY 10524.

The Hudson River Sloop Clearwater is an educational and environmental advocacy group. It uses its famous sloop, the *Clearwater*, first launched in 1969, to help promote appreciation of the river as a resource and awareness of issues affecting the river's health. The 106-foot-long *Clearwater* is a replica of a nineteenth-century Hudson River sloop. More than eighteen thousand people each year, mostly schoolchildren, experience and learn about the river at first hand aboard the *Clearwater*, through its Classroom of the Waves program. Through its educational programs, Clearwater also works with schools and the general public. Largely supported by membership contributions and grants, it sponsors numerous festivals and events, many located along the riverfront, and utilizes the talents of renowned local musicians like Pete Seeger (the folksinger and one of the founders of the *Clearwater* project) to raise money for its programs and promote awareness. Clearwater has been very active, including in lobbying efforts, on a number of environmental issues, particularly PCB contamination. It has also been a strong advocate for increased public access to the riverfront. Their address is Hudson River Sloop Clearwater, Inc., 112 Market Street, Poughkeepsie, NY 12601.

Scenic Hudson was also founded in response to the plan that threatened Storm King. Today Scenic Hudson is an environmental organization focused on, among other things, land preservation, mainly through acquisitions and easements. Through its efforts 11,000 acres of land have been protected from development and eighteen new parks and preserves have been created. Scenic Hudson is also involved in monitoring development activities, testifying at hearings, improving access to the riverfront, issues affecting the health of the river such as PCB contamination, grassroots organizing, lobbying, and public education. It is funded largely by foundations and individual donors as well as corporate and government sources. Their address is Scenic Hudson, 9 Vassar Street, Poughkeepsie, NY 12601.

THE HUDSON RIVER VALLEY GREENWAY

One of the biggest challenges facing those trying to improve the area's environment is the region's host of political entities. Besides straddling two states and eleven counties, the Hudson Estuary borders a multitude of towns, villages, and cities. The river often acts as a political barrier rather than as a unifying factor. Communities are usually conscious of their own rights and prerogatives and highly suspicious of (and sometimes hostile to) the concept of regional planning. Getting these communities to work cooperatively for the benefit of the entire region is a daunting task.

A greenway is a kind of linear park that links parks, open-space areas, natural landmarks, historic sites, and cultural centers into one identifiable entity. In 1991 the New York State Legislature established the Hudson River Valley Greenway, whose goals are resource protection, coordinated regional planning, economic development, improved public access, and education, and which is designed to improve the quality of life within the greenway. Its primary purpose, however, is to create a sense of community for the entire region.

The greenway encourages all communities within the area to develop their own plans consistent with its overall objectives. The plans are then combined and, through a twenty-five-member independent Hudson River Valley Greenway Communities Council, an overall greenway plan is developed.

The Greenway Conservancy for the Hudson River Valley supplies technical assistance and funding to communities for greenway projects, one of the big projects being the development of a Hudson River Greenway Trail. The conservancy also promotes tourism, economic development, agriculture, cleanup and revitalization of waterfronts, and other efforts that enhance the greenway model.

5 How To

Walking

THE ART OF FOOT TRAVEL

To me walking is about balance and perspective, the body moving gracefully through space while focusing attention on oneself and one's relationship to everything around one. Walking is also about physical and mental health. Though walking doesn't put undue stress on the body, it helps keep it in optimum shape. It is an exercise most people can do, no matter what age or physical condition. The positive mental health benefits of getting outdoors and walking have been recognized for centuries. In our stress-filled world the benefits of getting out, getting away, and walking—for even short periods—cannot be emphasized enough.

For me walking means taking one's time—an opportunity to relax and enjoy a slower-paced existence than the one we usually experience. Walking also affords an opportunity to learn about patience and the idea that even if we don't rush, we'll still get where we're going eventually.

Don't overextend yourself. Trying to do more than you can leads only to frustration, muscle pain, blisters, and fatigue. I've met people doing eight to ten miles on rough terrain for their first hike, and they didn't look happy. (Most, I suspect, will never try it again.) My advice is to start small and gradually work your way up to bigger things. Muscles usually get in shape quickly, and feet toughen up with experience. Before you know it your body and mind are ready for the bigger challenges.

Walking trails covered in this book include paved pathways (primarily used for strolling, jogging, biking, skateboarding, or in-line skating), shoulders of roads (where one will have to contend with traffic), carriage roads, old rail beds, and woods roads (well-graded, wide unpaved paths, closed to motorized traffic, though you may have to share them with mountain bikes and equestrians; the Old Croton Aqueduct Trailway is an excellent example), and hiking trails designed specifically for day hikers and backpackers. Note that some trails, particularly in the Hudson Highlands and Palisades, are relatively steep, and some may involve scrambling (using one's hands as well as feet) to traverse logs, rocks, and boulders. Also, most (though by no means all) trails are marked with paint blazes or colored metal or plastic disks spaced far enough apart for the hiker to see the next marking up the trail. Cairns—piles of stones— are sometimes used to mark trails, especially where trees are absent. (Bushwacking, or hiking off trail, is not covered in this book. Only those with good wilderness skills, especially in the use of a compass, should attempt to bushwack.)

Some basic rules for walking outdoors: You are responsible for yourself. Accept the risks inherent in outdoor recreation and try to minimize them through care and thought. Do not deface rocks or trees with graffiti. Leave animals and plants alone. Do not litter. Dispose of your own trash. Respect any land you walk on, whether it's private or public property. Where trails are marked or well defined, stay on them. Creating your own path encourages others to follow, trampling vegetation and causing erosion.

PACKS

Those going for day walks won't need much equipment. Besides obvious clothing and footwear, the only other essential item is a daypack or rucksack to carry your supplies. Daypacks come in all sizes and shapes, and which one is most suitable for you depends on your plans. For an easy half-day hike on a fine day in late spring, you won't have to bring much, so a small pack should be adequate. Longer hikes or hikes in tougher conditions require more supplies and equipment, so bigger packs will be necessary. Packs come in many designs and may have such features as special pockets, cushioned straps, and hip belts. The two things I pay attention to when buying a day pack are durability and the quality of the zipper. Zippers seem to be the first feature of the pack that breaks. Repairing a zipper may cost as much as the pack itself, so it pays to get one with a good zipper. Keep in mind that though most of us treat our equipment roughly, we expect it to endure such treatment.

Fanny packs and belt packs are good but only sufficient for short hikes. I find that they don't hold enough water, food, and extra clothing for full-day hikes, unless somebody else is carrying most of the supplies.

When one is also carrying a day pack or backpacking, a belt pack is a convenient place to store a map, compass, snacks, water bottle, and camera—things you might want readily available, so you won't have to stop and take your backpack off each time you need them.

PLANNING AND MAPS

Careful planning usually results in a better outing. I don't feel that one loses anything in terms of spontaneity when one plans: In the outdoors, no matter how much you plan, most of your experiences will still be unanticipated. Good planning puts you in a place where pleasurable and meaningful experiences can happen. Planning means asking yourself what you would like to do and estimating how much you can do where and how best to do it.

Maps provide an idea of what to expect before you actually visit a site. They are the key planning tool for any outdoor experience. Before I go on a trip I always study the map, trying to familiarize myself with the terrain and the location of landmarks and sights. Contour lines on a map will provide a sense of a trail's difficulty—when they are squeezed closely together, it usually indicates a dramatic change in elevation.

Maps more detailed than the ones in this book may be desired by some walkers and bicyclists. The New York/New Jersey Trail Conference publishes an excellent series of trail maps covering the Palisades, Hudson Highlands, and Catskills. These maps are generally accurate, easy to follow, and made of tough, water-repellent, tear-resistant material. They can be purchased at many camping and sporting goods stores, as well as some bookstores. They can also be ordered directly from the Trail Conference.

Many individual sites have their own maps, which may ordered by calling or writing whoever manages the land. (For example, Scenic Hudson has a number of maps for its various properties.) Maps may also be available at the entrance to a park, but don't count on it: Places often run out of maps. Road maps and atlases, available from most grocery stores, pharmacies, and convenience stores, may be useful for locating trailheads or if you're riding a bike and planning to visit places beyond the physical scope of this book.

EQUIPMENT AND SUPPLIES

I always carry a compass even though I rarely use it. Don't get lost in the first place, and you probably won't need one, but learn how to use a compass, and if you do get lost, it may help lead you to safety.

Some people prefer to carry a walking stick. A walking stick will take some weight off your legs by acting as a third one. It also provides a prop you can use to steady your balance. I've heard they are especially useful when walking uphill, and they can be used to probe for loose rocks or poisonous snakes. A walking stick can be anything from a stick you find lying on the trail to one that is intricately carved and superexpensive.

Water is the primary sustenance the human body requires, and I take some whenever I walk anywhere. Given how essential water is, we probably don't drink enough. However, outdoor exertion, especially in heat, requires large amounts of water. Even in cool temperatures one can work up a good sweat with enough exertion. Lack of water can cause dehydration and fatigue. Water is heavy and takes up a lot of space in your pack, so most people don't like to carry too much. Nonetheless I feel it is better to carry a lot, even if you don't use it all, than to end up short somewhere far from any source. My rule of thumb is, for a full-day hike bring at least one quart of water per person. On a hot or very strenuous day, two quarts are preferred.

Water is best carried in containers made of nalogene, a nearly indestructible plastic that is able to take rough treatment. I've found that regular plastic containers and canteens puncture easily, especially the larger ones. As to water sources along the trail, the only ones I trust are water pumps. Springs, where the water obviously comes straight out of the ground, can dry up in the middle of the summer and aren't always safe; there's no way of really testing them. Stream, pond, lake, or river water in the Hudson region is likely to be infected by pollutants or by the microscopic protozoan Giardia. Giardia can be found in streams far from any human developments. A stream may look clear and the water may taste good, but there's no way a hiker can know if it's really safe. A reaction to Giardia—called giardiosis—usually hits seven to ten days after the protozoan has been ingested. Common symptoms include diarrhea, cramps, and loss of appetite. To purify water of Giardia you can utilize a portable water filter, available in most camping and outdoor recreation stores. It's important to keep water filters clean. Boiling water for several minutes also effectively kills all Giardia. (Neither method, of course, is effective with water that is polluted by chemicals.)

Food can be anything from a snack to an elaborate gourmet feast. Keep in mind that exerting yourself is liable to build up a big appetite, and you may want to eat more than you usually do, so bring more food than you normally eat: You'll be surprised how fast it disappears. Also, remember that some foods spoil or get soggy more easily than others, so try to bring things that keep their freshness well. Package most food in plastic bags for protection and to keep them better organized and easily accessible. Carbohydrates are considered especially good for high-energy activities. Energy bars and trail mix (usually a combination of various nuts, raisins, dried fruit, and cereals) make excellent snack material.

CLOTHING

Because weather conditions in the Hudson region are fairly predictable and rarely extreme, one need not splurge on the best protective garments available. A wool sweater or light jacket may be necessary in the spring and fall; and regular casual clothing, such as jeans, is suitable for most hikes in this book as long as the conditions are fairly mild and dry. Chances are that you'll encounter some mud, however, so prepare for the fact that your clothes will probably get soiled.

Whatever you wear, the best approach is layering, so you can easily take off or put on the various items, one piece at a time. Conditions are likely to vary over the course of the day. Generally it's cooler in the morning and hotter in the afternoon. Your body temperature may also vary depending on what you're doing. You need to have the right kind of clothing to address these possible changes in conditions. Bright colors will certainly help others spot you should you get lost. Be forewarned: Cotton clothing, which is fine in hot or mild weather, is worthless for protection once it becomes damp or wet. It also takes forever to dry.

In the past ten years there's been a revolution in outdoor wear, and today many people wouldn't think of going out except in hiking outfits. Many of these were originally designed for people who hike or climb in extreme conditions of cold and moisture. Usually lightweight, these outfits provide good protection from the elements. Their bright colors and other attractive design features have made them fashionable even with those who aren't "into" the outdoors.

I don't recommend going out and purchasing a new hiking outfit all at once. Acquiring the right gear should be a slow process of experimentation, finding out what works best in what conditions. Polyester pile and fleece jackets and sweaters have the advantage of being extremely lightweight, warm, and fast drying; relatively cheap ones are sufficient for hiking in the Hudson region anytime except winter. The only problem is their bulk. Rather than fill my day pack up with one, I tend to carry mine wrapped around my waist. The elasticized sleeves are perfect for wrapping. Pile and fleece do not afford much protection in wind, in which case a nylon shell or light jacket will be useful. Some shells are water resistant or even waterproof but not breathable. You may find yourself swimming in sweat if the temperature rises or you exert yourself. Gore-Tex shells and jackets, as well as some of the newer synthetics, are fairly waterproof and somewhat breathable but are also a lot more expensive.

Nylon pants, available only through some camping stores or catalogs, seem to be the ideal option as far as outdoor legwear goes. They're lightweight, comfortable, and warm in the cold and cool in the heat; they also dry superfast. The only problems are durability and cost: The lighter ones rip and puncture easily and they're not cheap. Nylon or Gore-Tex leg gaiters provide waterproof protection for legs and boots. These are most useful for snowshoeing, cross-country skiing, or hiking in tall wet grass or deep mud. Shorts are popular in warmer weather, especially the new nylon ones. However, that much exposed skin makes a perfect target for ticks and other pesky insects, is subject to sunburn, and provides more surface area for poison ivy to scrape against.

Polypropylene underwear keeps the body warm and dry and is useful protection in colder weather. A lot of heat is lost through the head, and so wool hats or those made of fleece are necessary when temperatures are cold. A wool scarf or a gaiter made of fleece provides protection for the neck area. For my hands I prefer polypropylene glove liners. They're warm enough for anything but severe cold, are very flexible, and dry fast. In severe cold I'll add heavy wool mittens over the liners.

FOOTWEAR

Good footwear is primary: Nothing takes the joy out of walking like sore feet. The kind of footwear you use should depend on what feels comfortable as well as the conditions you're anticipating. If you're going for a stroll in Riverside Park in New York City, you certainly won't need the kind of footwear required for backpacking in the mountains. For half-day hikes on level-to-moderate ground in good conditions, a wide assortment of sneakers, tennis shoes, and related athletic or running shoes are more than suitable. In the past several years light hiking boots have become popular, even with folks who never hit the trail. Such boots provide firm ankle support and have thick rubber soles with deep treads to improve traction. They should be ideal for day-long hikes even in rugged conditions. Many are not waterproof, however. That's something to keep in mind if you're expecting rain or have to walk in deep mud. Unless you're backpacking, light hiking boots should be sufficient for all the trails in this book. Because of the heavier loads they carry, backpackers usually require heavier, more durable, stiff leather hiking boots.

Thick wool socks are necessary if you're wearing stiff, heavy boots. They will stay warm even if your feet get wet. I find that thin polypropylene sock liners, worn underneath wool socks, make them more comfortable. In moderate-to-warm conditions, regular cotton crew socks or athletic socks worn under sneakers or light hiking boots are probably sufficient. In cooler weather or on longer hikes, medium wool socks are probably best.

SANITATION

Sanitation needs to be planned for before you hit the trail. Whenever possible use the available facilities. Go right before the hike starts, and if you pass any facilities along the way, such as outhouses, stores, or restaurants, use them. Owners are generally gracious toward hikers in need. In the backcountry, far from roads, any secluded spot should suffice. Use common sense. Don't use what looks like a potential campsite. Don't use areas right beside trails or near streams or other bodies of water. If you're defecating, always dig a hole and bury it; a plastic shovel may be useful for this, and cheap ones are available at most camping and sporting goods stores. Used toilet paper may be stored in a plastic bag for disposal once you return to civilization. People—especially children—who are novices in the woods may need a little encouragement.

COMPANIONS

Walking with another person or persons requires the same kind of cooperative effort any indoor activity might. The one thing to keep in mind is that people have different needs, expectations, and abilities. Some people enjoy tranquillity and prefer to walk in silence; others see it as primarily a social opportunity and talk nonstop. Some prefer vistas or historic sites; others are captivated by wildflowers or birds. As you get to know people you'll learn what their interests are. Some people need to take more rest stops or bathroom breaks or need to walk more slowly or eat more frequently. It may be helpful to let the slower walkers go in front so that the pace set is comfortable for everyone. Also, many groups employ a "sweep," one strong hiker who trails the slowest hikers and ensures they don't get left behind. Some people may need extra help scrambling over rocks or fording streams. Companions should be able to communicate their needs and be willing to accommodate one another. The joys of sharing your experience are reason enough to make the effort.

PETS

Never bring a pet into the woods unless the animal is trained and you're reasonably sure you can control it. Being in the wild can excite a pet's instincts, making it more difficult to control. Most places require that dogs be leashed, a sensible idea on the trail. When you have a pet with you, avoid areas where you're likely to encounter wildlife, such as the edge of a wetland. Many sites mentioned in this book do not allow pets, so check ahead of time.

THREATS AND DANGERS

Walking or biking along the Hudson for the most part entails fewer risks than may be encountered in more rugged mountain or desert regions. Injuries can occur, though sunburn, blisters, rashes, and mosquito and tick bites are generally the worst things anyone ever gets. Nevertheless, one should still act cautiously and respect the environment. It's when one doesn't that accidents happen. One should always be prepared in case of serious injury.

Sunburn and Heat

We all know that sun exposure can cause red itchy skin and, in severe cases, swelling and pain. Sunburn, probably the most common malady one may suffer as a result of outdoor activity, always develops faster than one thinks. It can usually be avoided by wearing protective clothing: long pants, long-sleeve shirts. A brimmed hat will protect the face, ears, and neck (a cap provides less protection but is preferable to nothing). A liberal application of sunscreen is also a good idea, and an anti-itch ointment should be applied once the sunburn occurs.

Heat cramps, heat exhaustion, and heatstroke are all potential maladies that can occur on hot days when people overexert themselves and don't drink enough water. Fatigue, lethargy, headaches, and muscle cramps are all symptoms. Water, shade, rest, and salt are the best treatments. Heat exhaustion and heatstroke, in which the body temperature soars, resulting in vomiting and convulsions, require medical attention. Paring back your physical activity on hot days and drinking plenty of fluids will eliminate the risks.

Lightning

The chance of being struck by lightning is minute. However, lightning, which strikes just about everywhere, kills more people than hurricanes or tornadoes do. There are no safe outdoor places in the event of a thunderstorm. Be aware of potential risk, and avoid going out when thunderstorms threaten. Should one strike when you're out, lie or crouch as low on the ground as possible (inside a vehicle is probably the safest place to be). Avoid open areas—especially trees in open areas—as well as open summits and ridges. Damp, narrow caves are not considered safe in a storm.

Hypothermia and Frostbite

Hypothermia, which can be brought on by cold, wet, damp, or windy conditions, is the result of falling body temperature. A sweaty body exposed to cold or wind is at risk for hypothermia: The temperature does not have to be freezing. Symptoms include shivering, chattering teeth, fatigue, disorientation, stumbling, difficulty balancing, and sometimes irrational, even reckless behavior. The best way to treat hypothermia is to warm the victim. Finding shelter, changing into warmer clothes, climbing into a sleeping bag, ingesting warm liquids and foods, taking exercise, and having contact with other people's body warmth are all helpful measures. Hypothermia can be prevented by not going out when conditions are too cold. If you do go out, you must wear the proper clothing for the conditions and add clothes as the temperature drops. Never wear cotton in wet or damp conditions.

Frostbite is the result of frozen skin, which will looked discolored and feel numb to the victim. Heat frozen skin by contact with warmer body parts; do not rub it. Badly frozen limbs must be carefully treated in a hospital.

Insects, and So On

Walking or biking, one may encounter biting or stinging insects such as mosquitoes, black flies, ticks, bees, wasps, and hornets. Protective clothing helps prevent bites and stings. Use insect repellent sparingly. One hundred percent Deet, for example, should always be watered down. It has been known to cause a number of harmful effects and is considered toxic to children. Walking in midsummer, especially in fields or near swamps and wetland areas, you'll be likely to encounter more insects. Mosquitoes are usually most active around sunset. Bees and other stinging insects, pollen gatherers, tend to be prevalent in the vicinity of flowers. Use extra caution in those areas, and be careful not to disturb them. Bees and other stinging insects rarely attack unless accidentally or intentionally provoked. Those who are allergic need to be particularly cautious.

Lyme disease is an infection caused by spirochetes, a kind of bacterium. It is carried by deer ticks, tiny arachnids barely visible to the naked eye that become more visible when engorged with a victim's blood. Not all ticks carry the disease. Ticks in the nymph stage are the most common infectors of Lyme disease. Ticks tend to occur in vegetation, and when someone brushes by, the tick attaches itself to its intended victim. Ticks may crawl around on the victim's body looking for a suitable place to attach. A tick must be attached for at least twenty-four hours in order to transmit the disease. Deer ticks infected with Lyme disease are very prevalent along the Hudson River, and anyone going outdoors should be especially vigilant. Wearing light-colored protective clothing will improve tick visibility, and rolling your socks over the bottoms of your pants legs will prevent most ticks from planting themselves on you. After any outdoor excursion, it's a good idea to inspect your body for ticks. (If you have a partner, he or she can help with the inspection.) If you find a tick, carefully remove it with a tweezer or by rotating its body. If the head or other body parts should break off in the process of removal, these may transmit the disease.

Early signs of infected tick bites include a spreading rash, flulike symptoms, fever, fatigue, muscle ache, and chills. However, many victims never develop these early symptoms. Later symptoms include a host of serious maladies including severe fatigue, heart irregularities, meningitis, arthritis, and neurological problems. Lyme disease can be successfully diagnosed only through blood tests and clinical examination. In its early stages Lyme disease is relatively easy to treat with antibiotics. For more information contact the Lyme disease hotline at 914-431-1538.

Rabies

Rabies is unfortunately prevalent among the region's mammal population, especially raccoons, skunks, woodchucks, and bats, as well as dogs. Avoid close contact with any wild mammal, especially those that behave in a docile or aggressive fashion. If you're bitten or scratched by a wild mammal, get prompt medical attention.

Poison Ivy and Other Plants

Poison ivy is extremely common in the area along the Hudson River, and while rarely dangerous, the severe rash it produces is an extremely high price to pay for a good time. Distinguished by clusters of three pointed leaves, poison ivy can occur as a vine or shrub. Skin irritations, caused by oils that are present throughout the plant, produce an itching or burning sensation that almost cries out to be scratched or rubbed. Some people appear to be more allergic to poison ivy and contract it more easily than others, but hardly anyone is totally immune. If you have touched poison ivy, wash thoroughly with cold water and non-oil-based soap. If a rash develops, use calamine lotion or cortisone cream. Scratching may spread the irritation further.

Poison oak and sumac can also produce rashes similar to those of poison ivy. Stinging nettles are covered with hairs coated with an acid that can produce a temporary itching or burning sensation.

Blisters

Foot blisters, caused by abrasion and heat, are another common malady suffered by walkers. If allowed to develop, they can become very uncomfortable or even painful. Feet that haven't walked much are good candidates for blisters. Also, inadequate footwear or new, stiff boots can cause blisters. If you have a sore reddened area on your foot, you should increase the number or thickness of socks you're wearing to provide an extra cushion. Polypropylene sock liners also help prevent blisters.

You may also consider applying moleskin to the sore area. Moleskin is a sheet of felt with an adhesive coating on one side. Cut the right size moleskin patch from the sheet. Place it over the wound to cover it, but with a hole cut out of the moleskin to expose the sore. This enables the sore to breathe while it's protected on each side. The adhesive should keep the moleskin fastened to you until you're ready to remove it. If the blister swells (which they're prone to do), then it will probably need to be lanced. This is best done in a physician's office in sterile conditions.

Venomous Snakes

Though venomous snakebite is such a rare occurrence in the Hudson region that it's barely worth mentioning, it remains the number-one fear many people have going into the woods. While it is such a rare occurrence, that's little comfort to somebody who is actually bitten by a venomous snake. The Hudson region has only two species of venomous snakes: the copperhead and the timber rattlesnake. Both have the ability to strike quickly and have relatively long fangs that inject venom deep under the skin. Neither snake is very common or very aggressive, however, and their venom is not considered highly toxic compared with those of other species of snakes found outside the region. Both have camouflage colors, which often makes them difficult to see. These snakes would prefer to be left undisturbed. If you do come upon one, it's always best to give it a wide berth. A snake can strike farther than you think. While few people are skilled at identifying snakes, and chances are the snake you're observing is one of the more numerous nonvenomous species, never corner a snake. All snakes deserve respect, and even nonvenomous species can inflict a painful bite. A good way to avoid snakebite is to wear protective footwear and pants, watch your step, and never put your hands or feet anyplace where you can't see them.

If you should get bitten, the primary thing to remember is not to panic. Adult deaths from snakebites are almost as rare as the snakebites themselves. Children, however, are more at risk. Once bitten, expect extreme pain and inflammation (if these symptoms don't develop then chances are no venom was actually injected or you were bitten by a nonvenomous snake). Stay calm and get to a hospital right away. Treatment of snakebite is usually with antivenin. Walking unfortunately raises the metabolism, which spreads the venom through your system. A child that has been bitten should be carried if possible. If you're alone and have to walk more than an hour to be rescued, then first aid should be considered. If you plan to use first aid, it should be applied immediately after the bite. Snakebite kits, available at most camping and sporting goods stores, have the necessary tools and instructions. First aid involves cutting the wound with a sterilized instrument and sucking out the venom with a suction device included as part of the kit. A tourniquet may be tied above the wound (not so tight it cuts off the circulation of blood and only while the operation is being performed). First aid at best only limits the venom's impact, however; a visit to an emergency room as soon as possible will still be necessary.

Getting Lost

This is another primary fear, but in a densely populated area like the Hudson region, people rarely get so seriously lost as to require rescue. Those who are inexperienced should stick with the more popular places where they're likely to see other people if they become confused and need to ask directions. Also, if you're inexperienced it's a good idea to hike with a more experienced partner or to go on an organized outing led by one of the local hiking clubs. Inexperienced hikers should only walk on well-marked trails. Even if you're with a larger group, always bring a map you can follow, as there's a danger of getting separated. A compass may be useful if you've lost your bearings; and a whistle may also signal for help. Telling people where you're going and when you expect to return may alert them to trouble if you don't appear on time.

If you do get lost, don't panic. If you don't have a compass or map, stay put, conserve your energy, and try to stay warm. The longer you survive, the greater the likelihood you'll be rescued. If you have matches, a small fire may be used to signal for help (it will also keep you warm). A flashlight will also be useful in signaling. Some people may wish to bring a cell phone in case such emergencies occur. Be forewarned, though—in rugged mountainous terrain, cell phones are often inoperable.

Hunting

Hiking in the woods during deer-hunting season is dangerous. Accidents occur every year, and there have been fatalities. Deer-hunting season takes place in late fall. Find out the hunting schedule and regulations for the area you're interested in visiting.

Assaults

One of the greatest dangers one faces when walking is from other human beings. This is particularly true where other human beings congregate, such as in urban areas, but those walking in isolated places away from civilization are at some risk too. Smaller urban centers along the Hudson have their share of urban problems as New York City does, so one should exercise caution there as well. Common sense is your best tool. When hiking in urban areas, avoid high-crime-rate sections, where the number of assaults reported is high. Steer clear of such places at night. Go with a partner or a protective dog; always maintain your composure—acting nervous or agitated will only draw attention your way, and acting in a brazen or disrespectful manner is liable to attract hostility. Keep valuables such as cameras or jewelry hidden. Don't wear your most expensive jacket. Be especially vigilant in isolated areas—such as alleyways, vacant lots, and unpopulated parks—in urban centers.

In the backcountry, far from roads, the risks are considerably lower, but to be confronted by a threat in an isolated area where there's no hope of rescue is a nightmarish experience indeed. Again, those who might feel threatened in such places should consider going with a partner or a larger group or bringing a protective dog—usually enough to deter most potential attackers. A loud whistle is another safety device in backcountry areas. Be cautious with strangers, especially those offering or asking for help. Martial arts skills and self-defense training may provide some protection in certain situations.

Traffic

One of the biggest threats when walking on roads or streets is from traffic. In New York State, some twenty thousand traffic-related pedestrian injuries and six hundred deaths occur each year. About half occur in urban areas, but the rest happen in less crowded environments. It's always best to walk facing oncoming traffic and walk as far to the left as possible. Use sidewalks whenever possible; never walk in the middle of the street or road. Be especially careful at intersections. Drivers are unpredictable, so try to anticipate possible dangerous moves. Some drivers may even go out of their way to harass or frighten walkers, and others, unfortunately, may be impaired by alcohol or drugs. Drivers, who tend to concentrate on other vehicles, find walkers less visible, so wear bright-colored clothing, and avoid walking on roads in the dark or very early in the morning or late in the day, when visibility is poor. If you do, wear reflectors.

First Aid

Except for insect bites or sunburn, most people have very positive experiences outdoors. Good planning, common sense, and preparation help. Carry a first-aid kit that includes antiseptic cream, anti-itch medication (antihistamine or cortisone), aspirin or other pain relievers, alcohol, swabs, surgical tape, Band-Aids, gauze, bandages, butterfly closures, scissors or a knife, and of course a first-aid handbook.

In the event of fractured bones, dislocations, back or neck injuries, or other major problems, the primary rule is to keep the victim as immobile and comfortable as possible and get him or her to a hospital. In most cases that means having someone go get help. Trained personnel can transport a victim on a litter in a way that avoids further injury. Fractured limbs should be splinted. To avoid shock, keep the victim as warm as possible. Wounds should always be cleaned with soap and water and then properly dressed with a bandage. In the event of bleeding, pressure should be applied to the wound, and the wound area should be elevated above the heart.

DAY PACK PACKING LIST

- water
- food
- first-aid supplies
- rain jacket or poncho
- map
- matches
- compass
- tissues
- toilet paper
- plastic bags
- sunscreen
- insect repellent
- extra socks and sock liners
- extra clothes
- flashlight and extra batteries
- sanitary pads/tampons (for women)
- cell phone (optional)

BACKPACKING AND TREKKING

Backpacking involves trips of at least one overnight stay or more. Backpackers must carry sufficient supplies and equipment to make these overnight stays possible, including tents, sleeping bags, extra clothes, enough food, stoves, and fuel. Opportunities for backpacking are limited in the region, primarily because of very limited facilities for camping along the river, and most backpackers prefer to walk on trails as opposed to roads. Options do exist, however. My wife and I completed a three-day adventure, backpacking from the Franklin Delano Roosevelt Estate in Hyde Park up to Clermont, thirty miles to the north, camping at Mills/Norrie Park and Ferncliff Forest. Almost half the route was on trails and the rest was primarily on scenic rural roads. Opportunities also exist along the Appalachian Trail where it crosses through the region and in the Catskill Forest Preserve.

Ideally backpacking along the Hudson River would be more similar to backpacking in Europe, where overnight stays in villages in hostels, small hotels, dormitories, or shelters are utilized. There it is referred to as trekking, a form of recreational travel that would be more feasible here if more options for affordable overnight stays were available.

Backpacking in the Catskills may involve overnight stays in the back-country, perhaps miles from the nearest road. Practically any well-drained level piece of ground reasonably clear of vegetation and sheltered from weather will suffice as a campsite. A reliable water source should be within easy walking distance, but not too close. If possible, try to uti-lize sites that have already been cleared. Some, however, are being al-lowed to return to their natural state, and a sign will usually indicate if camping is not permitted at a particular site. Lean-tos—rustic covered shelters usually made of logs—are available in some places on a first-come basis. They usually have capacity for several individuals, and back-country etiquette decrees that they must be shared. In a rainstorm, such shelters are especially appreciated. Sites of lean-tos are usually indicated on maps. Backpackers should always bring tents, though, just in case the lean-tos are filled to capacity.

There are certain rules regarding backcountry campsites. Camping is only permitted on state-owned land; camping on private property is by permission only; camping is forbidden above 3,500 feet in the Catskills. Except in the vicinity of lean-tos, camping is not permitted less than 150 feet from trails or water sources. Backpackers should always pack out what they pack in: leave no trash or waste. Because of the limited supply of downed wood, campfires are discouraged. If you do have a campfire, do not cut any fresh wood. Make sure the campfire is located far enough from any flammable materials and thoroughly doused when no longer in use.

HIKING CLUBS

Hiking with organized groups can provide social opportunities, safety, and an introduction to the activity—as well as to new places—for new-comers. Besides scheduled outings, hiking clubs often are involved in conservation work, trail maintenance, and building new trails. A few of the bigger local clubs are listed below.

The New York/New Jersey Trail Conference is a nonprofit federation of 9,500 individuals and hiking clubs whose memberships total 106,000. Primarily a volunteer organization, its primary focus is on building and maintaining trails as well as protecting the lands where the trails are lo-cated. It is also a resource for information about trails and hiking and publishes excellent maps and hiking guides for the region. Solely through volunteer efforts, the conference maintains thirteen hundred miles of trails, including all the marked trails on lands managed by the PIPC, in-cluding Harriman State Park and Storm King. It also maintains trails in the Catskill Forest Preserve, as well as the Long Path and the Highlands Trail. For information, call 212-685-9699, write GPO Box 2250, New York, NY 10116, or visit their website at www.nynjtc.org/~trails.

The Appalachian Mountain Club (AMC) has an active New York/New Jersey chapter. The club is involved in trail maintenance, building trails, and preservation and conservation efforts. The AMC also conducts numerous outings: hiking, canoeing, and bike trips. For information, call their New York City office at 212-986-1430.

The Sierra Club, founded in 1892 by John Muir, is an environmental group active throughout the United States and Canada (the Hudson region has the largest concentration of members outside California). The club addresses environmental issues of global and national concern. New York's Atlantic Chapter, as well as many local groups, also address local environmental issues. Raising appreciation of nature and the outdoors and sponsoring outings (hikes, cross-country skiing, backpacking, canoeing) are a big part of the Sierra Club's focus. If you contact the national organization, it will put you in touch with the local group. The address is 85 Second Street, San Francisco, CA 94105, or call 415-977-5500; the website is www.sierraclub.org.

The Adirondack Mountain Club, though it focuses on the Adirondacks, has very active local chapters that offer numerous outings—hikes, backpacking, canoeing, and bike trips—in the region. To get in touch with a local chapter, contact their Lake George office at 518-668-4447.

Biking

Biking was a popular form of transport around the turn of the century, when the population was more concentrated in urban areas and before automobile use became widespread. Today it is primarily a recreational activity, though bike use for transport, especially in urban areas, seems to be on the rise. Like walking, biking provides a wonderful opportunity for outdoor experience and exercise with the advantage of being able to cover more ground and sample more of the region's pleasures in a shorter time. With its wide assortment of country roads, scenery, and natural and historical landmarks, the Hudson region has much to offer the bicyclist. Multiday trips covering the entire region on both sides of the river are possible, an exciting and rewarding way to explore the area.

Bike travel requires a certain level of riding proficiency as well as sufficient physical ability. By starting small with relatively easy trips, one can gradually work up in terms of skill and physical ability to longer, more challenging outings.

Most of the bike routes covered in this book are on roads, mostly paved back roads that have plenty to offer in terms of scenery and interest, and that also see less automobile traffic. Occasional short stints on busy two- and four-lane highways are unfortunately necessary to complete the linear path. Traffic will be a factor in these places, but usually the shoulders are sufficiently wide for safety. The bike routes often pass through urban areas, where there tend to be a number of hazards, including automobiles and pedestrians. Biking is also permitted along stretches of wide unpaved paths, such as old woods roads, carriageways, and old roads or railroad beds now closed to traffic. The durability of the bike, especially its tires, will be a factor in these places.

Two basic types of bikes are suitable for outdoor recreation and travel: touring bikes, which are used primarily on roads, and all-terrain or mountain bikes, which are primarily for off-road use. One should note that these bikes were designed for vastly different purposes. However, there is considerable overlap in their use, and in bikes that combine the characteristics of both.

TOURING BIKES

Most touring bikes are lightweight ten-speeds designed for traveling long distances on primarily asphalt surfaces. The metal frames of touring bikes must be lightweight but strong enough to withstand lengthy use, including carrying extra gear, which puts a lot of stress on a frame. Frame breakage can best be avoided by purchasing a bike that has a strong, dependable frame and strong joints. Good frames consist of sturdy, seamless steel-alloy tubing, made of such materials as chrome, molybdenum, and manganese. The frame size should accommodate *your* size: Bike riders should be able to straddle the frame in an upright position comfortably with at least one inch clearance.

Quill-type pedals, with toe clips and straps, are used on standard touring bikes to keep feet firmly in place. Toe clips give your feet added leverage, especially when going uphill; straps should be kept loose enough to allow you to remove your feet easily. Derailleurs are attached to cables, which are connected to control levers. By shifting gears, the bicyclist can adjust the level of thrust and resistance, thus conserving muscle effort.

Most touring bikes have caliper brakes. These are operated with cables connected to brake levers located on the handlebars. Saddles should be narrow to allow your thighs to move without chafing. Touring bike handlebars generally slope downward.

TRAFFIC SAFETY

Although this book tries to focus on roads that don't see a lot of automobile traffic, encounters with traffic inevitably happen and create challenging if not dangerous situations for bicyclists. In the United States, nearly fifty thousand bicyclists a year are involved in traffic accidents, and approximately one thousand die. Many city streets as well as country roads have no shoulders to ride on. These are some good things to remember: Bicyclists are obliged to follow the same rules as automobiles. Ride on the right side of the road with the traffic, never on the left against it. Never ride in the middle of the road. Some automobile drivers are hostile to bicyclists and will deliberately cause problems. Others fail fully to appreciate the presence of a bicyclist and will unconsciously create danger. As much as possible give yourself a wide cushion of space, and ride outside the main flow of traffic as close to the shoulder as possible. Of course be courteous and don't obstruct traffic unnecessarily.

It's important to be aware of everything going on around you. Be alert and anticipate trouble, so your reactions don't surprise motorists. Use hand signals. You should be extravigilant in densely populated areas with many intersections and a lot of traffic. Parked cars are a potential threat from passengers suddenly opening doors in your path. In areas where there's high-speed traffic and no shoulder, consider walking your bike on the sidewalk or taking another route. Trucks are a potentially grave threat, partly for the amount of space they take up on the road and the blast of wind they create when they rumble by. Be especially vigilant early in the morning and late in the day when the sun is low and visibility poor.

Street and road conditions vary considerably in the Hudson region. Potholes, bumps, railroad crossings, and animals are among the many hazards you might encounter. If you anticipate trouble, it won't surprise you and you'll have time to react safely. Getting off the seat when you hit a bump helps reduce the shock. Avoid storm sewers with grates. Never ride diagonally across railroad tracks: Your tires may get snagged, and it's better to walk your bike across. Brakes are less effective when wet, and bikes can skid on wet pavement the same way other vehicles can.

ACCESSORIES

A luggage rack is obviously essential for longer, overnight, and multiday trips. Panniers, carrying cases specially designed for touring bikes, will help carry supplies. Lights and reflectors are required for riding after dark. Mirrors attached to your helmet, eyeglasses, sunglasses, or the handlebars will improve visibility, and you won't have to turn your head so often. A kickstand will aid in the parking dilemma when there isn't a rack or something to lean your bike against. Fenders will provide partial protection from spray and mud during a rainstorm. Dog repellent, the kind mail carriers use, may be handy in case there's a dog attack; a spray bottle of ammonia may provide similar protection. (In most cases outrunning the dog is the easiest way to protect yourself. Repellent should always be a last resort.) A handy water bottle attached to the frame will eliminate some stops. A chain or cable lock will provide some protection for an unattended bike, but will not thwart a determined thief with the proper equipment.

MAINTENANCE AND REPAIR

The first step in keeping a bike properly maintained is to read the owner's manual. The next is to keep it clean. Adjust parts, such as the brakes and cables, as necessary, and lubricate parts like chains, cables, and bearings regularly. On longer trips it may be useful to carry a small amount of solvent and a lubricant. Replacement cables and spokes should always be carried in case they break. Tire punctures, unfortunately, are fairly common. No matter what the length of your trip, it's a good idea to bring a deflated spare tube, always an easy thing to carry. Before hitting the road, a bicyclist should know how to remove a tire, replace a tube and/or patch holes, pump up a tire, and reinstall it. Such repairs, practiced at home, can then be performed more easily on the road. A six-inch adjustable wrench, both Philips and standard screwdrivers, tire irons, tire-patch kits, air pumps, and pliers are some of the standard bike-repair tools you might consider carrying.

CLOTHING

Helmets may seem like an imposition, but by absorbing a great deal of shock in an accident, they help protect the head from injury. A helmet is composed of a tough outer shell and a snug foam inner liner. A good helmet should be light, comfortable, and well ventilated, factors that will encourage the bicyclist to use it. Bicycle shoes with thick soles and cleats help hold the foot in place on the pedal and allow the bicyclist to pedal with greater power. Colorful, durable clothing that increases visibility is preferred. Tuck pant legs into your socks to prevent them from snagging in the gears or chain. Tight-fitting bike shorts with legs that extend to midthigh are useful for maintaining comfort. Tights may be worn in colder weather, or early in the morning before the sun has warmed things. Rain gear is essential equipment on extended multiple-day rides or when the weather is inclement. Fingerless cycling gloves improve the grip on the handlebars and reduce muscle cramping.

ALL-TERRAIN AND MOUNTAIN BIKING

Off-road biking opportunities are limited in the Hudson region since most trails are reserved for hikers only. There are a few good, relatively easy sites, such as the Shore Trail north of Nyack, Tallman State Park south of Piermont, the Old Croton Aqueduct Trailway, the Hudson/Mohawk Trail, the trails in Mills/Norrie State Park in Dutchess County, the Blue Mountain Reservation in Westchester, and the Stewart Airport Buffer Zone west of Newburgh. Fishkill Ridge by Mount Beacon has some tough, challenging trails for experienced mountain bikers. Black Rock Forest has an excellent network of trails suitable for mountain bikes but is restricted to members only. There are also a number of excellent opportunities just outside the region, such as Bluestone Wild Forest; Jockey Hill, located just north of Kingston; and Minnewaska State Park and the Monhonk Preserve, both located in the Shawangunk Mountains west of New Paltz. The region has a number of old woods roads, carriage paths, and old railroad beds no longer in use that would make excellent bike trails. Some are currently being planned or developed for such use.

All-terrain or mountain bikes are ruggedly constructed and lightweight for challenging off-road use. These bikes are also suitable for asphalt roads, but are less comfortable and efficient than touring bikes on longer road trips. Like good-quality touring bikes, all-terrain bike frames are constructed of highly durable steel alloys, though the tubing is generally larger and stronger. The frame is usually longer and lower on all-terrain bikes; the wheels are also smaller. However, the tires are wider and thicker to prevent sinking into loose sand, dirt, or mud and to provide maximum traction and to cushion bumps. Lower tire pressure gives better performance for off-road riding. All-terrain and mountain bikes utilize bold, knobby treads for maximum grip. Some have a raised center ridge, which provides a smoother ride on pavement. All-terrain bikes lack the straps and toe clips that touring bikes have. This enables free use of your feet for thrust or to prevent spills. Handlebars are flat in an all-terrain bike. These allow the bicyclist to steer better and to sit upright and observe the trail ahead as well as enjoy the scenery. When purchasing an all-terrain bike, allow for at least three inches between the top tube and your crotch. Adult bikes should be less than thirty pounds.

Clothing for off-road biking should include long sleeves, long pants, and gloves to protect from scrapes and scratches should you fall or brush against vegetation, as well as to provide protection from sun and insects. I've noticed that in practice, most riders seem to prefer short pants and short sleeves, primarily to stay cool. You can judge what is a priority. Light hiking boots are perfect footwear for all-terrain bikes.

BIKE CLUBS

Bike clubs sponsor organized rides, as well as providing networking possibilities for riders. They are a source of information about routes and resources such as repair shops.

The Five Borough Bicycle Club, based in New York City, features day rides, weekend trips, and bicycle repair courses. To contact them, write: Five Borough Bicycle Club (located at the International Youth Hostel), 891 Amsterdam Avenue, New York, NY 10025, or call 212-932-2300, ext. 115.

The New York Cycle Club, also based in New York City, is a nonprofit volunteer organization with more than a thousand members. They have a monthly newsletter and meetings, social activities, weekend day rides outside the city, overnight trips, and recommended routes. To contact them, write: POB 20541, Columbus Circle Station, New York, NY 10023, or call 212-828-5711.

The Country Cycle Club, Inc., based in Westchester, offers regular weekend road and off-road rides and some weekday rides in warmer weather as well as special events. Rides generally start in Westchester but may also include Rockland, Orange, and Putnam Counties, and Connecticut. There are monthly meetings and a monthly newsletter. It is affiliated with the League of American Bicyclists and Adventure Cycling. To contact them, write: 182 McLain Street, Mount Kisco, NY 10549.

The Westchester Mountain Bike Association has educational programs promoting mountain-bike safety and good etiquette. They help create new mountain-bike trails as well as doing trail maintenance. To contact them, write: POB 286, Croton-on-Hudson, NY 10520.

The Mid-Hudson Bicycle Club, primarily for road riders, offers weekend rated rides, weekday evening rides in warmer weather, social activities, picnic rides, and other special events. There are monthly meetings, a newsletter, and courses on bike maintenance and riding skills. To contact them, write: POB 1727, Poughkeepsie, NY 12601-1707, or their website: www.mhv.net/~mhbc.

Fatz in the Cats Mountain-Bike Club, based in Kingston, offers weekly rides, trail maintenance, races, monthly meetings, and social activities. To contact them, call Peter Brink at 914-236-7649 or write: 48 Laggsmill Road, Lake Katrine, NY 12449.

Call the Mohawk-Hudson Cycling Club at 518-439-3267 for a lengthy recorded message listing all their outings.

Trails

To be recognized a trail must have a persuasive presence. It should be obvious and interesting. It should provide clear linkages between sites. It should have a focus like the Hudson River. It should offer access to compelling diversions like scenic views, and historic and cultural sites. Trails need to be publicized in order to promote use and gain legitimacy.

Guidebooks like this one, maps, brochures, educational programs, and special events all help to publicize existing trails.

Trails don't just happen. They are usually the result of arduous efforts of planning, fund-raising, and implementation. Considering the relatively low material costs of building most trails, it is surprising how long it can take. Major construction projects like bridges and high-rises are often completed in less time than it takes to create a new trail. That is because trail development tends to be a low priority for most government bodies and agencies. It usually takes a number of very dedicated individuals and groups to create trails. Most new trail construction is primarily the result of volunteer efforts. Funding sources for new trail construction are limited and usually result from grants and private donations. There are also maintenance costs and liability issues, especially when trails cross private land.

In the old days a handshake was usually sufficient to negotiate a trail crossing somebody's private land. Today most landowners are reluctant to allow trails to cross their land. Easements, which protect landowners from liability issues and maintenance concerns, must often be negotiated with private landowners, these responsibilities being assumed instead by the trail-building organization. There may also be tax write-off incentives for landowners to agree to trail easements.

The Hudson region is crossed by four major trails that extend beyond the region: the Appalachian Trail, the Long Path, the new Highlands Trail, and the Greenway's Hudson River Trail.

The Appalachian Trail is 2,150 miles long and runs the length of the Appalachian Mountain Range all the way from Springer Mountain, Georgia, to Mount Katadin in Maine, crossing fourteen states. Often nicknamed the AT, it is the nation's oldest extended hiking trail and certainly one of the most famous in the world. Sections of the AT that run through the Hudson Highlands are featured in later chapters of this book. The idea for the trail came from a 1921 article by Benton MacKaye, entitled "An Appalachian Trail: A Project in Regional Planning." In 1923 the newly formed New York/New Jersey Trail constructed the first official section of the AT in Harriman State Park, between Bear Mountain and Arden. In 1925 the Appalachian Trail Conference formed to market the trail and to coordinate planning and construction efforts. The AT was completed in 1937. Because of encroachments by developments that threatened the trail, it received protection and designation as a National Scenic Trail in 1968. Efforts to protect the AT include the purchase of a thousand-foot-wide corridor through which the trail runs. Protection of the Appalachian Trail corridor is part of the impetus behind efforts to preserve Sterling Forest.

The AT is usually marked by white paint blazes. Some 162 miles of the AT are located in New Jersey and New York State. Millions of people hike sections of the AT every year. There are facilities for camping along the entire route. Each year at least a thousand through-hikers attempt to hike the entire trail, a journey that usually takes several months. Usually a few hundred make it the whole way. Maintaining the AT is accomplished primarily through volunteer efforts coordinated by the Appalachian Trail Conference. For information about the Appalachian Trail Conference, call 304-535-6331.

The Long Path is 329 miles long and extends from the George Washington Bridge in Fort Lee north to Thatcher State Park, southwest of Albany. It is hoped that this trail will eventually extend north into the Adirondacks. It is usually marked by turquoise-colored paint blazes. The Long Path was first conceived in the early 1930s by Vincent and Paul Schaefer as an unmarked bushwacking route located in a 10-mile-wide protected corridor of forest land. In 1935 the first section of the trail was completed in the Palisades Park. The trail project lost momentum, and little was done up to the 1960s. At that point developments had made the idea of the 10-mile-wide corridor unfeasible, and the idea of a marked pathway was born. Most of the construction took place in the sixties and seventies through the efforts of the New York/New Jersey Trail Conference, and the trail was completed as far north as Route 23 in the Catskills. In the nineties the trail has been extended north, and efforts are presently under way to extend it into the Adirondacks. Sections of the Long Path are featured in chapters on the Palisades, the Catskills, High Tor, and Schunemunk Mountain.

The new 150-mile-long Highlands Trail links the Hudson and Delaware Rivers from Sparta, New Jersey, to Cornwall, New York. It is being developed by a volunteer Highlands Trail Committee that includes a number of private individuals, groups, organizations, and public entities. The National Park Service Rivers, Trails, and Conservation Assistance Program is providing technical assistance for this project. In this section the Highlands Trail follows basically the same route as the Stillman Trail through the Storm King section of Palisades Interstate Park and Black Rock Forest. It is marked with blue and yellow paint blazes. For more information contact the New York/New Jersey Trail Conference.

The Hudson River Greenway Trail was begun in 1992 as a project of the Greenway Heritage Conservancy. The trail is a key physical component of the Hudson River Valley Greenway's overall mission to preserve and develop the region's scenic, natural, recreational, cultural, and historic resources. It is envisioned as a 300-mile-long multiple-use trail system along both sides of the Hudson River, to provide physical and visual access to the river wherever possible. The Hudson River Trail will utilize already-existing trails, scenic highways, old railroad beds, and riverfront esplanades to increase opportunities for a wide assortment of non-motorized recreational activities for residents of the region as well as visitors.

State and local agencies, local communities, and private organizations will be involved in the planning and construction of the trail. The Hudson River Greenway Trail will be developed simultaneously with a Greenway Waterway Trail, a proposal of the Hudson River Waterway Association, a nonprofit volunteer group, to promote safe Hudson River access for paddling enthusiasts. According to the Greenway Conservancy, more than 275 miles of trail have already been designated as part of the Hudson River Greenway Trail. These include 21.91 miles of the Old Croton Aqueduct Trailway and 156 miles of Bike Route 9, a cooperative project of the New York State Department of Transportation and the Greenway Conservancy. For more information about the Hudson River Greenway Trail, contact the Greenway Conservancy, 1-800-TRAIL92 or 518-473-3835, or by E-mail at hrgreenway@aol.com.

Public Transport, Accommodations, and Food

PUBLIC TRANSPORT

Probably nowhere in the United States can so many wonderful hiking and biking opportunities be accessed through public transport. Using public transport saves fossil fuel and is less detrimental to the environment. A pleasant train or bus ride, to me, is less stressful than driving there in your car, and certainly better on the return trip, when you're likely to be tired.

One can use public transport not only to get to the trailhead or starting point, but through careful planning, to return to your starting point, thus minimizing car spotting or having to backtrack. Public transport is especially useful when one is on linear walks or rides parallel to public transport routes. When hiking sections of the Old Croton Aqueduct Trail, I was able to utilize train service to get to trailheads and to return home. I was able to do the same on the Long Path in the Palisades, utilizing bus service. Readers will find their own creative ways of using public transport for their outdoor adventures.

New York City has its own wonderful network of subway, bus, and cab service, described in the chapter on New York. Train service north of the city is mostly provided by Metro-North on its Hudson Line. Trains leave Grand Central Station and basically follow the east side of the Hudson with stops at all the major communities along the river. There is regular daily express service as far north as Poughkeepsie. There are even a couple of stops in the Hudson Highlands, with limited weekend service catering especially to hikers. The train ride along the Hudson is one of the most scenic in the country and is well worth doing for its own pleasure. Metro-North trains can accommodate bikes on weekends, but you must acquire a special permit, and there's also an extra fee for bikes. Call 1-800-METRO-INFO. In New York City, call 212-532-4900.

Amtrak also provides regular train service up the east side of the Hudson with stops in New York, Yonkers, Croton, Poughkeepsie, Rhinecliff, Hudson, and Rensselaer, opposite Albany. It is more expensive than Metro-North, but provides service to places north of Poughkeepsie not served by the former. There's an extra fee if you're carrying a bike. Long-distance bus service through Trailways, Greyhound (only stops at Albany), and Shortline provides access to most communities in the region, especially on the west side of the river. All leave from the Port Authority Terminal. Bicyclists will need to package their bikes for transport (call the bus companies for information). The Red and Tan Bus Company provides service from the George Washington Bridge Terminal in Manhattan, across the bridge and up the west side of the river, parallel to Palisades Interstate Park, the Long Path, and the Shore Trail. Regular daily service extends as far north as Nyack. Westchester, Putnam, Orange, Dutchess, Ulster, Albany, and Rensselaer Counties have their own local bus transport systems, described in subsequent chapters.

ACCOMMODATIONS

If you're planning overnight or multiple-day trips, it will be necessary to find suitable, affordable accommodations. Camping, hotel/motel, and bed-and-breakfast/inn facilities are available, but are not necessarily convenient or affordable. Youth or elder hostels or private dormitories, providing cheap but clean and relatively safe accommodations are largely absent from the region north of New York City. Campgrounds are also scarce. There are only two public campgrounds along the Hudson, at Croton Point, a Westchester County park, and in Mills/Norrie State Park, near Staatsburg. Both, which have the kind of facilities one expects in a campground, including bathrooms, showers, and public drinking water, are rarely full, except during major holidays and special events. (Call for reservations.) Harriman State Park also has camping, though not in the vicinity of the river. North Lake in the Catskills is another state campground convenient to excellent hiking and views of the river.

There are no private campgrounds along the Hudson River. There are a few in the Rhinebeck, New Paltz, and Saugerties areas, as well as a number in the Catskills. Backcountry camping opportunities are also limited. These are described in the section on backpacking.

Since the trails described in this book try to avoid commercial areas as much as possible, hotel and motel accommodations are limited and are often inconvenient for the best hiking spots. They may also be expensive, especially the nicer ones, which tend to be concentrated close to Thruway exits and major tourist attractions. Good downtown hotels in New York City and Albany are pricey. Cheap hotels and motels are often in poor condition and unfortunately tend to attract transients, rowdy parties, and illicit sexual liaisons. Inspect a place well before you agree to spend the night.

If modern conveniences are not a priority, then bed-and-breakfast and inn establishments often provide the best accommodations in terms of character and setting. These are generally small or family-run operations and offer very personalized service and a relaxing environment. Many are located in attractive locales in historic homes or buildings. Hudson region inns and bed-and-breakfasts compare favorably with those outside the region. A number of them are clustered in the Albany, Kingston, (Rondout), Cold Spring, Newburgh, and Rhinebeck areas. For more information about accommodations, contact local chambers of commerce and tourist information centers.

DINING

In terms of dining establishments, no area offers as much variety as the Hudson region. One can spend the day hiking or biking in nature and then sit down to a sumptuous meal in a fine dining establishment— the perfect blend of nature and civilization. New York City is well known for its large number of excellent top-of-the-line restaurants as well as numerous reasonably priced good places. Just about any kind of restaurant representing every ethnic cuisine on the planet can be found here, reflecting the ethnic diversity of the population. New York's fast-paced lifestyle was the primary impetus behind the development of fast, eat-it-standing-up food. New York is also the place where success is often celebrated with a fine meal. The good news is that the variety of eating establishments is superb throughout the region, not just in New York City, and great meals can found in seemingly unlikely places.

Those on a relatively tight budget will find no shortage of inexpensive places. Diners are very much a part of the Hudson region's dining landscape. They can be either tasteless kitsch or stylish art deco; menus are usually quite long and offer Greek and Italian specialities at low or moderate prices. Portions are typically huge, and desserts tend to be overwhelming. Many are open twenty-four hours. Ethnic restaurants, fast-food establishments, and chain restaurants are also fairly widespread. Much of the newer ethnic dining in the Hudson region is Latin American. Vietnamese and Thai restaurants are also becoming more commonplace. Pizza parlors exist in practically every community. Italian delis are good for sandwiches, salads, and other picnic fare. Bakeries have pastries that may serve as breakfast items, lunches, or snacks. Fresh Italian bread from a bakery is excellent for lunch or snack food. Muffins and Danish are popular for breakfast. These, too, often come in gigantic proportions. Most grocery stores offer takeout items, even dinners.

LOCAL CUISINE

There really aren't any foods that one would describe as local in origin, and given the abundance of wonderful immigrant food, one shouldn't mind. However, certain foods are especially prevalent in the region and are likely to be sampled. Pizza is about the most common, and many people feel that the New York–style pizza, a version of the Neapolitan original, is the best in the world. Pizzas first arrived here from Italy in the late nineteenth century. All-beef kosher hot dogs are an inexpensive local delicacy. Most are sold from pushcarts in New York City, but they can also be found in a number of establishments outside the city. New York bagels are world famous; they last quite well in a knapsack. Bagels are now pretty widespread through the Hudson region. Knishes, another treat of Jewish and Eastern European origin, are round or square-shaped dough pouches stuffed with mashed potatoes and sometimes vegetables or meat. They can be either fried or baked.

Falafel—spicy, deep-fried chickpea balls usually served inside pita— are a Middle Eastern specialty. Gyros feature spit-roasted meat served wrapped in pita. A Greek speciality, they can also be found in most Middle Eastern establishments and many diners as well as pushcarts in New York City. When it comes to dessert, if you're feeling especially decadent and can afford some calories and fat grams, go for New York cheesecake.

Visitors to the Hudson Valley may also want to sample the area's fresh fruit and cider. Pastries and pies filled with locally grown fruit are some of the region's more enticing treats, and apple cider doughnuts are one of the region's familiar delights. Hudson River wines are another highlight, a tour of local vineyards offering a pleasurable way to sample this regional specialty. Shad caught in the Hudson River, especially shad roe, are another delicacy and a feature at springtime festivals.

THE GUIDE

Note on Area Code Changes

Except for Westchester County, all 914 area codes have been changed to 845.

The City at the Mouth of the River

THE BATTERY TO RIVERDALE

New York, the nation's largest city and cultural capital and the world's corporate financial center, has come to mean many things. It isn't usually thought of as a destination for hikers and bikers. However, on an average day, ninety thousand bicyclists are out on New York streets for work or pleasure, and countless thousands are out walking for recreation. Those enthusiasts desiring outdoor adventure in an urban setting could not find a more captivating or thrilling environment than New York. The city has 350 miles of proposed greenway trails, more than half of which are already in place. The Hudson River shore from the Battery to Inwood has plenty to offer in terms of interesting sites, scenery, and views, and Riverdale in the Bronx is a less crowded, pleasant change of pace. Most of the seven and a half miles of riverfront north of Seventy-second Street is already parkland and provides a much-needed refuge from the rest of Manhattan's hustle and bustle. Current plans for redevelopment of the riverfront north of Battery Park City as the new Hudson River Park will mean a nearly continuous chain of parks, pathways, and open space along Manhattan's West Side.

For the most part the city at the mouth of the Hudson is also a city of islands. Of the five boroughs only the Bronx sits on the mainland. On January 1, 1898, the five boroughs were incorporated as New York City, which until then consisted solely of Manhattan. This political move more than doubled the population of the city while increasing its area severalfold. Twelve and a half miles long, the borough of Manhattan is the most developed and densely populated island in the world. Today it is only the third largest borough in terms of population after Brooklyn and

Queens, but it remains the center of most of New York's commercial and cultural activity.

To visit New York, whose population is one of the most diverse on the planet, is almost the equivalent of traveling around the world. It seems only natural that New York should be the headquarters of the United Nations. A large percentage of the city's residents are foreign born, and many of its neighborhoods exist as distinct ethnic enclaves. Visitors can enjoy the numerous ethnic shops and restaurants as well as the often distinct architecture of these neighborhoods. To walk New York streets is to experience a multitude of exotic languages, accents, different dress, hairstyles, and colors.

New York is the nation's wealthiest city, and its economic power is flaunted in its forests and canyons of skyscrapers. The nation's commercial capital ever since the early nineteenth century, the city has three major international airports, highways, railroads, and one of the nation's busiest ports. It lies in the heart of the country's most populated region, but New York's importance as a commercial center is worldwide in focus. The proximity of so many businesses, the availability of financial resources and other services (legal, communications, and so on) necessary to conduct business, and a highly trained, motivated workforce as well as nearby markets help make Manhattan the largest concentration of business activity in the world. To see New York at rush hour, when the gray suits descend from the numerous skyscrapers and flood the city's streets, is truly awesome.

Despite its corporate image (more corporations are headquartered here than anywhere else), New York's economy is primarily a multitude of small businesses and industrial enterprises. Mass media, banks, printing, publishing, advertising, and fashion are all areas in which New York plays a strong leading role.

Apparel remains the city's major industry. However, industrial activity, while still important, has been declining for much of the twentieth century. Much industry has shifted to the suburbs and to other sites throughout the nation and overseas. The loss of blue-collar industrial jobs has primarily impacted the city's middle- and lower-income and immigrant populations, who are forced to work at low-paying jobs in the service sector while struggling with New York's high cost of living. As a result the city is made up largely of rich and poor: Nowhere are poverty and wealth more conspicuously displayed than in New York.

The city is a leading cultural center. Museums, theater, music, dance, art, writing, and entertainment are all well represented here. New York's importance as a cultural center is due to a number of factors. Strong commercial and ethnic links between the region and the rest of the world helped create the kind of stimulating cosmopolitan atmosphere that attracts artists and intellectuals. The city's climate of tolerance has encouraged creativity and free expression; by the 1850s so-called bohemians had established an underground "community" that promoted alternative lifestyles and controversial writers, such as Walt Whitman. The presence of such institutions as the School of American Ballet and the Juilliard School of Music as well as already established communities of renowned artists continues to attract new ones to the city. Wealth accumulated by the city's business and commercial community has helped finance and promote the arts. New York's primary role in publishing, communications, and the mass media also supports numerous artists.

Along with other services, tourism plays a major role in the city's economy. New York is by far the leading tourist attraction in the Hudson region. Museums, galleries, cultural activities, historic sites, theater, entertainment, shopping, and an exciting cosmopolitan atmosphere are some of elements that attract twenty million visitors each year.

The city continues to suffer from severe congestion, a high cost of living, high taxes, racial tension, poverty, crime, and pollution, but given the intense concentration of such a diverse population, it's amazing that the city works as well as it does. As with the Hudson River, there's plenty of evidence that the city is improving, and New York continues to attract newcomers with its stimulating environment, its promise of opportunity, mobility, glamour, excitement, and culture: New York has both the best and the worst of what civilization has to offer.

While most of New York is paved over with asphalt and concrete, the city actually has an interesting geological history going back hundreds of millions of years. Evidence of that history can still be seen in numerous rock outcrops, mostly in the city's parks.

The rock that underlies New York City was originally deposited as sediment in seas more than 500 million years ago. Around 450 million years ago, a collision of the continents caused a chain of huge mountains to be formed, called the Taconian Orogeny. This mountain-building event pushed the sedimentary rocks, deposited millions of years earlier, deep beneath the earth's surface, where they were subjected to intense heat and pressure. These forces squeezed, folded, and greatly deformed the rock layers and also changed their granular structure, resulting in what would be called metamorphic rocks. The three bedrock formations found in New York City are the Fordham Gneiss, the Inwood Marble, and the Manhattan Schist.

The Fordham Gneiss is the oldest of the three rock formations. Believed to be metamorphosed sandstone, the rock is generally light colored, with quartz and feldspar the dominant minerals, and dark bands of mica. When exposed to the elements for a time, it becomes dark gray to black. The Fordham Gneiss underlies the Riverdale Ridge.

The Inwood Marble is younger; composed of calcium and magnesium carbonate, it appears sugary white to gray. The Inwood Marble was probably once dolomitic limestone. Exposed to moisture, it becomes unstable, turns brown, and eventually disintegrates into individual calcite grains. The Inwood Marble is thus softer and more erodable than the other New York City rock formations. It underlies the Spuyten Duyvil and the east side of Inwood Park.

The Manhattan Schist is the youngest of the three formations. Once shale, it appears light gray with thin dark bands. The rock turns rusty brown or dark brown or black when exposed to the elements. Manhattan Schist is composed of conspicuous flakes of mica, plus feldspar and quartz, and garnets in many places. It underlies most of Manhattan Island, with many exposures in Riverside Park, along the Fort Washington Ridge in Fort Tryon Park, and in Inwood Park. The rock is relatively hard and stable and provides a suitable foundation for the city's many skyscrapers. South of midtown it is buried underneath hundreds of feet of glacial sediment, but it reappears within forty feet of the surface in the downtown area.

It is estimated that 360 million years ago, intrusions of magma (hot molten rock) up to fifteen feet thick penetrated the Manhattan Schist formation. Later these magma intrusions cooled, forming coarse-textured light-colored bands and streamers of granite and granite pegmatite in the darker bedrock. Some of the latter, composed of larger grains and mineral crystals, which indicate slower cooling, have produced gem-quality crystals of beryl, garnet, tourmaline, and aquamarine (a blue-green variety of beryl). Some of the best are on display at the American Museum of Natural History on Central Park West.

The lofty mountains of the Taconic Range have long since weathered away, exposing New York's older bedrock. Twenty thousand years ago during the Pleistocene age, New York was invaded by glaciers, part of the huge ice sheets that covered much of eastern North America at the time. The glaciers left erratics, boulders transported—sometimes for many miles—by the moving ice. They also deposited thick layers of sediment that buried the older bedrock in a number of places. Where the bedrock is exposed it is often rounded and polished and may bear grooves and scratches made by the ice and other rocky debris the glaciers were carrying.

Four hundred years ago the New York City area was mostly forest and meadows populated by a myriad of wild creatures like deer, bears, and wolves. The shoreline around Manhattan Island was dotted with marshes, and porpoises and seals inhabited New York Harbor. Today New York is one of the most human-altered landscapes there is. Hardly a square inch hasn't been trampled, paved over, or built on. Despite that, nature is very much a part of the city.

While parks are a refuge for the city's human residents, they're also a haven for a variety of flora and fauna, including squirrels, chipmunks, and birds, including red-tailed hawks, which are now nesting on Fifth Avenue apartment houses across from Central Park. Tiny brown snakes that feed on grubs and worms can be found under rocks and logs. Deer occasionally wander into Riverdale. Even peregrine falcons, an endangered species, are residents of the city. Some of the most conspicuous nonhuman residents of the city—rats, cockroaches, and pigeons—were introduced by European settlers. Pigeons, also known as rock doves, nest and roost on high window ledges, roofs, and bridges and feed on fruits and grains they find in the city's parks as well as on generous handouts. They're very tolerant of human presence and thrive due to the lack of predators and competition from other birds. Their multicolored plumage was developed over centuries of domestication and breeding.

In its rush to become a great city New York has rarely looked back, mostly building over and erasing what existed before. A lot has transpired in the past four hundred years to create the exciting metropolis we see today, and New Yorkers are beginning to appreciate their heritage and even preserve remnants that tell the story of how the city came to be.

Lenape Indians inhabited the area of Manhattan, which was primarily a hunting ground. It's reported that on the north end of the island, along the Spuyten Duyvil, there was a Lenape village and lands were cultivated. Indian artifacts have been excavated from a former rock shelter in Inwood Hill Park. The Dutch first settled Walloon families on Governor's Island in 1624, and they may have used Manhattan to graze their cattle. By 1626 a permanent settlement had been established on the southern tip of Manhattan. That year the Dutch purchased Manhattan Island from the natives and made this community, called New Amsterdam, the capital of the new colony of New Netherland. New Amsterdam was primarily a trading outpost, and many of its inhabitants were non-Dutch. (By 1644 at least eighteen languages were spoken there.) The presence of windmills, a canal, narrow buildings with imported red tile roofs and gabled fronts gave the town a decidedly Dutch appearance, however. It was fortified against the possibility of Indian attack. As Dutch settlers spread beyond the walls of the town, tensions erupted with the indigenous population, who believed the Dutch to be encroaching on their land, and a number of raids took place. Dutch settlers were massacred and farms destroyed. Under the brutal leadership of Willem Kieft, the Dutch responded with armed reprisals, which escalated tensions and resulted in more raids and warfare. Under the new director general, Peter Stuyvesant, settlers were withdrawn to the security of the fortified town, and peace was made with the Indians. Stuyvesant was the first to try to improve the community's environment, which had grown squalid, restricting foraging swine, controlling overflowing privies, and removing trash heaps.

On September 8, 1664, New Amsterdam fell to the English. Its name was changed to New York, and it gradually transformed from Dutch to English. Its central location in the colonies and its naturally protected ice-free port made New York a thriving center of trade with Europe and the West Indies, exporting timber and agricultural products, primarily grain, from the Hudson Valley, and importing manufactured goods, cotton, indigo, mahogany, sugar, molasses, slaves, and rum. New York also became an important shipbuilding center. As trade grew, so did New York, and the city's political and social life was dominated by its wealthy merchants. The city became the second largest in the American colonies after Philadelphia. Problems of public health, poverty, crime, fire, and pollution grew faster than its limited services could deal with them.

Following the end of the French and Indian Wars, many of New York's citizens became discontented with British rule. A number of protests were staged that served as catalysts in the growing anticolonial sentiment that eventually led to the American Revolution. Once the war was under way, the strategic importance of New York's port was realized by both sides. The patriots built fortifications such as Fort Washington, to protect the city and guard the Hudson River. In July 1776 a large British force led by General Howe landed on Staten Island. On July 12, a pair of British vessels sailed up the Hudson, unimpeded by Fort Washington's guns. Later, to prevent the passage of British warships, Fort Lee was constructed opposite Fort Washington, and a chain of boats was sunk in the river near the present-day George Washington Bridge. On August 28 the British attacked the Americans guarding Brooklyn Heights. In what has become known as the Battle of Long Island, the inexperienced American troops, led by George Washington, suffered a huge defeat. Fortunately, under cover of darkness and fog, Washington was able successfully to withdraw the remainder of his army before the British could trap them.

On September 15, 1776, American forces suffered another reverse at Kipp's Bay and abandoned New York, which was then captured by the British. The following day Washington's troops rallied and turned back a British assault in the Battle of Harlem Heights. However, on November 16, 1776, Fort Washington, the last American stronghold in New York, fell, and the city remained in British hands for the rest of the war. During the British occupation New York's population swelled with Tory refugees.

Following the end of the war, the last British troops departed from the Battery on November 28, 1783. On December 4 Washington bade farewell to his officers at Fraunces Tavern. New York's population had shrunk to half its prewar level, and the city had been damaged by looting and two very destructive fires. Its recovery was aided by its temporary role as state capital, from 1783 to 1796, and as the nation's capital from 1785 to 1790. In April 1789 George Washington was inaugurated as the first U.S. president on the steps of the old Federal Hall.

In the new nation's economy New York's commercial importance grew. The Bank of New York was established in 1784, and the New York Stock Exchange in 1792. New York's financial infrastructure of banks and insurance companies aided its growth. It was the only city on the East Coast to receive its mail directly from Great Britain, thus it received news days or weeks earlier than did other ports, a big trade advantage. New York's deepwater port could handle the biggest ships with the largest cargoes. The city also had the nation's best port facilities and largest labor force.

American neutrality during the Napoleonic Wars enabled New York shippers to profit from supplying both sides in a war-ravaged Europe that was increasingly dependent on the United States for foodstuffs and other goods. The turmoil in Europe allowed New York merchants to secure much of the world's carrying trade. By the 1790s New York had surpassed Philadelphia to become the largest U.S. port, handling more than one-third of the nation's overseas trade.

New York also became a major shipping port for cotton grown in the South and shipped to the textile mills in Great Britain in exchange for manufactured goods (including textiles).

By 1820 the city's population reached 123,700. It had overtaken its rivals to become America's largest city. In 1825 the opening of the Erie Canal made the Hudson River and New York the main U.S. transportation corridor and the gateway to the West. New York banks helped finance the nation's expansion.

The city rapidly grew to 312,710 in 1840 and 696,115 in 1850, and more than a million inhabitants by 1860. New York was also the primary gateway for newcomers to this country, and nearly half the city's inhabitants were immigrants. Immigrants were a source of cheap labor, which along with the city's port encouraged the growth of industrial enterprises in the city. By the late nineteenth century New York was the leading industrial city in the nation and one of the leading industrial centers in the world.

New York's rapid growth led to a host of problems as well as extraordinary and sometimes monumental ways of addressing them. Major engineering achievements such as the Croton Aqueduct and later the Catskill Aqueduct brought freshwater into the city. Tunnels and enormous bridges like the George Washington helped link the city with wider transportation networks. The city's severe space shortage was addressed by huge buildings that soared into the sky. Increasing traffic congestion was partially solved by the construction of an elaborate subway system. Urban renewal and massive housing projects attempted to aid the city's poor. Modern public parks such as Central Park and Riverside Park provided city dwellers with seminatural environments and open space in the heart of the vast urban metropolis.

Throughout the nineteenth century, as New York's port grew, the waterfront along the Hudson was developed for shipping. By 1807 the Hudson had fifteen piers—less than half of the East River side, but growing rapidly. Following the end of the Civil War, most shipping activity transferred from the East River to newer facilities along the Hudson that would accommodate the deeper draws of the new transatlantic steamships. What once was a more irregular riverfront with marshes was rapidly transformed through landfill and the construction of piers and wharves and other facilities. Warehouses, shipping offices, markets, and factories along West Street and in TriBeCa and SoHo helped support this bustling waterfront. During the late nineteenth century New York's port shifted from primarily bulk goods to trade in manufactured goods.

In the twentieth century New York's importance as a port shrank. The numbers of passenger ships declined due to competition from the airlines. Other forms of transport, including trains and trucks, also competed with New York shipping. New York's strongly unionized labor force, high taxes, corruption, organized crime, and the expense of land—particularly on Manhattan's West Side—made the cost of shipping in New York Harbor prohibitive for many businesses. Other Atlantic ports, such as Norfolk and Baltimore, competed successfully. Much of New York's port activity shifted to the New Jersey side of the harbor, where modern facilities that could handle containerized cargoes were located. All this led to the eventual decline and abandonment of most port facilities along the Hudson, which were later demolished. Since the Clean Water Act of 1972, the quality of New York's Hudson River waters has improved greatly, and now numerous marine species have returned to the area.

In 1973 part of the aging elevated roadway along the Hudson collapsed, forcing its closure and eventual demolition. Plans were formulated to replace it with a huge 4.2-mile-long federally funded development project called Westway, which would have been constructed primarily on two hundred acres of landfill in the river. Parks, as well as intensive commercial and residential development, were planned to cover this new landfill. The estimated cost of the proposed project was $2.3 billion. Besides the obvious cost concerns, the project's impact on the environment was another source of controversy. The area to be covered by the landfill was a habitat for such fish as striped bass, winter flounder, and white perch. Opponents sued Westway's sponsors, stating that their environmental impact statement didn't adequately address the project's impact on the estuarine habitat. In 1982 the court ruled in favor of the environmentalists, and the project was halted. A new impact statement was written and presented to the court in 1985, but it too failed adequately to address the environmentalists' concerns, and again a judge halted the project. More recently a proposal for a considerably scaled-back land-based highway project with riverfront parks, pedestrian walkways, and bike paths has won acceptance. Those interested in learning more about the history of New York City should read the magnificent new volume *Gotham: A History of New York City to 1898* by Edwin Burroughs and Mike Wallace, published by the Oxford University Press.

New York is blessed with a dense network of public transport routes that make virtually any spot accessible within a few blocks at the most. For information about routes, fares, and schedules, call New York City Transit, 718-330-1234. Subways run twenty-four hours. Fares may be paid by means of tokens that can be purchased at newsstands and at booths located in most stations. A MetroCard, which will soon be available from machines in addition to booths in most stations, is good for multiple rides and is worthwhile if you're staying for a number of days. Free subway maps are available on request. The 1 and the 9 subway lines roughly parallel the route from the Battery to Inwood. The A line goes all the way north from the World Trade Center to 207th Street. Bus routes can also be utilized. Bus fares are payable by tokens, MetroCard, or exact change, and free transfers are available on request. The number 5 provides service from 72nd Street, follows Riverside Drive north to 120th, and continues to Washington Heights. The number 4 goes north from Penn Station to the Cloisters.

For information about accommodations, dining, and shopping, contact the New York City Convention and Visitor's Bureau, 800-NYC-VISIT. Numerous guidebooks also specialize in these areas. Also, a number of clubs listed in the "How To" chapter of this book have organized walking or bike tours of the city, with experienced leaders who are knowledgeable about the area's history, background, landmarks, and so on. Organized walking tours are also listed in the Weekend (Friday) section of the *New York Times*.

The Route

BATTERY PARK TO THE CHELSEA PIERS

Approximately three miles. The first mile and a half covers Battery Park and Battery Park City. A paved pedestrian and bike path continues north along the waterfront for another mile to a terminal of the New York City Sanitation Department. The last half mile unfortunately affords no views of the river.

Battery Park is a small refuge of trees and benches at Manhattan's southernmost tip. Located at the foot of the financial district, it provides relief from the downtown area's crowded towers and congested streets. From the park there are excellent views of New York Harbor, the Statue of Liberty, Ellis Island, and Staten Island, and ferries depart from there to all three. Boat rides to these popular tourist attractions offer exciting views and should not be missed.

During the colonial period, the Battery was fortified. Just south of Bowling Green was the site of Fort Amsterdam, later renamed Fort George by the English. In 1790 the fortifications were dismantled and a promenade erected, which became one of New York's first public open spaces. Young men and boys skinny-dipped from the shore, offending the genteel sensibilities of the city's upper class. In the early 1820s lawns, shade trees, and a decorative iron railing were added to the Battery, and it became New York's most popular and fashionable park, bordered by wealthy residences. Gradually the park was enlarged on landfill, eventually covering its present site.

Today one of the most prominent features of the park is Castle Clinton. During the War of 1812, as part of the city's defenses against a British assault, a fortress called the West Battery was constructed three hundred feet offshore. In 1824 the city acquired it from the federal government, and two years later it became a high-class theater, Castle Garden, and a reception area for dignified guests to the city. In 1855 Castle Garden was converted into the Emigrants Landing Depot, the country's major center for processing immigrants. Millions passed through its gates on their way to a new life in the United States until 1890, when Ellis Island took over that function. In 1896 it was redesinged by the firm of

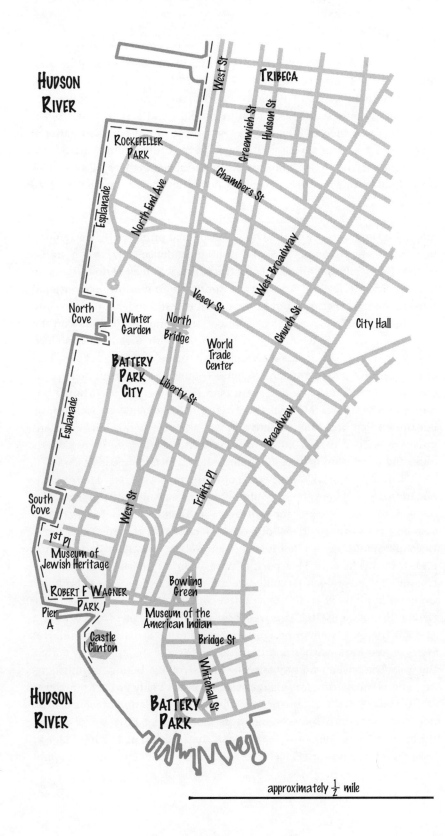

HUDSON
RIVER

TRIBECA

West St

Greenwich St

Hudson St

ROCKEFELLER
PARK

Chambers St

Esplanade

North End Ave

West Broadway

Vesey St

Church St

City Hall

North
Cove

Winter
Garden

North
Bridge

World
Trade
Center

BATTERY
PARK
CITY

Liberty St

Broadway

Esplanade

Trinity Pl

West St

South
Cove

1st Pl
Museum of
Jewish Heritage

Bowling
Green

ROBERT F WAGNER
PARK

Pier
A

Museum of the
American Indian

Bridge St

Castle
Clinton

Whitehall St

HUDSON
RIVER

BATTERY
PARK

approximately $\frac{1}{2}$ mile

McKim, Mead & White and became the city's first aquarium until the new one opened in Coney Island in 1942. In 1946 Castle Clinton was designated a national monument and restored to its original appearance. Today it sits landlocked, surrounded by landfill, and serves as the ticket office for the ferries to Ellis Island and Statue of Liberty (also national monuments), and most visitors lining up in the central courtyard are unaware of the structure's significance. For the curious, there's a small historical museum with three dioramas depicting the site in 1812, 1886, and 1941.

Just north of Battery Park is another significant New York City landmark. Bowling Green was the city's first official public park, designated in 1733. It was there in 1776, at a proindependence rally, that a statue of King George III was toppled. Later the statue was melted down to make bullets. Next to Bowling Green is the Smithsonian Institution's National Museum of the American Indian, located in the Alexander Hamilton Custom House. The museum has permanent and temporary exhibits on the art and culture of Native Americans, including both ancient and modern works. One may view baskets, ceramics, costumes, jewelry, carvings, and other beautiful and significant objects. Though the museum doesn't focus on Native Americans of the Hudson region per se, it certainly enhances one's appreciation of the artistic achievements as well as the culture and spiritual life of Native Americans in general. This excellent museum is open from 10:00 A.M. to 5:00 P.M. every day except Christmas, and admission is free. For information, call 212-668-6624.

From Battery Park's west end, continue northwest past Pier A, completed in 1886, where the city's firefighting vessels dock. At present it is being renovated as a pier for tour boats and historic vessels. There will also be a restaurant and visitors' center for the new Hudson River Park. Beyond it, make a sharp left into the new Robert F. Wagner Park, named after a former mayor. This park is part of Battery Park City, a ninety-two-acre mixed residential, office, retail, and recreation space, built entirely on landfill excavated during the construction of the World Trade Center during the 1970s. This was formerly an area of piers and wharves. Though the park's environment is rather sterile, it features wonderful views of New York Harbor and the Hudson River with Jersey City across the way. The paved walkway is perfect for strolling, biking, in-line skating, and skateboarding. It also provides a perfect sanctuary from Lower Manhattan's hustle and bustle, and the river is a calming presence. Just north on the right is the prominent, pyramid-shaped Museum of Jewish Heritage: A Living Memorial to the Holocaust, located at 18 First Place at West Street and Battery Place. It includes artifacts, documents, and photos of Jewish life before, during, and after the Holocaust, as well as special exhibitions. There is an admission charge. It is open Sundays through Thursdays from 9:00 A.M. to 5:00 P.M., and Fridays from 9:00 A.M. to 2:00 P.M. For more information call 212-945-0039.

Continue north past South Cove, an attractive inlet where a garden of boulders lines the path. Then enter the seventy-five-foot-wide paved esplanade that parallels the river. There are benches and views of the river and Jersey City across the way. Arrive at North Cove, an anchorage for expensive yachts, also the future site of the city police officers' memorial. Facing the center of the inlet is an impressive glass atrium, the Winter Garden, which contains palm trees, shops, and a host of restaurants and is the site for concerts and special events. Outdoor cafés line the plaza.

One block directly east, and accessible from inside the Winter Garden atrium via the North Bridge, are the twin 1,350-foot-high, 110-story towers of the World Trade Center, with nine million square feet of office space, covering twenty-three and a half acres of landfill, the tallest buildings in New York and among the tallest in the world. There's an observation deck on the 107th floor of the south tower, with an open promenade on the roof above. Depending on visibility, a spectacular vista of the Hudson, Manhattan, and the surrounding area may be enjoyed. It is open daily, 9:30 A.M. to 9:30 P.M. There is an admission charge. Expect about an hour wait. Call 212-435-4170 for information.

Continue north along the esplanade into Rockefeller Park, seven acres of lawns, gardens, and a children's playground; there are also restrooms. The whimsical brass sculptures by Tom Otterness are one of the highlights of the park.

The path turns right and leaves Battery Park City. At the corner of West Street, opposite Borough of Manhattan Community College, go north on an unadorned paved path that parallels the river. This also was once a busy area of piers, wharves, and waterfront activity. Today only the rotting remnants of a few remain, closed to the public for safety reasons. The area to the east is TriBeCa, which stands for "triangle below Canal." TriBeCa was once residential, but as the riverfront port grew, it became an industrial area crowded with factories and hundreds of warehouses that served the bustling waterfront. Many of the warehouses were designed in the then fashionable Italianate style with white marble or brownstone facades. When the waterfront declined, the warehouses were abandoned, and later, artists fleeing SoHo's rising rents converted them into loft space. The whole waterfront, from Battery Park City north to Riverside Park, is currently undergoing a massive 300-million-dollar facelift to become Hudson River Park that will include pedestrian and bike paths, landscaped areas, and other amenities. Right now the path is marred by eyesores and speeding traffic.

Pier 34, a pedestrian walkway with benches, has a superb view of Lower Manhattan. At the corner of Gansevoort Street, next to a rather hideous New York City Sanitation Department facility, the asphalt path along the river ends. Hard to believe, but this was once the site of a Native American fishing village, though it would be difficult to discern that now. Later it was the site of a battery during the War of 1812. Cross busy West Street—fortunately, there's a light—and continue north. You are now on the edge of Chelsea.

CHELSEA PIERS TO RIVERSIDE PARK

Approximately three miles. The first half mile passes the Chelsea Piers. The trail continues north past Jacob Javits Center, the *Intrepid* Air-Space Museum, and piers for cruise ships, before finally ending on the Upper West Side.

From 14th Street to 23rd Street on the left are the Chelsea Piers, an elaborate half-mile-long sports and entertainment complex built on the sites of former piers for ocean liners. This area is more populated than the previous section. Now West Street veers left and becomes Twelfth Avenue.

At 24th Street the view of the river opens up again. At 26th Street cross to the west side of Twelfth Avenue for another short walkway that ends at 29th Street. There are views across the river of Weehawken, New Jersey. Cross Twelfth Avenue again to the east side of the street, and continue north. At 34th Street you'll pass the Jacob Javits Convention Center on the right, 0.85 miles north of the Chelsea Piers, and be able to see the skyscrapers of midtown Manhattan. At 42nd Street you can cross Twelfth Avenue again to the Circle Line, Pier 83, where tour boats leave to circumnavigate Manhattan. Just beyond on the left is the *Intrepid* Air-Space Museum, one of New York's prime tourist attractions. The *Intrepid* is a 872-foot-long aircraft carrier built in 1943 and used in World War II. Its decks are packed with displays of naval aircraft and below are exhibits on space exploration. Nearby are a number of other naval vessels including the submarine USS *Growler,* open to tours. The museum is open in winter (Wednesdays through Sundays from 10:00 A.M. to 5:00 P.M.), and every day in summer, same hours except an hour longer on Sunday. There is an admission charge. Children under six are free.

Those who don't wish to pay the admission can stroll Armed Forces Plaza, which features excellent views of the ships as well as displays of weaponry (including Iraqi tanks captured during the Persian Gulf War).

Continuing north past cruise-ship piers, you may see one in dock. The pathway narrows, then enters a service road. Follow it north to the attractive entrance of another Sanitation Department building. From there you must detour right around the now vacant and somewhat desolate Pennsylvania Railroad yards, east on 59th Street underneath a viaduct to West End Avenue, where you make a left and head north. Continue north on West End past high-rise apartment buildings and a small park. This neighborhood is part of the Upper West Side. Hilly and swampy, the Upper West Side grew more slowly than did the East Side. Despite the construction of Riverside Park, in the late nineteenth century it was still an underdeveloped, primarily industrial area. In 1904 the arrival of subway service caused the Upper West Side suddenly to boom as a residential and commercial neighborhood. Two to three blocks east are Broadway and Columbus Avenue, which feature excellent restaurants, cafés, and boutiques. Also nearby is Lincoln Center, and the partially completed Riverside South, a huge residential project by developer Donald Trump. So far two forty-story condominium apartment buildings with facades by architect Philip Johnson have been constructed. At 70th Street the buildings turn older, and attractive row houses may be seen. Make a left at 72nd Street, and continue west to the corner of Riverside Drive, where you enter Riverside Park.

RIVERSIDE PARK TO THE RIVERSIDE VIADUCT

Approximately three miles through Riverside Park, passing the 79th Street Boat Basin, Riverside Church, and Grant's Tomb.

Riverside Park comprises 316 acres along the Hudson, originally designed by Frederick Law Olmsted. It opened in 1880 in an area that had previously been occupied by breweries, grain elevators, and slaughterhouses. In 1902 city engineer F. Stewart Williamson extended the park from 125th Street north to 157th. He employed the same naturalistic design principles that Olmsted did, but also built castlelike stone buttresses into the bluffs. At the time the West Shore Railroad was a continuous barrier between the park and the river. In 1937 Parks Commissioner Robert Moses buried the tracks underground and extended sections of the park out into the river on landfill. These new sections of the park used simple geometric patterns in the layout of paths and other features, in sharp contrast with the rest of the park, which was more natural and used less regular patterns. Access to the waterfront was improved, but the Henry Hudson Parkway was another unfortunate addition. Overlying the railroad tracks, it too presented a barrier to access as well as a major source of noise and pollution bisecting the center of the park.

Enter the park at the corner of 72nd Street and Riverside Drive. You're greeted by a statue of Eleanor Roosevelt. Follow the path to the left, through a tunnel underneath the Henry Hudson Parkway, to a promenade along the river. Continue north, passing the 79th Street Boat Basin on the left, a marina community of permanent and semipermanent boat dwellers. Just beyond, the asphalt path veers right. (Note: Though a well-defined dirt path continues north along the riverfront, I do not recommend it. The path follows a very narrow and desolate island between the highway and the river, and the constant assault of cars whizzing by and traffic noise more than detract from the open river views.)

Leaving the waterfront past the Boat Basin, the path goes east underneath the Henry Hudson Parkway again. A short walk uphill brings you to a pedestrian boulevard. Tall, stately apartment buildings on Riverside Drive loom overhead on the right. Make a sharp left and continue north. The boulevard is a popular place for bicyclists, in-line skaters, and pedestrians of all sorts. Beautiful flowering trees, forsythias, and daffodils bloom in the spring. In the summer it is an enchanting emerald path. There are partial views of the river through the trees. At 89th Street, up the hill to the right, is the Soldiers' and Sailors' Monument, an impressive Civil War memorial built in 1902.

Along the pedestrian boulevard at 91st Street is a lovely Community Flower Garden tended by local residents, each assigned a tiny plot. The path to the left descends to the waterfront again with more views, but you'll have to backtrack. The boulevard crosses 96th Street and continues for half a mile, turns into a paved trail that continues north, then veers to the right at tennis courts, and climbs uphill on steps. (Bicyclists will have to carry their bikes here.) The trail finally emerges from the park onto Riverside Drive at 120th Street, opposite Riverside Church and Grant's Tomb. This area is known as Morningside Heights.

Riverside Church is one of the largest churches in New York City— its steeple is 392 feet high—and one of the more impressive buildings along the river. Built in 1930 in a neo-Gothic style, it was criticized for its eclecticism. The Laura Spellman Rockefeller Memorial Carillon, donated by John D. Rockefeller, Jr., has seventy-four bells, including the largest tuned bell in the world. For a small admission, one can ascend the tower, climb 147 steps, observe the bells, and catch one of Manhattan's least-known best views. The carillon is played on holidays, on Saturdays at noon, and on Sundays, before and after the morning service and at 3:00 P.M. Call 212-222-5900 for information.

General Grant's Tomb is located just north of Riverside Church. You know who's buried there: the famous Civil War general and president of the United States, and his wife. The tomb, based on the design of a classical mausoleum in Turkey, was designed by John H. Duncan and completed in 1897, using more than two thousand tons of granite in its exterior. The interior replicates Napoleon's tomb in the chapel of the Hôtel des Invalides in Paris. Murals depicting Grant's victories in the Civil War were done by Allyn Cox in 1966. The largest mausoleum in the United States, it is a national monument. Grant's Tomb is open 9:00 A.M. to 5:00 P.M., Wednesdays through Sundays. Admission is free. Call 212-666-1640 for information. Around the perimeter of the monument is a colorful and whimsical mosaic bench, which was a community project.

This area of the Upper West Side/Morningside Heights has some other noteworthy attractions, including the campus of Columbia University at 116th Street and Broadway and the Cathedral of Saint John the Divine at 112th and Amsterdam.

Beyond Grant's Tomb, follow Riverside Drive north, through a rather desolate section where one should exercise proper caution. On the left is a small monument to St. Claire Pollock, a five-year-old who fell to his death from a rock in the vicinity in 1797. Around 125th Street Riverside Drive crosses the recently restored 1,688-foot-long Riverside Drive Viaduct, built in 1901. If you have time, check out the underside of the viaduct: The ironwork is a sight to behold. The Riverside Drive Viaduct crosses a valley created by a fault—a fracture in the rock that causes the rock beds on either side of the fault to move in opposite directions. Differential erosion of these rock beds formed the valley visible today, which has been partially filled with glacial sediment some two hundred feet deep. In the mid nineteenth century the area of 125th Street was populated by Irish immigrants who built small cottages and raised animals for sale to local markets. Hogs were so plentiful that the area became known as "Pig Alley." At the north end, at approximately 134th Street, Riverside Drive enters Hamilton Heights, named for the country estate of Alexander Hamilton. This area, which many consider to be part of Harlem, became accessible at the turn of the century once the subway line reached it. Originally a wealthy neighborhood with ornate, impressive apartment buildings overlooking the river, Hamilton Heights is now a mixed-income area.

HAMILTON HEIGHTS TO THE GEORGE WASHINGTON BRIDGE

Two and a half miles through Riverbank State Park, the north end of Riverside Park, and Fort Washington Park.

From the viaduct continue north on Riverside Drive, one quarter mile to 139th Street. A walkway on the left crosses over the highway to Riverbank State Park, completed in 1992. This popular but controversial park, which sits atop the North River Water Pollution Control Plant, was built to appease neighborhood concerns about the possible stench from sewage. The state-of-the-art plant treats the effluence from all of northern Manhattan, roughly a million people. The park is busy and well policed and has excellent recreational facilities and great views, particularly north toward the George Washington Bridge.

From Riverbank State Park one may continue north along Riverside Drive, which has a pleasant pedestrian sidewalk overlooking the river. If you go the Riverside Drive way, take a look at Trinity Cemetery, which climbs the hill up to Amsterdam Avenue, between 153rd and 155th Streets. The landscape design was done by Calvert Vaux in 1881. It was once part of a farm belonging to the great naturalist and painter John James Audubon (1785–1851), who is buried in the cemetery. On the north side of the cemetery on 155th Street are two small museums of the Hispanic Society of America and the American Numismatic Society. Access to Fort Washington Park from Riverside Drive may be gained via a walkway over the Henry Hudson Parkway, south of the bridge.

If you choose to go north by walking along the river, go to the northeast corner of Riverbank State Park and descend by elevator or stairway to Riverside Park below. There is a playground, basketball courts, a baseball field, and tennis courts. Unfortunately the condition of this section of the park is shabby, but it is being refurbished.

The park ends at a dirt road, blocked off to vehicular traffic. Though it appears very seedy, it is a popular fishing spot, where cars can drive right up to the river's edge. Towering overhead on the right are the ramps of the Henry Hudson Parkway. The roadway ends after a short stretch, and you enter Fort Washington Park. This park, which runs right along the Hudson, is well maintained, popular with Hispanic families and fishermen, and has great views of the George Washington Bridge and Fort Lee across the river. It is one of my favorite sections.

Follow the paved path north through the park, approximately one mile, approaching the George Washington Bridge, and finally crossing underneath the massive steel ramparts of the bridge.

The George Washington Bridge, designed by Othmar H. Ammann, was completed in 1931, the third automobile bridge across the Hudson. It was twice as long as any suspension bridge of its time, more than 4,760 feet across. Later it was expanded to include additional lanes of traffic and a lower deck. There are pedestrian walkways on both sides of the upper level, with rewarding views of the river in both directions, Manhattan Island, and the Palisades. The north-side pedestrian walkway may be accessed from Cabrini Boulevard and 179th Street, the south, from 178th Street.

Underneath the bridge is the Jeffries Hook Lighthouse, built in 1880 and originally located off Sandy Hook, New Jersey. In 1921 the Coast Guard moved it here, but construction of the bridge rendered it obsolete. It has not been in use for almost seventy years. In 1942 Hildegarde Hoyt wrote the children's classic *The Little Red Lighthouse and the Great Gray Bridge*, which probably saved the lighthouse from demolition. It is now a registered historic landmark, and there are twice-monthly tours between the end of March and October and on special occasions. Call 212-427-4040 for information. This was also the site of a chain of sunken ships the Americans used to try to block British warships from sailing up the Hudson—an effort that proved futile.

THE GEORGE WASHINGTON BRIDGE TO INWOOD HILL PARK

Approximately two miles, through the neighborhood of Washington Heights, Fort Tryon Park, the Cloisters, and Inwood Hill Park.

From the George Washington Bridge the trail continues north a short distance, then veers uphill to the right and bends south, coming out on a roadway. Go left, and follow the roadway east to the Henry Hudson Parkway. Just north is a pedestrian walkway and ramp over the highway. (The latter was closed when I last visited, so bicyclists may have to carry their bikes up and down the steps.)

After crossing the highway make a right onto Riverside Drive. Climb the hill to the corner of 181st Street, also labeled Lafayette Plaza. Make a left onto 181st, and continue east, uphill. Then, at the first intersection, make a left onto Cabrini Boulevard and head north. This takes you through the pleasant neighborhood of Washington Heights, which has been settled by various immigrant groups and today is populated mainly by immigrants from Eastern Europe, Latin America, and the Caribbean. One block east is Fort Washington–Bennet Park. Located between 183rd and 185th Streets, the park was the site of Fort Washington during the Revolutionary War. Together with Fort Lee across the river, it guarded the Hudson to prevent the passage of British warships up the river. After the capture of New York City by the British, Fort Washington remained the only American stronghold on Manhattan. It was bombarded by British warships and, despite a valiant defense, fell to a combined force of British and Hessian troops on November 16, 1776. Fifty-four Americans were killed and more than two thousand taken prisoner. The fall of Fort Washington was one of the worst American setbacks during the Revolutionary War.

Follow Cabrini Boulevard north till it bends east and enters Fort Tryon Park.

Sixty-six acres in a magnificent setting, beautifully designed by

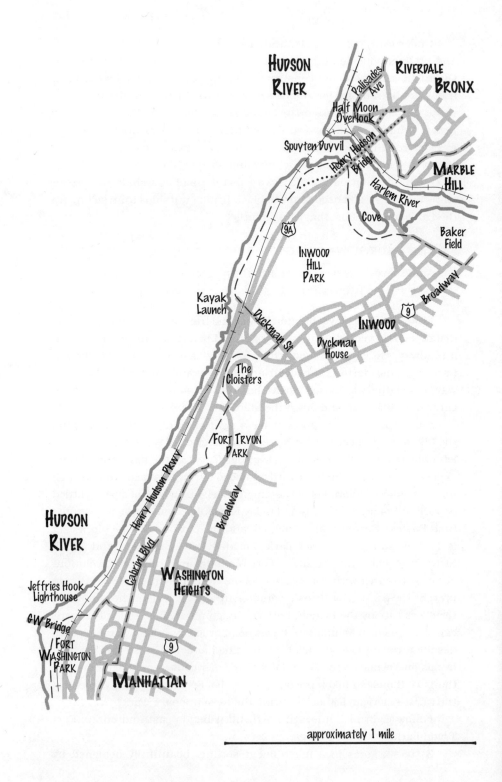

approximately 1 mile

Frederick Law Olmsted, Jr., son of the famous landscape architect, this popular park, one of the finest in New York City, was donated by John D. Rockefeller, Jr., in 1930. Fort Tryon was an American redoubt during the Revolution, protecting Fort Washington's northern flank. It fell to the British on the same day that Fort Washington did. (The first woman to fight in the war, Margaret Corbin, was among the patriots who defended the fort. She is buried at West Point, where a monument is dedicated to her.) A stone, fortresslike structure was built on the site of the former redoubt. At 267 feet, it is the highest point in Manhattan and has great views. It was named Fort Tryon by the British captors in honor of New York's last civilian governor, William Tryon.

Follow the paved path north through the park, past the lovely three-acre heath-and-heather garden, with a view of the river, the Palisades, and the George Washington Bridge in the distance. Tulips and daffodils bloom here—the city's largest free-access garden—in the spring. Continue north to the site of the former redoubt. Go down the steps or follow the paved path that skirts the redoubt to the west, and cross the bridge to an open lawn, which is a popular place for lounging. The medieval-looking Cloisters are just beyond.

The Cloisters, a branch of the Metropolitan Museum of Art, built in the style of a medieval cloister, was designed by Charles Collens and opened in 1938. It includes the collections of Charles Gray Barnard from the abandoned monasteries and churches of France brought here and reassembled. The collection is highlighted by seven unicorn tapestries dating from 1499, donated by John D. Rockefeller Jr. It also features a collection of medieval jewelry and an idyllic courtyard and herb garden that's one of Manhattan's most serene spots. Open Tuesdays through Sundays, March through October from 9:30 A.M. to 5:15 P.M., November through February, 9:30 A.M. to 4:45 P.M. There is an admission charge. For information call 212-923-3700.

From the Cloisters the path veers left, following the ridge, then bends sharply to the right and descends past large outcrops of Manhattan Schist down to Riverside Drive. Cross it and continue one block north on Payson Avenue to Dyckman Street. This area is known as Inwood. Nearby was an encampment of British and Hessian troops during the Revolutionary War. Poorly fed and supplied, they ravaged the area and denuded Manhattan's last virgin forest atop neighboring Inwood Hill for firewood.

At Dyckman House, located at Broadway and 201st Street, artifacts from the encampment are on display. This is the only remaining eighteenth-century farmhouse left on Manhattan Island. The Dutch-style colonial farmhouse with a gambrel roof and brick-and-fieldstone walls was typical of its time. It was burned by the British and rebuilt in 1783.

The Dyckman farm once included three hundred acres and was the largest farm on Manhattan until it ceased operating in 1868. The house now lies isolated in the heart of a densely populated urban neighborhood, appearing as out of place as possible. It was purchased by Dyckman descendants in 1915, restored, furnished with eighteenth-century furnishings, and donated to the city. It is open Tuesdays through Sundays, from 11:00 A.M. to 4:00 P.M. For information call 212-304-9422.

Dyckman Street is located in a valley that bisects the Fort Washington Ridge between Fort Tryon and Inwood Hill Park. This valley was created by a fault similar to the one that created the valley at 125th Street.

Across Dyckman Street is Inwood Hill Park, whose 196 acres cover the northernmost tip of Manhattan. It includes three sections: a landscaped area along the Hudson, built on landfill, with paved pedestrian paths and recreational facilities, mostly cut off from the rest of the park by railroad tracks and the Henry Hudson Parkway. There's a wooded middle section, the northernmost section of the Fort Washington Ridge, underlain by Manhattan Schist and bisected by the Henry Hudson Parkway. It has the only wild forest left on Manhattan Island, where hackberries, oaks, maples, cherries, tulip trees, cottonwoods, birches, and hickories may be seen. This was also the last site on Manhattan where wolves roamed and Native Americans hunted until the early eighteenth century. Native artifacts from the Woodland Period have been recovered from a rock shelter site in the park. Later, in the nineteenth century, Inwood Hill was an estate, and many exotic trees were planted, including copper beech and ginkgoes. Many of the outcrops of Manhattan Schist show characteristic evidence of glaciation: grooves and striations. Trails were constructed in the 1930s by the Work Projects Administration (WPA); they afford fine views of the river and the Palisades from meadows along the top of the ridge.

The last section comprises the flatlands east of the ridge. These are underlain by Inwood Marble, which erodes more easily than does Manhattan Schist. Today the flatlands are mostly devoted to recreation, but during the time of Dutch rule the area was settled and farmed by American Indians. A Wiechquaergeck village was located on the north side of the Spuyten Duyvil, named Shorakaprock, or "As far as the sitting-down place." It is reputed that this is where the Dutch purchased Manhattan Island from the Indians. The cove just north of the playing fields contains the last remaining wetland on Manhattan, an island that was once ringed by many wetlands.

At the entrance to the park you'll pass a playground on the right. Continue west on Dyckman Street toward the river, crossing underneath the highway and railroad bridge. At the end of the street is a kayak launch, parking, and a pedestrian pier with excellent views, especially of the George Washington Bridge. Go north on the pedestrian path, and enter the park. The pathway soon divides. Take the left fork, skirting a playing field, and follow the path along the river. There are views looking north of the Palisades across the river. The trail splits again; take the right fork to the pedestrian bridge over the railroad tracks. (If you're riding a bike, you'll have to carry it up and down the steps.) Once over, you'll enter a lovely deciduous forest, though unfortunately you'll still hear obnoxious traffic noise from the nearby highway. There are views of the river through the trees and an iron swing bridge used by Amtrak trains. Squirrels, chipmunks, and birds are abundant here. The trail splits; go left, and you'll soon reach another fork. Walkers may go right, uphill past a sumac field, an example of an area in the early stages of succession. It is also a rather desolate, rarely used stretch: Use caution. The trail emerges from the woods in front of a toll booth and the Henry Hudson Bridge, which was completed in 1936. Head for the pedestrian walkway on the left side of bridge. NO BIKES ALLOWED, warns a sign. I found the walk across the two-thousand-foot bridge over the Spuyten Duyvil tolerable at best because of the limited views and traffic noise; getting to the other side and Riverdale was a relief.

Since bicyclists cannot use the Henry Hudson Bridge, they should continue on the trail, which continues north and east, under the bridge. This will bring you down to the flatlands on the east side of Inwood Hill Park. Skirt the cove and continue east on 218th Street, past Baker Field, a Columbia University playing field, on the left, four blocks to Broadway. Go left, north on Broadway, and over the Broadway Bridge into Marble Hill. This small neighborhood was once a part of Manhattan, until construction of the Harlem River Ship Channel cut it off from the rest of the island. However, it is still administered as part of the borough of Manhattan. Continue north on Broadway to 231st Street. Make a left here and follow to the intersection with Waldo Avenue. The high ridge in front of you, the Riverdale Ridge, is composed of Fordham Gneiss. Go left on Waldo and follow it south, downhill to where it turns sharply right and becomes Palisades Avenue. Continue west underneath the Henry Hudson Bridge, soon reaching the intersection with Independence Avenue and the Walkers' Route.

RIVERDALE TO YONKERS

Approximately two miles, through Riverdale neighborhoods and parks, passing Wave Hill.

Riverdale is situated along the Hudson River on a high ridge. Perhaps the biggest surprise is that Riverdale is part of the Bronx. Located

in the extreme northwest corner of that borough, it is one of the most affluent and attractive residential neighborhoods in the city and has some
very posh homes. (John F. Kennedy lived here in 1928 while attending the
Riverdale Country School.) Bicyclists should be forewarned: Riverdale's
side streets are a maze and are often steep, narrow, winding, and poorly
maintained, with huge, gaping potholes. Use extra caution when riding.

After crossing the Henry Hudson Bridge, continue north on the
pedestrian path, parallel to the parkway, to a stop light at the intersection with Kappock Street. Cross the street and make a left onto Kappock
and head west, downhill one block to the corner by Henry Hudson Park,
which has a statue of the famed English navigator. Make another left
here onto Independence Avenue, and follow it to the end at Palisades Avenue. Make a right on Palisades Avenue and continue west, passing the
Half Moon Overlook on the left, with a superb open view of the Spuyten
Duyvil, the Hudson River, the Palisades, and the George Washington
Bridge in the distance. Palisades Avenue makes a sharp right and heads
north parallel to the river, past homes and apartment buildings to a less
crowded, quiet residential neighborhood of large homes, big yards, plenty
of trees, and little traffic. There are occasional glimpses of the Hudson
through the trees. At 0.4 miles from where Palisades Avenue turns north,
you'll reach Raoul Wallenberg Park on the right and Riverdale Park on
the left. Both are heavily wooded with mixed deciduous trees. Riverdale
Park extends from Palisades Avenue west to the railroad tracks that run
along the river. At an opening in the fence, walkers may enter the park
and take the trail that winds through the woods that run parallel to the
street and the river. Bicyclists should continue north on Palisades Avenue to 249th Street.

After a short distance, the walking trail ends at a driveway. Go right
and back onto Palisades Avenue where you go left and continue north.
Soon, you reach a second, larger section of the park. Again enter the park
through an opening in the fence and follow the trail through the woods.
After another quarter mile you'll reach a parking area. A few trails branch
off here. You can detour from here to Wave Hill. To do so, turn right at
the parking area, onto narrow 249th Street as it winds its way uphill to
Independence Avenue, and make a left.

Wave Hill, the most important and rewarding attraction in Riverdale,
is a public garden and cultural center donated to the city in 1960 by the
daughters of George W. Perkins, a Wall Street financier and conserva-
tionist who was one of the first presidents of the Palisades Interstate Park
Commission. The Wave Hill home was originally built in 1843. Perkins acquired it in 1903, enlarging it and adding greenhouses, gardens, and
stables. Teddy Roosevelt's family rented the estate for two summers when

he was an adolescent. Mark Twain leased it from 1901 to 1903 during the height of his career, and conductor Arturo Toscanini rented it in the 1940s.

The primary attractions are the beautiful gardens and the view of the Hudson with the Palisades in the background. The best vantage point is the Pergola Overlook. Another excellent spot is the stone pagoda, which overlooks the Wild Garden. There is the Herbert and Hyonja Abrons ten-acre woodland, with trails and a variety of native plants. On the lawn in front of the Wave Hill House are two stupendous copper beeches as well as other decorative exotic and native trees and shrubs. The house has a gift shop and café. Also on the property is the 1927 Georgian Revival–style Glyndor House, which serves as an art gallery. Wave Hill is open Tuesdays through Sundays, mid-May to mid-October, 9:00 A.M. to 5:30 P.M., Fridays till dusk, mid-October to mid-May, 9:00 A.M. to 4:30 P.M. Admission is free from November 15 to March 14. The rest of the year there is a small charge, with reduced rates for seniors and students. Children under six free. For information call 718-549-3200.

Walkers and bicyclists may return to the route by continuing north on Independence Avenue a short distance to the intersection at 252nd Street and making a left. Go one block west on 252nd Street and then turn right, north on Sycamore. Follow Sycamore all the way to 254th Street. Go left on 254th, west to Palisades Avenue, and turn right.

Back in Riverdale Park at 249th Street, hikers may go left diagonally and continue north, this time for more than a half mile in one of the park's most popular sections. It's hard to believe you're hiking in New York City through wild forest that looks as if it could be upstate.

The trail finally emerges from the forest at 254th Street. (To the left and down the hill is the Riverdale Metro-North Station.) Go straight on Palisades Avenue and continue north. Pass the Cardinal Spellman Retreat House on the left, followed by the Hebrew Home for the Aged. After more than a half mile Palisades Avenue turns sharply right and becomes 261st Street. Continue east a short distance to Riverdale Avenue, and make a left. There are bus stops located on the corner, and on the left is the College of Mount Saint Vincent. A short distance north on Riverdale Avenue is the boundary of Yonkers.

7 Palisades
FORT LEE TO STONY POINT

Only a bridge walk away from Manhattan, but what a difference! While the section covered in this chapter lies close to the heart of America's greatest urban center, many of the trails are blissfully tranquil and beautiful, have incredible views, and traverse a lush and varied landscape. This chapter explores the Palisades, one of America's most unique geologic formations. Much of the Palisades is parkland, open for recreational use, and protected. The Long Path provides a superb avenue for walkers, covering more than thirty miles from the George Washington Bridge up to High Tor. The Shore Trail in Palisades Interstate Park is by far the longest trail along the Hudson, rivaled only by the Shore Path stretching between Nyack and Haverstraw. Both are covered in this section. The Henry Hudson Drive is an excellent route for bicyclists and walkers, as is the rail trail between Piermont and Nyack. The Long Path and most other walking trails in this section are maintained by the New York/New Jersey Trail Conference. The Trail Conference's *Hudson Palisades Trails* maps, 4A and 4B, are useful when hiking this section.

The lovely communities of Piermont and Nyack have beautiful homes, shops, and cafés to lure visitors. Historic Revolutionary War sites, such as Fort Lee Historic Park and Stony Point, are located here as well as remnants of the river's early industries.

The Palisades is a ridge of volcanic diabase rock, also called trap rock, that was created when magma, hot molten rock that originated deep below the earth's crust, escaped upward through cracks that formed when the earth's continents split apart almost two hundred million years ago. Instead of reaching the surface, the molten rock spread between layers of sedimentary rock, forming a sill more than a thousand feet thick. The magma eventually cooled and hardened into the diabase, which contains augite, a dark-colored mineral, and plagioclase feldspar. Erosion from glaciers, the Hudson River, and the daily action of weather exposed the rocks and created the spectacular cliffs we see today. The Palisades got their name from the resemblance of the rock, which often erodes into six-sided pillars, to the walls of timbers the Native Americans used for their fortresses. This formation extends from Staten Island to just west of High Tor, a distance of about fifty miles.

Beneath the Palisades are layers of sedimentary rock from the Triassic, the early part of the Mesozoic era, the Age of Dinosaurs. Stony Point is part of an early Paleozoic igneous intrusion called the Cortlandt Complex. The Palisades section also faces the widest parts of the Hudson River: Haverstraw Bay and the Tappan Zee. This section of the river has the highest salt content, which affects the types of fish, animals, and plants that are found here.

The 2,472 acres of the New Jersey section of Palisades Interstate Park extends from Fort Lee north to the New York State line, approximately ten and a half miles. Relatively narrow for much of its length, the park includes the most spectacular section of the Palisades cliffs as well as miles of undeveloped shoreline accessible only to hikers.

This area along the Hudson was fished and hunted by indigenous peoples for at least seven thousand years prior to European settlement. During the colonial period, the river shore was inhabited by fishermen, boat builders and repairmen, woodsmen, tanners, and others who made their living off the river. Docks were established in a number of places where roads and trails ascended the cliffs, providing a means for farmers who lived west of the Palisades to get their produce to market, shipping it downriver to New York City. The thin soils on the top of the Palisades Ridge made it undesirable for farming, and much of it remained forested into the nineteenth century. During the 1800s New York's growing need for timber for building and fuel resulted in the destruction of the Palisades' forests. Wealthy residents built elaborate estates atop the cliffs. The Palisades Mountain House was a luxurious resort. The reddish sandstone at the base of the cliffs and the diabase itself were quarried for buildings, road materials, and other projects. As New York City grew, increasing demand for the materials, improved technology and the use of dynamite resulted in more and more of the cliff face being destroyed. In 1900 the New Jersey Federation of Women's Clubs fought to establish an interstate park commission, which then began to purchase the land along the Palisades. By 1910 practically all the land of the present-day park had been purchased by the Palisades Interstate Park Commission.

In the early days of the park, recreational facilities such as boat docks, camping grounds, bathing beaches, and trails were constructed. Many were WPA and Civilian Conservation Corps (CCC) projects during the Great Depression. Scores of visitors arrived from Manhattan, mostly by steamboat and ferry. In 1916 the Henry Hudson Drive was completed; in 1931, the George Washington Bridge; and in 1958, the Palisades Parkway. After World War II, all the Palisades beaches were closed due to pollution in the Hudson. The automobile allowed potential visitors to travel beyond the area, and thus the Palisades suffered a severe decline in popularity. Many of its facilities fell into disuse or were closed. However, since the 1970s, with renewed interest in nature and the environment, improvements in some facilities, plus efforts to clean up the Hudson River, this exceptional park has seen a resurgence in use.

The New Jersey Palisades present a mostly wild, diverse habitat that supports a wide variety of plant and animal life. The thin, mostly acidic soils on the ridge above the cliffs support primarily mixed deciduous forest dominated by oaks and hickories, but also black birch, ash, and in older sections of the forest, maples. Flowering dogwood and shrubs like the mapleleaf viburnum are also present. Along the rocky edges of the cliffs, red cedar, hackberry, sassafras, cherries, hawthorne, birch, and sumac take advantage of the presence of sunlight. Wildflowers like columbine and flowering pinks can often be seen decorating the rocks in spring. The lack of soil in the steep talus slopes underneath the cliffs presents a challenging environment for plants and animals. Nonetheless, roots of black birch, white ash, dogwood, slippery elm, and linden manage to wedge themselves into cracks. Ferns, wildflowers, vines, and shrubs like sumac and poison ivy can also be found. The paulownia, or princess tree, introduced from China, has lavender trumpet-shaped blossoms and is common on the talus slopes.

On the shady moist slopes and ravines, northern hardwoods like maples, tulip trees, beech, birch, and hemlock dominate. Along the shore of the Hudson, moisture, sunlight, and richer soil encourages a variety of lush vegetation: Cottonwoods, willows, maples, sycamores, hackberries, bayberries, aspens, dogwood, and box elders can be seen, as well as various grasses, vines, brambles, honeysuckle, raspberries, poison ivy and sumac, birch, and sassafras. In areas along the shore that were previously settled or developed, and in the area of former estates along the top of the cliffs, nonnative ornamental plants such as apple trees, lilacs, and rhododendron intermingle with native species.

Despite the park's proximity to New York City and suburbs, a number of bird and other animal species thrive. These include deer, woodchuck, snakes, and five-lined skinks—lizards that can be seen primarily on talus slopes and cliff edges, sunning themselves on the rocks—as well as squirrels, chipmunks, millipedes, and rabbits. Hawks and turkey vultures can be seen in the air and on ledges of the cliffs. Foxes, frogs and toads, various songbirds, and abundant insect and arachnid life may also be observed. Geese, ducks, and shorebirds are common in the river.

Fort Lee Historic Park comprises thirty-four acres just south of the George Washington Bridge. The Revolutionary War fort was built in 1776. On November 12, 1776, George Washington watched the fall of his namesake fort from Fort Lee. Eight days later the landing of six thousand British troops under the command of General Lord Cornwallis, north of Fort Lee, threatened the security of the fort and made its position untenable. Washington ordered a hasty retreat to Hackensack, saving the garrison but losing valuable cannon and other supplies. The Americans departed so quickly that food was found cooking in still-smoldering campfires when the British arrived.

The northern portion of the fort has long since been buried by urban development, but the southern end has been restored by the Palisades Interstate Park Commission as Fort Lee Historic Park. Part of the fort's artillery batteries have been reconstructed. There is also a reconstruction of a soldiers' hut, designed to sleep eight troops during the winter, with a stove and other equipment used by the Continental Army. A guide in period costume explains the display and answers questions. A new museum and visitors' center has exhibits on Fort Lee's role in the American Revolution along with artifacts, films, uniforms, a gift shop, and rest rooms. Trails on the property have excellent views of the Hudson, Manhattan across the way, and the George Washington Bridge. There is a charge for parking. For information call 201-461-3956.

The Palisades are easily accessible from Manhattan via public transportation. Red and Tan Line provides regular hourly bus service from the George Washington Bridge Bus Terminal up 9W to Nyack, daily including weekends. There are numerous stops along the way, including Palisades Park and Piermont. For schedule and fare information call 201-384-2400. Shortline provides bus service from the Port Authority in Manhattan to Haverstraw and Stony Point, three times a day during the week and four times a day on weekends and holidays. For information call 1-800-631-8405, extension 111. For information about shopping, dining, and accommodations in the Piermont/Nyack area call 914-353-2221.

The Route

Heading north from Fort Lee, there are three options: The Shore Trail and the Long Path are both restricted to walkers. The Henry Hudson Parkway is an excellent bike route, but walkers can use it also. All three routes link up in the northern part of the park near the New York State border.

FORT LEE HISTORIC PARK TO THE LAMONT NATURE SANCTUARY VIA THE SHORE TRAIL

The Shore Trail is the single longest trail along the Hudson's shoreline (13.5 miles) and, I believe, one of the most magnificent trails in the entire book. It traverses a variety of different terrains including shorelines, woodlands, and talus slopes. Walkers will experience many types of vegetation as well as wildlife. Along the way there are also historic sites, natural landmarks, geological formations, and wonderful views of the river and the opposite shore from Upper Manhattan to Dobbs Ferry. Spotting cars or using public transport (buses), it can be accomplished in a single day, but most will prefer to break it up into shorter stretches. It is relatively flat, but the northern section does include some tough scrambling over talus slopes and a steep, narrow ascent just before reaching the end—a section that can be slippery and hazardous when wet. Those who have balance difficulties or are afraid of heights, novice hikers, children, and those who are out of shape may wish to avoid this segment. Walkers should also beware of ticks, poison ivy, and sumac, all of which are plentiful along the trail. By utilizing either the Long Path or the Henry Hudson Drive, one can fashion loop hikes (those in which one is able to return to the starting point without backtracking), that are quite satisfying. The Shore Trail is marked with white paint blazes and is always easy to follow.

From the entrance to Fort Lee Historic Park, go south on Hudson Terrace a short distance to the entrance to the Palisades Park on the left. Descend the roadway to steps veering to the right. Continue down to the river shore and the remnants of the Dupont Dock. There are beaches of reddish sand, and above to the right the impressive steel structure of the George Washington Bridge. To the left are exposures of reddish and gray

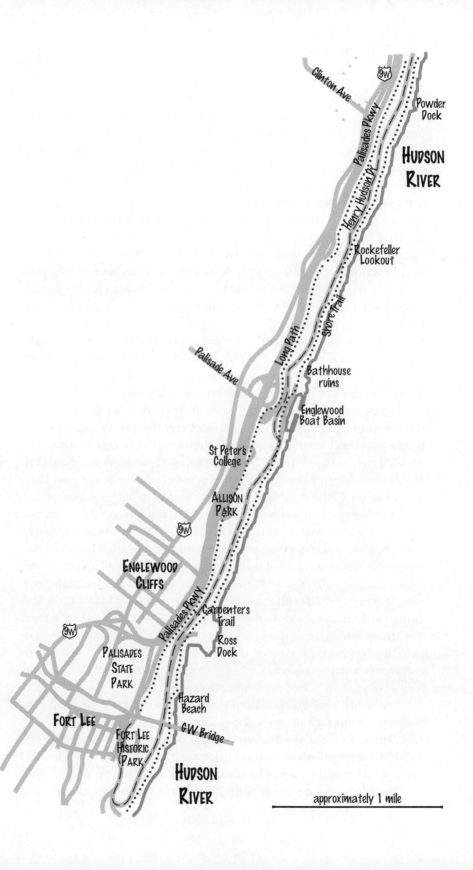

Clinton Ave

9W

Palisades Pkwy

Powder Dock

HUDSON RIVER

Henry Hudson Dr.

Rockefeller Lookout

Shore Trail

Palisade Ave

Long Path

Bathhouse ruins

Englewood Boat Basin

St Peter's College

ALLISON PARK

9W

ENGLEWOOD CLIFFS

Palisades Pkwy

Carpenters Trail

Ross Dock

9W

PALISADES STATE PARK

FORT LEE

Hazard Beach

FORT LEE HISTORIC PARK

GW Bridge

HUDSON RIVER

approximately 1 mile

Triassic sandstone where the partial skeleton of a phytosaur—a two-hundred-million-year-old crocodilelike aquatic reptile—was unearthed by Columbia University students in 1910. It is on display in the American Museum of Natural History in New York City.

On the right is a boat-launching ramp. Just beyond it, pass underneath the bridge, a truly extraordinary sight towering overhead. The next half mile is paved roadway with more red sand beaches along the shore until you reach Ross Dock, where there are picnic grounds, restrooms, and parking. Just before Ross Dock, there's a path to the left, the Carpenter's Trail, which zigzags up to the top of the cliff and the Long Path. The Shore Trail goes through a short tunnel underneath the roadway and continues as a trail along a beautiful, undeveloped, mostly quiet stretch of shoreline with forest and beaches. The Hudson provides a welcome barrier between here and Manhattan across the way, preserving the tranquillity of this area.

Less than three miles from the beginning of the trail is the Englewood Boat Basin, where there are more picnic grounds, parking, boating, rest rooms, and a refreshment stand in season. Views opposite are of Inwood Hill Park at the extreme northern tip of Manhattan.

The Shore Trail passes stone ruins of an old bathhouse on the left—testament to the popularity this area once enjoyed as a swimming beach before pollution forced its closure. Continue north through an area thick with shrubs and apple trees. There are exposed outcrops of reddish Triassic sandstone in a number of places. Cross Lost Brook and pass Lambier Dock on the right, with views opposite of Riverdale and Yonkers.

Just beyond is a lovely secluded beach and gorgeous Greenbrook Falls, 250 feet of nearly continuous falls. (From here one is able to observe only the lower section, which is impressive enough.) A short distance beyond, a red-marked trail veers to the left. It climbs upward and joins the Long Path. The trail, the former Huyler Road, was supposedly used during the Revolutionary War by Cornwallis and six thousand British and Hessian troops who were ferried here from across the river. The troops scaled the cliffs in an attempt to surprise and trap the Americans, led by General Washington, who were stationed at Fort Lee. American scouts warned Washington of the British advance, and Fort Lee was hastily evacuated before the British troops arrived.

The Shore Trail ascends from the shoreline on stone steps and enters a beautiful area of steep slopes and rock outcrops of volcanic diabase. Huge oak trees, maples, birches, and mountain laurel are prevalent. There is a marker dedicated to John Jordan, the first superintendent and patrol captain of the park, who died here in 1915 while on duty.

The Shore Trail descends to the Alpine Boat Basin, about eight miles from the beginning of the trail. There are parking, restrooms, a boat basin, a playground, picnicking, a refreshment stand in season, and views opposite of Yonkers. Notice the historic Yonkers Pier on the waterfront facing you. The Blackledge-Kearney House, a historic site, is located here. Part of the original Flemish-style dwelling was built in 1750 as a home for the schoolmaster who settled here to teach the local Dutch children English. During the Revolutionary War, General Cornwallis may have visited the home while scouting the area for trails up the cliffs. However, it is unlikely that he stayed in the house or used it as a headquarters. The plaque just north of the house, indicating that this is where the British troops scaled the cliffs, is also likely to be false.

The Blackledge-Kearney House was enlarged during the nineteenth century and later served as a riverside inn. A gristmill just north of the house on the neighboring creek processed grain that farmers west of here brought by wagon down the Closter Dock Road. The flour was then shipped south to New York City by boat from a nearby dock. The area was also a ferry landing and was a popular recreation area (with beaches) during the early days of the Palisades Park. The Blackledge-Kearney House served as the park's first headquarters.

Today the house has been restored with period furnishings and historical exhibits. A silent black-and-white video provides a glimpse of the Palisades beaches in the early, prepollution days of the park. What a joyful center of activity this once was. There are also exhibits on Skunk Hollow, a nineteenth-century community of free blacks who lived in the northern section of the park. Guides on duty can explain much about the history of the area as well as provide information about planned events and so on.

Just north of the house, ascend the wide path. Soon you'll reach an intersection. The trail on the left gently climbs the old Closter Dock Road, zigzagging up to the Henry Hudson Drive and the Long Path. It joins them just south of the park's main administrative center.

Continue right on a wide path through a mature forest of maples, birches, oaks, dogwood, tulip trees, and others. The trail forks again. The left fork goes up to the Excelsior Grove picnic area. Go right and descend past the old Excelsior Dock on the right, which is now overgrown. The trail continues down to the river shore, thick with shrubs and brambles. There's an excellent open view of Yonkers and Hastings-on-Hudson.

Cross another small stream, and arrive at a lovely secluded sandy beach on the right. This is part of Twombley Landing. Archaeological excavations nearby revealed an ancient camp dating back to the Archaic period more than seven thousand years ago, one of the oldest Archaic sites along the Hudson.

The upper trail then rejoins the lower trail. Continue north to Forest View, a former community of farmers and fishermen that was later developed as a recreation area with ferry access from Yonkers. The recreation area was subsequently abandoned and today is populated by stately willow and cottonwood trees, though evidence of the recreation area remains. The trail ascends briefly past talus slopes. These boulders have fallen from the cliffs over the past several thousand years; those that have fallen more recently lack vegetation.

The trail descends again to the river's edge with amazing views looking up at the sheer cliffs towering hundreds of feet overhead like a fortress wall. Nowhere else along the shore can this be viewed so dramatically. You'll soon reach the intersection with the blue-and-white-marked Forest View Trail. The Forest View Trail veers to the left and climbs uphill on steps to the Long Path, the Women's Federation Monument, and the State Line Lookout. At this point you've come approximately ten miles. Those wishing to avoid the extremely rugged section of trail that crosses the steep talus slopes should exit here.

Just beyond the intersection, the Shore Trail begins to ascend a sloping talus rock field, where you'll have to scramble over huge boulders following white paint blaze markers. After considerable time, but less than a mile, reenter the forest for a brief stretch before coming to another precipitous talus slope with a superb open view. Cross it and continue on the narrow path through woods on a vertical incline. The trail descends to a rocky shore. Carefully make your way over the rocks, skirting a rocky headland with a view north of the distant Tappan Zee Bridge. By now you've entered New York State.

The trail continues along the shore, then veers to the left, climbing steeply, zigzagging upward on a very narrow path on precipitous slopes. Climb a ladder and continue, finally reaching the level floor of a ravine and junction with the Long Path. This is the end of the Shore Trail.

One can either go left on the Long Path or take a detour north to the "Italian Gardens." To visit the "Italian Gardens," follow the red-marked trail, which is very rough. It ascends briefly, then makes a very steep descent, passing an impressive diabase rock column on the right, finally reaching a stream after less than a quarter of a mile—that seems longer. Cross the stream and intersect another, better trail. Continue to descend past Half Moon Falls and to a beach at the base of the cliffs. The area is graced by picturesque ruins of a former estate with the waterfall providing the perfect romantic backdrop. This, I believe, is one of the most beautiful and secluded spots along the entire river. When my wife, niece, and I were there, the only other visitors had arrived by canoe. To exit, ascend the same path to the intersection and continue west through the ravine, ascending more gradually parallel to the stream. This area is part of the twenty-three-acre Lamont Nature Sanctuary. The ravine is deliciously tranquil and thickly populated with old-growth northern hardwoods such as maples, ashes, oaks, and some hemlocks. After less than a quarter mile, the trail intersects with the Long Path.

THE GEORGE WASHINGTON BRIDGE TO THE
NEW YORK STATE BORDER VIA THE LONG PATH

A second option for walkers starting from Fort Lee is to take the Long Path. The Long Path generally follows the top of the Palisades cliffs, from the George Washington Bridge north to just beyond the New York State line, where it intersects with the Shore Trail, a distance of approximately twelve miles. This is the very beginning of the Long Path, which extends north from here to the Helderberg Plateau and eventually reaches the Adirondacks.

This Palisades segment has many splendid views of the Hudson River and opposite shore as well as the cliffs themselves. There are some mixed deciduous hardwood forests and ruins of old estates. Flowering plants from the old estates intermingle with native species to create a rich gallery of colors in many spots. Unfortunately much of the trail closely parallels the Palisades Parkway, and the constant din of traffic detracts from the experience.

The Long Path through the Palisades Park is generally level and easy for walking. It is marked with turquoise-colored paint blazes. The entire Palisades Park segment can be hiked in a single day, parking cars at both ends or using public buses. Hikers can combine the Long Path with sections of the Henry Hudson Drive or the Shore Trail to create rewarding loop excursions. The primary hazards are ticks and poison ivy and sumac, which are plentiful. One should exercise caution at the edges of cliffs since there may be drops of hundreds of feet, and people have lost their lives in accidents.

The Long Path begins just north of the interchange for the George Washington Bridge. There's an enclosed walkway and a sign that indicates the pedestrian entrance to the bridge. Climb the steps. The pedestrian walkway turns off to the right. The Long Path continues up and into the forest and becomes a regular trail. For the first half mile, the trail is a relatively smooth level path through a young, mixed deciduous forest with occasional remains of former estates, stone walls, and foundations. Numerous side paths lead to cliff-top views of the Hudson, Manhattan, and the George Washington Bridge. The Carpenters Trail veers off to the right and zigzags down to the Shore Trail. The Long Path continues north, closely paralleling the Palisades Parkway and at times coming right up to its shoulder. The number of walkers quickly thins as you get farther north from the bridge.

After a mile of easy walking, you reach an iron fence, the boundary of the popular William O. Allison Park. The Long Path skirts it, but it is well worth visiting its beautifully landscaped grounds, scenic paths, exotic shrubbery, and spectacular views of the river. This was the former site of the Palisades Mountain House, a three-hundred-room retreat for wealthy New Yorkers who arrived via steamer and ascended the cliffs by carriage road. This was one of the famous mountain house resorts, like the Catskill Mountain House and the present-day Mohonk Mountain House. It burned down in 1884 and became part of the William Allison Estate until it was donated to Palisades Park in 1967. Just beyond it is the campus of Saint Peter's College. The Long Path bypasses it by following the shoulder of the parkway and then reenters the woods to the north. Two miles from the beginning, the path crosses a stream and then Palisades Avenue. A zigzagging yellow-marked path with steps descends here, parallel to the roadway, to the Englewood Boat Basin, the river, and the Shore Trail. (For a description of the Englewood Boat Basin, see the Shore Trail section.)

Cross Palisades Avenue, ascend the steps, and continue north. Pass the ruins of the former Dana Estate, the oldest of the cliff-top estates, built in the late 1850s by a rich New York publisher. High Tom, a rock cliff with an open vista looking north, with Yonkers in the distance, is just beyond.

About three miles from the beginning of the trail you'll reach the Rockefeller Lookout, a drive-up viewpoint with a classic view looking south of the George Washington Bridge, with the Manhattan skyline behind it.

Reenter the woods and continue north to Clinton Point, another spectacular view with breathtaking sheer cliffs more than a hundred feet high. Pass more ruins and cross a marshy area on wood planks. About five miles from the beginning you'll encounter a chain-link fence on the right that marks the boundary of the Greenbrook Sanctuary, a 165-acre special-use nature preserve. It is open to members and their guests and occasionally to the general public.

The Long Path goes around the fence, continuing closely parallel to the parkway, making brief descents into ravines along the edge of the sanctuary. Pass the intersection with the red-blazed Huyler Road on the right, which descends to the Henry Hudson Drive and the Shore Trail and the river. (See the section on the Shore Trail for a description of the Huyler Road's role during the Revolutionary War.) Six miles from the beginning of the trail, you'll reach the Alpine Lookout, another drive-up viewpoint with an amazing panorama of cliffs, rock pinnacles, and Yonkers across the river.

Continue north, passing the well-preserved ruins of the former Zabriskie Estate. There are wonderful vistas and ornamental shrubs such as lilacs, as well as an assortment of wild and exotic flowers in spring and summer. Pass tunnels on the left underneath the Palisades Parkway to Route 9W. Cross the stream and reach the Henry Hudson Drive. (The tunnel underneath the roadway was closed off when I last visited, in May 1997. However, crossing the Henry Hudson should present no problem.) Just beyond, intersect the unmarked Closter Dock Road, that descends to the Alpine Boat Basin and the Shore Trail. (See the Shore Trail section for a description of the Closter Dock Road and the Alpine Boat Basin.) The Long Path continues north, closely parallel to the Henry Hudson Drive, a short distance to the main park headquarters. You've now come approximately eight miles from the George Washington Bridge.

Just past the headquarters, the trail reenters the woods near the former Ringling Estate, owned by the famous circus family, continuing through a mature forest of oaks, maples, and hickories. On the right is Gray Crag, the largest isolated section of the Palisades cliff. It is more than three hundred feet long and can be reached via a bridge that crosses the narrow ravine that separates it from the main cliff. Again, use extra caution, as there are many steep dropoffs. Pass through a quiet old-growth area with woods roads and marshy depressions that support insect and amphibian life. In the past, cut timbers were tossed from various pitching points on the nearby cliffs, down to boats waiting below to transport the wood south to New York City. A couple of miles north of the headquarters, the trail passes more estate ruins with ornamental trees and shrubs, including Norway spruce, cedars, magnolia, and large stands of rhododendron. The Long Path reaches an intersection with the blue-and-white-marked Forest View Trail. The Long Path continues to the right, passing the small castlelike monument, erected in 1927, to the New Jersey Federation of Women's Clubs, which played a crucial role in the formation of the Palisades Park in 1900. There's another open cliffside view from here, an excellent place to picnic. The Long Path then descends into a ravine, and the Forest View Trail splits off to the right to descend on steps down to the river and the Shore Trail. The Long Path crosses the stream, veers left, up steps, past rocks decorated with beautiful flowering pinks in season, finally reaching the road (Old 9W). The actual 9W was relocated west of the Palisades Parkway.

Go right and follow the old roadway for about a quarter of a mile until you reach the State Line Lookout, another drive-up viewpoint, more than ten miles from the beginning of the trail. There are a snack bar and rest rooms and spectacular views of the river, Hastings-on-Hudson, cliffs, and talus below. Much of southern Westchester County can be seen, all the way to Manhattan and Long Island, even Long Island Sound. At 530 feet this is the highest point in the New Jersey Palisades, and it is a very popular place for walking and biking. In winter there are cross-country ski trails and ski rentals. The trail continues north, following a section of old Route 9W that has been closed off for bicycle and pedestrian use.

The trail leaves the roadway on the right and continues as a wide forest path. This section is wonderfully peaceful, far from the Palisades Parkway, and includes many examples of large old-growth trees, including hemlocks. About one mile north of the State Line Lookout, you'll reach a chain-link fence, the boundary with New York State, and an 1882 monument. The trail passes through an opening in the fence to High Gutter Point, an amazing cliffside view, especially looking north toward the Tappan Zee Bridge, Hook Mountain, and the Piermont Pier and Marsh. (The last was another former pitching point, where cut timber was tossed from the top of the cliffs.)

The trail descends via a long series of stone steps to a ravine and the junction with the Shore Trail. The other red-marked trail goes north to the "Italian Gardens." (See the Shore Trail section for a description.) Continue west through this beautiful ravine, part of the twenty-three-acre Lamont Nature Reserve. Cross the stream and reach a juncture with another trail that goes east, also to the "Italian Gardens," a longer, easier path. The Long Path continues west another quarter of a mile to Route 9W and a parking area and bus stop at the entrance to Columbia University's Lamont-Doherty Geologic Observatory, a 150-acre property that once was the home of the famous botanist John Torrey. In 1928 the property was acquired by a financier, Thomas W. Lamont, and in 1949, following his death, it was donated to Columbia University for use as a research center in the earth sciences.

FORT LEE TO THE NEW YORK STATE BORDER VIA THE HENRY HUDSON DRIVE

This eleven-mile route is the third option. This is the only one of the three that permits bikes. It is a superb bike trail, very popular, with many viewpoints and access to the river in a number of places. Vehicular traffic is limited, which means a safer, more enjoyable ride. For most of the way it is a shady emerald path through mature deciduous forest below the cliffs and talus slopes and above the Hudson's shoreline. Much of the forest appears as it did hundreds of years ago. The road is also popular with walkers, in-line skaters, and joggers—in fact, anyone who prefers to walk on smooth asphalt. The road is open daily from April through November.

The Henry Hudson Drive was built in 1916 to provide access to the park's bathing beaches. The entrance is just south of Fort Lee Historic Park. The road descends toward the river and heads north, passing beneath the great structure of the George Washington Bridge. After a mile it passes the entrance to Ross Dock. (See the Shore Trail section for a description.) The road continues another mile and a half to the Englewood Boat Basin, crossing Palisades Avenue. (The Englewood Boat Basin is described in the section on the Shore Trail.) Follow the road another three miles, passing the Undercliff Picnic Area, where there's an early-nineteenth-century cemetery, and crossing Greenbrook Falls, a spectacular 250-foot series of waterfalls and cascades, one of the most arresting sights in the whole park. Another mile brings you to a fork, the right branch leading down to the Alpine Boat Basin. (See the Shore Trail section for a description.) The road continues left, gradually ascending past the park headquarters and under the Palisades Parkway to Route 9W and the end of the Henry Hudson Drive.

One can continue further north on 9W approximately one mile to a pedestrian bridge on the right, crossing the Palisades Parkway. After traversing the span, a trail on the left leads out to the beginning of the entrance road to the State Line Lookout. Go right and follow this, less than a quarter mile, to State Line Lookout. (See the section on the Long Path for a description.) After stopping to admire the view or visiting the snack bar and rest rooms, continue north on Old 9W, blocked from vehicular traffic, now a fine bike and pedestrian path, approximately a mile and a half back to 9W at the entrance to the Lamont-Doherty Geologic Observatory, just south of the New York State border.

LAMONT-DOHERTY GEOLOGIC OBSERVATORY TO PIERMONT

This relatively easy 3.15-mile segment includes some unpleasant walking or riding along 9W in its first half and then a very lovely stretch though Tallman State Park, with excellent views toward the end. Walkers can use the section designated as part of the Long Path.

From the entrance of the observatory, continue north along 9W for about a mile through pleasant surroundings, but unfortunately there's a lot of traffic. On the left you'll pass a historic marker for Skunk Hollow, once a small farming community established by free blacks, most of whom were former slaves, in 1806. It lasted until 1905, when it was abandoned. Most of it is now part of Palisades Park.

Continue north on 9W to the intersection with Oak Tree Road. There's a bus stop on the corner. Oak Tree Road leads to Snedens Landing, formerly the western terminus of the Dobbs Ferry. The land was first settled in 1701 and primarily populated by the Sneden family, descendants of Dutch immigrants. Molly Sneden (1709–1810), who operated the ferry, lived to be 101. She and all her children were infamous Tories during the Revolutionary War. The patriot side built a fortification here that fell to the British after a fierce fight. Following the end of the hostilities, on May 7, 1783, General Washington was rowed from here out to a British warship anchored in the Hudson, to meet with Gen. Sir Guy Carleton, to plan the British evacuation of New York City. The British gave Washington's boat, which displayed an American flag, a seventeen-gun salute, the very first British salute to an American flag. Today it is an area of exclusive private homes.

A quarter mile beyond that intersection is the entrance to Tallman State Park on the right, a very popular 687-acre section of the Palisades Interstate Park. (The parking lot here tends to overflow on weekends.) The bike path is designated part of the Hudson River Greenway Trail. The trail heads east on a broad, shady pedestrian and bike path, through lovely serene forest of young oak trees and dogwoods. After a quarter mile the Long Path leaves the broad path and heads north. Bicyclists and walkers may continue east on the broad path, which links up again with the Long Path after another mile.

The Long Path continues north, passing a shallow pond on the right. This area was once planned as an oil-tank "farm" in 1923 by the Standard Oil Company, and oil-seepage ditches were excavated with earthen berms. Fortunately the project was abandoned, and the ditches and berms gradually filled with water, creating marshes and ponds—the most extensive wetlands atop the Palisades. This area supports a rich variety of plant and animal life: sweet gum, red maple, spicebush, pin oak, elm, tupelo, skunk cabbage, and many varieties of ferns, mosses, and wildflowers. These wetlands are an important breeding area for amphibians. They are also an excellent habitat for turtles and snakes.

The trail continues north for more than half a mile, then veers eastward through more mature oak forest, finally crossing the bike path. It continues a short distance and then bends to the left, north again, following the edge of the ridge, with partial views of the river through the trees. After another half mile a picnic area is reached, with rest rooms located conveniently right next to the trail. The trail then crosses a bike path and a view on the right of the park swimming pool below, with the

Hudson and Piermont Marsh beyond it. Just beyond is a traffic circle. The road descending on the right is closed to traffic but is ideal for walkers or bikers heading down toward the gorgeous path along the marsh. The Long Path ascends the hillside to a large upper picnic area with the fragrance of barbecue, blaring radios, and a cacophony of different languages. There is a superb panoramic view on the right of the Piermont Marsh, Piermont Pier, and the Sparkill Creek, where it enters the Hudson. Just beyond, the trail descends steeply to the bike path which continues east past the marsh. Go left, west, and cross the Sparkill Creek to Paradise Avenue. A right turn here takes you to the Piermont Pier. A left takes you a short distance into the village of Piermont. Scientists believe that Sparkill Creek and the Hackensack River once formed part of the original course of the Hudson River, which drained into the Atlantic west of its present course. Just west of here, Sparkill Creek forms the only sea-level gap in the fifty-mile-long Palisades Ridge. In 1841 the Erie Railroad took advantage of this gap in the Palisades as a route westward, making Piermont a major railroad terminus.

Piermont Marsh is a 940-acre wetland and wildlife sanctuary, one of four wetlands that make up the Hudson River National Estuarine Research Reserve. The marsh extends for nearly two miles along the river from the Piermont Pier to Snedens Landing. Piermont Marsh is owned and managed by the Palisades Interstate Park Commission, the New York State Department of Environmental Conservation, and the village of Piermont. The marshes are human-made, the result of the construction of the Piermont Pier, which served to protect the shallows south of the pier, slowly transforming them into the marsh we see today. This is the largest brackish water marsh in the Hudson River. Extensive subtidal shallows, only a foot or two deep at low tide, border the marsh. These are home to benthic (bottom-dwelling) organisms that serve as food for a variety of young fish. In deeper waters, hydroids—colonial animals closely related to sea anemones—live in bushy clumps on the river bottom. Pipefish, relatives of the sea horse, sway gracefully with the currents, and luminescent comb jellies drift with the tides.

The introduction of freshwater from Sparkill Creek as well as brackish water from the Hudson creates a very diverse environment here. Piermont Marsh has areas of salt meadows where salt has become concentrated through evaporation. The marsh harbors a number of plant species that thrive in salt conditions but are absent from the more freshwater sections of the river. These include four species of cordgrass. Cordgrass was harvested during colonial times as salt hay for animal fodder and bedding. Today it makes up only 3 percent of Piermont Marsh. Other plants include swamp rose mallow, seaside goldenrod, three-square sedge, common reeds, also known as Phragmites, narrow-leaf cattails, wild rice, spike grass, and water parsnip. Fiddler and blue-claw crabs, shrimp, striped bass, muskrats, snapping turtles, and occasionally a northern diamondback terrapin inhabit the marsh. There's also great bird-watching in the marsh itself and in the neighboring woods. Ducks, herons, gulls, bitterns, American kestrels, rails, kingfishers, pileated woodpeckers, wrens, vireos, redwing blackbirds, orioles, goldfinches, cormorants, ibis, ospreys, terns, plovers, snipe, grebes, loons, peregrine falcons, and possibly bald and golden eagles are among those that may be spotted, depending on the season. The marsh is best observed from the path in Tallman State Park that skirts its edge as well as from the Piermont Pier.

The village of Piermont lies at the foot of Tallman Mountain. It is a picturesque gem, one of the loveliest communities along the Hudson. From the Piermont Pier and the marina along the waterfront, the town rises steeply, houses and narrow streets clinging to slopes overlooking the town. With its salt smells and pounding surf, Piermont resembles a seaside community. Many exquisite Victorian homes may be observed along Piermont Avenue, which follows the riverfront north to Nyack. Lavish modern homes are located on the bluffs above the town. The charming center of town has upscale shops, antique stores, galleries, restaurants, and a nightclub. At the Piermont Library one can purchase a walking guide that highlights the town's history and architecture. Woody Allen used Piermont as the setting for his 1983 film *Purple Rose of Cairo.*

Piermont's quaintness and beauty are hardly undiscovered. It is already a major stop and watering hole for bicyclists, and on weekend nights swarms of visitors crowd its busy center and finding convenient parking may be problematic. New retail and condominium developments located on the Piermont Pier may eventually overshadow this community.

Piermont was once known as Tappan Landing, the location of a store and gristmill. In 1841 Tappan Landing became the eastern terminus of the Erie Railroad. A mile-long pier was constructed on ninety acres of landfill to handle the transfer of passengers and freight from the trains to steamboats for the journey south to New York City, or vice versa. The name of the town was changed to Piermont. Piermont briefly experienced a period of rapid growth and became an important center of commerce. In 1852 the rail line was rerouted to Pavonia, New Jersey, to avoid the train/boat transfer, and Piermont's importance rapidly diminished. The pier was later abandoned and subsequently decayed. Now the pier is undergoing a major redevelopment with condominiums and retail establishments. Piermont's importance is on the rise again.

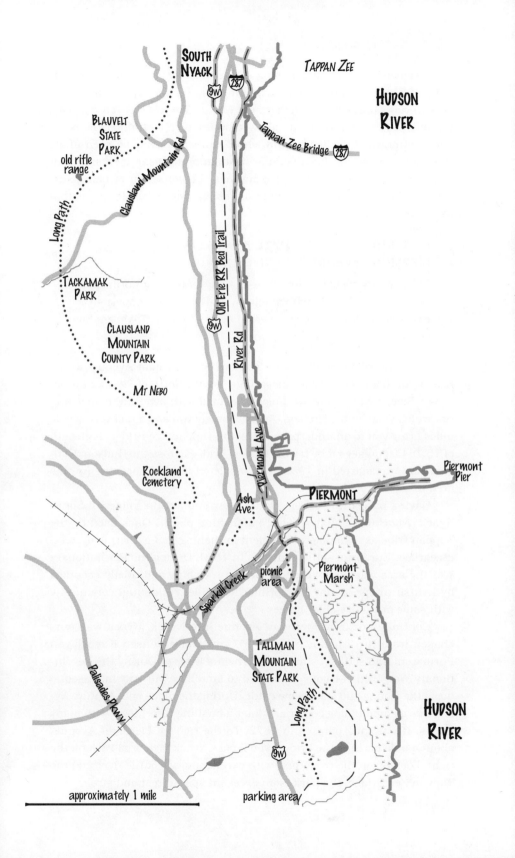

SOUTH NYACK

TAPPAN ZEE

HUDSON RIVER

BLAUVELT STATE PARK

old rifle range

Long Path

Clausland Mountain Rd

Tappan Zee Bridge

787

9W

787

Old Erie RR Bed Trail

Tackamak Park

CLAUSLAND MOUNTAIN COUNTY PARK

Mt Nebo

9W

River Rd

Piermont Ave

Rockland Cemetery

Ash Ave

PIERMONT

Piermont Pier

Sparkill Creek

picnic area

Piermont Marsh

TALLMAN MOUNTAIN STATE PARK

Palisades Pkwy

Long Path

9W

HUDSON RIVER

approximately 1 mile

parking area

Piermont Pier is one mile long and extends eastward into the wide Tappan Zee, providing excellent walking and biking opportunities and superb views of the river and Piermont Marsh. There's a paved roadway, but only cars with permits are allowed on the pier, so traffic is no problem. Cottonwoods, willows, and white mulberries can be seen along the road. The pier is also a popular destination for fishermen and birdwatchers. At the end of the pier one has the sensation of being surrounded by a wide body of water and crashing waves; the feeling is that this is really an arm of the ocean.

PIERMONT TO NYACK STATE BEACH VIA PIERMONT AVENUE AND RIVER ROAD

This five-mile route is one of three options for traveling north to Nyack and Nyack State Beach. Entirely on roads in densely populated areas, it goes through the commercial heart of Nyack. There are fine views along the first half of the route.

From the village of Piermont, go north on Piermont Avenue, which runs right along the river for most of its length. North of Piermont it becomes River Road, a narrow, busy lane lined with beautiful homes and rewarding views of the Hudson. Approximately two and a half very scenic miles bring you to an underpass below the Tappan Zee Bridge. Its length of 15,764 feet makes it by far the longest bridge across the Hudson. Construction was started in 1952 and completed in 1955, opening up this area to rapid growth.

Having passed the bridge, you've now entered the village of South Nyack. *Nyack* is the native word for "fishing place." Once used by the Tappan tribe as a summer settlement for fishing and gathering oysters, its earliest European settlement was in 1689. During the Revolutionary War the area was bombarded by British warships and briefly occupied by British troops. Today it is primarily a quiet residential community with some attractive older homes.

Continue north on Piermont Avenue into Nyack. Nyack was purchased from the Tappan tribe in 1671 by Claes Jansen Kuyper van Purmarent and settled by his son Cornelius Kuyper. During the Revolutionary War, British troops attempted to land here but only managed to do a little looting and steal some cattle. During the nineteenth century Nyack was a shipbuilding center and later a bustling resort town with many hotels. It was incorporated in 1872. To the right of Piermont Avenue, about a mile north of the bridge, you'll pass Nyack Memorial Park on the right. Located on the riverfront, with excellent views of the river and the Tappan Zee Bridge, the park is an excellent spot to rest and stroll.

Just beyond the park, you'll reach the end of Piermont Avenue. From here go left on Main Street to the heart of Nyack's downtown area at Broadway and Main Streets. This area is packed with stores, upscale shops, antique dealers, galleries, arts and crafts shops, cafés, bakeries, restaurants, and an excellent library, children's museum, and the Helen Hayes Performing Arts Center. Many establishments seem to have a New Age focus. Downtown Nyack is perfect for strolling, hanging out, eating, or shopping. There are street fairs five or six times a year.

Just north of downtown Nyack, on the left at 82 North Broadway, is the Edward Hopper House, the birthplace and boyhood home of the famous realist painter. Built in 1858, the house is a registered New York State Historic Site and is being restored by the Edward Hopper Landmark Preservation Foundation. Today it serves primarily as a gallery for works by local artists, though some Hopper prints are on display as well as books about the painter. It is open Thursdays through Sundays, from noon to 5:00 P.M. There's a small donation. Call 914–358–0774 for information.

North Broadway continues a little less than two miles through the community of Upper Nyack to the entrance of Nyack State Beach. During the Revolutionary War three failed attempts to land British troops here resulted in many losses. To avenge their defeat the British set fire to the home of Henry Palmer, an infamous smuggler of supplies for the patriot side. Today, Upper Nyack is a quiet residential community with many elaborate homes along North Broadway overlooking the river. On the right side of North Broadway is the Old Stone Church, a tiny chapel built in 1813 of native maroon sandstone, the oldest surviving church in Rockland County. Detour left on Old Mountain Road, and on the north side of the street is a tiny cemetery, the oldest in Rockland County, which contains the graves of Revolutionary War veterans.

PIERMONT TO NYACK VIA THE OLD ERIE RAILROAD BED

A second alternative route follows an abandoned commuter rail line that connects these two towns. This 3.38-mile-long path, which is suitable for both bikes and walkers, exists thanks to the communities of Piermont, Grandview, and South Nyack. It is designated part of the Hudson River Greenway Trail. This shaded route is quieter and safer than the first alternative, though it doesn't offer as much in terms of views. One could easily take one route one way and return via the other route. To find this trail follow turquoise blazes of the Long Path from Piermont Avenue, west and uphill to Ash Street, where it crosses the obvious former railway bed.

This commuter rail line first opened in 1870, operating until 1965. The railroad tracks have been removed. The former station, now a private residence, is on the right, just west of the path. Go right, north on the trail, passing numerous homes along the way and partial views of the Hudson River. As you enter South Nyack the trail becomes the Raymond G. Esposito Memorial Trail. Route 9W runs closely parallel to the trail at this point. The trail crosses the road, and just beyond, the trail crosses the New York State Thruway on an old railroad bridge, now reserved for pedestrian use. Getting this far will take walkers approximately one hour. From here the trail runs through densely populated residential neighborhoods and finally ends in Nyack at the Franklin Street Park. Continue north, passing a community garden on the right and reaching Main Street. Turn right. Three blocks east through the heart of downtown Nyack is Broadway, where you can join the first alternate route.

PIERMONT TO NYACK STATE BEACH VIA THE LONG PATH

This is by far the longest and most strenuous alternative. It is more than seven miles and follows the ridge of the Palisades, where it goes inland away from the river. This route takes from three and a half to five and a half hours. There are few vistas, but you get to explore a four-mile nearly continuous stretch of tranquil, seemingly remote section of forest that you wouldn't think could exist in the heart of a highly developed, densely populated region. You will encounter stands of relatively old-growth forest where rattlesnakes, porcupines, and barred owls have been reported. This route is for walkers only.

From the railroad crossing in Piermont, follow turquoise blazes north and west on Tate Avenue, one block uphill, to a staircase on the opposite side of the street. Climb to the top of the staircase, facing Ash Avenue. You'll pass the old railroad station on the right and cross the old railroad grade, now the rail trail. Continue northwest to Piermont Place, and make a left. Then go right, west, uphill on Crescent Road. The road veers to the left and becomes a wide asphalt path. On the right the Long Path heads west, but do not follow it: It leads to a section that's closed. Instead go straight a short distance to a school, from which you can access Route 9W. Go south on 9W less than a quarter mile to the first light, Hickey Street. Make a right on Hickey and then immediately another right onto the King's Highway. Go north on the King's Highway one-half mile to the entrance of Rockland Cemetery. Go right, and follow the road into the cemetery a short distance to the first intersection. Go left and just past it, make a sharp right. Follow the road as it bends to the left and goes uphill, approximately one-half mile, to a view on the right through the trees of the river and the Piermont Pier below. The grave of John Charles Frémont (1813–1890), the famous pathfinder of the American West, is located here. The road bends to the left, and just beyond, the trail leaves the road and continues into the woods as a level path skirting the summit of Mount Nebo. Looking south, there's a partial glimpse of the Manhattan skyline in the distance. The trail veers right, crosses a stone fence, and enters the 513-acre Clausland Mountain County Park, which was acquired in 1969.

Follow the trail along the ridge through open parklike woods. Pass a shallow pond on the right (it is home to amphibians in the spring). Descend; cross a seasonal brook. The trail veers right and left, ascending through younger forest, then bends to the left again. Cross the ridge, with its huge outcrops of diabase, and descend through a thick forest of birches, maples, and beech. The trail enters 105-acre Tackamack Town Park. Continue your descent to a stream, and cross it on a wooden bridge. There are large hemlocks, birches, maples, and hickories in the vicinity. The trail ascends, zigzagging up to Clausland Mountain Road. There's a sizable parking area on the north side of the road. At this point you've come a little more than two miles from Piermont. Continue north through the parking lot and into a young second-growth forest of aspens, gray birch, cherry, and hackberry trees. The trail continues on a broad excellent track, then descends to a small dammed pool on the left, surrounded by large mature beech trees. Cross the stream on a wooden bridge, and enter 590-acre Blauvelt State Park.

The trail bends to the right, east, and passes an area thick with hemlocks, severely damaged by blowdowns but beautiful nonetheless. The Long Path crosses a number of other trails; mountain bikers frequent this area. Enter a secluded area of white pines and other evergreens. The trail then crosses an old field that's returned to a young forest of dogwoods, aspens, hawthornes, gray birches, cherry, sassafras, and blackberry bushes, and sumac and honeysuckle, with plentiful bird and insect life. The trail can be muddy in places. The Long Path traverses a concrete wall that was part of an old New York State National Guard rifle range, built in 1911. (The walls supported targets.) The range lasted only three years before neighborhood complaints about stray bullets forced its closure.

The trail makes a sharp right onto an old dirt road, passing more ruins on the right. Go left at the next intersection. Follow the turquoise blazes, descending through thick stands of young hemlocks. Cross a small seasonal stream near graffiti-damaged trees, and begin a slow ascent through a mature forest of tall majestic trees: beech, elms, tulip trees, and maples with an understory of smaller, younger trees. Cross

Tweed Boulevard and ascend a ridge with birches, oaks, and hickories. Pass garish graffiti on rocks and ascend to a 640-foot-high view of the Hudson, the Tappan Zee Bridge, and Piermont Pier in the distance. The trail descends on steps and continues on the ridge parallel to the road. There are many wildflowers in the spring. Cross a gravel road by a storage tank and ascend the ridge again, with partial views of the Hudson through the trees. The trail veers right and then left, past outcrops of diabase with dogwoods, ashes, elms, oaks, and wildflowers. The Long Path crosses an old dirt road and makes a sharp right, then descends gradually to Bradley Hill Road. You've now come a little more than four miles from Piermont. Cross Bradley Hill Road and continue north following markers. Ascend a hill covered with oaks and ash trees and many shrubs. The trail crosses a stone fence at the tree-covered summit. Descend to a intersection where the trail veers sharply to the right. Pass another stone fence on the left and arrive at the end of a cul-de-sac. Continue north on Waldron Road to a busy intersection of Route 59, less than a quarter mile away. There are a number of fast-food restaurants in the vicinity. (Route 59 continues east into the heart of Nyack.)

The Long Path crosses the New York State Thruway and continues north on Mountainview Avenue. About a quarter mile north of the Thruway, the trail leaves the road to the right, just past a thirty-miles-per-hour sign. The trail is clearly marked. It goes a short stretch through the woods, then crosses another road, continues uphill, passing an apartment complex on the right, levels, and then descends to a road in the corner of Oak Hill Cemetary, where the artist Edward Hopper is buried. There's an excellent view of the Hudson, Nyack, and the Tappan Zee Bridge.

The trail continues on the roadway, which ascends in switchbacks, passing a green storage tank on the right, and then veers left, becoming a narrow path again. Ascend to the right, and pass an apartment complex on the left. About a mile past the cemetery, the trail reaches Christian Herald Road. Go east on the road less than half a mile to 9W.

NYACK STATE BEACH TO HAVERSTRAW VIA THE SHORE PATH

This very popular trail is 4.91 miles long, mostly smooth dirt, well graded, with excellent views of the Hudson in the first two miles. The Shore Path is the second longest trail that runs right along the river shore. It is designated part of the Hudson River Greenway Trail.

Nyack State Beach is at the very end of North Broadway in Upper Nyack, about two miles north of Nyack's business district. Parking is available here, and there are restroom facilities. There's a parking fee between Memorial Day and October. The park is open daily, year round. Call 914-358-1316 for information. Nyack Beach is part of four contiguous parks owned and managed by the Palisades Interstate Park Commission—Rockland Lake, Hook Mountain, Haverstraw Beach—which total nearly two thousand acres. The Nyack State Beach section is sixty-one acres. The land was acquired in 1915, in an effort to halt quarry operations and save the cliffs. (The shoreline here was the site of intensive quarry activity as well as a landing for steamboats and ferries.)

The path is best suited for bikes with wide tires. Helmets are required. In addition to bicycling and hiking, fishing and picnicking are other popular activities. Once I saw a man playing the bagpipes along the trail here. The presence of many pedestrians and especially young children means that bicyclists should use extra caution.

Begin the trail from the north end of the parking lot. On the left impressive cliffs of the Palisades diabase tower above. Once these cliffs were heavily quarried by the Manhattan Trap Rock Company. Along the base of the cliffs are piles of giant boulders. In places not covered with talus, cliffs of pink-and-orange Triassic sandstone and shale may be seen. Where the diabase meets the sedimentary rock, the once-hot magma metamorphosed the sandstone and shale into quartzite and hornfels. This area is of particular interest to geologists studying the ways in which the earth's powerful natural forces can transform rock. Echoes of the river's waves may be heard emanating from the cliffs. From the trail superb views of the Tappan Zee, from the Tappan Zee Bridge in the south to Croton Point in the north, may be observed along the next two miles of trail. This is one of the easiest and most rewarding sections in the entire book. There are also benches and barbecue grills.

The fauna and flora of this section of the riverfront are basically the same you might encounter along the Shore Trail in the New Jersey Palisades. Pay particularly close attention to the talus slopes, where black birch, white ash, black locust, Dutchman's breeches, and columbine may be seen. Be careful of poison ivy and sumac, which are also plentiful. In the areas of former quarries, pioneer trees, weedy shrubs, and vines are numerous. White pines and Norway spruces have been planted by park personnel. Along the riverfront are elms, maples, willows, and cottonwoods.

About two miles north of the entrance, there's a lovely picnic area on a tiny peninsula on the right. From here the trail climbs to an intersection with Rockland Landing Road. Unfortunately bicycles cannot use this road, which continues west to Rockland Lake State Park. However, it provides walkers with a useful link to the Long Path for a relatively easy loop hike over Hook Mountain. This area is part of Hook Mountain

State Park, 676 acres of mostly wild forest land, which includes Hook Mountain.

From the intersection the path descends to an area once known as Slaughter's Landing. It was first settled in 1711 by one John Slaughter. By 1831 the Knickerbocker Ice Company was cutting blocks of ice from nearby spring-fed Rockland Lake, then transporting it down through Trough Hollow to docks along the Hudson, whence it was shipped to New York City. A cog railway had been installed by 1860 to aid in the shipment of ice. Two thousand men were employed in this operation at its height, and more than two hundred thousand tons of ice were shipped from here every winter. Plentiful ruins of buildings, docks, and transporting equipment remain today. From Slaughter's Landing there are excellent views of the river and Westchester County on the opposite shore.

The trail climbs again and remains about 50 to 150 feet above the river for the rest of the way, along steep, forested slopes, with mountain laurel in places. Trees block the view except in early spring, late fall, and winter. The trail passes more ruins and quarries. Less than a quarter mile from the end, the trail becomes paved. Just beyond, there is a white-marked trail, for walkers only, ascending on the left, which connects with the Long Path. There is a ruined cottage to the right of this trail juncture, and a white marker painted on the asphalt road. A short distance up the road, a historical marker indicates that on this site in 1780, Benedict Arnold and Maj. John André plotted the surrender of West Point to the British. Below is Snedekers Landing where André landed. During the nineteenth century it served as a shipyard and steamship dock. It burned in 1854. The Shore Path ends just beyond the sign in a parking area.

UPPER NYACK TO HIGH TOR STATE PARK VIA THE LONG PATH OVER HOOK MOUNTAIN

The Long Path proceeds north on 9W from its intersection with Christian Herald Road for about a quarter of a mile before it veers to the right off the highway. There's a telecable warning sign at this juncture, but also follow the markers carefully. You have now entered Hook Mountain State Park (see above for a description). A continuation of the Palisades Ridge, the mountain got its name from its hook shape, which is obvious from the air. The ridge that includes Hook Mountain has seven summits called the Seven Sisters, the highest of which is 736 feet. No single one is that challenging, but taken together they require some effort. The trail is well marked, and hardly any scrambling is necessary. Plan three to four hours to cover the six miles to Haverstraw.

A very short distance after the Long Path leaves the road, it arrives at a juncture with a white-marked trail. This quarter-mile-long trail provides a very useful link with the Shore Path in Nyack State Beach for those wanting a loop trip over Hook Mountain and along the Hudson. The white-marked trail heads east, descending past people's backyards, crossing a small seasonal brook with plentiful skunk cabbage. It ends near the intersection of North Midland Avenue and Larchdale. This trail is muddy in places, and downed vegetation caused this author a few moments of confusion in one spot. From the corner of Larchdale and North Midland, continue east on Larchdale to the intersection with North Broadway. One block northeast is the entrance to Nyack Beach State Park and the beginning of the Shore Path. (See above for description.)

To continue on the Long Path, from the intersection with the white-marked trail proceed north, parallel to 9W and the constant din of traffic, gradually ascending through a mixed deciduous forest of oaks, maples, and tulip trees. There are abundant wildflowers in the spring and partial views through the trees looking south of the Tappan Zee Bridge and the Palisades Ridge. The trail veers to the right, away from 9W and traffic noise, and climbs steeply to the top of the ridge. A short, nearly vertical ascent from here leads to the bare summit, the highest point on the ridge. You've come approximately one mile from the intersection of Christian Herald Road.

This summit has panoramic views in every direction from the Hudson Highlands in the north to the New Jersey Palisades in the south, Rockland Lake, the Tappan Zee, and the bridge. Rockland Lake is the centerpiece of the popular 1,079-acre Rockland Lake State Park, which is contiguous with Hook Mountain State Park.

This summit of Hook Mountain is most famous for viewing the annual fall hawk migration. The local chapter of the Audubon Society and other nature groups observe the migration of hawks, ospreys, eagles, and vultures from here. Sometimes hundreds can be observed in a single hour if the wind conditions are right.

The dry rocky summit area supports prickly-pear cactus, scrub oak, chokecherry, columbine, Dutchman's breeches, prickly ash, and lichens; be careful not to trample them. The trail descends past a bed of cactus, then climbs to another excellent view from the top of a sheer dynamite-blasted cliff that looks straight down on a picnic area hundreds of feet below. Be extra careful.

The Long Path descends again through a mixed deciduous forest with ash, hickory, sassafras, many varieties of oak, flowering dogwood, hackberry, and mountain laurel. Intersect an old woods road and continue your descent on the road; the route is clearly marked. The trail levels and continues north, intersecting the ridge again. You pass old stone walls. Just before a major fork in the trail, an unmarked trail ascends to the right and another amazing view from the top of a quarry cliff. One can see Croton Point across the river and the Hook Mountain Ridge, including a dramatic view of the cliffs. Again exercise extreme caution, since it's a long drop to the bottom.

From the intersection the Long Path veers sharply left, while the unmarked trail heads right. The Long Path descends from here to Rockland Lake Road. The final stretch is fairly steep. You've now traveled more than two miles from the first bare-summit view. You pass old foundations just before you reach the road. There's convenient parking along the side of the road. This road continues west to Rockland Lake State Park and 9W, or east to the river and the Shore Path. Those wishing to make a loop trip via the Shore Path may exit here.

The Long Path crosses the road, continuing north uphill, passing a tiny nineteenth-century cemetery on the right with the headstones all lying on the ground faceup. The trail continues its ascent to another open view above a quarry face. Directly across the river is the town of Ossining and Croton Point to the north. Again, watch your step.

The trail continues through Trough Hollow, where it skirts a filtration plant. Through this low point in the ridge, ice was once transported from Rockland Lake to Slaughter's Landing. (See description of the Shore Path.) Past stone walls on your left, you'll encounter tennis courts and parking lots, part of Rockland Lake State Park. There is informal access from the parking lot. Rockland Lake State Park has bike trails, cross-country skiing, a host of other recreational activities, a refreshment stand, and a boardwalk with descriptive signs through a woodland swamp, in case you wish to detour here.

Continue north along the ridge, which features more brief ascents and descents. There is another view from one of these summits of points north and west, and partial views of the Hudson through the trees in late fall, winter, and early spring. Two miles after crossing Lake Rockland Road, the Long Path finally makes its descent from the ridge, reaching an intersection with another white-marked trail, the same one described in the section on the Shore Path. The white-marked trail descends the steep slope to the right in a series of switchbacks. It passes a short side trail to the rim of a quarry with an open view north of the river toward Croton Point. Just beyond is a railroad tunnel on the left. About a quarter mile, or ten to fifteen minutes, after leaving the Long Path, you'll reach the Shore Path. From the white trail's intersection with the Shore Path to the parking lot north, it's only about an eighth of a mile. Going south, it's about four and a half miles to the Nyack State Beach entrance.

HAVERSTRAW BEACH STATE PARK TO STONY POINT

This 6.6-mile stretch ending at the entrance to the Revolutionary War historic site is entirely on roads. The northern stretch, particularly around Grassy Point, has stunning views of Haverstraw Bay. Much of the area was once the scene of huge brick works.

From the parking area at the north entrance of Haverstraw State Beach, go north on Riverside Avenue through Dutchtown, a crowded but pleasant residential enclave. After 0.4 miles traverse the huge complex of Tilcon Corporation, a stone-and-gravel company. Continue another 0.4 miles to a stop sign at the intersection of Short Clove Road. Go right and continue north on Riverside. After another 0.3 miles there's a historical marker on the right dedicated to Haverstraw's role as a brickmaking center. A short distance beyond you enter the village of Haverstraw.

Haverstraw comes from the Dutch *haverstroo* ("oatstraw"), which was abundant in local swamps. The land was first settled in 1681. It was the site of the famous Treason House, where Benedict Arnold sold Major André the plans for West Point. The Helen Hayes Hospital is now located on the site. Followers of Robert Owen established the Franklin Community here in 1825, America's first socialist experiment in communal living. During the early nineteenth century, red sandstone in the area was quarried for building material. The presence of abundant clay deposits and cheap transportation via the river made Haverstraw ideal as a center for brickmaking. By the late nineteenth century the the area was home to the Hudson's largest concentration of brickyards. The town was incorporated in 1854. High Tor State Park, described in chapter 14, is located just west of the town.

From Riverside Avenue make a right onto Elk Street, a narrow one-way street. Make the first right onto West Street. Follow West Street a short distance to a view of the river and a marker indicating that this is the widest point in the river, about four miles. The street turns to the left and becomes First Street, lined with old Victorian mansions in various stages of disrepair, a testament to the period when Haverstraw was a prosperous brickmaking center. Follow First Street 0.2 miles to the entrance to Emeline Park, named after a side-wheel ferry that was used in the area. Today this small park is popular with local children. There's a playground, fountain, portable toilet facilities, and an excellent view of the river. At this point you've traveled slightly less than two miles from the beginning. Thanks to Scenic Hudson and the village of Haverstraw, the recent acquisition of Vincent's Landing, a neighboring parcel, will allow for an expansion of the park and an increase in recreational opportunities.

Continue north on First Street, one block to its end. Make a left onto Broad Street. Go a short distance on Broad Street to the intersection with Broadway. Turn right on Broadway and continue north, 0.8 miles, to the intersection with Samsondale Avenue. Go right, and after a short distance make another right onto Tanneyanns Lane. Follow to the end of the road and make another right. There's another historical marker on the left denoting the site of the Benson House, home of a patriot arrested and executed by the British.

Pass a small park with a pond on the right. Behind it is the Bowline Power Plant. Just beyond, the road bends sharply to the left and continues north, to the right of Minisceongo Creek. Follow the road 0.9 miles, passing a marina on the right. There are extensive wetlands on the left side of the road. This entire area was once heavily populated by brick-making plants; all are gone now. After another 0.2 miles pass underneath a pipe conveyor that leads to a gypsum plant. Pass a waste-treatment facility on the right and then an open view of Haverstraw Bay, a popular spot for locals to sunbathe and enjoy the view. Just beyond is Grassy Point. The road makes a sharp left here and becomes County Road 108. There's a town park open to town residents only. Pass more marinas on the right, and cross the small bridge over Minisceongo Creek. The road continues north as Beach Road (County Road 110), right along the Hudson's shore, finally making a left onto Tompkins Avenue. Pass underneath the Conrail tracks and continue west a short distance, making the first right, and continue north about 0.3 miles through a residential neighborhood to an intersection. Go either way, about 0.2 miles, to the intersection of Battlefield Road. Go right on Battlefield, a short distance to the entrance of Stony Point Battlefield State Historic Site.

The historic site is located on Stony Point, a high, rocky headland overlooking a narrow, barely half-mile wide section of the Hudson opposite Verplanck's Point. This narrow point separates two of the Hudson's widest sections; Haverstraw and Peekskill Bays. The underlying bedrock here is part of the Cortlandt Complex, an igneous intrusion from the early Paleozoic age. It is primarily exposed on the east side of the Hudson. Located just south of the southern gateway to the Hudson Highlands, Stony Point was the site of the King's Ferry, one of the main communication links between New England and the rest of the colonies during the Revolutionary War. It was considered very strategic and both sides of the river here were fortified by the Americans. On July 1, 1779, six thousand British troops under the personal command of Gen. Henry Clinton captured Stony Point after the small American force retreated without bloodshed. The British strengthened the fortifications and left a large garrison commanded by Lieut. Col. Henry Johnson. Because it was bounded on three sides by the Hudson and connected to the mainland by only a narrow causeway, Johnson believed the fortress was immune from attack.

Gen. Anthony Wayne was convinced he could capture the fort in a carefully coordinated surprise attack and persuaded General Washington to allow him the command of 1,350 handpicked troops. On July 14, 1779, they marched south from their encampment near Fort Montgomery, crossed the mountains, and arrived late that day. Just before midnight of the fifteenth, the Americans, with sheets of paper in their hats for identification, and using only fixed bayonets, surprised the British and captured the fort. The Americans lost fifteen troops; the British suffered heavier casualties, and 543 were captured, along with supplies and cannon. Only two British officers managed to escape. The British had underestimated the ability and daring of the Americans to stage such a raid.

Failing to capture the British fort across the Hudson at Verplanck's Point, the Americans abandoned Stony Point three days later, after destroying it. General Wayne earned a gold medal ordered by Congress. The British reoccupied the fort, but later abandoned it, and the Americans reclaimed the site. Humiliated, Colonel Johnson was later returned to the British and court-martialed at his own request.

Although today nothing remains of the fort, the site is preserved and maintained as a park by the Palisades Interstate Park Commission. There's a small museum with Revolutionary War artifacts excavated in the New York area and Hudson Highlands, including utensils, tools, buttons, buckles, and weapons. One of the fifteen English bronze eight-inch howitzers captured in the Battle of Stony Point by the Americans is on display. A twelve-minute slide show recounts the course of the battle. Demonstrations of musketry, artillery, and Revolutionary War camp life by guides dressed in period costumes also take place here. An informative brochure is available and there are signs throughout the site as well as excellent views of the river, especially south toward Haverstraw and across the river of Verplanck's Point. The site also includes the Hudson River's oldest lighthouse, built in 1826 and used up to 1925; it is open on weekends to tours. This is also the site of the King's Ferry Landing.

The 0.44 miles of trail in the park are designated part of the Hudson River Greenway Trail. The park is open from April 15 through October 31. The museum is open Wednesdays through Saturdays from 10 A.M. to 4:30 P.M., Sundays from 1:00 to 4:30 P.M. The grounds are open a half hour longer, till 5:00 P.M. Admission is free except for special events; no pets or bikes are allowed. For information call 914-786-2521.

8 Lower Hudson East
YONKERS TO PEEKSKILL

When people think of this area, all of which lies within Westchester County, suburbs usually come to mind. In fact, this area offers extraordinary variety for both the walker and bicyclist.

Remnants of Westchester's natural landscapes may be seen in a number of parks and preserves, including the Graff Audubon Sanctuary, George's Island Park, and the Crawbuckie Nature Preserve. The railroad severely limits access to the Hudson's shoreline. However, there are notable exceptions, such as Croton Point, George's Island, and Oscawana Island, which offer superb shoreline access. There are dramatic views of the Hudson's widest points as well as the Palisades across the river and the Hudson Highlands to the north. Rockwood Hall is another park with excellent views well worth checking out. Some of the area's historic sites, including Lyndhurst; Washington Irving's home, Sunnyside; the Van Cortlandt Manor; and the Philipseburg Manor, are among the highlights of the region; and towns such as Tarrytown, Irvington, and Peekskill offer many attractions that cater to visitors.

As part of the Manhattan Prong, the geology of the Lower Hudson East is similar to that of the New York section in terms of age, history, and types of rock. The Manhattan Schist, the Fordham Gneiss, and the Inwood Marble underlie much of this section. The Inwood Marble has been quarried commercially, especially in the Ossining area. In the area of Cortlandt Township there is a large intrusion of younger igneous rocks into the older rocks of the Manhattan Prong. Exposures of this rock may be seen in George's Island Park and in the Blue Mountain Reservation, which is described in chapter 14. These dark gray and black igneous rocks (pyroxenite, gabbro, diorite, and periodotite), which were once magma, are approximately 435 million years old. One rock of the Cortlandt Complex, the Peekskill Granite, is a beautiful white and pink and has been used as a building material for such structures as the Cathedral of Saint John the Divine. The hot magma heated the surrounding rock and in some cases turned it into emery, a mixture of very hard minerals that has commercially valuable abrasive qualities. The only emery mines in the Western Hemisphere are located here.

Thousands of years ago, Westchester was settled by Native Americans, who left piles of discarded oyster shells (middens) along the Hudson's shores in what are now Croton Point and George's Island Parks. Under British colonial rule Westchester land along the Hudson was primarily divided into two large land grants. Land from the Croton River south belonged to the Philipse family, and that north of the Croton River belonged to the Van Cortlandt family. Both estates were cultivated by numerous tenant farmers. During the American Revolution, Westchester was contested by both sides, neither of which was able to gain full control. There were numerous encampments, small fortifications, troop movements, and skirmishes.

Following the war Westchester's large estates were broken up, and the area prospered as an agricultural region served by numerous small ports along the river. The area's rural ambience attracted artists and writers from the city, such as Washington Irving, as well as many wealthy residents who built fabulous homes overlooking the Hudson. By the mid-nineteenth century the introduction of railroad service accelerated these trends, and Westchester towns along the river became industrial centers. By the late nineteenth century, New York City was expanding beyond its boundaries north into Westchester. New residents first clustered near train stations, but with the advent of the automobile, they spread inland. The area experienced a long period of commercial and population growth, which has continued to the present, making this the most populated and developed area along the Hudson north of New York City.

The Old Croton Aqueduct Trailway, the longest in the region for both hikers and bikers, stretches twenty-seven miles from Van Cortlandt Park in the Bronx to the Croton Dam. This incredible linear trail is the ideal route for walkers and bikers to follow the river. It traverses a number of varied settings, including some of Westchester's poshest neighborhoods, and links a number of points of interest along the way. It is wide, relatively level with hard-packed dirt, fine gravel, and occasionally asphalt surfaces, perfect for walking or riding. Some segments are quite popular, and some communities have made the trail a part of efforts to attract tourists. The Audubon Society reports that the Aqueduct Trailway has excellent bird-watching and serves as a migration route for a number of species. The Old Croton Aqueduct Trailway is a designated National Historic Landmark. The segment from Philipse Road to Croton is officially part of the Greenway Conservancy's Hudson River Trail. Most of the trail runs atop the Old Croton Aqueduct.

During the early nineteenth century New York City was growing rapidly, and getting enough fresh water to the city presented a huge problem. Epidemics and destructive fires emphasized the need for a reliable water supply. A plan was devised to bring one hundred million gallons of water per day from the Croton River, forty-one miles to the north, via an aqueduct. One of the chief engineers of this ambitious project was John B. Jervis, who also worked on the Erie and the Delaware & Hudson Canals and later on the Hudson & Mohawk Railroad, some of the most impressive engineering feats of the time. Work was begun in 1837 and took five years and thirteen million dollars to complete. The aqueduct project was one of the earliest uses of hydraulic cement, which dries quickly and lasts a long time. At the height of construction, more than three thousand workers, mostly Irish immigrants, were employed. On October 14, 1842, there was an official celebration of the aqueduct's opening, which included the ringing of church bells, cannon volleys, a five-mile-long parade, and the plying of fountains.

The water was carried through an eight-and-a-half by seven-and-a-half-foot brick-and-mortar-lined tube. The water flow was driven by gravity, as it dropped thirteen inches per mile. Bridges and earthen fills carried the aqueduct over streams and valleys, with conical ventilating towers placed every mile or so to relieve pressure and keep the water fresh. The structure was built to last and was supposed to meet New York City's water needs for at least a hundred years. However, the city's population grew faster than expected, and the growing use of water closets and baths saw the average daily use per person rise from thirty to seventy-eight gallons. By 1885 a second, larger Croton Aqueduct was constructed. It, too, would prove inadequate, and in 1917 a giant water system, the Catskill Aqueduct, would begin bringing water from the Catskill Mountains to the city. Construction of these other aqueducts rendered the Old Croton Aqueduct obsolete, and by 1955 it saw only very limited use. In 1968 it was purchased by the state. Today it is managed by the OPRHP as a recreational and cultural resource. Exhibits on the history and construction of the aqueduct may be viewed at the Ossining Urban Cultural Park Visitors' Center. For information about the trail, guided tours, and so on, write Old Croton Trailway State Park, 15 Walnut Street, Dobbs Ferry, NY 10522, or call 914-693-5259.

A new map of the trailway has recently become available. To order it, write the Friends of the Old Croton Aqueduct, Inc., Overseer's House, 15 Walnut Street, Dobbs Ferry, NY 10522.

Those hiking or biking in this area are blessed with Westchester's superb public transportation system, which makes virtually any site mentioned in the book readily accessible. Metro-North trains run along the Hudson, making regular stops at Yonkers, Glenwood, Greystone, Hastings-on-Hudson, Dobbs Ferry, Ardsley, Irvington, Tarrytown, Philipse Manor, Scarborough, Ossining, Croton, Cortlandt, and Peekskill. Call 1-800-METRO for schedule and fare information. There's also local bus service via Bee-Line; call 914-682-2020 for schedule and information.

Those interested in information about tourist destinations, lodging, and dining should contact the Westchester Convention and Visitors' Bureau, Ltd., at 1-800-833-WCVB. The Historic River Towns of Westchester is a consortium of riverfront communities working and planning together to promote economic development and tourism, as well as provide information for visitors. You may contact them by calling 914-271-2238.

The Route

NEW YORK CITY/YONKERS BOUNDARY
TO HASTINGS-ON-HUDSON

Four and a half miles through the city of Yonkers, passing Philipse Manor Hall, the Hudson River Museum, and other sites. The last 1.8 miles is on the Old Croton Aqueduct Trailway.

Yonkers is located on the Hudson just north of New York City and opposite the Palisades. It was once a thriving industrial center, river port, and suburb. Yonkers is the fourth largest city in New York State, and if you count Jersey City, the third largest along the Hudson. The city has a long and colorful history. It was the home of the Otis Elevator Company, and the first American game of golf was played here in 1888. Jerome Kern, Art Carney, Sid Caesar, Anne Bancroft, and Ella Fitzgerald all resided in Yonkers at one time or another. The city has many attractions, including the historic Philipse Manor House and the Hudson River Museum, and it is where walkers and bikers can start along the Old Croton Aqueduct Trailway.

Yonkers was the site of a summer fishing settlement the Indians called Nappeckemack, named after the cascades of the Nepperhan River, meaning "town of swift water." In 1646 the Dutch West India Company awarded the 24,000-acre Kekeskick Tract to Andriaen Cornelissen van der Donck, the first lawyer and historian in New Netherland, for his help in negotiating a treaty between the Dutch and the Mohawk. Born in the Netherlands in 1620 of wealthy parents, van der Donck came to the New World when he was twenty-one. In 1652 he was granted the title of patroon of the colony he named Colen Donck, meaning "Donck's colony." He was nicknamed *jonker* or *yonkeer*, meaning "young lord." He established his plantation and erected a mill on the Nepperhan River, which he renamed the Sawkill (it was later renamed the Saw Mill River). Van der Donck tried unsuccessfully to attract settlers to his property. Colen Donck was split up when the British took over New Netherland in 1664.

Frederick Philipse (1626–1702) purchased the land as part of his great 52,500-acre estate, which stretched north along the Hudson from the Spuyten Duyvil to the Croton River. Philipse came to New Netherland in 1647 and by 1653 was serving Peter Stuyvesant, the director general, as a carpenter and architect. In 1662, his marriage to a rich widow, Margaret Hardenbrook de Vries, who owned ships and a thriving trading company, made Frederick wealthy. The Philipses traded in grain, tobacco, furs, molasses, rum, and slaves. By 1674 he was the richest man in the colony. In 1693 William and Mary granted him a royal charter to the manor of Philipsborough for an annual fee of fourteen pounds and twelve shillings. He built mills at Poncantico, Yonkers, and on the upper Nepperhan River.

For most of the war Yonkers was held by the British, and in 1780, sixteen thousand British troops were camped nearby. By 1781 the British withdrew, and the Americans occupied it. Following the war, Yonkers continued as an important grain- and lumber-milling and wool-processing center and river port. Lemuel Wells was instrumental in bringing steamboat traffic to Yonkers. By 1849 the Hudson River Railroad reached it, and the town became an important industrial center. In 1854 Elisha G. Otis established his famous elevator works here. Otis, a mechanic in a Yonkers bedstead factory, designed a successful elevator for the plant. Planning on moving to the California goldfields, he received orders for his new elevator and realized his fortune lay in New York City, where buildings were shooting up higher and higher. In 1855 Yonkers was incorporated as a village, and in 1872 as a city. In the late nineteenth century, as neighboring New York City filled its boundaries, population and commercial activity spilled over its borders into Yonkers, which saw rapid growth. In the 1870s and 1880s many of New York's wealthiest citizens established residences in Yonkers. By the mid-twentieth century the decline of riverfront industry and the migration of population to newer suburbs in the north resulted in a long period of stagnation and decay. Much of the riverfront became occupied by abandoned or dilapidated buildings and low-income residences. Efforts to revitalize the area and convert old factories into offices and condominiums is currently under way.

Primary access to the riverfront and views of the river and the Palisades are from the historic Yonkers Pier and JFK Memorial Park.

Metro-North express trains stop at the Yonkers station. There is also local train service to the Glenwood and Greystone stations. Bee-Line Transit makes stops along Broadway (Route 9).

Having entered Yonkers from Riverdale, proceed north 1.3 miles on Riverdale Avenue to the city center. There's a large supermarket here if you need supplies. Just beyond, one can detour left on Main Street to the Yonkers Pier. To reach the Yonkers Pier, take South Main Street just south of the Yonkers train station, through the tunnel under the railway to the parking area. The Yonkers Pier is just beyond. Just north of this site, the Saw Mill River enters the Hudson.

From the intersection with Main Street, continue north a short distance on Riverdale Avenue, which becomes Warburton Avenue. At the intersection of Dock Street, pass Philipse Manor Hall on the left.

The Philipse Manor Hall is a New York State–designated historic site, operated by the OPRHP. The original building dates back to the 1680s, probably a small simple Dutch-style stone house built by Frederick Philipse. There was a nearby mill located on the Saw Mill River. Frederick primarily resided in New York City and probably used the house for storage and for occasional visits. His grandson, Frederick II (1695–1751), who was active in politics and served in the provincial assembly, inherited the house, which he expanded and remodeled in the Georgian style. It served as the family's summer residence. His son, Frederick Philipse III, who lived a carefree life of leisure, remodeled the house again and added the north wing, which tripled its size. A Tory, Philipse abandoned the house during the Revolutionary War, fleeing with his family to British-held New York City. After having several private owners, it was acquired by the village of Yonkers in 1868 as a village hall. In 1872 it became Yonkers City Hall. In 1908, thanks to Mrs. Eva Smith Cochran, it was purchased by the state and saved from demolition. In 1912 it opened as a museum.

Today, the opulent home remains one of the few surviving examples of Georgian-style architecture in the United States. The Rococo-style papier-mâché-on-plaster ceiling, installed in 1750, is one of the earliest examples of this style of decoration in the American colonies. There are exhibits on the history of Philipse Manor Hall, locally excavated artifacts, and an excellent photographic exhibit on the history of Yonkers. There is also the Alexander Smith Cochran Collection of portraits of American presidents and heroes of the Revolution. The museum is open

Wednesdays and Thursdays from 11:00 A.M. to 2:00 P.M., and between April 1 and October 31, Sundays from 2:00 to 5:00 P.M.. Between November 1 and March 31, it is open Sundays from 1:00 to 4:00 P.M. Call 914-965-4027 for information.

Continue north on Warburton 1.4 miles to the intersection with Philipse Road. On the right leads to the Croton Aqueduct Path. On the left is the Hudson River Museum.

The Hudson River Museum features changing art exhibits and Glenview, built in 1876–1877, the former Victorian summer home of John B. Trevor, a wealthy New York stockbroker. Gen. William Tecumseh Sherman often dropped by to play billiards with Trevor. The house was purchased by the city of Yonkers in 1924. It is partially restored, with original Victorian furnishings and decorative arts, exquisite walnut and maple woodwork, painted ceilings, and imported floor tiles. Paintings of artists of the Hudson River School are on display. There are hands-on exhibits of Victorian lifestyle. The museum also features prints by Andy Warhol and Robert Rauschenberg and Red Grooms's 3-D cartoon creation *Gift Shop.* There are also the Troster Hall of Sciences and the Andrus Planetarium. A fine view of the Hudson River and Palisades can be observed from the Watercolor Café. It is open October through April, Wednesdays through Sundays from 12:00 to 5:00 P.M.; from May through September it stays open till 9:00 P.M. on Fridays. There is a small admission fee for the museum as well as one for the planetarium. Call 914-963-4550 for information.

The Hudson River Museum is located in JFK Memorial Park. Just beyond the museum on the left, JFK Memorial Drive leads to the waterfront and open views of the river and Palisades. Across from the museum entrance, go east on Philipse Road, uphill a short distance, and cross the Old Croton Aqueduct Trailway. There's a small sign prohibiting motorized vehicles. Make a left onto the trail. Follow the trail north one block, crossing Shonnard Terrace. Continue north through a quiet residential neighborhood with views of the Hudson and Palisades on the left through the trees. Pass the first of many ventilating towers. The trail crosses Arthur Avenue after 0.6 miles, and after another 0.3 miles passes Untemeyer Park on the right. The park is located on the former Greystone estate, 125 acres with a huge ninety-nine-room mansion once owned by Samuel Tilden, who served as governor of New York State and was an unsuccessful candidate for president (1876). Samuel Untermeyer (1899–1940), a wealthy attorney, purchased the mansion and property in 1899. Untermeyer made Greystone's mansion and gardens a showplace. He hired the beaux-arts landscape architect William Welles Bosworth, who also designed the grounds of Kykuit, the Rockefeller estate, to design the

Greystone's fabulous gardens. These included flowerbeds, fountains, canals, and greenhouses that displayed the world's largest private collection of tropical plants, including more than three thousand orchids. Presidents Grover Cleveland and Woodrow Wilson were among the many famous visitors to the estate, and the dancer Isadora Duncan performed outdoors on the grounds. Following Untermeyer's death vandalism and a lack of maintenance caused the mansion and gardens to decline. They were purchased by the city of Yonkers in 1946, and the mansion was demolished two years later. Most of the property was sold, though fifteen acres were maintained as the current park. The park's gardens are currently being restored, and plans are eventually to connect the park with the Aqueduct Trailway. Right now you can enter the park from the trailway by scrambling up a steep hillside.

Some of the park's highlights include a columned amphitheater built in 1924 for Untermeyer's wife, nine thousand square feet of mosaics, one of the nation's largest outdoor collections, flowerbeds, and twin pairs of Ionic columns topped with winged marble sphinxes by Paul Manship, the famous art deco sculptor who did the Prometheus at Rockefeller Center.

Just beyond the beginning of Untermeyer Park is a weir, and there are numerous outcrops of the Fordham Gneiss along the trail here. Continue north another 0.4 miles, passing ruins of the Untermeyer estate on the right, including the caretaker's cottage and a gate flanked by a sculpted stone lion and a now decapitated unicorn. Up the hill is the old amphitheater. Continue north on the trail, passing another ventilating tower. A short distance beyond, the trail crosses Odell Avenue. To the left and down the hill is a bus shelter for Bee-Line Transit and also the Greystone train station. The trail continues north past high-rise apartment buildings with occasional views of the river, and the forty-acre Lenoir Preserve, a wildlife refuge on the right behind a fence. One-half mile north of Odell Avenue, the trail enters Hastings-on-Hudson.

HASTINGS-ON-HUDSON TO TARRYTOWN

Nine miles on the Old Croton Aqueduct Trailway, passing through the communities of Hastings, Dobbs Ferry, Ardsley, Irvington, and Tarrytown. Lyndhurst and Washington Irving's Sunnyside are both located in this segment.

Hastings-on-Hudson was named after the English birthplace of local manufacturer William Saunders. The waterfront was primarily industrial and included the only deepwater facility in this section of the river. Much of that industry is now closed, and the waterfront is mostly a collection of abandoned, dilapidated buildings, vacant lots, and refuse. Some parts are contaminated with PCBs. Efforts to clean up and restore the waterfront are currently under way. MacEachron Waterfront Park, next to the Hastings train station, offers spectacular views of the river and the Palisades. Beyond the waterfront, Hastings is a very attractive, intensely developed commuter suburb.

Hastings-on-Hudson was the home of many famous people, including Adm. David Farragut, the commander of the Union fleet that defeated the Confederates in the Battle of Mobile Bay during the Civil War. It was also the home of the influential publisher Horace Greeley, and actress Billie Burke and theater impresario Florenz Ziegfeld had an estate nearby. William Shatner of *Star Trek* fame resided here. The Hudson River School painters Jasper Cropsey and Worthington Whittredge also lived here. The modern sculptor Jacques Lipchitz had a studio in Hastings, and one of his works graces Fulton Park, near the library and train station.

Hastings-on-Hudson was first settled by Europeans in 1650. During the Revolutionary War, there were skirmishes in the area, and it was occupied by a division of American troops in 1777. At the end of the war, General Washington briefly had his headquarters here, at the Van Brugh–Livingston House. It was there that he met with New York governor George Clinton and British commander Sir Guy Carleton to confer on the fate of prisoners of war, Tories, and the British evacuation of New York City. In the late nineteenth century, Hastings-on-Hudson became an industrial center and wealthy suburb, attracting artists, writers, and performers.

Metro-North has a station at Hastings-on-Hudson for local service; there is also Bee-Line Transit service, which stops along Broadway (Route 9). For information about shopping, dining, and special events, contact the Hastings-on-Hudson Chamber of Commerce at 914-478-0839.

The Old Croton Aqueduct Trailway continues north through lovely neighborhoods, crossing Pinecrest Avenue, where there's a parking area, then passes another ventilating tower. Less than a mile beyond, the trail crosses Washington Avenue. The Gothic Revival–style Jasper F. Cropsey home and studio is on the left at 49 Washington Street. It is open weekdays, by appointment. Call 914-478-1372 for information.

A short distance beyond, the trail crosses a busy intersection of Main Street and Farragut Parkway, just west of Hastings-on-Hudson's downtown area. Pass a playground and recreation field on the right. The trail continues north through another affluent area (Notice how many private residences have opened up their own access to the trail). About 0.6 miles north of downtown Hastings, you'll enter Dobbs Ferry.

Dobbs Ferry was originally named Wysquagua, meaning "place of the bark kettle." Archaeological excavations at the mouth of Wicker Creek along the Hudson north of the riverfront park revealed that Dobbs Ferry was the center of Wiechquaesgeck lands that extended south to Manhattan. One of the earliest European settlers was William Dobbs, a Swede from Delaware, who established a ferry here in 1730. Originally part of the Philipse Patent (estate), it was purchased by the Livingstons in 1796 after the government confiscated it in 1785. In 1777, during the American Revolution, British forces landed here on their way to attack Washington's troops at White Plains. During the war both British and American troops were stationed here at different times. In 1781 Washington briefly established a headquarters in Dobbs Ferry where he met with Count Rochambeau, the commander of French forces allied with the Americans, to plan the decisive Yorktown campaign. Today Dobbs Ferry is primarily a quiet suburban community with lovely views of the Hudson and the Palisades. It serves as the headquarters of the Old Croton Aqueduct Trailway State Park.

Dobbs Ferry has a Metro-North station for local service and bus service via Bee-Line Transit along Broadway (Route 9). For more information about shopping, dining, and special events, contact the Dobbs Ferry Chamber of Commerce, 914-421-6456.

The trail crosses Broadway (Route 9) and continues through the heart of Dobbs Ferry. After 0.6 miles you'll pass the Overseers' House on the right, a simple two-story Italianate-style home built in 1845, which served as the residence for the overseers of the Old Croton Aqueduct, and their families, for 110 years, until 1955. The design of the home was based on one proposed by Calvert Vaux in his book *Villas and Cottages.* This residence is currently being renovated and will eventually be used as an educational center. Just across the street is the headquarters of the trail. A short distance beyond on the right is the Zion Episcopal Church at Cedar and Main, erected in 1834. Washington Irving served as the vestryman here from 1837 to 1843.

The trail continues north, crossing the drainage of Wickers Creek. Just beyond is the campus of Mercy College, one of the prettiest spots so far. As you leave the campus grounds, you pass another ventilator tower. Continue into Ardsley-on-Hudson, a small but very wealthy community. After a short distance you'll enter a beautiful property owned by Columbia University. On the left is the sprawling Nevis mansion, the home of James Alexander Hamilton (1788–1878), the third son of Alexander Hamilton, who named the house after his father's birthplace in the British West Indies. Built in 1836, originally a simple Greek Revival home, it was lavishly remodeled in the 1890s by Stanford White. In 1934 it was donated to Columbia University as a horticulture and landscape design center. Fifty-six varieties of trees are planted here and 1,928 ornamental shrubs, making this one of the largest arboretums in the United States. The house itself now serves as Columbia University's Nevis Laboratory for physics research.

Continue a short distance, entering the small village of Irvington-on-Hudson. The town was named after its most famous resident, Washington Irving. However, Sunnyside, Washington Irving's home, was later incorporated into adjacent Tarrytown. Irvington was originally settled in 1650 and became part of the Philipse family estate. During the Revolutionary War, British troops camped nearby. By the 1830s, the area's rural charm had attracted romantics like Washington Irving. Arrival of the railroad made this an attractive country retreat for the wealthy, who built elaborate homes here. Irvington was also home of the famous landscape painter Albert Bierstadt and the stained-glass designer Louis Comfort Tiffany. Like many of Westchester's other riverfront communities, Irvington became an industrial center. Like the others, too, Irvington's waterfront suffered years of pollution and was lined with dilapidated structures once those industries finally abandoned the area. Through the efforts of Scenic Hudson, Inc., the village of Irvington, and a grant by the state, a fourteen-acre section of the riverfront is being cleaned up and converted into a public park with a waterfront promenade.

Irvington-on-Hudson has a Metro-North station with local service. It also has bus service via Bee-Line Transit with stops on Broadway (Route 9). For more information about shopping, dining, and special events, contact the Irvington Chamber of Commerce at 914-591-6006 or stop in at 64 Main Street.

The first place you'll pass on the left is the incredible eight-sided Octagon House, one of the most distinctive homes in the entire region. It was originally built in 1860 by the wealthy meat tycoon Philip Armour. Joseph Stiner, a tea importer, expanded the residence in 1872 and added the prominent dome and porch. The late Carl Carmer, the author of a popular book on the Hudson and a strong and active opponent of Con Ed's plans to build a power plant at Storm King, also lived here.

Cross Clinton Avenue. Detour to the right and on the corner of Broadway you'll see the Harmes-Conklin-Odell Tavern, which was built in 1690. The New York Committee of Safety met here in 1776 to discuss Washington's defeat at the Battle of Long Island.

Continue north another half mile and cross the Station Road Viaduct, where the aqueduct traverses a very deep ravine. A road passes underneath. Walkers and bikers should use caution and stay in the middle of the path since there are huge drops on both sides. Bicyclists are warned to walk their bikes through this section.

A short distance beyond, the trail crosses Irvington's Main Street, which slopes westward toward the Hudson. The charming thoroughfare is lined with shops and restaurants. The Irvington Town Hall Theater is a replica of Ford's Theater. Down at the west end of the street is Irvington's train station. Detour east one block and north on Broadway, and you'll pass the Presbyterian Church on the left, built in 1869. Louis Comfort Tiffany designed the stained-glass windows. A short distance beyond, also on the left, is Villa Lewaro, once the home of Madame C. J. Walker, a black woman who invented a hair-straightening lotion and made a fortune. Despite hostility from the neighbors, she built the mansion—designed by Vertner Tendy, the first black admitted to the American Institute of Architecture—in 1917. It is now a private residence.

Continue north another mile and you cross a road from which a detour left takes you to Sunnyside, Washington Irving's home from 1835 to his death in 1859. Irving was the first popular American author to win national and international acclaim. The house was originally built around 1690 by Wolfert Ecker, a tenant farmer on the Philipse Estate. Irving mistakenly believed it dated back to 1654. During the Revolutionary War it was a popular gathering spot for patriots and was burned by the British. The home was rebuilt. Irving, born and raised in New York City, had visited the area as a youth and was attracted to its rural, romantic character. He also had a lifelong fascination for the Hudson River and surrounding region. He purchased the house in 1835 when he was fifty-two years old and already rich and famous from his writings. Irving had many interests including architecture, art, and agriculture. He remodeled the home cleverly, combining features of English, Spanish, and Dutch styles he encountered in his travels and remembered, including a stepped-gable roof, a skylight, and a Spanish tower. He also designed trails, planted trees and shrubs, and introduced other features to enhance the property's scenic and aesthetic character. He affectionately called the cottage his "pile." Irving never married, but he invited his widowed brother and his children to move in, and two of his nieces stayed on and helped run the place. Guests included Louis Napoleon, Martin Van Buren, Oliver Wendell Homes, and William Jennings Bryant. Currier & Ives prints touted this as the most picturesque country house in America. In 1945 Sunnyside was purchased by John D. Rockefeller, Jr. Today it is operated by Historic Hudson Valley.

Besides the home, there is an icehouse and root cellar, a wonderful view of the Hudson and attractive grounds, gardens, trails, and picnicking. There is a 350-year-old horse-chestnut tree on the property. There are also a gift shop and a snack bar. There's an admission fee for the house. Tours last up to an hour; the guides dress in period costumes and are wonderfully informative. A grounds pass is available for a small

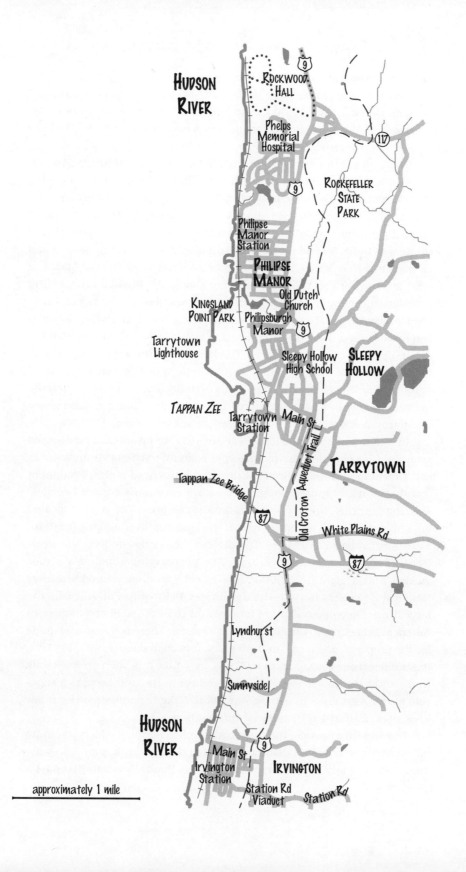

HUDSON
RIVER

ROCKWOOD
HALL

⑨

⑰

Phelps
Memorial
Hospital

⑨

ROCKEFELLER
STATE
PARK

Philipse
Manor
Station

PHILIPSE
MANOR

Old Dutch
Church

KINGSLAND
POINT PARK

Philipsburgh
Manor

⑨

Tarrytown
Lighthouse

Sleepy Hollow
High School

SLEEPY
HOLLOW

TAPPAN ZEE

Tarrytown
Station

Main St

TARRYTOWN

Tappan Zee Bridge

Old Croton Aqueduct Trail

⑧⑦

White Plains Rd

⑨

⑧⑦

Lyndhurst

Sunnyside

⑨

HUDSON
RIVER

Main St
Irvington
Station

IRVINGTON

Station Rd
Viaduct

Station Rd

approximately 1 mile

fee. The house and grounds are open daily except Tuesday in March, November, and December from 10:00 A.M. to 4:00 P.M., and from April through October from 10:00 A.M. to 5:00 P.M. Last tours are an hour before closing. Ask about ticket combinations for other area sites. Call 914-591-8763 for information.

The trail continues north through old estate lands returning to wild forest, finally crossing the beautiful open lawn of Lyndhurst, a Gothic Revival residence designed by Alexander Jackson Davis, the greatest exponent of the Gothic Revival style. Many consider Lyndhurst the finest surviving example of Gothic Revival architecture in America. The original estate was built in 1838 by William Paulding, a former congressman and ex-mayor of New York City. It was later purchased by George Marrit, a wealthy New York merchant, who hired Davis, the original architect, to redesign and enlarge the home. In 1880 it was bought by famous railroad financier Jay Gould, who used it as a summer home. In 1964 Duchess Anna of Talleyrand-Perigord, a Gould descendant, donated the estate in memory of her parents. The home features a collection of Victorian decorative arts, including furniture designed by Davis and wood painted to resemble marble, which was actually more expensive than using real marble but was considered more stylish; Tiffany stained glass; and parquet floors with a different design in every room.

In addition to the mansion, there are sixty-seven acres of landscaped grounds that combine the picturesque romantic style of Andrew Jackson Downing and more formal, European-influenced styles. Prominent among the many huge specimen trees are enormous copper beeches, weeping beeches, Norway spruces, and sycamores. The house, located on a hillside, has an excellent view of the Hudson River looking north toward the Tappan Zee Bridge. The driveway runs down along the riverfront in a quiet, tree-shaded area. The property also includes a rose garden and a gigantic 19,000-square-foot greenhouse modeled after Roulault's Conservatory in the Jardin des Plantes in Paris. It was the largest private conservatory of its day and the first steel greenhouse in America. It is currently undergoing restoration. There is a map and guide for the property, and a café and gift shop. It is open daily except Mondays, in summer from 10:00 A.M. to 5:00 P.M. In winter it is open on weekends from 10:00 A.M. to 4:15 P.M. There are house tours, and there is a separate fee for a grounds pass only. Ask about ticket combinations for other area sites. Call 914-631-4481 for information.

Leaving the grounds, the trail soon reaches Route 9, which you must follow north, left, a short distance, crossing the New York State Thruway. Just beyond, make a right onto White Plains Road, then left, just past a shopping center, and you're back on the trail again. Continue north through a residential neighborhood, passing another ventilator tower.

According to Washington Irving, Tarrytown's name was derived from the habit of local farmers of tarrying in the town's saloons when they came here to market. It could have also gotten its name from the Dutch word *tarwe*, which means wheat, which was grown locally. During the Revolutionary War, Tarrytown was the site where, on September 23, 1780, the famous British spy Major André was captured by American militia. His capture, and the discovery of plans for the American fortress at West Point in his boot, foiled Benedict Arnold's attempt to sell the fort to the British. A statue dedicated to his captors is located on Main Street north of the library. Tarrytown was also the home of Comm. Oliver Hazard Perry, the hero of the Battle of Lake Erie during the War of 1812; his brother, Comm. Matthew Calbraith Perry, who opened up Japan to U.S. trade and was an early advocate of an all-steamship navy; and the home of Gen. John C. Frémont, one of the greatest explorers of the American West.

Tarrytown was incorporated as a village in 1870. Today, it is the home of Marymount College. Tarrytown is part of a major corridor of business, research, and industry located in the heart of Westchester County. Christ Church on North Broadway, built in 1838, was where Washington Irving worshiped from 1843 until his death in 1859, and where his funeral ceremony was held, an event that attracted more than a thousand people, including celebrities. The Warner Library on North Broadway was built in 1928 in the beaux-arts style. The Tarrytown Lighthouse was built in 1883 and operated until 1955. It is located in Kingsland Park, which is only open to town residents.

The Historical Society of Tarrytown has changing exhibits and displays of native artifacts, on the capture of Major André, and on Washington Irving. It is located at 1 Grove Street and is open Tuesdays, Wednesdays, and Saturdays from 2:00 to 4:00 P.M. For information, call 914-631-8374.

Tarrytown has a Metro-North railroad station with express service as well as bus service via Bee-Line Transit. For information about dining and lodging contact the Sleepy Hollow Chamber of Commerce at 914-631-1705 or stop in at 80 South Broadway.

TARRYTOWN TO SCARBOROUGH STATION

Five miles, mostly following the route of the Old Croton Aqueduct. The trail passes historic Philipsburg Manor and the Old Dutch Church of Sleepy Hollow. It also traverses Rockefeller State Park. For walkers a side trip to Rockwood Hall is very worthwhile.

The trail continues north, crossing Prospect Avenue and then ending in a parking lot by Leroy Avenue. Go left one block to Broadway, and then go right, north. After less than a quarter mile, you'll cross Franklin Street. A left here takes you down to the Tarrytown Metro-North station. Continue north to the intersection of Main Street in Tarrytown's bustling downtown area. There are antique shops, restaurants, and a music hall with live shows. Go right, east, on Neperan Road a short distance to pick up the trail again on the left. A short distance north and you'll pass another ventilator tower.

The trail continues northward, apparently ending in a courtyard of Sleepy Hollow High School. Go right to the end of the building, around the corner, and down the steps to the parking lot. Continue to the left through the parking area, which then continues north, to the left of the playing field. The trail resumes after crossing Bedford Road. Just beyond is an excellent view of the Hudson overlooking a twentieth-century neighborhood, part of the village of Sleepy Hollow.

Continue north past another ventilator tower, crossing Gorey Brook Road. A detour left on this winding road will bring you to New Broadway, then west on Gordon to Broadway (Route 9), and both the Philipsburg Manor and the Old Dutch Church of Sleepy Hollow, located a short distance to the north.

Philipsburg Manor Upper Mills is located on the left side of Broadway. First constructed in 1682 by Frederick Philipse and completed in 1720 by Adolph Philipse, one of his sons, it served primarily as an office and operations center as well as a weekend and summer retreat for the family. The Pocantico River, a tributary of the Hudson, provided the necessary waterpower to operate a gristmill, which could grind up to five thousand pounds of grain daily. Sloops owned by Philipse would transport the flour and biscuits down the Hudson to New York City. The Dutch-style manor house contains seventeenth- and eighteenth-century Dutch furnishings. The estate was worked by eleven hundred tenant farmers and twenty-three slaves, who performed various duties including operating the mill. It was confiscated by the Americans during the Revolutionary War because the Philipse family were prominent Tories.

Today the site is a replica of an eighteenth-century working farm with farm animals, an herb and vegetable garden, and demonstrations of eighteenth-century farming methods. One of the highlights is the demonstration of the gristmill, which grinds grain into flour as it did in 1682, the only such working mill along the Hudson. There is also a reconstruction of an eighteenth-century barn and a replica of a tenant farm. Guides in period costumes provide tours of the grounds and buildings as well as demonstrations of eighteenth-century crafts. There is a picnic area on the grounds. The visitors' center offers a documentary film about the estate, a gallery, an open-air café with a view, and an excellent gift shop. It is operated by Historic Hudson Valley. It is open from 10:00 A.M. to 5:00 P.M. on weekends in March, and from April through December, daily except Tuesdays. Ask about combination tickets for other sites. Call 914-631-3992 for information.

On the right-hand side of Broadway is the Old Dutch Church of Sleepy Hollow, built by Frederick Philipse and his second wife, Catherine van Cortlandt, in 1699. The simple stone chapel was remodeled in 1837 in the Gothic style with help from Washington Irving. The original bell was cast in the Netherlands in 1685. Sleepy Hollow Cemetery contains the graves of Washington Irving, Andrew Carnegie, and other notables.

One can continue west from here toward the river and the Philipse Manor train station. The station includes one of the original set of sixteen cast-iron eagles that stood atop Grand Central Station in New York City in the nineteenth century.

Continue north from Gorey Brook Road and enter Rockefeller State Park and Preserve, 850 acres of forest that was once the private grounds of the Rockefeller family for carriage riding, donated to the state in 1983. The preserve includes twenty-two miles of hiking trails. This beautiful and relatively tranquil section is the only large segment of wild forest along the Old Croton Aqueduct between Yonkers and Ossining. For more information about the park, call 914-631-1470. At the beginning of the park, there's a playground with restrooms.

After a short distance Sleepy Hollow Cemetery appears on the left. Just beyond, the Aqueduct Trail crosses a deep ravine with a stream via a tall earthen embankment. Once you reach the other side you'll encounter a weir, a rectangular stone structure once used to control the water flow. The trail continues through mixed deciduous forest with glimpses of the river through the trees. With the growing sound of traffic, you approach Route 9, eventually reaching the busy highway below the steep embankment on the left. Just ahead is the intersection of Route 9 and Route 117. The trail veers to the right past dark rock outcrops, dips, and continues east. Just beyond, a pedestrian bridge appears on the left. (The trail on the right continues into the Rockefeller Preserve. No bikes are allowed.)

Cross the pedestrian bridge over Route 117. On the other side the trail makes a sharp left, then gradually bends to the right. (The land to the right of the trail is privately owned; no trespassing.) The trail straightens and continues north, roughly parallel to Route 9 for about a quarter mile, passing another stone ventilator tower. Just beyond, the trail reaches an intersection. Bear left and go a short distance to the new Archville Pedestrian Bridge, constructed in 1998, that crosses Route 9.

Cross the bridge. On the opposite side is a marker commemorating an arch constructed in 1839 that carried the aqueduct over the roadway at this point. It was removed in 1924 and the aqueduct buried under the roadway.

About 300 feet past the bridge, the trail intersects a dirt road on the left. The road leads to Rockwood Hall, an extremely worthwhile detour (for those on foot, since bikes are not permitted). Rockwood Hall is a two-hundred-acre property owned by the Rockefeller family, but open to the public though a special arrangement with the Taconic State Park System. One of the best places in this chapter for viewing the river, it is administered by the OPRHP.

To get there follow the dirt road as it bends to the left, reaching a gate after a short distance, and intersecting a second dirt road on the right. Follow this road as it descends, bends to the left and then right, soon reaching another intersection and a sign indicating you've entered Rockwood Hall. Go right. The dirt road descends, following a lovely stream, crossing it four times via small wooden bridges, and passing large stands of rhododendron. The road bends to the left where the stream enters the Hudson and an expansive view opens, overlooking the railroad tracks and the Tappan Zee with Hook Mountain, Nyack, Croton Point, and Haverstraw in the distance. The roadway continues south, shaded by tall trees, parallel to the tracks and river with nearly continuous views the whole way. After a quarter mile from where the road reaches the river, a second dirt roadway on the left ascends to a prominent hilltop where William Rockefeller, younger brother and business partner of John D., Sr., the famous oil magnate, built an elaborate mansion he hoped would surpass any of the others along the Hudson. When he died in 1922, the property became a private country club with a golf course. The country club went bankrupt during the Great Depression and the land was acquired by John D. Rockefeller, Jr., William's nephew. He demolished the huge mansion and left the land largely undeveloped with woods, imported specimen trees, meadows, terraces, and cinder paths. The foundation of the once-great mansion is a wonderful vantage point for viewing the river, and the Tappan Zee Bridge. The surrounding meadows are perfect for picnicking, hanging out, and enjoying the views. The roadway along the river continues south, eventually linking again with the other roadway.

The main entrance to Rockwood Hall is off Rockwood Hall Road between Phelps Memorial Hospital and IBM, which can be reached from Route 9, a quarter mile south of the intersection with Route 117. There's parking and a Bee-Line bus stop with regular service. The park is open in the daylight hours, year round. For more information, call the park office at 914-631-1470.

From the detour to Rockwood Hall, the Croton Aqueduct Trailway veers right and continues north for about a quarter mile through the woods, then reaches a gate and crosses a road. The trail continues as a narrow path to the right of a colonial-style home, goes a short distance to a driveway, then makes a left onto a broad marked path, which you follow till it reaches River Road. Make another left here on River Road, which you follow for about half a mile till the road bends to the right past fabulous homes with river views. Cross a bridge over a picturesque brook. A short distance beyond you'll reach the intersection with Scarborough Road. If you detour straight, descend to the Scarborough Metro-North train station (local service). To the left over a bridge is tiny Scarborough Park, which has expansive views of the river and surrounding area.

SCARBOROUGH TO CROTON

A walk or bike of 6.6 miles, mostly following the Old Croton Aqueduct Trailway. The trail passes right through the village of Ossining, and an Urban Cultural Park with an excellent visitors' center, and crosses the famous Aqueduct Bridge.

From Scarborough Park, backtrack over the bridge and up the hill. Make a left onto Scarborough Road, and follow it for less than a quarter mile to Route 9, Broadway. On the corner is the impressive Scarborough Presbyterian Church, built in 1893 of rubble fieldstone and sandstone. Just north of the intersection, on Route 9 on the left, is the Sparta Burying Ground, a graveyard dating back to colonial times.

Just beyond the church make a left onto Scarborough Road, and follow it for about half a mile. Past the firehouse, the trail goes left into the woods. Follow it for one and a half miles, crossing a stream on an embankment and a short distance beyond, pass some apartments and a rather muddy, rut-filled section. Informal access is on the left via a parking lot: You've now entered Ossining.

Ossining derived its name from the Sinck Sinck tribe. The village of Sing Sing was incorporated in 1813, the first to become incorporated in Westchester County. Sing Sing Prison was established here in 1825 because of its remote location, easy access via the river, and the presence of Inwood marble, which would be quarried by the prisoners who then used it to build their own cellblocks. Being sent "up the river" meant being sent to Sing Sing, which became the largest and best-known prison in New York State. Some two thousand prisoners are still incarcerated there. The village of Sing Sing also developed as a river port, and other diverse industries grew in the area. Many Italian immigrants came to work in the marble quarries. In 1903 the village of Sing Sing changed its name to Ossining after a boycott of prison-made goods hurt businesses in the town. Ossining is the home of the Maryknoll Catholic Missions. The town is one of fourteen New York State Urban Cultural Parks, its theme is reform movements, and its focus is on the prison and the Old Croton Aqueduct.

Ossining has a Metro-North train station with express service. There is also bus service via Bee-Line Transit with many stops in the town and connections to other Westchester communities. For information about lodging and dining, contact the Greater Ossining Chamber of Commerce at 914-941-0009.

The trail continues for another quarter of a mile over another tall embankment and finally ends in a parking lot off North Highland Avenue (Route 9). Go right, and pass lovely Nelson Park on the left. Just beyond, go left, west, on Washington Avenue. Pass another park on the right, and a school. Make a right onto Spring Street at the T-intersection. There's a ventilator tower on the corner of the school property. Continue north to the downtown area, and make a right onto Maple Place. The path is on the left, paved with bricks. You've now entered the Ossining Urban Cultural Park. Continue north one block to Main Street. An impressive array of nineteenth- and early-twentieth-century facades line Main Street, referred to as the Crescent. One of the key features of the area is the aqueduct, which has been transformed into a tree-shaded linear path in the heart of the town's center.

If you wish to detour to the waterfront, go left down Main Street, about half a mile to the Ossining train station. Just beyond is the Louis Engel Memorial Park, from which there are excellent views of the river, Croton Point, the Palisades, and Sing Sing Prison.

The Croton Aqueduct Trailway crosses Main Street. A short distance on the left is Overlook Park, which provides a platform for viewing the Aqueduct Bridge (I found the view from here somewhat limited). On the right and down the hill is the community center, part of which is the Ossining Urban Cultural Park Visitors' Center. The Visitors' Center has rest rooms and a drinking fountain. There are also excellent imaginative exhibits on the Old Croton Aqueduct and Sing Sing, including a walk-through replica of a brick- and mortar-lined section of the aqueduct complete with a gushing-water soundtrack. There are also replicas of an electric chair and cellblocks as well as a display of weapons made by prisoners. The Visitors' Center is open every day of the year, from 10:00 A.M. to 4:00 P.M. Call 914-941-3189 for information.

Just beyond, the trail crosses the Aqueduct Bridge, probably the most impressive feature of the Old Croton Aqueduct. Here the aqueduct crosses the Broadway Bridge and the deep ravine of the Sing Sing Kill, creating the famous double arch within an arch. The Aqueduct Bridge was constructed using a honeycomb design, unique for its time. The arch within an arch is best seen from the Visitors' Center. You can also cross over the top of it, which is where the trail goes anyway. For many pedestrians it's not just an engineering wonder but the easiest and most direct way to get from one side of town to the other, a truly functional structure.

On the opposite side of the Aqueduct Bridge is another weir, built in 1882. From here the path climbs a series of steps, levels, and continues north on a paved path. The trail crosses a street and becomes a grass-covered path. Cross another street, and continue one block. Cross Snowden Avenue, and continue on the upper, level trail just to the right of the fire station. The trail veers right and continues about a quarter mile through dense woods, passing another weir, and finally emerging at Beach Road. Walkers may detour left to the Crawbuckie Nature Preserve. Beach Road winds down to a cul-de-sac and a small parking area. From there a loop trail begins. The preserve is twelve acres and slopes down to the railroad tracks along the Hudson. There is a variety of vegetation, including woodlands with trees nearly two hundred years old, and marshland with aquatic plants. The loop trail can be walked in ten minutes, but if you have the time, take longer and enjoy the solitude of this small but relatively wild place.

From Beach Road the trail continues north and enters a huge lawn in front of a stone-and-brick building. The trail veers to the right and goes a short distance, bending right and ending up on Route 9. (The Croton Aqueduct Trail crosses Route 9 here and continues north three miles to the Croton Dam, a scenic detour.) Follow Route 9 north for about half a mile to the entrance to the pedestrian walkway on the left. (Bicyclists will need to cross Route 9 here at the intersection of Quaker Bridge Road in order to access the walkway.) The pedestrian walkway takes you over the Croton River with wonderful views of the mouth of the river where it enters the Hudson and a mature brackish water marsh with plentiful cattails. There are interpretive signs along the way.

The Croton River was named Kitch-A-Wan, which means "swift current," by the Native Americans. Croton Bay was supposedly the site where Henry Hudson docked on October 1, 1609. The Dutch named it Croton in honor of an eponymous native sachem. Much of the bay is quite shallow, the result of a flood that took place in 1841, destroying the Croton Dam and dumping huge quantities of sediment in the bay.

CROTON TO OSCAWANA ISLAND PARK

A distance of 4.2 miles, mostly on roads. There are worthwhile detours
to the historic Van Cortlandt Manor and Croton Point Park.

Croton Harmon Metro-North Station has express service and is
within easy walking distance of Croton Point Park and the Van Cortlandt
Manor. There is also bus service via Bee-Line Transit in the village of
Croton-on-Hudson to other Westchester–Hudson River towns, White
Plains, and so on. For information about dining in the Croton area, con-
tact the Croton Chamber of Commerce at 914-271-2196.

Having crossed the mouth of the Croton River, the pedestrian walkway continues north to the interchange for Croton Point Avenue, a total
distance of 0.8 miles from the beginning of the walkway. To visit Van
Cortlandt Manor go north on Croton Point Avenue a short distance to a
T-intersection with Riverside Avenue. Go right on Riverside, passing a
shopping center on the right. At the end of the road on the left is the entrance to Van Cortlandt Manor.

Van Cortlandt Manor is a superb example of an elegant eighteenth-
century house. The foundation was originally built by a Dutchman,
Stephanus van Cortlandt, in 1680 as a hunting lodge and trading post
for an 86,000-acre tract of land he acquired. This included almost all of
the property north of the Croton River up to what is now the Putnam
County line. In 1697 he received a formal charter from King William III
of England to the land. The charter is on display in the house. Stephanus
divided his land among his sons. His grandson Pierre acquired the property in 1750, about 2,500 acres and the house, which he enlarged into
its current form. The house combined elements of the Dutch and Georgian styles of architecture. Pierre van Cortlandt was New York's first lieutenant governor and also served in Congress. His sister Catherine and her
children also resided there. The Van Cortlandts were among the most
prominent and powerful of Hudson Valley landowning families, and they
associated with and married others like the Philipses, Rensselaers, and
Livingstons. The property was a working farm, and the Van Cortlandts
were slave owners who usually kept about eight, mostly women, who performed domestic duties. The house was abandoned during the Revolutionary War and occupied by troops of both sides, who vandalized it.
Following the war the family returned, restored the home, and continued to reside there until 1941. It was later purchased by John D. Rockefeller, Jr. and opened to the public. The first tours began in 1959. It is
now owned and operated by Historic Hudson Valley and is designated a
National Historic Landmark.

The house has Georgian- and Federal-period furnishings, many of them originals owned by the family. Most are American-made but copies of refined European style. There are decorative imported European and Asian items as well. The kitchen downstairs has original hearth and cooking equipment, and demonstrations are given. There's a scenic brick trail called the Long Walk, which follows the original seventeenth-century path that connects the property's three main buildings. There's also a formal garden that displays flowering bulbs in spring and herbs and vegetables in summer. Also on the grounds is a restored 1720s inn on the site of the original Croton River ferry crossing of the King's Highway, a small section of which has been restored. The inn includes a taproom, where locals and guests would have gathered and the typical dormitory-style accommodations that were prevalent then. The simple, sparse furnishings and decorations of the tavern stand in sharp contrast to those of the main house. The beautiful grounds include picnic areas, rest rooms, and a gift shop. Van Cortlandt Manor is open from April through October, daily except Tuesday, from 10:00 A.M. to 5:00 P.M., and in November and December on weekends from 10:00 A.M. to 4:00 P.M. There are tours, and a grounds pass is available. Call 914-271-8981 for information.

To visit Croton Point Park, backtrack to the interchange of Route 9 and Croton Point Avenue. Continue south on Croton Point Avenue one-half mile to the entrance to the park.

Croton Point Park, the largest park along the Hudson in this chapter, includes 504 acres. It is a peninsula that separates Croton Bay from the Hudson's main channel. It is surrounded by water on three sides, and so there are wonderful views of the river and surrounding region from the Hudson Highlands in the north, south to the Tappan Zee and the Palisades, including the Hudson's widest sections. Croton Point was once part of a delta where the Croton River emptied into a large Ice Age lake one hundred feet higher than the present Hudson. Today most of the peninsula is highly developed for recreation uses. You can pick up a rough map of the park at the headquarters by the entrance. To the left of the entrance is a large, rounded hill that was a huge landfill that since has been capped and covered with grass. The park has extensive campgrounds, with a nightly fee for tents. (Note: This is one of only two public campgrounds along the river.) There are also rest rooms, a refreshment stand, telephones, and two shaded picnic grounds. One of the main features of the park is the beach. It is the southernmost swimming beach along the Hudson, and, despite the imported sand, one of the Hudson's most popular. Fishing is another favored activity in many parts of the park. The southeast side of the peninsula is marshland with varied bird life, muskrats, and other creatures. It is reputed to be the best birding site along the Hudson in Westchester County, and certain rare species such as the golden eagle, the yellow-nosed albatross, the American avocet, and the royal tern have been spotted. In the spring you might see grebes, cormorants, snowy egrets, swans, sandpipers, gulls, thrushes, warblers, indigo buntings, and sparrows. In the summer look for sandpipers and glossy ibis. In the fall loons, herons, egrets, Virginia rails, plovers, and grosbeaks can be seen. In the winter loons, grebes, gulls, owls, and an occasional bald eagle may be observed. On the narrow neck of land that connects Croton Point to the mainland, there was an ancient native fortress built by the sachem Croton. Just east of the fortress was a native burial site. The Nature Center is in the old superintendent's residence on the end of a road past the picnic ground on the right. It has educational natural history exhibits. The building also serves as the Materials Archives and Laboratory for Archaeology (MALFA), founded by Louis A. Brennan, a famous archaeologist, in 1963. On display is an extensive collection of native artifacts from Croton Point and Piping Rock, at the mouth of the Croton River, as well as an excavation of an eighteenth-century tenant farmer's residence. Behind the house is a short-loop nature trail that follows the top of the cliffs overlooking a rocky beach. Prehistoric native oyster-shell middens that date back around six thousand years can be seen along the trail.

The southern tip of the peninsula is known as Teller's Point, the dividing point between the Tappan Zee and Haverstraw Bay. The point was named for William Teller, who purchased it from the Native Americans—who had named it Seasqua—for a barrel of rum and twelve blankets. During the Revolutionary War a volley of patriot cannon fire from here drove the British ship the *Vulture,* from which Major André was to be picked up, downriver and away from its appointed rendevous with Benedict Arnold. André's having to take an alternate overland route resulted in his capture near Tarrytown and the failure of Arnold's attempt to sell West Point to the British. In 1827 Robert Underhill devoted eighty acres of the peninsula to growing grapes, the first commercial winery along the Hudson. Remains of old wine cellars can be seen along the south-facing road between Teller's Point and the entrance.

Admission to the park is free to pedestrians and bicyclists. It is open from 8:00 A.M. until dusk, every day. Call 914-271-3293 for information.

From the intersection of Route 9 and Croton Point Avenue, go right a short distance to the intersection with South Riverside Avenue. Make a left and go one-half mile to intersection of Route 129. Go straight on Route 9A, a busy road with a lot of traffic, north another 2.2 miles to the intersection of Warren Road and Scenic Lane. Walkers may go left on Warren Road to the Graff Audubon Sanctuary. Bicyclists should continue north on 9A another half mile to the intersection of Furnace Dock Road and make a left there. This road is part of the 4.8-mile Town of Cortlandt Shoreline Trail, which is designated part of the Hudson River Greenway Trail. Continue west, passing underneath Route 9. After another three-tenths of mile, pass the Graff Audubon Sanctuary on the left. There is a small sign and trailhead and limited parking on the right side of the roadway.

From Warren Road walkers will pass underneath Route 9, then make an immediate right onto Briggs Lane. Follow to the very end of the road, a cul-de-sac; there's limited parking here. On the left is a driveway. Continue up the driveway, veering to the left just before the house. Pass a sign labeled SMRAS (Saw Mill River Audubon Society). I found the trail to be quite overgrown (I hope it is better maintained by the time you visit it). The trail is well marked with red paint blazes and easy to follow. Be forewarned, though, there are some relatively steep sections. Among the lush undergrowth are jack-in-the-pulpits and other spring wildflowers. The trail is appropriately named Jack-in-the-Pulpit Trail.

The Graff Sanctuary comprises thirty acres and has 0.8 miles of hiking trails. There are no facilities, and bikes and motorized vehicles are prohibited. Dogs must be kept on a leash. It is open year round from dawn till dusk. The land, donated to the National Audubon Society in 1975, has been since then managed by the Saw Mill River Audubon Society, the local affiliate. Ownership of the sanctuary was transferred to the SMRAS in 1991. For more information about the sanctuary call 914-666-6503.

Continue on Jack-in-the-Pulpit Trail about a tenth of a mile, passing a stone wall on the left, to an intersection with the Tulip Tree Trail in an area of towering upland hardwoods. You may detour left on Tulip Tree Trail, marked with white paint blazes, crossing a ravine with a seasonal stream and then reaching the intersection with the blue-marked Riverview Trail. Make a left here on the Riverview Trail, continuing through a small meadow, then making a sharp right. There's a view from the top of a bluff of the Hudson and a small privately owned lake just east of the railroad tracks. The trail continues north through a hemlock grove to an intersection with the white-marked Tulip Tree Trail.

The Tulip Tree Trail crosses another ravine and continues north through open woodlands with many tulip trees. Reach the intersection with the red-marked Jack-in-the-Pulpit Trail. Going right here will take you a short distance through a very-steep-sided ravine and then back to Briggs Lane and the entrance. Go straight on the white-marked Tulip Tree Trail, descending into another ravine, then climbing up a steep slope to the entrance on Furnace Dock Road.

From the Graff Sanctuary entrance on Furnace Dock Road, go left about three-tenths of a mile. The road veers sharply right and becomes

Cortlandt Street. After another tenth of a mile, there's an open view of the river on the left and a small parking area that's rarely full. After three-tenths of a mile there's a parking area and the entrance on the left to Oscawana Island Park, which is well worth a visit.

Oscawana Island Park is a Westchester County park, nine acres of which border the Hudson. No longer a true island, it is a peninsula connected to the mainland by railroad tracks and landfill. The railroad tunnels underneath the park, which is primarily undeveloped and heavily wooded, with dense vegetation in places. Occasional trashcans, benches, and trails are the only amenities. From the entrance there's a quarter-mile-long dirt-and-gravel road, with a barricade at the beginning. Just inside the entrance there are views of wetlands both north and south of the peninsula. A short distance beyond, a trail on the right leads to an excellent view of the wetland around the shallow mouth of Furnace Creek. Various birds, including swans, may be observed there. (Oscawana Island is within the Haverstraw Bay Significant Coastal Fish and Wildlife Habitat.)

The main trail crosses over the railroad tunnel and passes an old chimney ruin on the left. It then descends to the shore, where one can walk out on smooth white-and-pink boulders of Fordham Gneiss to the river's edge and dramatic views of Hook Mountain and Croton Point Park to the south, Haverstraw and High Tor on the distant opposite shore, and Verplanck's Point and Stony Point to the north. The area is fairly secluded, and despite the sound of motorboats and jet skis, I think it provides some of the best views and shoreline access along the Hudson. A narrow walking path follows the northern edge of the peninsula to its juncture with the railroad tracks, with beach access along the way.

OSCAWANA ISLAND PARK TO PEEKSKILL

Six miles on roads and trails through Crugers, Verplanck, and the city of Peekskill. The waterfront park at FDR Veteran's Memorial Hospital and George's Island Park are the two highlights of this section. A 1.5-mile-long trail linking the two parks is rough in places and those on bikes will have to walk them to get through this stretch.

From the entrance to Oscawana Island Park, continue north on Cortlandt Street, crossing a small bridge over Furnace Creek, making a sharp left onto Crugers Street, and then winding through a residential neighborhood. After 0.4 miles, you'll reach an intersection, the old Crugers Metro-North station (no longer in operation). Go left and cross the bridge over the railroad tracks. Continue to a gate, likely closed, but easily bypassed. You've now entered the grounds of Franklin D. Roosevelt Veteran's Memorial Hospital. The entrance to the waterfront park is on the left.

The park is landscaped and has benches, sheltered picnic areas, an elevated walkway, (handicap accessible), a beach, and superb views of Haverstraw Bay. The park primarily exists for the hospital's patients and guests so please use the utmost respect and follow all of the park rules. Bikes are not permitted on the elevated walkways so use the roadway instead.

About a quarter mile from the entrance to the park, go right at a gate. A trail ascends the hillside, passing a restored WPA picnic structure on the left (no trespassing). Just beyond, there is an open gate and a small reservoir. Follow the trail on the left (south) side of the reservoir. Just beyond the reservoir is another open gate. Passing through the gate you've entered George's Island, a Westchester County park. The park has 3.25 miles of hiking trails that are designated as part of the Hudson River Greenway Trail. There's a map available at the main entrance to the park or you can get one by calling 914-737-7530 or 914-242-PARK. Besides hiking trails, the park has picnic areas, restroom facilities, and a boat launch. There's a parking fee during the summer months. George's Island was formerly a rocky island, later connected to the mainland by artificial fill.

From the gate, descend a steep hillside on a rough informal path. Bicyclists will have to dismount here and walk their bikes the rest of the way. The path soon intersects a more established trail at the bottom of the hill. A short detour to the left will bring you out to secluded VA Point, which has a wonderful panoramic view of Haverstraw Bay, prehistoric shell middens, and exposures of Manhattan Schist.

From the intersection go right and cross a small wooden bridge. The trail ascends to the top of the cliff for an exciting walk to another rock promontory with another superb view. On the right is Pearlman's Harbor and Sundance Point. The trail continues to ascend to a parking area. The entire length of the trail from the boundary of the park to the parking area is less than a mile and a half.

To hike to Sundance or Dugan Point, follow the road all the way to the end, another 0.3 miles, to a second large parking area, where there is a swimless beach at Shasta Cove, restrooms, a boat launch, shelter, and a picnic area. From here a short trail leads to Sundance Point, which separates Shasta Cove from Pearlman's Harbor, where the boat launch is located. There are fine views of the Hudson and Haverstraw Bay, the Hudson Highlands to the north, the village of Haverstraw and High Tor across the river, and south toward Croton Point and Hook Mountain.

From the north side of the parking area, the Whoopee Lake Trail goes north for a half mile, skirting wetlands and Whoopee Lake. It continues for three-quarters of a mile, around neighboring forested uplands and past JK Pond, climbs up a small rise, and becomes the Dugan Point Trail, which continues another half mile through the forest and ends at a secluded beach on Dugan Point, with a prehistoric oyster-shell midden located nearby.

From the George's Island Park parking area, go one-half mile and make a left onto Sunset Road. Continue north 0.9 miles to Kings Ferry Road. Go left on Kings Ferry Road 0.3 miles to a causeway separating Lake Meahagh on the right and the Hudson on the left. You've reached the small community of Verplanck.

Verplanck's Point was called Merchagh by the Native Americans. Henry Hudson supposedly anchored here and got into a skirmish with them, in which one was killed and another drowned. The land was purchased in 1683 by Stephanus van Cortlandt, who named it after his granddaughter's husband, Philip Verplanck. It was the eastern terminus of the King's Ferry, an important east-west communication and transportation link. It had great strategic value during the Revolutionary War, linking New England with the rest of the colonies, and was contested by both the English and American sides. To protect this link the Americans built Fort Lafayette here. Together with Stony Point across the river, the two forts guarded the narrowest section of the river south of the Hudson Highlands. Both forts fell to the British, led by Gen. Henry Clinton, on July 1, 1779. Two weeks later American troops under General Wayne recaptured Stony Point but failed to recapture Fort Lafayette. In October of the same year the British abandoned the fort and it was reoccupied by the Americans. In 1782 General Washington camped here and reviewed American and French troops led by Count Rochambeau. A large military banquet was also held.

The Cortlandt Heritage Museum is in the old town hall, which also used to serve as a jail. It is located at 137 Seventh Street. It is open on the second Saturday and third Sunday of the month, from 1:00 to 3:00 P.M.

From the causeway continue north on Sixth Street, 0.4 mile to Broadway. Go right on Broadway. After 0.9 miles enter the village of Buchanan. On the left, 0.3 miles beyond, is the main entrance to Indian Point. Indian Point is the site of a large ninety-million-dollar nuclear reactor and steam- and electricity-generating plant, owned and operated by Consolidated Edison, completed in 1963 and expanded in 1978. Conservationists have long been concerned about the potential threat nuclear reactors pose to the environment and people's health. They've also been anxious about the impact on fish and wildlife of warm water being returned to the Hudson. In 1963 large numbers of striped bass fingerlings were sucked into the water intake system and killed. The plant also sits right atop the Ramapo fault line, another potential hazard. Indian Point was once the site of a popular 320-acre park, owned and operated by the Hudson River Dayline.

Continue north another 0.7 mile, passing Lents Cove Park on the left. There are restrooms there. The road crosses Lents Cove and continues north 0.3 miles through the Charles Point Business Park with the Charles Point Power Plant on the left. Just beyond, the Charles Point Pier Park, a city of Peekskill park, is on the left; it has fine views of Peekskill Bay and the Hudson Highlands. Right past the entrance to the park there's a light. Make another right onto Louisa Road, and cross the New York Central railroad tracks. After 0.3 mile, make a left onto South Street and continue north into the city of Peekskill.

Peekskill was named Appamaghpogh by the Kitchawong who lived here. In 1655 the Dutch government granted it as the Ryck Patent, an enclave later surrounded by the Van Cortlandt Patent. Jan Peek, a Dutch trader, ran his boat aground in Annsville Creek and later started a settlement there in 1697. During the Revolutionary War a small American fort was located just north of the mouth of Annsville Creek. A Tory spy, Edward Palmer, was captured in Peekskill and despite British pleas for clemency, was hanged on nearby Gallows Hill.

Peekskill was incorporated as a village in 1816 and as a city in 1940. Iron foundries used to line the waterfront. It is the location of the Fleischman's Distillery and Yeast plant, the largest such factory in the world. T. Coraghessan Boyle, the author of numerous acclaimed satires, such as *World's End*, grew up there, and it was the birthplace of Australian actor Mel Gibson. Like other cities along the river, Peekskill experienced a long period of decline in the twentieth century as industries and the community's more affluent residents moved to newer suburbs. Businesses abandoned the downtown area for shopping malls on the outskirts of town. Today it is seeing a resurgence as home to a thriving artistic community. The resulting gentrification has brought an influx of art galleries and upscale restaurants and shops into Peekskill's downtown area, centered around Jan Peek Square. Many Peekskill artists open their downtown studios and lofts to visitors on the third Saturday of the month. For information call the chamber of commerce.

Peekskill has an impressive waterfront park called Riverfront Green, located next to the Metro-North train station. There are outstanding views of Peekskill Bay and the southern entrance to the Hudson Highlands in the distance. The park is currently expanding onto three and a half acres of former industrial land purchased by Scenic Hudson in 1998. This land may eventually include a riverfront walk, a canoe/kayak launch, a wooden-boatbuilding center, and a maritime history museum. For information about special events, call 914-724-PARK. The Peekskill Museum, located at 124 Union Avenue, a shingle-style Victorian, was built in 1877, designed by William Mead, who later helped found the prestigious McKim, Mead & White architectural firm. The house is currently being restored and contains an eclectic collection of clothing, furnishings, decorative arts, tools, industrial products, and other Peekskill artifacts. It is open from 2:00 to 4:00 P.M., Saturdays, Sundays, and holidays, from March through December. Call 914-737-6130 for information.

The Metro-North train station has express service. Peekskill also has bus service via Bee-Line Transit. For information about sites, dining, shopping, special events, and lodging, contact the Peekskill/Cortlandt Chamber of Commerce, 914-737-3600, or stop in at the Visitors' Center at 1 South Division Street, next to Jan Peek Square.

From the corner of Louisa and South Street, go north 0.4 miles, passing the entrance to the Peekskill train station on the left, also the entrance to Riverfront Green. Continue another 0.2 miles and make a right on Hudson Street. Go east underneath a Route 9 overpass and make an immediate left onto South Street. South Street climbs a hill with views of Peekskill Bay on the left and continues east 0.6 miles to Division Street. Go left on Division one block to Jan Peek Square in the heart of Peekskill's bustling downtown section. The tourist information center is on the right.

9 Hudson Highlands West

STONY POINT TO CORNWALL

The Hudson River cuts through the billion-year-old granites and gneiss of the Appalachian Mountain Chain in a deep narrow gorge fifteen miles long. Many believe that the gorge and the mountains surrounding it, known as the Hudson Highlands, are the most spectacular section of the river. Whether you agree or not, this relatively small section has a lot to offer the visitor. Much of the land is state owned and open to the public. There is a dense network of excellent scenic trails that are among the best in the entire book. Among them the famous Appalachian Trail and the new Highlands Trail cross through the Highlands here. Because of the ruggedness of the terrain, many of the trails are physically challenging, but there are easy ones as well. Many spots offer dramatic aerial views of some of the Hudson's most magnificent landmarks. Also there are superb walks through tranquil forests with opportunities to observe plant and animal life. Iona Island Sanctuary is one of the Hudson's richest marshlands and an excellent site for bird-watching; the rare bald eagle has been sighted. Routes 9W and 218 offer the privilege of bicycling in spectacular settings. The New York/New Jersey Trail Conference map sets *Harriman/Bear Mountain Trails* and *West Hudson Trails* are useful when hiking this section.

One of the primary features of this area is Bear Mountain/Harriman Park, by far the largest park that borders the Hudson and the largest within a hundred miles of New York City. Comprising fifty-one thousand acres, it has more than two hundred miles of hiking trails. The park's varied topography, which includes steep mountains often with rocky faces, forests, deep valleys and gorges, open fields, bogs, and marshes, is a haven for a wide assortment of plant and animal life. Deciduous trees include oaks, maples, hickories, ashes, tulip trees, beeches, tamaracks, and sweet and sour gums. Evergreens include cedars, pitch pines, hemlocks, balsams, and white pines. Mountain laurel, witch hazel, spice bush, wild azaleas, prickly pear cactus, and blueberries are among the common shrubs and groundcover. Deer, foxes, muskrat, squirrels, chipmunks, various snakes including rattlesnakes and copperheads, and five-lined skinks—a lizard—and box and painted turtles are among the plentiful wildlife. Two hundred and fifty species of birds have been reported, including turkey vultures, various hawk species, ruffed grouse, wild turkeys, cuckoos, owls, hummingbirds, several woodpecker species, several varieties of flycatchers, wrens, thrushes, gnatcatchers, vireos, and wrens.

Bear Mountain/Harriman Park is jointly managed by the Palisades Interstate Park Commission. Edward H. Harriman, the railroad magnate, and George W. Perkins, then president of the Palisades Interstate Park Commission, proposed the development of a park in the Hudson Highlands. In 1908 the state purchased the land around Bear Mountain to build a prison, and convicts were, in fact, transported there to begin clearing the site. There was a great public outcry from those opposed to this use of the site. In 1910 Mary A. Harriman (the widow of Edward Harriman), donated ten thousand acres of nearby land to become Harriman Park, stipulating that the prison project be abandoned. Later this became part of the park as well. For information about Bear Mountain/Harriman State Park, call 914-786-2701.

Some rocks of the Hudson Highlands date back 1.2 billion years, making them by far the oldest in the region. Originally they were sedimentary rock deposited in seas. However, after being subjected to intense heat and pressure for hundreds of millions of years, the rocks were entirely transformed into gneiss and granite, the hard crystalline rocks we see today. The Storm King Granite is the youngest and hardest rock in the Highlands, and forms the crests of many of the Highlands' highest ridges and summits such as Storm King, Dunderberg, and Bear Mountain. Glaciers smoothed the rugged features of the Highlands, and glacial striations (scratches), can be seen on some exposed surfaces in the area.

With little arable land, the Highlands remained largely undeveloped long after other parts of the region were fully settled. Highlands forests were a great source of fuel for the Hudson region's growing industries and population, and at some point in the nineteenth century, the last stands of virgin forest were cleared. Much of what is seen today is second- or third-generation growth.

The Highlands was an area of great strategic importance during the

Revolutionary War. Because of the river's narrowness here and the rugged terrain, the patriot side fortified this section of the river to counter the threat of a British invasion. Forts Clinton and Montgomery (located north and south of the present-day Bear Mountain Bridge) were the primary components of this defense system. These forts were garrisoned by militia troops led by Governor Clinton and his brother, James. An iron chain was stretched across the river here to block the passage of British warships. In their failed attempt to control the Hudson and divide the colonies, British general John Burgoyne and his army were trapped near Saratoga. Hoping to create a diversion that might free Burgoyne, British general Henry Clinton sent a large force up the Hudson. Under the cover of fog, two thousand British and Hessian troops landed at Stony Point on the morning of October 6, 1777. Guided by Beverly Robinson, a Tory landowner, the British followed an overland route through the mountains, arriving at the twin forts by midafternoon. Outnumbered and unprepared for a land-based assault, the two American forts capitulated after a fierce fight. More than three hundred American militia were killed, wounded, or captured in the disaster. The iron chain was dismantled by the British and later used to guard the harbor at Gibraltar. Governor Clinton and his brother, James, both managed to escape, James reputedly sliding down the steep slope to the river to boats waiting below.

Following the British withdrawal, the Hudson Highlands were refortified by the Americans. West Point became the site of America's strongest fortress during the war; the British never challenged its supremacy. Following the war it became America's military academy. Easy access from New York City by steamboat and later via the railroads, as well as historic sites and spectacular scenery, attracted visitors. The wealthy built opulent mansions along the river here. Later, city dwellers came in search of fresh air and a refuge from the city and seeking cures for various maladies. Today the Highlands are still a popular destination for city dwellers. The Bear Mountain Trailside Museum and Zoo is one of the best exhibits on the Hudson River area's history and natural history. Also be sure to visit the Museum of the Hudson Highlands in Cornwall.

Shortline provides regular daily bus service from the Port Authority Terminal in Manhattan to Tompkins Cove, Bear Mountain, Fort Montgomery, Highland Falls, and West Point. There's also daily service to Cornwall. For information about fares and schedules, call 1-800-631-8405, extension 111. Metro-North provides limited warm-weather train service on weekends to Manitou, just north of the Bear Mountain Bridge on the east side of the river. For information call 1-800-METRO-INFO. There's also weekend ferry service from Peekskill to Bear Mountain and

West Point. For information call 914-365-1964. For information about accommodations and dining, call Orange County Tourism, 914-294-5151, extension 1647.

The Route

STONY POINT TO JONES POINT

This two-and-a-half-mile-long segment, which is almost entirely on Route 9W, brings one to the southern boundary of Bear Mountain/Harriman Park. There are numerous hiking possibilities in the park, as well as many views of the river along the way.

From the intersection leading into Stony Point Battlefield State Historic Site, go right 0.2 miles, climbing up through a ravine to Route 9W. Go right and continue north on 9W 1.2 miles to Tompkins Cove. Tompkins Cove has a small area of Paleozoic dolomite and shale, similar to rocks north of the Hudson Highlands—the only occurrence of these rocks south of the Highlands on this side of the river. (A large quarrying operation just north of Stony Point is extracting the dolomite.) Continue north another 0.7 miles, passing an open view of the river on the right and a parking area. The view is marred somewhat by the Con Ed Indian Point Nuclear Plant, which looms right across the river. For the next half mile the road makes a gradual descent, passing the trailhead for the 1777 Trail on the left, with triple red-on-white markings, just before reaching the base of the hill (see below for a description).

Route 9W ascends again and after another half mile passes, on the right, an anchor monument with a plaque dedicated to the 189 World War II cargo and passenger ships that rested here from 1946 to 1971 as the Hudson River National Defense Reserve Fleet, storing grain as a floating silo. There's another open view of the river here, also dominated by the Indian Point plant.

Some 0.3 miles farther up 9W is the intersection leading to Jones Point, named for the Jones family, who first settled here in 1692. Make a right and continue about a quarter mile into this quiet riverfront community of modest homes. There is parking here, and it is an excellent place from which to hike into Bear Mountain/Harriman Park.

HIKING TRAILS FROM JONES POINT

The Ramapo-Dunderberg Trail, which extends more than twenty miles from Jones Point to Tuxedo, can be hiked one way to the summits of Dunderberg and Bald Mountains, which have views. Returning via the

1777 Trail to Jones Point (three and a half miles), will take at least a half day, covers a distance of about five miles, and some steep ascents and descents, and can be rather strenuous.

From Jones Point go west on the Ramapo-Dunderberg Trail, marked with a red circle on white blazes, crossing 9W and beginning a gradual ascent of the east face of Dunderberg Mountain, which is more than a thousand feet high. In 1889 a scheme was developed to build a palatial hotel, which was to be served by a pair of inclined railways, on top of the mountain. Grading for the railways was begun in 1890, but the project fell through a year later. Remnants of the railroad grade are still present, and the trail crosses them several times.

The thousand-foot climb up the rocky east face of Dunderberg Mountain is steep and unrelenting, with only occasional partial views of the river through the trees, looking east toward Peekskill and Anthony's Nose. As you approach the first of four summits, the trail begins to mellow. Descend briefly, and then climb to a second, taller summit with a limited view. Descend again, and follow the ridge, with brief ascents and descents but basically staying fairly high along the ridge. After two to three hours and two and a half miles, you'll reach the intersection with the blue-marked Cornell Trail, heading north. This trail can be followed to 9W opposite Iona Marsh and then returning to Jones Point for a strenuous but rewarding journey (see below for a description of the Cornell Trail).

The Ramapo-Dunderberg Trail continues west a short distance to the open summit of Bald Mountain with an excellent view of the Hudson Highlands Gorge looking north toward Iona Marsh and Island, Bear Mountain, Anthony's Nose, the Bear Mountain Bridge, and so on. Nearby is the old Cornell Mine, one of several nineteenth-century iron mines in the area. Remnants of pits, trenches, and a shaft are still present. In the late nineteenth century the famous inventor Thomas Alva Edison attempted to revive iron mining in the area through new techniques of separating the ore, which he developed. He purchased a large tract of land on the north slope of Dunderberg and Bald Mountains but was never able to get his iron mine to produce much ore. Descend three-quarters of a mile west to the low point between Bald Mountain and the Timp (just west), to the intersection of the 1777 Trail. The forest in the gap is very open, with few shrubs and plenty of grass. On October 6, 1777, this gap was undefended, allowing two thousand British and Hessian troops an easy passage on their way to their surprise attack on the two American forts, Fort Clinton and Fort Montgomery. (The 1777 Trail was created as part of the Bicentennial celebration with the help of the Palisades

FORT MONTGOMERY

HUDSON RIVER

Popolopen Torne

Timp Torne Trail (b)

Popolopen Gorge Trail (r)

Popolopen Brook

Palisades Pkwy

Major Welch Trail (r)

Conrail

Bear Mountain Bridge

museum & zoo

Perkins Memorial Dr.

BEAR MOUNTAIN

Hessian Lake

Bear Mountain Dock

Perkins Memorial Tower

Appalachian Trail (w)

Bear Mountain Inn

Doodletown Bight

ORANGE COUNTY
ROCKLAND COUNTY

Seven Lakes Dr

Iona Island

Iona Marsh

Suffern-Bear Mountain Trail (y)

Salisbury Meadow

1777 Trail (r)

Cornell Mine Trail (b)

Jones Point Path

Doodletown Lake

BEAR MOUNTAIN/ HARRIMAN STATE PARK

9W

WEST MOUNTAIN

DUNDERBERG MOUNTAIN

Ramapo-Dunderberg Trail (r)

JONES POINT

BALD MOUNTAIN

The Timp Brook

Shelter

Timp Torne Trail (w)

Anchor Monument

Timp Torne Trail (b)

1777 Trail (r)

THE TIMP

HUDSON RIVER

9W

approximately 1 mile

Interstate Park Commission and the Boy Scouts. For the most part it follows the route of British and Hessian troops.)

Go left on the 1777 Trail, marked with red blazes inside a white diamond. The trail veers left, then right, descends rather steeply, and crosses a talus slope. The trail gently zigzags down, then levels, passing some private homes on the right, just outside the park boundary.

The trail bends to the right and continues to descend, crossing an old roadway and descending more steeply; then sharply left, descending more gradually to a wooden bridge over a seasonal brook. Then the trail veers left, south, crosses a ravine, and follows the edge of the ravine through thick stands of mountain laurel. It crosses an old railroad grade, then narrows and descends steps down to 9W and the trailhead. (To follow this trail as the British and Hessian troops did in 1777, one would have to go in the opposite direction.) To return to Jones Point, go left, north, up 9W, 0.8 miles.

JONES POINT TO BEAR MOUNTAIN

A bikers' and walkers' route of 2.5 miles on an old dirt-road trail and on 9W, with a possible side trip to the Bear Mountain Dock. There are also views of Iona Island and Marsh and access to hiking trails in Bear Mountain/Harriman State Park.

From the north end of the hamlet, the 1.91-mile-long Jones Point Path begins. Part of the Hudson River Greenway Trail, it traverses a section of Bear Mountain/Harriman Park. There are barriers at both ends to prevent vehicular use. The smooth dirt path is shaded the entire way and is popular with both walkers and bicyclists. From one end to the other should take approximately one hour to walk. This trail is ideal for walkers as part of a loop that includes either the 1777 Trail or the Ramapo-Dunderberg Trail, as well as the Cornell Trail. Allow a whole day, though, for any of the above excursions. There are no open views along the trail, but during the last mile, partial glimpses of the river and Iona Marsh and Island add to the pleasure.

The trail ends on 9W across from Iona Marsh and Island. Beautiful two-hundred-acre Iona Marsh, also known as Salisbury Meadows, lies between the west bank of the Hudson River and Iona Island in what may once have been the main channel of the river. It is a brackish tidal marsh and has dry hummocks at low tide. The marsh began to form some six thousand years ago, though construction of the West Shore Railroad in the late nineteenth century provided a barrier that hastened the deposit of sediment that creates and sustains the marsh. Shallow tidal creeks meander through the marsh, and large areas of mudflats are exposed at low tide. Narrowleaf cattails predominate in the intertidal areas; there are also small stands of purple loosestrife along the causeway, and extensive patches of exotic reeds. Swamp rose mallow, iris, water chestnut, water celery, and Eurasian water milfoil are some of the other aquatic plants that occur here. A few saltwater cordgrasses manage to survive, in what is their northernmost outpost along the river. Elm, willow, ash, and red maple occur along the edges of the marsh and where tidal flow is more restricted.

The marsh is an important feeding site and incubation center for a variety of marine life: killifish, grass shrimp, barnacles, blue crabs, and occasionally fiddler crabs. It is also a significant bird feeding and nesting site. Cormorants, nesting herons, bitterns, geese, ducks, rails, swans, gulls, terns, swamp sparrows, common nighthawks, willow flycatchers, yellowthroats, belted kingfishers, swallows, marsh wrens, turkey vultures, overwintering rough-legged hawks, and bald eagles and golden eagles are just some of the species that may be seen here. (Iona Marsh is one of the best sites along the Hudson to see eagles.) Muskrats, turtles, and frogs also inhabit the marsh. The marsh was acquired in 1915 by the Palisades Interstate Park Commission, which today manages it as a bird sanctuary. There are excellent views of the marsh from 9W and along the causeway that links Iona Island with the mainland, 0.3 miles from the north end of the Jones Point Path. The marsh is also part of the Hudson River National Estuarine Research Reserve and is a designated National Natural Landmark.

East of the marsh is 118-acre Iona Island, owned by the Palisades Interstate Park Commission, which maintains research and educational facilities there. The island is connected to the mainland by a causeway. Except for the causeway Iona Island is, for the most part, not open to the public. The West Shore Railroad cuts across the island. Archaeologists have recovered a number of Woodland Age artifacts from a couple of rock shelters on the island, including nearly complete ceramic pots now on display in the Trailside Museum and Zoo. During the mid-nineteenth century the noted horticulturist W. C. Grant began extensive vineyards and orchards here, producing the famous Iona grape, for which the island was named. At the time it was a major source of grape production in the United States. In the 1870s the island was a popular resort served by excursion steamers from New York City and ferries from Peekskill; it also had train service. Between 1900 and 1945, it served as a U.S. naval arsenal and supply depot. In 1964 it was the first headquarters of the Hudson Valley Commission, established by Governor Nelson A. Rockefeller. In 1965 the island was acquired by the Palisades Interstate Park Commission, becoming part of Bear Mountain/Harriman Park. The island is especially noteworthy in that the sea breeze is reputed to reach here—its northernmost extent on the river—warming the island's vege- tation. The spring season begins here two weeks earlier than it does in Newburgh, only fourteen miles to the north.

About 0.3 miles north of the causeway entrance, cross a small bridge over lovely Doodletown Creek. The blue-marked Cornell Trail enters the roadway here. Plenty of parking is available—rarely full—along both sides of 9W. From here the Cornell Trail continues south to the summit of Bald Mountain, or north about three-quarters of a mile, to the parking area by the Bear Mountain Inn.

Continue to follow 9W north; 0.2 miles past the Iona Marsh cause- way a road on the right leads to a parking area and short trail through a tunnel underneath the railroad tracks, to the Bear Mountain Dock. This dock for excursion boats also has a small landscaped area ideal for picnicking, fishing, and other leisure activities. The main attraction is the wonderful view of the river in all directions, especially of the Bear Mountain Bridge, Anthony's Nose, and other features.

Just beyond, a clearly marked road on the left leads to the main en- trance to Bear Mountain/Harriman Park. There is a huge parking lot and a parking fee. The lawn area around the parking lot is very popular and crowded on summer weekends, with picnickers and others pursuing var- ious recreational activities. North of the parking area is the rustic Bear Mountain Inn, built in 1922. The inn has restrooms, snack machines, a snack bar and restaurant, and overnight lodging. Call 914-786-2731 for information.

FIVE EXCITING HIKES FROM THE BEAR MOUNTAIN INN

Some of the best hikes in Bear Mountain/Harriman (especially those with Hudson River views) start from the Bear Mountain Inn. Most are relatively strenuous and involve steep climbing in rocky terrain. The one exception is the short excursion to the Trailside Museum and Zoo. Most of this segment follows the famous Appalachian Trail, probably one of its busiest and most popular sections, as well as the 1777 Trail.

Much of the Trailside Museum and Zoo covers the site of Fort Clin- ton, a former Revolutionary War fort. To get there go north of the park- ing area and Bear Mountain Inn, east of picturesque Hessian Lake, called Lake Sinnepink by the Native Americans. It's reputed to have got- ten its present name from the corpses of Hessian soldiers allegedly tossed into it following the assault on the nearby Revolutionary War forts. Today it is an often-crowded recreation area for hordes of city dwellers and others. East of the lake the trail makes a sharp right turn and enters a tunnel underneath busy 9W. On the other side you'll pass Bear Mountain's famous giant, more-than-Olympic-size pool, which on hot days is always jammed and noisy. Just beyond, the trail splits. To the right it descends a short distance down to the Bear Mountain Dock, described above.

The left-hand trail immediately enters the Trailside Museum and Zoo, established in 1927. There's a small admission charge. Along the paved path there are natural history exhibits, a statue of Walt Whitman, and live animals, including bears, deer, wild turkeys, waterfowl, beaver, foxes, and coyotes (most are reputed to be crippled and unable to survive in the wild). The zoo also has a fine raptor collection, including a bald eagle, turkey vultures, red-tailed hawks, owls, and rare peregrine falcons. The first building on the right has exhibits on Hudson River ecology as well as live reptiles, amphibians, and fish. Various trees and shrubs along the path are labeled. There's a small wetland with ferns, jack-in-the-pulpits, and skunk cabbages. The Geology Trail has interpretive signs and leads to a superb view looking south of the river. There is also a small building devoted to geology, with a fine collection of locally collected minerals and a partial skeleton of an Ice Age mastodon excavated near Balmville, north of Newburgh.

One of the highlights of the Trailside Museum is the building dedicated to local history and archaeology. The artifacts and exhibits on prehistoric native life, which are by far the best specific to the Hudson region, include some complete Woodland Age ceramic pots as well as weapons and tools. There is also an excellent display on the two Revolutionary War forts, Clinton and Montgomery; nearby are the remnants of Fort Clinton's western redoubt.

From the Trailside Museum and Zoo, pedestrians may access the Bear Mountain Bridge. Built in 1924 to attract more visitors to the new Bear Mountain Park, it was the first automobile bridge across the Hudson and at the time, the longest suspension bridge in the world. It is 2,252 feet long, and the central span is 1,632 feet. The success of the bridge's design led to the construction of other, longer suspension bridges such as the George Washington Bridge and the Golden Gate. There are pedestrian walkways on both the north and south sides of the bridge, with terrific views of the Hudson and the Highlands Gorge looking in both directions. The Appalachian Trail crosses the Hudson here, the lowest point in its entire 2,155-mile length.

An excellent but strenuous eight-mile loop hike originating from the Bear Mountain parking area takes the Cornell Trail up nine hundred feet to the summit of Bald Mountain. One can return via the 1777 Trail described above. This walk can be accomplished in a half day by those who are physically fit, but it's not a bad idea to stretch it out and make it a full day.

From the parking lot south of the Bear Mountain Inn, proceed south on a blue-marked trail, crossing underneath the Seven Lakes Drive through a tunnel. At this point the Cornell Trail is also a cross-country ski trail and the 1777 Trail. After approximately one-half mile, the Cornell Trail veers left and downhill to 9W, where there is parking and views of Iona Marsh and Island (see above for description). The trail climbs steeply back to the right and continues south about an hour, the elevation rising very gradually to four hundred feet. The final half mile, the trail rises steeply more than five hundred feet to an intersection with the Ramapo-Dunderberg Trail, marked red on white. Go right, one-eighth of a mile, to the open summit view looking north (described above).

To return via the 1777 Trail, follow the Ramapo-Dunderberg Trail west three-quarters of a mile as it descends into the gap between Bald Mountain and the Timp (see above for a description). Here you will intersect the 1777 Trail (described above), marked with red dots on white triangles. The 1777 Trail continues north, descending past stands of mountain laurel and groves of hemlocks, and passing an embankment on the left, thickly covered with ferns, and the unmarked Timp Pass Road. The 1777 Trail crosses a cross-country ski trail and continues through a gorgeous landscape of meadows, ferns, trees, and ruins along Timp Brook. The trail passes a stone shelter on the right, then crosses the stream, and follows a relatively level dirt road, passing an open field on the left. About a mile and a half north of the gap, the 1777 Trail splits. In 1777 there was a small skirmish here between British and American forces. The British forces divided, half proceeding west around the backside of Bear Mountain to attack Fort Montgomery, the rest continuing north on their way to Fort Clinton.

The site where the trail splits was also the location of the onetime small community of Doodletown, based on a corruption of the Dutch words for "dead valley," supposedly for the number of dead trees in the vicinity. First settled in 1776 by French Huguenots, it later supported a population of woodcutters who provided timber for nearby shipyards and brickworks until the forests were depleted. By 1945 approximately a hundred people resided here, primarily employed at Iona Island or by the Palisades Interstate Park Commission. Incorporated into the park, the community was vacated, and except for some foundations, driveways, and the presence of ornamental trees and shrubs, much of the town has returned to a more natural state.

An unmarked roadway on the right leads to the town's cemetery. The roadway turns asphalt and crosses another cross-country ski trail. The

1777 East Trail intersects the Doodletown Road and another ski trail, and veers right, east. At the next intersection, a short distance away, the trail turns left, north, and immediately crosses a bridge over a stream and passes a lovely reservoir on the right, a perfect picnic spot. Just beyond, pass another intersection and go straight, north. The 1777 Trail branches off to the left, and an unmarked trail continues straight, crossing the blue-marked Cornell Trail, and going right, then descending to 9W opposite Iona Marsh.

The 1777 Trail continues north, intersecting the blue-marked Cornell Trail about a half mile north of the reservoir. The 1777 Trail continues north another quarter mile, crossing the Seven Lakes Drive and finally reaching the parking area just south of the Bear Mountain Inn.

A longer and more strenuous eight-to-ten-mile loop hike includes West Mountain, the Timp, and Bald Mountain. A somewhat shorter version, skipping Bald Mountain and returning via the 1777 Trail, is another possibility. What makes this daylong venture worthwhile is the incredible stretches of forest one travels, as well as the spectacular views from the Timp and from West and Bald Mountains.

From the main parking area at Bear Mountain, just south of the playing field, head west uphill on the wide but steep path with white and yellow markers. This is part of the Appalachian Trail and the Suffern-Bear Mountain Trail. This first part can be quite excruciating if you're out of shape or you're running to catch up with the group you just missed. After one-half mile the Appalachian Trail veers to the right. Continue left on the Suffern-Bear Mountain Trail, blazed yellow. After another half mile, cross Seven Lakes Drive and continue southwest. One mile past Seven Lakes Drive brings you to Doodletown Road, just a woods path. The abandoned community of Doodletown is nearby (see above for a description).

The yellow-marked trail crosses the 1777 West Trail, where one column of British and Hessian troops headed west and north in their surprise assault on Fort Montgomery. The yellow-marked trail continues south, climbing the north side of West Mountain. There's a steep, rocky section before the trail levels off near the summit plateau. Observe the open meadows and forest-fire damage. The trail then intersects with the Timp-Torne Trail, marked blue. Go left on the blue-marked trail. A very short hike from here will bring you to a stone shelter with a panoramic view looking south of Haverstraw Bay, High Tor, and the northern Palisades; the Timp to the left; and on particularly clear days, one can see Manhattan skyscrapers directly south in the distance. There are even more views a short way up the trail. The shelter is a perfect resting and picnicking spot.

The Timp-Torne Trail continues east, descending into a steep col, or gap, between West Mountain and the Timp called Timp Pass. Next it climbs to the imposing red granite face of the Timp, with an excellent view looking west just above the cliff. This is a very popular viewpoint and is likely to be crowded. The trail continues southeast a short way and crosses the red-on-white-marked Ramapo-Dunderberg Trail. Go left on this new trail as it descends northeast into the gentle col between the Timp and Dunderberg Mountain. At the base of the col, the trail crosses the 1777 Trail again. You could exit north here, following the description above, or you could hike east and north to the summit of Bald Mountain and return via the Cornell Trail. This section of the Ramapo-Dunderberg Trail and the Cornell Trail is described above.

A shorter half-day but still very strenuous and steep five-to-six mile loop follows part of the Appalachian Trail to the summit of Bear Mountain, which has wonderful views. Incidently, this section of the Appalachian Trail is part of the twenty-one-mile segment from Bear Mountain to Arden that was constructed in 1923, the very first section of the trail to be built. You may have to use your hands to scramble in a few steep rocky sections of this loop. Because of relatively easy automobile access via Perkins Drive, the summit can be overflowing with humanity on a nice weekend day. There are other more secluded views, however, and some areas may be relatively peaceful. Bear Mountain may have been named after the bears that were once very common in the area. Today they're absent, though it's always possible that at some point, if we leave them alone, they might recolonize the area. Another possible origin of the name is a corruption of "bare mountain," referring to its bald summit.

One begins this loop on the Appalachian Trail from the parking lot by the playing field south of the Bear Mountain Inn. Follow the yellow-and-white-marked trail. The first half mile is described above. From where the Suffern–Bear Mountain Trail branches to the left, stay on the white-marked Appalachian Trail, cross a ravine, and after twenty to twenty-five minutes of steady uphill climbing, you'll reach a meadow and just beyond, the first partial view. The trail levels among stands of pitch pine and white pine and a view of West Mountain, Bald Mountain, and the Timp. Cross underneath power lines. Reach a dirt road, and make a right, following white markers to a parking area. Then follow the paved road north. A short distance beyond, there's a classic panoramic view of the Hudson looking south including Dunderberg and Bald Mountains, Iona Island and Marsh, and Peekskill in the distance.

The trail leaves the roadway to the left and climbs a hill to another viewpoint and then reaches a second road. Cross the road and continue west, mostly level, through a very open forest setting with abundant huckleberries and a picnic area. Cross the road again, and five minutes later reach a paved path and the 1,305-foot summit with Perkins Tower and a large parking lot. Perkins Tower commemorates George Perkins, one of the founders of Harriman Park, and first president of the Palisades Interstate Park Commission. A water fountain and rest rooms are available at this spot. There's a spectacular view south of the tower, on smooth granite boulders, of West Mountain, the Timp, Bald Mountain, Dunderberg, and Haverstraw Bay and Manhattan in the distance.

To return, go north past the tower and across the parking lot till you encounter red markers: the Major Welch Trail. The trail follows Perkins Drive east to a picnic area, where it makes a sharp left onto a dirt road just before the drive itself makes a sharp right turn. Cross the dirt road, and head into the forest. Beware of unmarked side trails. There are many huge rock outcrops. The trail descends very steeply on rocks through pitch pines, shrub oaks, and huckleberries; the footing is very questionable in places and may be treacherous when wet. There are open views looking north of Popolopen Torne, the Hudson River Gorge, Breakneck, Storm King, Garrison, West Point, and the Bear Mountain Bridge. The trail crosses Perkins Memorial Drive again (it shifts slightly west here; follow markers to the sign for the Bear Mountain Inn and descend from roadway). The trail continues its steep descent on rocks, reaching the base of the mountain with the echo of traffic from Route 6 reverberating through the forest. The trail bends to the right, levels, and continues east, then veers to the right again and continues south. It finally turns left and descends to the paved roadway around Hessian Lake. From the south end of the lake, continue south to the parking area and playing field.

Bear Mountain can also be climbed by bike by going west on the Seven Lakes Drive about three miles, then making a right turn onto Perkins Memorial Drive. This road winds its way to the summit and spectacular views. (For a description of the summit, see above).

The last loop, starting from the Bear Mountain parking lot, goes to the top of Popolopen Torne following Popolopen Brook and its spectacular gorge. It is approximately six to seven miles long and should take at least half a day. Most of the hiking is relatively easy except for the short but steep climb to the summit. Much of the first half of the hike follows the route the British and Hessian forces followed on their way to attack Fort Montgomery. It was also the route the American general "Mad" Anthony Wayne and his troops followed in 1779 on their march to attack the British fort at Stony Point.

The area of the gorge is notably rich in bird species as well as other wildlife. Hawks, ruffed grouse, woodcocks, pileated woodpeckers, flycatchers, swallows, wrens, gnatcatchers, vireos, warblers, orioles, and indigo buntings are among the many bird species you might spot through careful observation.

From the parking area, hike north past the Bear Mountain Inn and Hessian Lake on the left to 9W. Follow the shoulder of 9W north about a quarter of a mile to the traffic circle, and continue north on 9W. You'll soon cross a bridge over Popolopen Brook with a wide, open view of the Hudson and the Bear Mountain Bridge and Anthony's Nose across the river. Just beyond the bridge on the right is a historical marker indicating the nearby site of Revolutionary War Fort Montgomery.

At this point the blue-and-red-marked 1777 and 1779 Trails and the Timp-Torne Trail leave the roadway on the left. There's a large stone alongside the road marking this trail juncture. Follow the trail a short distance till it intersects a roadway. Follow the road and markers another short distance to where the trail enters the woods again. Several minutes later the trail intersects Mine Road. Go left, west, a short distance, till the trail leaves the road on the left-hand side. The trail continues west, following the fairly level route along the north side of Popolopen Brook's deep gorge. About a half hour later, the blue-marked Timp-Torne Trail leaves the main trail and heads north to the summit of Popolopen Torne. (Note: this intersection is easy to miss, so pay attention.) Hikers will have to scramble to the rocky bare summit, where there are excellent views in all directions. The Hudson River, Bear Mountain Bridge, and Anthony's Nose are particularly prominent to the east, as well as the view of Popolopen Gorge below. The peak has pitch pine, pear cactus, and other summit vegetation that's typical of the region. Among the fauna, I have observed five-lined skinks sunning themselves on the granite boulders.

Continue on the Timp-Torne Trail as it circles around to the west and south and makes a steep descent, soon rejoining the 1777 and 1779 Trails. The route then continues to descend into the gorge to an idyllic spot by the stream, where there's a wooden footbridge. Cross the bridge and continue southwest a short distance, ascending to an intersection with the red-marked Popolopen Gorge Trail. Go left here and head east, following the route of the old Bear Mountain Aqueduct. The trail makes a steep descent into the narrow, deep gorge, enshrouded with hemlocks, known as Hell Hole, named by West Point cadets who performed maneuvers here. The gorge has precipitous rock cliffs, and the stream tumbles over huge boulders, drowning out all noise from the nearby highway. This scene is reminiscent of wilderness sites in the Catskills and Adirondacks, and it's amazing to encounter it here so close to civilization.

About a mile east of the intersection, you'll reach lovely Roe Pond. There's a view of Popolopen Torne towering over the pond to the west. Below the dam that forms the pond, there's a series of small waterfalls as the stream continues to plunge east toward the Hudson. Less than a half mile past the pond, the trail ascends toward growing traffic noise and finally reaches 9W. From there one can return south to the Bear Mountain Inn parking area.

BEAR MOUNTAIN TO WEST POINT

A walkers' and bicyclists' route. This 7.1-mile segment is entirely on roads and goes through the villages of Fort Montgomery and Highland Falls and through the West Point Academy. The sites of West Point are the highlight of this section.

From the Bear Mountain Inn parking area, return to Route 9W. Go north about a quarter of a mile to the traffic circle. The Bear Mountain Bridge is just east of here, clearly visible. See above for description. Continue north crossing the bridge over Popolopen Gorge, also described above, and passing the site of former Fort Montgomery on the right.

The route continues north on 9W, passing through the small village of Fort Montgomery. At 1.7 miles north of the traffic circle, go right onto the Old State Route. About 0.7 miles later, you enter the village of Highland Falls, once called Buttermilk Falls, after the scenic falls located in the heart of town. It was officially incorporated as Highland Falls in 1906. In 1871 banker and railroad magnate John Pierpont Morgan purchased a home here called Cragston, which he used as a summer residence. Another 0.7 miles farther north, the road intersects Route 218, Main Street. There's a YIELD sign. Go right, bearing right again at the WEST POINT sign, 0.7 miles north of the last intersection. Enter the commercial district of Highland Falls. There's parking here and an information board on area businesses. Just beyond is Thayer Gate, the main entrance to the West Point Military Academy. On the right is the old campus of Ladycliffe College, which closed in 1980. Cozzens Hotel, once one of the most renowned resorts along the Hudson, was formerly located on this site. It could accommodate three hundred to five hundred guests and was famous for its lovely grounds overlooking the river. The Prince of Wales, later Edward VII, was one of the guests. Today the grounds are part of the West Point Academy.

West Point is the region's primary tourist attraction. It is the nation's first and most renowned military academy and the oldest continually occupied military post in the nation. The West Point campus includes three thousand acres of prime Hudson Highlands real estate. About four thou-

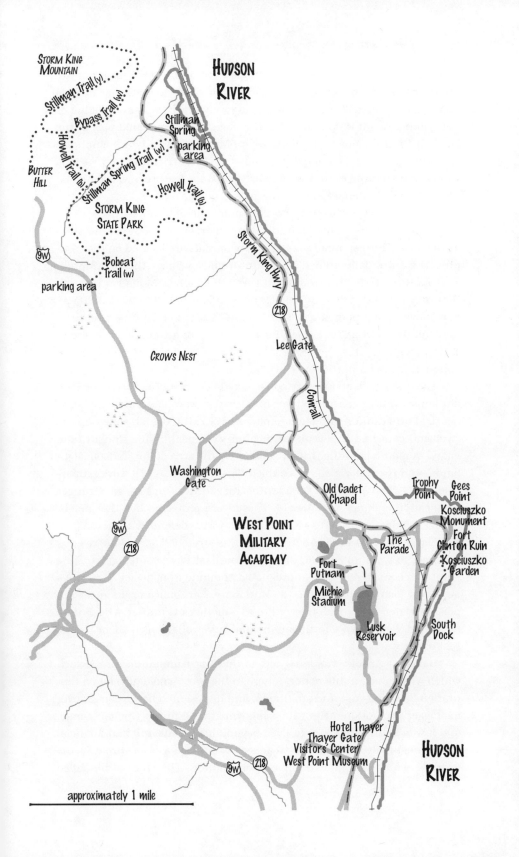

HUDSON
RIVER

STORM KING
MOUNTAIN

Stillman Trail (y)

Bypass Trail (w)

Howell Trail (b)

Stillman
Spring

parking
area

BUTTER
HILL

Stillman Spring Trail (w)

Howell Trail (b)

STORM KING
STATE PARK

9W

Bobcat
Trail (w)

parking area

Storm King Hwy

218

Lee Gate

Conrail

CROWS NEST

Washington
Gate

Old Cadet
Chapel

Trophy
Point

Gees
Point

Kosciuszko
Monument

9W

WEST POINT
MILITARY
ACADEMY

The
Parade

Fort
Clinton Ruin

Kosciuszko
Garden

218

Fort
Putnam

Michie
Stadium

Lusk
Reservoir

South
Dock

Hotel Thayer
Thayer Gate
Visitors' Center
West Point Museum

HUDSON
RIVER

approximately 1 mile

sand cadets attend here every year. Views of and from West Point are among the Hudson's most famous and have come to epitomize all this region has to offer. West Point is also a lovely place for easy strolling or bike riding. About 6.05 miles of paths have been designated part of the Hudson River Greenway Trail. At West Point there is a heavy emphasis on sports and physical activity in the school's curriculum and various games and sporting events are a nearly constant feature of weekend visits. Cadets will often greet you with a "sir" or "ma'am."

The West Point Museum, Fort Putnam, the old Cadet Chapel, Trophy Point, and the picnic grounds along the river are some of the main attractions. Thirteen monuments and memorials are located on the campus. There are daily guided bus tours from November through March, 11:15 A.M. to 1:15 P.M.; from April through October, Mondays through Saturdays, 10:00 A.M. to 3:30 P.M. and Sundays, 11:30 A.M. to 3:30 P.M. For information about tours call 914-446-4724. For all other information call 914-938-2638. Except for bus tours, all attractions are free to the public. Hours may be limited, however, so it's worth checking first if you plan to visit a particular site.

The first fortifications were constructed here in 1775, during the Revolutionary War to guard the river from British warships. After the fall of nearby Forts Clinton and Montgomery in 1777, the British sailed up the river and captured the weak fortifications on neighboring Constitution Island. A month later the British abandoned the area of the Hudson Highlands, and the Americans reoccupied West Point. In 1778 work, supervised by Polish patriot Tadeusz Kościuszko, was begun on stronger fortifications named Fort Arnold. These were protected by other neighboring fortifications such as Fort Putnam, which defended against a possible land-based assault. An iron chain was stretched across the river as a barrier to warships attempting to sneak past West Point's guns. West Point was considered to be impregnable, immune from attack. America's strongest fortress during the Revolutionary War, guarding its most important waterway, it was referred to as America's Gibraltar. The British respected West Point's fortifications and never challenged them for the rest of the war.

Benedict Arnold was assigned as the first commander of the fort, which was named in his honor. A hero in the war, Arnold also had a reputation for being vain and ambitious, and he resented being passed over for bigger promotions. His wife was sympathetic to the English cause, and it was known that Arnold lived beyond his means and had financial difficulties. Only through his treachery was there a brief threat to the fortress, which was later renamed Fort Clinton. The story of his failed attempt to turn the fortress over to the British is described in other sections of the book.

In 1793 George Washington suggested West Point as the site of a military academy. The following year thirty-two cadets were assigned to an artillery corps there. In 1802 Congress formally authorized the founding of a military academy. Maj. Sylvester Thayer was superintendent from 1817 to 1833. He was a strict disciplinarian and the rigorous program he developed helped make West Point a military school of the first order. Many of America's most famous generals, including Ulysses S. Grant and Robert E. Lee, Douglas MacArthur, George Patton, and Dwight Eisenhower, graduated from here.

The early nineteenth century, part of the romantic period, was also a time of intense nationalistic fervor. West Point, with its renowned military school, its importance during the Revolutionary War, and its spectacular setting, had much to offer visitors. The introduction of the steamship provided a very pleasant and comfortable three-and-a-half-hour excursion for those traveling up from New York City. For many European visitors, the Point was the first stop on the tour of America's scenic wonders. To accommodate such guests the Hotel Thayer was built on the grounds. Later the construction of Gothic-style buildings, with thick, locally quarried granite walls, towers, and embattlements, decorated with shields and other ornamentations, helped enhance West Point's image as a medieval fortress. Reviews on the parade grounds by the uniformed cadets, as well as concerts, fireworks, and sporting events, are some of the special activities that have attracted visitors here for nearly two centuries.

Begin at the Visitors' Center, 0.3 miles south of the Thayer Gate, on the right. It's a prominent building that's hard to miss; there's also ample parking. You can get information there, as well as maps, brochures, and tour tickets. Tours also begin here. The Visitors' Center has exhibits, videos, and a replica of a cadet dorm room as well as an enormous gift shop. Behind the Visitors' Center is the West Point Museum, certainly one of the best military museums in the Western Hemisphere. The museum has exhibits on military history from ancient Rome to Desert Storm, specializing in campaigns related to the U.S. Army. There's a superb collection of memorabilia, mostly weapons and uniforms, including Kościuszko's sword, George Washington's pistols, a British drum and cannon captured at the Battle of Saratoga, the metal casing of the "Fat Man" atomic bomb, a German army Eagle emblem captured and donated by General Patton, Sioux Indian arrows used in the Battle of the Little Big Horn, and the spacesuit of astronaut Frank Borman, a West Point graduate. There are some excellent dioramas of famous battle scenes. The history of West Point as a fortress and military academy is also featured, including a model of the infamous *Vulture*, the British warship on which Benedict Arnold escaped. The museum is open daily from 10:30 A.M. to 4:15 P.M. Admission is free.

From the Visitors' Center, follow the road north through the Thayer Gate. Continue north, passing the Hotel Thayer on the right. Just beyond it is an open view of the river with Sugarloaf and Castle Rock on the opposite shore. Just beyond, 0.2 miles from the Thayer Gate, there's a turnoff for Williams Road, which leads to the West Point South Dock and Depot. This is a worthwhile detour for bicyclists since it leads to a lovely picnic area right by the river, with excellent views. Walkers may use this as the main route. From the intersection to the picnic ground is less than a mile. Follow the road as it descends. Walkers may enjoy the wide sidewalk and nearly constant views of the river, including the village of Garrison, Castle Rock, and Sugarloaf. At the bottom of the hill, the road splits. Straight ahead is the old West Point train station. Go right and cross the tracks. Just beyond is the South Dock. According to different accounts, when fresh recruits would arrive by train, they had to run up this hill as their first reception to West Point. This was also a regular landing site for the Hudson River Dayline, and it still is for tour boats and ferries. Beyond the dock is a boat-launching area, and beyond that is the picnic area right next to the river, one of the most beautiful and popular picnic areas on the entire Hudson. The views of the river and the Highlands from here are amazing.

The picnic area continues north for some distance, finally ending in a loop just south of a small beach area. No swimming is allowed. Walkers can backtrack from here across the playing field to a ramp that ascends the cliff, passing a small waterfall. The ramp becomes steps and continues its steep ascent, reaching a lovely small alcove known as Kościuszko's Garden, reputed to be a favorite spot where he meditated on a regular basis. There's a fountain and grotto here. Flirtation Walk begins here on its three quarters of a mile descent to Gee's Point on the river. Unfortunately it is off limits to the public unless accompanied by a cadet.

Continue up the steps to a parking area behind Lincoln Hall. Go north through the parking area behind the building. North of the building the road ascends to Cullum Road, or you may climb steps beside the gas turbine lab. Go right on Cullum Road. A short distance to the right are the Kościuszko Monument, erected in 1828, and the remains of Fort Clinton.

Tadeusz Kościuszko (1746–1817) was born in Poland. He became a military student and was inspired by America's struggle for independence. At the age of thirty, he volunteered to help the American forces. He impressed General Washington, who assigned him as chief of the Engineer Corps and gave him the rank of colonel. Kościuszko supervised the construction of West Point's fortifications. After the Revolution, Kościuszko returned to his native Poland, where he was involved in a failed attempt to gain independence from Russia. Imprisoned, he was later released; in 1797 he returned to the United States with great fanfare and was awarded a gift of land by Washington.

Underneath the monument is the site of Fort Clinton; some of the surviving earthworks remain of this fortress, which was once the heart of the West Point fortifications. It was 1,800 feet around the perimeter, with fourteen-foot-high, twenty-one-foot-thick walls. It could be manned by up to seven hundred troops, and it had twelve cannon and eleven mortars, ready to destroy any enemy ship that should attempt to pass underneath. The fort was used until 1802.

There is a view from here of Constitution Marsh and Island, Dick's Castle, and Mount Taurus. Below is World's End—between Gee's Point and Constitution Island—at 216 feet the Hudson's deepest point, made infamous in the satirical novel *World's End* by T. Coraghessan Boyle about Hudson River life. During the Revolutionary War an iron chain was stretched from here to Constitution Island to block the passage of British warships. Thirteen of the original links can be seen on display at Trophy Point.

Constitution Island is opposite Gees Point. It was first garrisoned in 1775 and named Fort Constitution after the British Constitution. In 1777, it was easily captured by the British. In 1778, as part of the overall plan to strengthen West Point, an iron chain was stretched from here to Gees Point. Ruins of batteries and an old blockhouse where gunpowder was stored may still be observed there.

Henry Warner, a New York attorney, purchased the island in 1836 and, after the Panic of 1837, which ruined him, lived here in a 1774 farmhouse with his two spinster daughters, Susan and Anna, who rarely left the island, but became best-selling authors. The island was donated and added to West Point in 1908. Today it is accessible only by boat or canoe. The house, with original furnishings, Victorian garden, and fortifications is open to the public. There are tours via ferry from South Dock, Wednesdays and Thursdays, at 1:00 and 2:00 P.M. from June 20 through September 30. There's an admission fee. Call 914-446-8676 for information.

Bicyclists and walkers may also arrive at the Kościuszko Monument by going straight at the intersection for the South Dock, just past the Hotel Thayer. (This is Thayer Road.) From the intersection continue north, passing a long, open view of the river on your right. After a half mile the road splits. Go left, uphill, passing huge granite fortresslike buildings on the right. You've entered the main part of the campus, with cadet barracks on the left. About 0.3 miles later, the roadway ends at a large open grassy area known as the Plain, which serves as the academy's parade ground. General Baron von Steuben used this area to drill American troops during the Revolutionary War. Go right here, passing the library on the right. On the left is the Patton Monument, in memory of the famous World War II general. Just beyond, intersect Cullum Road. Go left, north, passing Cullum Hall on the right, designed by the firm of McKim, Mead, & White in 1896. The balcony of this building provides more excellent river views. South of the building, steps lead to Kościuszko's Garden and eventually down to the picnic ground and the South Dock. All are described above. Continue north, passing Lincoln Hall on the right, followed by the gas turbine lab. The top of the building is a bus shelter. Just beyond is the Kościuszko Monument and remains of Fort Clinton, 1.3 miles from the Thayer Gate.

From the Kościuszko Monument, continue west 0.2 miles to Trophy Point. This park area has some of West Point's most famous and memorable views, looking north toward Storm King, Breakneck, Cold Spring, Mount Taurus, Bannerman's Island, and Newburgh Bay. This was once the site of the West Point Hotel. There are cannon representing five major wars in which the United States has been involved. A thirteen-link section of the iron chain that stretched from Gees Point to Constitution Island during the Revolutionary War is on display here. The West Point Band plays in the amphitheater below. The most beautiful and prominent feature of Trophy Point is the Battle Monument. It was erected in memory of the 2,230 soldiers of the Regular Union Army killed in the Civil War. The tall, smooth pink shaft is the largest single section of granite in the Western Hemisphere. Atop it sits a statue of a winged angel, called *Fame.*

Continue west on Washington Road. On the left, you'll pass the Thayer Monument. Beyond it on the left are the residence of the superintendent and the commandant's quarters. At the next left, Miles Road (the Catholic Chapel is on the corner), you can detour to visit Fort Putnam. Follow the road uphill, passing the gymnasium on the left and the Cadet Chapel, probably the most impressive building on campus. Miles Road bends to the right as it reaches Lusk Reservoir. The American Soldier statue is on the right. Just beyond is a trail on the right that goes a short distance uphill to the fort, bearing left at the first intersection. Those on bikes may have to walk them.

Fort Putnam was built in 1778 as part of a series of fortifications to protect Fort Arnold, the main fortification, from a land-based assault. Fort Putnam, located five hundred feet above the river, was the largest and most critical of these fortifications. It was named for Colonel Ruthus Putnam, whose troops built the fort. Enlarged in 1794, the fort was restored in 1909 to its 1794 condition. Today it displays original casements (bombproof living quarters and storage), and walls, and reproductions of eighteenth-century artillery and mortars. There is a sweeping view of the West Point campus, the Cadet Chapel, the Plain, the river, Constitution Island and Marsh, and a view south of Anthony's Nose and Dunderberg. The McLean Historical Museum Building has maps and models explaining the history of the West Point fortifications. It is open Thursdays through Mondays from mid-May to mid-October, 10:00 A.M. to 3:00 P.M.

From the corner of Miles Road and Washington, continue west on Washington Road, less than half a mile to the Old Cadet Chapel on the right. Built in 1837, it was relocated in 1911 from its original site by the library. The chapel is in the Renaissance Revival style, with a Greek Doric portico. Inside is an oil by Robert Weir, entitled *Peace and War.* Black marble shields commemorate every American general in the Revolutionary War. The name of Benedict Arnold has been conspicuously omitted, leaving just his rank and birthdate. Today, the chapel is used for funeral services. It is open Mondays through Saturdays from 8:00 A.M. to 4:15 P.M.; and Sundays from noon to 4:15 P.M. The neighboring cemetery dates back to 1817 and includes graves of veterans of the Revolutionary War.

Just beyond the chapel on the right are a grave and monument dedicated to Margaret Corbin, the first woman to fight in the Revolutionary War. From the cemetery continue to follow Washington Road north 0.3 miles to the intersection with Lee Road. Go right on Lee Road through a beautiful residential area. There's a view of the river on the right after less than half a mile. From the intersection with Washington Road, it's 0.7 miles to Lee Gate, which is almost always closed. However walkers and bicyclists can easily bypass it on the left and continue out to Route 218 to exit the academy.

WEST POINT TO CORNWALL VIA THE STORM KING HIGHWAY

A bicyclists' and walkers' route, 4.1 miles.

The cliff-hugging Storm King Highway took almost twenty years of controversy and challenges to build, the formidable topography being only one of the difficulties. Actively supported by the Palisades Interstate Park Commission as a way to make its parklands more accessible to the public, the road was finally completed in 1922. Since the construction in

1940 of 9W made it obsolete as a north/south artery, and rock slides and snowfall keep it closed in wintertime. With long, steep ascents and descents, speeding traffic, many blind curves, little shoulder, and sheer cliffs, it is both strenuous and potentially treacherous particularly in wet weather. However, the extraordinary views make this a worthwhile ride for the experienced cyclist.

From the Lee Gate, go right, north, on the Storm King Highway (Route 218), 0.8 miles to an open view on the right of the river, of Mount Taurus and Breakneck Ridge. Huge granite cliffs tower above. The road descends and after another half mile brings you to a parking area; just beyond on the left are trailheads for the Howell and Stillman Spring Trails (see description below). Just north on the left is the Stillman Spring.

For the next half mile the road climbs, gradually at first and then more steeply, with views of the river and Highlands Gorge. A parking area is reached, with a panoramic view, from the top of a cliff more than four hundred feet above the Hudson, of the river itself, West Point to the south, Newburgh Bay to the north, Breakneck Ridge and Mount Taurus across the river. The island in the river, just north of Breakneck, is Bannerman's Island, also known as Pollepel Island. Native Americans reputedly believed the island was haunted. It is also believed to have been used by the Dutch as a dropoff for drunken sailors, giving them time to sober up before the voyage home. In 1777, during the Revolutionary War, the patriots, as part of their strategy for defending the river, stretched a chevaux-de-frise line between the island and Plum Point. However, the British, under Gen. John Vaughn, had little trouble bypassing this barrier and sailing upriver to burn Kingston. In 1900, Francis Bannerman (1851–1918), a wealthy New York arms dealer, purchased the island and built the huge Scottish-style castle, which was used as both a home and arsenal. Bannerman died before the castle was finished. In 1920 it was damaged by an explosion. In 1967 the family sold the island to the state and in 1969, the castle was destroyed in a fire. Today, the Hudson's most famous and spectacular ruin is part of Hudson Highlands State Park and remains the most impressive ruin along the river. It is accessible only by boat.

In addition to the highway, Storm King Mountain was the scene of another, better-known environmental controversy: a 1961 proposal by Consolidated Edison—the utility that supplies New York City and Westchester with electric power—to build a hydroelectric-pump-storage facility there that would be the largest privately owned one in the world. The proposed plant would pump six billion gallons of river water through a two-mile-long tunnel, uphill a thousand feet to an artificial storage reservoir, and release that same water downhill, during peak demand, to power a turbine generating electricity. Because of its access to the river and steep topography, Storm King Mountain was considered an ideal location for such a project.

After the proposal, a small group of citizens opposing the project formed the Scenic Hudson Preservation Conference. Hearings were held by the Federal Power Commission (FPC) in February 1964 to review Con Ed's permit application to build and operate the plant. Meanwhile the controversy was gaining national attention. Scenic Hudson launched a media campaign, and events were staged to generate publicity.

In March 1965 the FPC completed its review and decided to grant Con Ed the license. Later, in December, the Circuit Court of Appeals, recognizing Storm King's value as a scenic landmark, ruled that the FPC should give equal consideration to aesthetic and environmental concerns as to purely economic ones. It was the very first time an appeals court had rejected an FPC power plant license.

The FPC scheduled new hearings for November 1966. Among others, sport and commercial fishermen came out strongly against the proposed project. Concern over the effect the project might have on the striped bass population, which spawned at the foot of Storm King, led Robert Boyle to form the Hudson River Fishermen's Association (HRFA), which joined other environmental groups in a lawsuit against Con Ed.

In August 1970 the FPC once again decided to approve the project. Scenic Hudson and the HRFA both appealed the decision, but this time it was upheld by the court of appeals. The Supreme Court refused to hear the case, allowing the decision to stand. The controversy did not end, however. In December 1973 Scenic Hudson and the HRFA argued in the court of appeals that the Con Ed studies failed to account for the river's being tidal. In July 1974 the court ordered further studies, and the project was put on hold again.

Leadership at Con Ed changed, and the issue of power generation was addressed by gas-operated turbines, constructed in Brooklyn and Queens. Con Ed finally agreed to mediation to settle a variety of disputes with the environmental groups, the state, and the federal government. An agreement was reached in December 1980, in which Con Ed agreed to abandon its plans for the pump-storage facility. Instead the land was donated to the Palisades Interstate Park Commission and the town of Cornwall. In addition the settlement called for the utility to provide a twelve-million-dollar endowment for a new Hudson River Foundation to fund independent research for long-term conservation purposes.

The Storm King controversy did more than any other issue to raise public awareness of the Hudson's value as a scenic resource and to galvanize efforts to protect it.

A half mile later, the road begins to descend, crossing the Catskill Aqueduct buried far below, which is described in the next chapter on the Hudson Highlands East. In less than a half mile you arrive at the village of Cornwall-on-Hudson. It and its neighboring community of Cornwall (actually, the two villages seem to meld into one another) provide a pleasant stopover as one descends from the mountains. Another mile brings you to a gazebo in the center of town.

Cornwall was chosen by *Outside* magazine as one of the top ten communities in the country for outdoor recreation. It hardly looks like a mecca for outdoor enthusiasts, though. It is a very attractive, mostly residential community, well situated on a shelf below Storm King Mountain. The town has some arts and crafts and antique shopping as well as fine eating establishments. There are numerous hiking possibilities nearby on Storm King Mountain, part of the Palisades Interstate Park, and neighboring Black Rock Forest and Schunemunk. The Storm King Highway is a scenic bike route, and there are boating and windsurfing on the river. North of Cornwall is the Kowasee Unique Area and historic sites in New Windsor that relate to the Revolutionary War. Just west of town is the renowned Storm King Art Center, where many famous modern sculptures form an impressive outdoor display.

In the nineteenth century Cornwall was a popular resort town for city dwellers who came by the thousands for the healthy air and country atmosphere. Many were convalescing from illnesses and disease. One such visitor was Nathaniel Parker Willis, an acclaimed author, who wrote about the community and helped publicize its attributes. A romantic, he was also instrumental in changing the names of local landmarks such as Butter Hill to Storm King. He ended up settling on his estate, called Idlewild, whose grounds were designed by Calvert Vaux.

Cornwall has a fine waterfront park, Cornwall Landing, one of the very best along the Hudson, with superb views of the river, Breakneck Ridge, and Bannerman's Island. Parking is restricted to town residents only. However, those on bike or foot are welcome.

The Sands-Ring Homestead at the corner of Academy Avenue and Main Street is an eighteenth-century clapboard farmhouse once used as a general store and as a Friends' meeting house during the Revolutionary War. It has been restored and is open by appointment: Call 914-534-8422 for information.

The Museum of the Hudson Highlands is a small but interesting nature and art museum with changing exhibitions. A range of different local habitats utilizing live plants and animals is on display. Outside the museum are short, easy nature trails. The museum is open from September through June, Mondays through Fridays from 2:00 to 5:00 P.M.,

Saturdays and Sundays from noon to 5:00 P.M., and from June through August, Mondays through Fridays from 11:00 A.M. to 5:00 P.M., and Saturdays and Sundays from noon to 5:00 P.M. There is a small admission fee. It is located in Roe Memorial Park on the Boulevard. The Kendridge Farm off 9W is also part of the Museum of the Hudson Highlands and is currently used for outdoor programs and educational workshops. For information call 914-534-7781.

HIKING TRAILS ON STORM KING

Storm King is only 1,340 feet high, but is one of the best known and most dramatic of all the Hudson Highlands summits. Storm King forms the western flank of the "Wey Gat," Dutch for "wind gate," later called the North Gate, which forms part of the northern entry to the Hudson Highlands. The mountain itself was originally called Butter Hill by the Dutch skippers who navigated this stretch of the river, ostensibly because it resembled a huge lump of butter. The western extension of the ridge is still called Butter Hill. Later, during the nineteenth century, the mountain's name was changed to the more dramatic-sounding Storm King at the urging of Nathaniel Willis. The mountain is part of the Storm King section of Palisades Interstate Park and is open to the public. Much of the land was donated in 1922 by Dr. Ernest Stillman, a New York City physician. There are several miles of excellent, rugged hiking trails with wonderful views of the river and surrounding peaks, as well as pleasant walks through the forest. About 5.9 miles of the Stillman and Howell Trails have been officially designated as part of the Hudson River Greenway Trail. Be forewarned, though: These are mountain trails with great relief and steep ascents and descents, and it may be necessary to scramble a bit in rocky sections, but the rewards are also great.

From the parking area on Route 218 south of Cornwall by the Stillman Spring, go west on the blue-marked Howell Trail as it ascends. William Thompson Howell (1873–1916), for whom the trail was named, was an explorer, photographer, and writer, and Storm King was one of his favorite haunts. Follow the trail to an old woods road, clearly marked. Follow it to the left until the trail departs the road to the right and continues as a narrow path zigzagging upward. Finally emerge from the forest on rocks with dwarf trees to an open vista looking north of the rocky face of Storm King, with Breakneck Ridge, Sugarloaf North, and Newburgh Bay beyond. The views grow more panoramic as you ascend. Climb a series of stone steps to another open view. The trail then veers sharply right. Just beyond there's an excellent view looking south of Cold Spring, Mount Taurus, and Little Stony Point, with Constitution Marsh and Island in the distance. There's another vista looking north, which includes a fine view of Bannerman's Island. The Catskills may be seen from here on a clear day. Pass through a meadow of scrub oak. The trail briefly descends and bends to the right and then continues to climb. The trail veers left with a view of Breakneck Ridge, Mount Taurus, and the Hudson below. Cross the grassy summit of North Point (there are blueberries in season). Descend along the ridge, with its abundant mountain laurel; there are views on the right of Butter Hill through the trees. Reach an intersection with the white-marked Bobcat Trail. By going left and following the Bobcat Trail less than half a mile you'll reach a parking area on 9W, another possible access point.

To continue on the Howell Trail, go right on the blue-marked trail, slowly descending through dense stands of mountain laurel to the right of an ever-deepening ravine. Just before crossing a seasonal brook, you'll see an intersection with the white-marked Stillman Spring Trail on the right. The Stillman Spring Trail descends for three-quarters of a mile back down to the parking area off the Storm King Highway. It is a useful alternate for loop hikes. To continue on the Howell Trail, follow the blue-marked trail for approximately one mile on a fairly level tract through the forest. The trail crosses a boulder-strewn gully with barely a trickle of water—except following storms when it is likely to gush. The Howell Trail ascends a series of switchbacks and continues to climb steadily for another half mile to an intersection with the white-marked Bypass Trail.

Go left on the blue-marked trail, which climbs steadily for less than half a mile to the intersection with the yellow-and-blue-marked Stillman Trail, which is also part of the Highlands Trail, which extends all the way from Storm King west to the Delaware. A short detour to the left will bring you to the summit of Butter Hill. The exposed top has 360-degree panoramic views, including north of Newburgh Bay and the Newburgh/Beacon Bridge as well as wonderful views of Schunemunk, the Shawangunks, and the Catskills, with Stewart Airport in the foreground. You may watch planes take off and land below you. Hawks and turkey vultures circling in the air currents below are also common sights. One can also follow the Stillman Trail west for another quarter mile as it descends to a parking area off Route 9W.

From the intersection of the Stillman Trail and the blue-marked trail, continue right, east, on the yellow-and-blue trail, soon reaching the summit of Storm King and a spectacular open view looking north, with Bannerman's Island prominent in the foreground and the village of Cornwall-on-Hudson far below. Pitch pines appear as you head east, passing an intersection on the right for the white-marked Bypass Trail, and finally reaching the steep precipice of the mountain's prominent east face. There are wonderful views from here looking south toward Cold Spring and Constitution Marsh and Island. The trail swings back to the left and begins a descent through a canopy of hemlocks with mountain laurel lining the path. It continues its steady descent with a nearly vertical slope to the right and occasional views. Finally, after a couple of switchbacks, a small wooden bridge is reached and a more moderate descent follows. The trail then veers right and levels off, reaching an open area with a fire pit. The trail veers left again and joins a dirt woods road, part of an old abandoned estate with ruins. The road walk is mellow and relaxing, and there's interesting stonework whenever it crosses a stream. Approximately a mile down the road you'll reach a small parking area flanked by two stone pillars, the old entrance to the estate. From here you're on Mountain Road. About a one-mile walk to the right leads down into the village of Cornwall-on-Hudson.

10 Hudson Highlands East

PEEKSKILL TO BEACON

In terms of grandeur and natural beauty, the Hudson Highlands east of the river are hardly less spectacular than those on the west side. They also rival the west side of the Highlands in terms of their wealth of historic sites and opportunities for outdoor recreation. Geologically this rugged area is similar to the Highlands west of the river, also part of the Reading Prong. It includes very old metamorphic rocks as well as igneous intrusions like the Storm King Granite, which can be found on Mount Taurus and Breakneck Ridge.

Like the other side of the Highlands, much of the land on this side is state owned and open to the public. The 4,200-acre Hudson Highlands State Park is administered by the Taconic Region of the OPRHP. It was acquired through donations and land purchases since 1938 and has been expanding ever since. There are also numerous privately owned preserves that allow public access. These include Manitoga, Manitou, Constitution Marsh, Fishkill Ridge, North Redoubt, and Arden Point. Information about these sites is given below. Constitution Marsh, one of the Hudson's largest tidal wetlands, provides the best opportunities for birdwatching.

There are a profusion of excellent hiking trails in this section; some are the most popular in the book. Many are quite strenuous and involve steep climbs with dramatic changes in elevation; one may have to scramble on rock using hands as well as feet in some places. Other trails in this section are fairly easy. The New York/New Jersey Trail Conference map series East Hudson Trails, maps 1 and 2, covers this section. To acquire these excellent maps call or write the Trail Conference. The bike route is relatively simple. It primarily follows Route 202/6 to the Bear Mountain Bridge and then Route 9D north. Scenery abounds along this route, and there are a number of incredible views of the river and surrounding mountains. The 9D section is designated part of the Hudson River Greenway Trail. However, there is a considerable amount of traffic along these roads, and there are narrow, curvy sections with blind corners, steep dropoffs, and narrow shoulders, especially along the Route 202/6 stretch.

This section has excellent train service from Metro-North's Hudson Line, with major stops at Peekskill, Garrison, Cold Spring, and Beacon. There is also limited weekend service especially for hikers with stops at Manitou and Breakneck. For information call 1-800-638-7646.

The Route

PEEKSKILL TO THE BEAR MOUNTAIN BRIDGE

A distance of 5.7 miles, mostly on highways with spectacular views of the south entrance to the Hudson Highlands. Bikers and those walking the roadway should use extra caution. This is one of the most perilous sections in the entire book. For hikers there's the Camp Smith Trail and the summit of Anthony's Nose, which offer amazing views and a safer— though more strenuous—alternative to walking along the highway.

From Jan Peek Square in the heart of Peekskill (Peekskill is described in chapter 8), go north on Division Street, 0.4 miles to a fork (there's a monument). Bear left at the fork, on Highland Avenue, and continue north 0.7 miles to the intersection with the Bear Mountain State Parkway. Go left at the intersection. Be extra careful! This is a dangerous intersection with speeding traffic and poor visibility. Go west on the Bear Mountain Parkway, 0.7 miles to the intersection with Route 9. Go right on Route 9, crossing the bridge over Annsville Creek. Continue north to the traffic circle, and head west on Route 202/6. After 0.3 miles you'll pass the entrance to Camp Smith on the right.

Camp Smith is a 1,900-acre summer training ground for the New York State National Guard. Both artillery and infantry units are trained here. The land was acquired between 1885 and 1923; the camp was named in honor of the late governor and unsuccessful candidate for president Alfred E. Smith. Camp Smith includes the area immediately east of the Bear Mountain Bridge. Except for Anthony's Nose and the Camp Smith Trail, the camp is strictly off limits to the public.

From the entrance to Camp Smith, continue west on 202/6. After 0.3 miles the highway starts to climb. Just 0.7 miles past the entrance to Camp Smith, the trailhead for the Camp Smith Trail is on the right, just before the old abandoned tollhouse.

From the trailhead for the Camp Smith Trail, continue to follow Route 202/6 west. About 0.6 miles past the old tollhouse, views of the river open up on the left. One can also see Dunderberg, Iona Island and Marsh, and the south entrance to the Hudson Highlands. Some 1.8 miles past the tollhouse, there's a parking area on the left with views. In winter this is one of the best vantage points along the Hudson for observing bald eagles, which patrol the river from nearby Iona Island. Continue another 0.8 miles to the east entrance of the Bear Mountain Bridge (described in chapter 9).

CAMP SMITH TRAIL

This trail on Camp Smith property opened in November 1995. Constructed by New York/New Jersey Trail Conference volunteers and students from a special military-type program, it was made possible by cooperative agreements among the Trail Conference, the Greenway Conservancy, and Camp Smith that took nearly fifteen years to negotiate. The entire trail is 3.7 miles long and runs roughly parallel to the highway, finally ending at the juncture with the Appalachian Trail, 0.6 miles east of Route 9D. It is for walkers only. The trail is rough in places and steep, and there are dangerous cliffs. Overall, I would say the trail is moderately strenuous, but the views make it well worthwhile. Traffic noise from the highway below is sometimes a minor distraction. The entire hike should take from two and a half to three and a half hours. Really fit individuals could probably complete it in less time. There are options for shorter or longer hikes.

From the parking area on the right (north) side of Route 6-202, hike northwest into the woods on the trail marked with light blue paint blazes. Pass the register with brochures, then climb steeply, closely parallel to roadway. Descend past rocks and cross a small broken dam. Then climb again to views looking west and south of Dunderberg, Iona Island, Jones Point, and Indian Point. The views improve as you ascend. At 0.9 miles you reach Two Pines View, with more spectacular open views, especially of Iona Island and Bear Mountain Park across the way. In wintertime there's a possibility of observing bald eagles from here. Part of this area was cleared by a large fire in 1993. Such summit fires are common in the Hudson Highlands and were even noted by the early explorers.

At 1.9 miles, after a quarter-mile descent, you reach a stream crossing, just a hundred feet from the roadway and a second parking area. You can either end your hike here and return via the roadway, or you can continue. If you choose to continue, ascend slowly to another viewpoint at 2.5 miles. After this the trail becomes steeper. The Bear Mountain Bridge comes into view at 2.7 miles; the trail then zigzags another steep 0.3 miles to the summit of Anthony's Nose, approximately nine hundred feet above sea level. A short, precipitous drop just beyond it leads to a dirt road, and to the left an open area of steep cliffs and the best views so far. There is a dramatic view looking straight down at the Bear Mountain Bridge, hundreds of feet below, and superb views of Bear Mountain, the Bear Mountain Inn, Popolopen Torne, Hessian Lake, Bald Mountain, Dunderberg, Iona Island, and of course the Hudson River in one of its most awe-inspiring settings. This is also a perfect vantage for observing the sites of the two Revolutionary War forts: Fort Clinton and Fort Montgomery flanking both sides of the mouth of Popolopen Brook.

From Anthony's Nose continue north on the dirt road descending another 0.6 miles to the intersection with the Appalachian Trail. The intersection with the Appalachian Trail is just a half mile east of 9D where there's parking by the Bear Mountain Bridge. If you get an early start and you're reasonably fit, you might consider going farther north on the Appalachian Trail as it descends to South Mountain Pass, or continue farther climbing over Canada Hill, just north of which is the intersection with the Osborn Loop. From there you can continue on to either Manitoga or Castle Rock Unique Area, or hike to Graymoor, which is located off Route 9.

APPALACHIAN TRAIL FROM THE
BEAR MOUNTAIN BRIDGE TO WHITE ROCK

Roughly 4 miles, with only limited views and considerable changes in elevation. There's a very worthwhile side trip to the summit of Anthony's Nose, and also camping at Hemlock Springs.

From the east entrance of the Bear Mountain Bridge, begin Route 9D north, also the Appalachian Trail, marked with white paint blazes, which crosses the Hudson on the bridge. There is parking north of the bridge entrance. Continue north for about 0.2 miles, where the Appalachian Trail leaves the highway and enters the woods on the right, part of Hudson Highlands State Park. Follow the markers as the trail climbs. Approximately one-half mile after leaving the roadway, the Appalachian Trail intersects the blue-marked Camp Smith Trail, heading south and up to the summit of Anthony's Nose (see description above). The Appalachian Trail continues northeast to a partial view, then descends as a roadway and then a trail, and passes a spur trail to the Hemlock Spring Campsite, where there is a spring. Finally the Appalachian

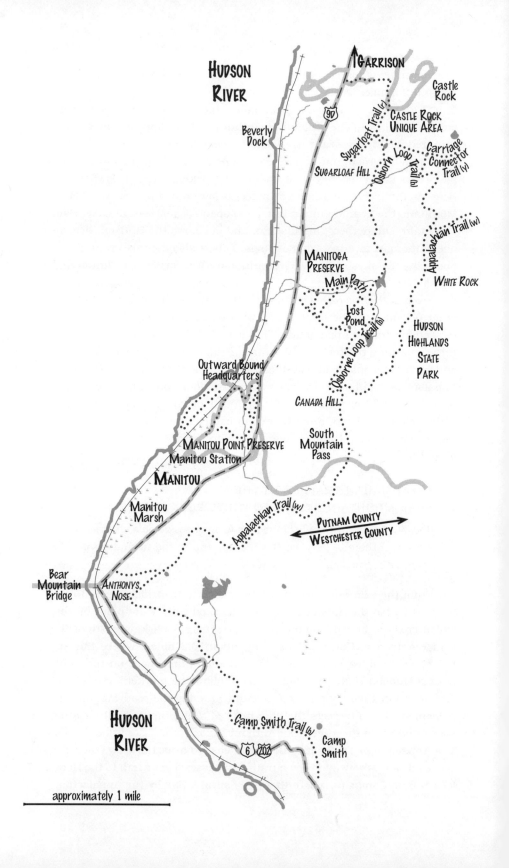

HUDSON
RIVER

Garrison

Castle
Rock

9D

Beverly
Dock

Castle Rock
Unique Area

Sugarloaf Trail (r)

Carriage
Connector
Trail (y)

Osborn Loop Trail (b)

Sugarloaf Hill

Appalachian Trail (w)

Manitoga
Preserve

White Rock

Main Path

Lost
Pond

Osborne Loop Trail (b)

Hudson
Highlands
State
Park

Outward Bound
Headquarters

Canada Hill

Manitou Point Preserve
Manitou Station

South
Mountain
Pass

Manitou

Manitou
Marsh

Appalachian Trail (w)

Putnam County

Westchester County

Bear
Mountain
Bridge

Anthonys
Nose

Camp Smith Trail (w)

Camp
Smith

HUDSON
RIVER

6 202

approximately 1 mile

Trail reaches South Mountain Pass, a dirt road with limited parking, a little more than a mile and a half from where the trail left 9D. The South Mountain Pass used to be the main highway prior to the construction of Route 9D.

The Appalachian Trail crosses the road and continues north, climbing over Canada Hill, elevation 820 feet, covered with dense mountain laurel, no views, but a relatively tranquil and pristine forest environment that sees few visitors. Descend briefly to the intersection with the blue-blazed Osborn Loop Trail, about a mile north from the road. The Osborn Loop Trail bears left and continues north to the Manitoga Preserve, about a quarter mile. An hour and a quarter north is the Castle Rock Unique Area. The Appalachian Trail, now a broad path, stays on a fairly level ridge through young forest of birch, oak, and hickory for slightly more than a mile, or about a half hour to forty minutes of walking, to White Rock, elevation 885 feet, with partial westward views on the left, off the trail. From here the Appalachian Trail continues east toward Graymoor and Route 9 and eventually Maine. Or one can continue north on the now-blue-blazed Osborn Loop Trail to Castle Rock Unique Area or follow the loop south back to the intersection with the Appalachian Trail.

ROUTE 9D FROM THE BEAR MOUNTAIN BRIDGE TO GARRISON

This 4.75-mile walk or bike ride on a scenic roadway, part of the Greenway, is quite pleasant despite the summertime absence of river views. This segment isn't nearly as curvy as the last, and the shoulder is fairly wide. Traffic, though, is usually plentiful. This section can be combined with other routes to make reasonable and enjoyable loop hikes. Walkers may want to detour for the Manitou Nature Preserve, the Manitoga Preserve, or Castle Rock Unique Area.

From the east entrance to the Bear Mountain Bridge, continue north on 9D. At one and a half miles, there's a historic marker on the left commemorating the first iron chain to span the Hudson. It was used by the Americans during the Revolutionary War to prevent the passage of British warships up the river. On October 6, 1777, the British captured the two American forts, Fort Clinton and Fort Montgomery, and subsequently broke the chain.

On the left, two miles from the beginning, pass the entrance to the Manitou Point Nature Preserve (it is also the entrance to the Outward Bound Headquarters). There is a parking area and kiosk once you enter the property, off to the left. Dogs must be leashed, and no bikes are permitted. The 155-acre preserve was formerly the property of Edward

Livingston, who purchased it in 1894. Edward was a direct descendent of Chancellor Livingston. Edward and his wife built the colonial revival home in 1897. Renovated in 1984, it now serves as the Outward Bound Headquarters. Outward Bound is an international company that provides wilderness adventures as well as personal-growth training. The land was purchased in 1990 by the Beaverkill Conservancy, Inc., a subsidiary of the Open Space Institute, and the Scenic Hudson Land Trust, Inc., funded in part through Lila Acheson and DeWitt Wallace, the cofounders of the *Reader's Digest*. The New York/New Jersey Trail Conference maintains the preserve's 3.7 miles of trails, which are also designated part of the Hudson River Greenway Trail.

The preserve has a large area of mature upland forest, huge rock outcrops, a steep-sided ravine through which Copper Brook flows, as well as portions of the Manitou Marsh. The main feature is the 32-acre peninsula that lies west of the railroad tracks and is accessible via a stone arch bridge over the tracks. The Outward Bound Headquarters is also located on the peninsula. Much of the peninsula is wild forest. The River Loop Trail, one of six trails in the park, follows the edge of the cliffs overlooking the river with astounding views. It is one of the finest riverside walks along the Hudson's eastern shore, similar to Mills/Norrie Park. One will see hemlocks and cedars growing right out of the cliffs above the river. To get there an interesting roundabout way, take the Hemlock Forest Trail, marked with white blazes, which runs south from the parking area, closely parallel to Route 9D and traffic noise. After a half mile it bends to the right (west), away from the road, crosses Copper Brook, and descends to a fine dirt road that runs along the edge of Manitou Marsh. Go right and follow the road another three-quarters of a mile to an intersection. Go left and follow the road over the tracks and onto the peninsula. Pass the Outward Bound Headquarters on the left, with fine views looking north and west of the Highlands and the river. Just past the house on the left and beyond a huge stand of rhododendron, an obvious trail continues south along the river for about a quarter of a mile to a junction with the white-marked trail. The white-marked trail continues south, passing a secluded pebble beach, then loops around and heads north, meeting a carriage road that takes you back to the mansion. To return to the parking area, backtrack over the bridge and go straight up the road about a quarter of a mile, to the entrance and the parking area. There are four other short trails through the center of the preserve that may be worth exploring as well.

From the entrance to Manitou, continue north on 9D another 0.7 miles to the entrance to the Manitoga Preserve on the right. The Manitoga Preserve was the former private estate of the industrial designer

Russel Wright. It was here he built his modern experimental home Dragon Rock in 1942 on seventy-nine acres that were devastated by lumber and quarry operations. Wright, through thoughtful planning and careful arrangements of "natural" features, restored the property to its "wild" state. He named it after the Algonquian word for "place of the Great Spirit." The pond next to Dragon Rock was formerly a granite quarry. (Rock from here was used to construct the New York Public Library.) Today it is fed by an artificial waterfall. From Mary's Meadow near the entrance, the Main Path winds 1.8 miles mostly uphill to Lost Pond. Along the way you'll pass an open meadow of blueberries and mountain laurel that in June becomes an enchanting cascade of lovely white and pink blossoms. Spring-fed Lost Pond is surrounded by giant granite boulders. Blooming mountain laurel are reflected in the pond's waters. From Lost Pond a trail connects to the Osborn Loop. The trail continues downhill for about one mile back to Mary's Meadow. An offshoot on the left leads to the Chestnut Oak Ridge Osio (*osio* is the Algonquian term for "beautiful vista"), which features a bench and a panoramic view of the Hudson and surrounding highlands.

Dragon Rock is open to tours by special arrangement. During summers and weekends the Nature Center schedules a regular program of environmental lectures, nature walks, and other special events. There's a small admission charge. It is open from 9:00 A.M. to 4:00 P.M. weekdays year round and from 10:00 A.M. to 6:00 P.M. on weekends from April through October. For information, call 914-424-3812.

From the entrance to Manitoga, continue north on Route 9D 0.8 miles, passing the prominent Sugarloaf South on the right (not to be confused with Sugarloaf North, near Breakneck Ridge, or Sugarloaf Mountain in the Catskills), elevation 730 feet. It was named after the old-fashioned conical sugarloaf that was suspended by string over the center of Dutch dining tables and used primarily to sweeten tea. Sugar was imported and a precious commodity in the Hudson region in colonial times. There's a trail to the summit of Sugarloaf, with a view. It can be reached from the Castle Rock Unique Area or by a longer route via the Manitoga Preserve.

Just 3.9 miles from the Bear Mountain Bridge, you'll see a state historical marker for the Beverly Robinson House, which was located nearby, overlooking the Hudson. Built in 1750, it was the home of the Tory landowner who, during the Revolutionary War, served as a guide for British troops that surprise-attacked Fort Clinton and Fort Montgomery. The home later served as a headquarters for American general Benedict Arnold, commander of West Point. It was just below the house, at Beverly Dock, on the river, that on September 24, 1780, following Major André's arrest in Tarrytown and the discovery of the plot to sell West Point to the British, Arnold escaped by boat to the British warship *Vulture*, eventually reaching British lines. General Washington arrived at the house minutes later and uncovered Arnold's treachery. The house burned down in 1892.

About 4.2 miles from the beginning, Route 9D passes the entrance to the 129-acre Castle Rock Unique Area on the right, owned and managed by the New York State Department of Environmental Conservation. The prominent two-and-a-half-story castle overlooking the entrance was built in 1881 by railroad magnate William Henry Osborn. The design of the house and estate was inspired by Frederick Church, the famous Hudson River School painter, who was a childhood friend of Osborn's. It remains privately owned, and the four and a half acres that surround it are off limits to the public, but distant views of the castle are quite impressive. In 1988 the Osborn family donated the Castle Rock Unique Area to the state. The Castle Rock Unique Area provides convenient access to Hudson Highlands State Park, Sugar Loaf South, and the Appalachian Trail, which are part of the 1,033 acres William Henry Osborn II, past president of the Hudson River Conservation Society, donated in 1974. Except for Sugarloaf South, the area lacks good river views. However, it is an extremely lovely varied forest tract. The trails are generally wide and easily walked and seem to stretch on forever, and there are relatively few visitors, making this an ideal place to enjoy a degree of solitude in a superb natural setting.

From the entrance parking area behind a picturesque old red barn (follow the signs), head south on a dirt road to a closed gate. Continue south another hundred yards to an arrow pointing east. The trail crosses a lovely open field, gradually ascending, with a panoramic view looking north of West Point, Storm King, and Breakneck. A short steep climb into the woods leads to a T-intersection in front of an old gazebo. Go right, south, on the red-marked Sugarloaf Trail, a carriage road, as it climbs a series of switchbacks to the right of a stream, through lovely stands of hemlocks. After approximately a mile and a half, you'll reach a four-way intersection with the blue-blazed Osborn Loop Trail. If you continue left on the Osborn Loop Trail, you go about half a mile past a shallow pond surrounded by mixed deciduous forest with gorgeous wild azalea, to the intersection with the yellow-blazed Carriage Connector Trail. At the intersection the Osborn Trail goes right and climbs for about one mile through thick mountain laurel up to the intersection with the Appalachian Trail at White Rock (see description above).

From the four-way intersection with the Osborn Loop Trail you can reach the summit of Sugarloaf South by climbing one-half mile on the red-marked Sugarloaf Trail steeply to a level ridge and then continuing on to the summit. Just beyond is an open view, looking south, of the Bear Mountain Bridge, Bear Mountain, Dunderberg, and Anthony's Nose. Retrace your steps down to the four-way intersection. If you go right from here on the blue-marked Osborn Loop Trail, you'll climb steeply from the ravine, pass a stone fence on the right with partial views, and then descend and cross a few tiny streams. Walking about a mile and three-quarters from the four-way intersection you'll reach trails on the right that lead into the Manitoga Preserve, which is well worth a visit. A half mile beyond that, the blue-blazed trail reaches the intersection with the Appalachian Trail, from which you could loop back to the four-way intersection. The entire loop could take anywhere from three to five hours and is approximately seven miles long.

From the entrance to the Castle Rock Unique Area, continue north on Route 9D 0.3 miles to the entrance to the village of Garrison, a picturesque little community and designated National Historic District, located between the railroad tracks and the Hudson River. It has a commuter train station with regular service and many quaint nineteenth-century homes, and superb views of one of the Hudson's more spectacular sections, across from West Point. It is also the headquarters of the Hudson Riverkeeper. During the Revolutionary War, American troops of the Northern Continental Army were stationed here, hence the name. In 1821 ferry service was begun between West Point and here, and in 1849 the railroad reached here and provided passenger service. Between the trains and the ferries Garrison became a small bustling transport hub. The area between Garrison and Cold Spring, the site of numerous estates owned by some of America's wealthiest businessmen, was called "Millionaire's Row." Garrison was also used for filming a scene for the movie *Hello, Dolly!* because it supposedly resembled Yonkers (the musical's original setting) in the 1890s.

Just south of Garrison is Arden Point, a sixteen-acre peninsula owned and managed by the Open Space Institute and acquired in 1992. Though Arden Point has marked trails and excellent views of the Hudson, West Point, and neighboring peaks, it sees relatively few visitors. The main reason for the low utilization is the difficulty of getting to the site. At the time of this writing, the state is developing a better access route directly from the Garrison train station. For more information call the Open Space Institute at 212-505-7480.

At the light make a left-hand turn and descend the hill. Pass the railroad station parking on the left after a little more than a quarter mile. Just beyond, make a sharp left and cross the bridge over the railroad tracks, then another sharp left into the village. There's a beautiful waterfront park on the right with a gazebo and splendid views of Hudson

Highlands and West Point. The old railroad station, built in the early twentieth century, has been converted into a community theater.

GARRISON TO COLD SPRING

This section for both walkers and bicyclists is on scenic roadways, primarily busy Route 9D. The primary attractions along the way are the Constitution Marsh Sanctuary and Boscobel, but the entire stretch is rewarding. One can also detour to North Redoubt, the site of a Revolutionary War outpost.

From the Garrison train station, backtrack over the railroad bridge. Bear left at the fork and climb the hill. At 0.6 miles from the Garrison waterfront, you'll reach 9D again. Make a left onto 9D, and follow it north for a little more than half a mile to the intersection with Bill Brown Road on the right. From here, walkers can visit North Redoubt, a tiny 14-acre nature preserve owned by the Open Space Institute. It is 0.3 miles east of 9D and opposite the entrance of the Walter Hoving Home, a residential program for children. There is informal parking along the roadside. A mile-long red-marked trail passes a steep ravine on the left, eventually bending to the right and climbing to the summit of a five-hundred-foot hill. There's a good view looking north toward Constitution Marsh and the remnants of an American outpost used during the Revolutionary War, of which only some earthworks and stone piles remain. For more information call the Open Space Institute at 212-505-7480.

From the intersection of Bill Brown Road, continue north on 9D 1.3 miles to a bridge over Indian Brook; 0.3 miles beyond the bridge, make a left onto a dirt road for Constitution Marsh Sanctuary and Indian Brook Falls. From the intersection bear left on the narrow dirt road. Follow the road 0.3 miles to a parking area for both sites, part of the same 270-acre sanctuary, owned and operated by the National Audubon Society. Parking is limited to reduce the number of visitors. Constitution Marsh is a sensitive habitat that can tolerate only so much use. The sanctuary is open from 8:00 A.M. to 6:00 P.M. every day. No pets are allowed, and there's no smoking.

To get to Indian Falls from the parking lot, follow the dirt road to the left (east), one-quarter mile to beneath the 9D bridge. Just beyond it is a metal gate on the right, where the rough trail begins. Cross the stone bridge over the stream and descend to the creek. Another quarter mile on the rough path brings you to the picturesque falls. They are often referred to as "Fanny Kemble's Bath," after the famous nineteenth-century English actress who fell from a rock while climbing the falls and nearly drowned.

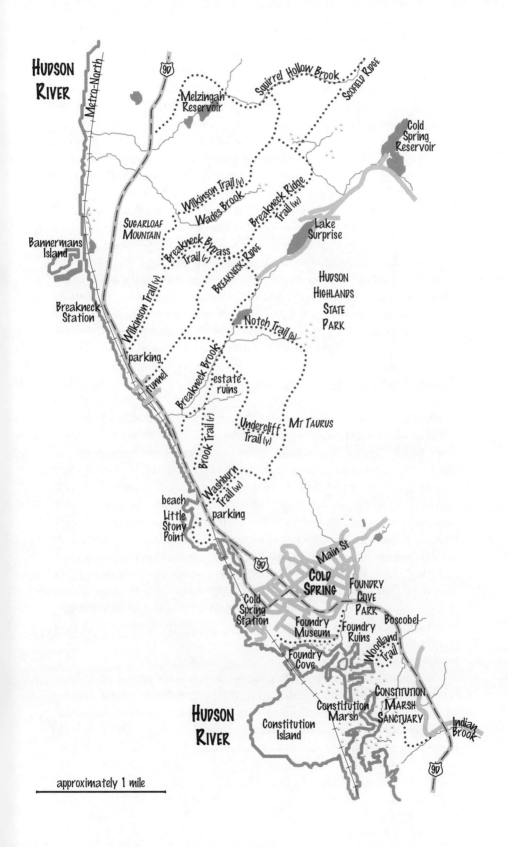

HUDSON
RIVER

Metro-North

90

Melzingah
Reservoir

Squirrel Hollow Brook

SCOFIELD RIDGE

Cold
Spring
Reservoir

Wilkinson Trail (y)

Wades Brook

Breakneck Ridge
Trail (w)

Lake
Surprise

Sugarloaf
Mountain

Bannermans
Island

Breakneck Bypass
Trail (r)

BREAKNECK RIDGE

Wilkinson Trail (y)

HUDSON
HIGHLANDS
STATE
PARK

Breakneck
Station

parking

tunnel

Breakneck Brook

Notch Trail (b)

estate
ruins

Undercliff
Trail (y)

Mt TAURUS

Brook Trail (r)

Washburn
Trail (w)

beach
Little
Stony
Point

parking

90

Main St

COLD
SPRING

FOUNDRY
COVE
PARK

Boscobel

Cold
Spring
Station

Foundry
Museum

Foundry
Ruins

Woodland
Trail

Foundry
Cove

CONSTITUTION
MARSH
SANCTUARY

Constitution
Marsh

Indian
Brook

HUDSON
RIVER

Constitution
Island

90

approximately 1 mile

Backtrack to the parking area. Follow the dirt road on the right, descending one-quarter mile to the bottom of the hill. A nature trail, with markers that label trees, forks to the left. On the right is the Nature Center. It has a butterfly/hummingbird garden and an excavation of a prehistoric native settlement. A trail nearby leads a short distance to a rock shelter inhabited by Native Americans since the Archaic age, more than four thousand years ago. It was excavated in the 1950s under the auspices of the Museum of the American Indian.

Another hiking trail continues one-quarter of a mile past a rare tidal swamp with marsh marigolds and snapping turtles. The trail then veers right (north) up a steep promontory with a handrail for assistance. Here there are pitch pines and a view of West Point opposite. Then descend onto a boardwalk with extraordinary views overlooking Constitution Marsh, a Significant Coastal Fish and Wildlife Habitat Area. Constitution Marsh is a mature brackish water marsh, primarily populated by cattails. Two hundred species of birds have been observed here. Thirty-one species actually breed in the marsh including wood ducks, marsh wrens, clapper and Virginia rails, pileated woodpeckers, gnatcatchers, cerulean warblers, and redwing blackbirds. Straight channels were constructed in 1837 by Henry Warner for growing wild rice (see chapter 9 for Warner's story). The marsh and its varied plant and animal life may be better observed via nonmotorized water craft, such as canoes, kayaks, or rowboats. The sanctuary leads guided canoe trips into the marsh. For more information and reservations, call 914-265-2601.

From Constitution Marsh Sanctuary backtrack 0.4 miles to route 9D. Make a left, and go north on 9D. After 0.2 miles pass the entrance for Boscobel on the left. Boscobel is the restoration of the home of States Morris Dyckman (1755–1806), who made his fortune supplying the British during the Revolutionary War. The house was constructed between 1804 and 1808. Dyckman died before it was completed, but his descendants continued to occupy it until 1952. Originally located fifteen miles south, at Crugers, when it was threatened with demolition in the 1950, it was saved and moved piece by piece to its new location on forty acres of land bought and donated by Lila Acheson Wallace. Boscobel is owned and operated by Boscobel Restoration, Inc., a private organization.

Boscobel was patterned after the style of houses prevalent in late-eighteenth-century London. Known in the United States as the Federal style, it was popular here from roughly 1780 to 1820. Many consider Boscobel to be one of the finest surviving examples of a Federalist-style residence. The house's decor has numerous neoclassical influences. Many American eagle symbols are used, reflecting the patriotism of the times. The home includes the Dyckmans' original English china, silver-

ware, library, and some furniture. Many exceptional Federal-period furnishings are on display as well. Whale-oil Argand lamps, a barrel organ
that actually plays, a portable field bed, a snuffbox made out of a frag-
ment of wood from the "royal oak" that hid Catholic king Charles II from
his Protestant pursuers, and paintings by Benjamin West and Thomas
Doughty are among the thousands of interesting, beautiful, and/or unusual items you'll encounter here. The basement features a museum
gallery of Federal-period decorative arts and a replica of a period kitchen.
There's no museum home in finer condition anywhere along the Hudson.

The grounds are well maintained and include beautiful formal rose
and herb gardens. However, the real highlights are the outstanding
panoramic views of the river and the Hudson Highlands. Just below is
Constitution Marsh, and downriver is West Point. The Woodland Trail,
which opened in October 1997, thanks to grants from the Greenway Conservancy and the Hudson River Improvement Fund, winds through a relatively young forest of locust, ash, birch, and hemlock to an excellent
view of the river at a rustic summerhouse pavilion surrounded by lovely
shade trees. Squirrels, chipmunks, deer, pileated woodpeckers, red-tailed
hawks, nuthatches, and chickadees may be observed. This mile-long loop,
marked with orange triangles, is well graded and relatively easy for just
about anyone to walk. A brochure and map are available at the Visitors'
Center.

Boscobel has a picnic ground and gift shop. Pets are not allowed.
Boscobel is open daily except Tuesdays, Thanksgiving, Christmas, January, and February. In March it is open on weekends only. Hours are
from 9:30 A.M. to 5:00 P.M. from April to October, and in November, December, and March from 9:30 A.M. to 4:00 P.M. The admission charge includes guided tours of the house. Admission to the grounds only is less.
(Children under six are admitted free.) For more information call 914-
265-3638.

From the entrance to Boscobel continue 0.6 miles north and enter the
village of Cold Spring, a relatively small community (fewer than a thousand inhabitants) but a significant destination for visitors. Multitudes of
city dwellers and others are lured by the easy accessibility (there's a
Metro-North station located right in the heart of town), awesome scenery,
and quiet, laid-back small-town atmosphere. Cold Spring is situated right
on the river at the foot of some of the Hudson Highlands' most majestic
peaks, making this a truly spectacular setting. Some of the region's best
hiking trails are located nearby. The village itself is very pleasant, with
many beautiful examples of nineteenth-century homes and buildings in
many styles. Numerous shops, antique stores, and restaurants line Main
Street, and there are a number of good, though not cheap, places to stay.

For more information call the Cold Spring Area Chamber of Commerce, 914-265-9060.

The town got its name from a large spring that supplied boats plying the Hudson with fresh water. The spring may still be observed just west of the railroad tracks in front of the Depot Restaurant. During the 1800s the West Point Foundry, located north of Foundry Cove, gave impetus to the town's growth. It also became a popular resort and attracted literary figures such as Fitz-green Halleck, Washington Irving, and Joseph Rodman Drake. It was the residence of Thomas Prichard Rossiter (1818–1871), a Hudson River School painter who lived here from 1859 until his death.

The town's main parking area is located at the train station. Just south and east of the train station is Foundry Cove, which forms the northern boundary of Constitution Marsh. Along the north side of the cove was located the famous West Point Foundry, which operated here from 1817 to 1884. During the War of 1812, President James Madison ordered the construction of four foundries. Because of its proximity to West Point, the presence of nearby iron deposits, and the river as a transportation corridor, Cold Spring was chosen as one of the sites. The foundry employed up to twelve hundred workers, many of whom were Irish immigrants. The foundry manufactured weapons, steam engines, pipes, and even decorative garden benches. It pioneered modern technology, including America's first iron ship, the engine for the first American-made locomotive, and the Parott gun, designed by Robert Parott, which was used widely during the Civil War. Gouverneur Kemble was the first head of operations. His nearby home, Marshmoor, was a hub of social activity and attracted Hudson River painters and Knickerbocker writers. Jules Verne chose Cold Spring as the site where his fictional projectile that would travel to the moon was manufactured. The invention of steel made the foundry obsolete, and it eventually closed; today little of it remains.

Foundry Cove was later the site of a battery factory constructed by the Army Corps of Engineers in 1952. Until 1979, when the factory closed, twenty-five metric tons of cadmium, a highly toxic heavy metal, known to cause kidney damage and suspected of causing cancer, were dumped in the cove, making this the worst deposit of cadmium anywhere in the world and one of the worst hazardous-waste sites in the United States. In 1981 the EPA placed Foundry Cove on the National Priorities List, calling for the dredging of the contaminated areas of the cove, removal of the contaminated sediments to landfills outside the area, and restoration of the site. Between 1991 and 1993 agreements were made between the EPA, the Army Corps of Engineers and former operators of the site, to fund the cleanup. The dredging, cleanup, and restoration of the site has since taken place and in November 1996, Foundry Cove was declared no longer a toxic waste site.

The eighty-five-acre site is now owned and managed by Scenic Hudson and being developed as a park and historic site. Today there is informal access to the site from the corner of Route 9D and Chestnut Street right after crossing the bridge, on the left side of Chestnut, with parking along Chestnut Street. A half-mile-long blue-marked loop hiking trail (steep in places), sometimes paved with bricks, descends into the ravine beside the creek and winds through lovely forest, passing the interesting foundation ruins of the old foundry, including walls, chimneys, and furnaces. A mile-long dirt-and-gravel road follows the north shore of Foundry Cove with views of the cove, mature cattail marshes, and Constitution Island and Marsh in the background. The bird-watching is excellent. This trail eventually links with the east platform of the Cold Spring Metro-North railway station. Walkers may use this as the main route to the Cold Spring waterfront. Scenic Hudson plans to expand the trail system, to build a bird observation tower by the marsh, and to restore the 1865 foundry administration building, currently abandoned and dilapidated, as a museum and interpretive center, including displays of foundry artifacts discovered during the dredging of the cove. Currently Foundry Cove is the site of a project called Building Boats, Building Bridges, where local teenagers are building a full-size replica of a shad boat. Call Scenic Hudson, 914-473-4440, for more information.

West of the train station parking lot and perched on a bluff overlooking the river is the quaint chapel of Our Lady of Cold Spring, built in 1828 in the Greek Revival style and believed to be the oldest surviving Catholic church along the Hudson north of New York City. Its congregation included skilled Irish mechanics smuggled into the United States to work at the West Point Foundry. Gouverneur Kemble donated the property, funds, and plan for the church. The construction of a second, larger Catholic church in 1907 caused this building to become obsolete. In 1931 it was purchased by the Catholic Church, restored, and reopened in 1977 as a house of worship for all faiths.

The Foundry School Museum, located at 63 Chestnut Street, was formerly a schoolhouse for foundry workers' children. It displays a wide variety of artifacts, antiques, and memorabilia relating to Cold Spring's history and the West Point Foundry. It has Hudson River School paintings, including John Ferguson Weir's famous dramatic canvas *The Gun Foundry*. There's a reproduction of a nineteenth-century classroom, a general store, and a colonial kitchen. Dinnerware Abraham Lincoln used when he visited Robert Parott is also on display. The museum is open

Wednesdays from 9:30 A.M. to 4:00 P.M., Sundays from 2:00 to 5:00 P.M., and by appointment. There's a small admission charge. Call 914-265-4010 for information.

Continue on Route 9D, winding through town to Main Street. Make a left and head west down toward the river. This a National Historic District, with many fine nineteenth-century buildings. There is also a large assortment of antique shops, arts-and-crafts stores, and cafés. It is an excellent place for strolling. Call the chamber of commerce for information about walking tours.

Continue through the underpass beneath the railroad tracks to the scenic waterfront area. There is a formal park with excellent views, benches, an old-fashioned early-nineteenth-century gazebo, and one of the famous Parott guns (see above). It is a popular spot for both tourists and residents. Directly across the river is the 1,350-foot east face of Crow's Nest Mountain. This sheer granite cliff provided a convenient target to test the guns manufactured at the nearby West Point Foundry, including the Parott gun. To the south are West Point and Constitution Island, and to the north are Storm King and Breakneck Ridge.

Next to the park is the Hudson House, an inn in continuous operation since 1832, making it the second oldest in New York State. It is a designated National Historic Landmark. There are other quaint inns and bed-and-breakfasts nearby.

COLD SPRING TO BREAKNECK

About 1.6 miles on mostly straight highway with an adequate shoulder. There are fine views of the river and Breakneck Ridge and Storm King. This route offers numerous walking opportunities in Hudson Highlands State Park, including Little Stony Point, the Cornish Estate, Mount Taurus, and Breakneck Ridge. These include some of the most rewarding—and challenging—hikes in the entire book.

Backtrack up Main Street, making a left at Fair Street. Follow this 0.6 miles until it reconnects with 9D. From this intersection, go straight. A short distance on the left is Little Stony Point. There's parking on both sides of the road for it and for the trail up Mount Taurus. These parking lots can be very busy on weekends and often fill up, so get there early if you're driving.

Owned and managed by OPRHP, Little Stony Point is a thirty-acre peninsula jutting into the river. The bridge over the railroad tracks was rebuilt in 1995, allowing pedestrian access to the site. The area was once the site of a major quarrying operation, remnants of which are still quite apparent. There was also a huge dock from which rock quarried here and at nearby Mount Taurus was loaded on barges and floated downriver. It was purchased by the state in 1967.

Today Little Stony Point has mostly returned to its natural appearance. There's a 0.59-mile-long foot trail (designated part of the Hudson River Greenway Trail) that circles around the south side of the peninsula, passing an abandoned early-nineteenth-century iron mine, cliffs, and superb views of the river in all directions. Another shorter trail leads to a spectacular view from the edge of the quarry face. The major highlight of the park is an easily accessible sandy beach, reputed to be one of the Hudson's best, located on the north side of the peninsula. It's a popular place for sunbathing and admiring the amazing view north of Storm King, Breakneck, Bannerman's Island, and Newburgh Bay. One can often see the Catskills in the distance. As of this writing, swimming is still not permitted, but there are plans for supervised swimming in the future.

From the parking area on 9D begins a trail from which there are excellent hiking opportunities, including climbing Mount Taurus, also known as Bull Hill. It was renamed in the nineteenth century by essayist Nathaniel Willis, who bestowed new, more romantic names on a number of the area's landmarks. Beginning in 1931 Mount Taurus was the site of a huge quarry for crushed stone, which provoked intense public opposition because of the huge scar it created on the side of the mountain. But the protests failed to halt it until 1944, when the quarry ceased operating. In 1968 it was purchased by the state and became part of Hudson Highlands State Park.

To hike a worthwhile loop that takes three to four hours and includes both the old Cornish Estate and Mount Taurus, begin from the parking area on 9D, proceed north on an unmarked trail that runs parallel to route 9D for about a quarter of a mile till it intersects a paved roadway by the former main entrance gate to the Cornish Estate. (Edward G. Cornish, chairman of the board of the National Lead Company, built his elaborate estate in 1900. Only thirty years later, it was abandoned. The buildings quickly fell into disrepair and the mansion burned in 1956.) Continue up the roadway, still in superb condition, for one mile as it climbs past the ruins of the mansion and other structures. Notice the mansion's four brick chimneys, with many fireplaces now apparently suspended in midair. The paved roadway ends soon after. Just beyond, it intersects the red-marked Brook Trail and continues as a rough dirt track. After a short distance, it crosses the Catskill Aqueduct and soon afterward crosses the yellow-marked Undercliff Trail, which crosses a wooden bridge here over Breakneck Brook. The new Undercliff Trail (constructed in June 1997 by the New York/New Jersey Trail Conference), connects

Breakneck Ridge with Mount Taurus, providing a steep, rugged shortcut to either peak.

A half mile, or twenty to thirty minutes, after joining the red-marked Brook Trail, you'll cross a wooden bridge over Breakneck Brook. Just beyond the bridge is the well-marked intersection of the blue-blazed Notch Trail. The trail to the left, which is less steep than the Undercliff Trail, climbs up to Breakneck Ridge. Go right (east) on the Notch Trail, which rises very gradually (about 600 feet in a little more than a mile), less than an hour of hiking, to an intersection with another rough dirt road. From here the road and trail run roughly parallel, intersecting three times. One can follow either, zigzagging south and east up to the intersection with the white-marked Washburn Trail. The blue-marked Highland Trail continues east one mile to North Highland Road, where there's parking. To continue to the summit, go right on the Washburn Trail and follow the last half mile through thick stands of mountain laurel and scrub oak. From the 1,420-foot summit there are views in every direction. The road ends here in a circle. Before you reach the end of it, there's a view of Manhattan's skyscrapers in the far distance.

From the summit of Mount Taurus, descend on the white-marked Washburn Trail, heading south. After less than a quarter mile, or ten to fifteen minutes, there's a superb open view over huge boulders named Table Rock, which takes in the most spectacular section of the Hudson Highlands Gorge, including West Point, one of the finest lesser-known views in the whole book.

The Washburn Trail veers sharply to the right. Another unmarked trail goes straight. Following the white markers, continue to descend. You'll soon pass an intersection with the yellow-marked Undercliff Trail on the right. The Washburn Trail plunges westward for another ten minutes to the rim of the huge granite quarry that scars the mountains's eastern flank. The trail makes another sharp right, which brings one to the floor of the quarry where there is old rusting equipment. The trail then veers left and continues its descent less than ten minutes back to Route 9D and the parking area.

From the parking area for Mount Taurus on Route 9D, continue north another mile with open views looking west of the river and Storm King Mountain's prominent dome. Straight ahead is an open vista of Breakneck, an imposing vertical granite cliff towering high above. This magnificent landmark forms the east end of the Northern Gate and the beginning of the Hudson Highlands Gorge from the north. The sheer rock cliffs and rugged scenery seem almost more like some western landscape. According to legend Breakneck got its name from a runaway bull that rampaged through farms in the valley below. Pursued by angry farmers and their dogs, the bull fell from the cliff and broke its neck. Approaching Breakneck, continue through the tunnel drilled through the mountain's west flank. There's parking just beyond the tunnel on the left. Breakneck Ridge, Sugarloaf North, and Mount Beacon are some of the many prominent peaks featured in the Wilkinson Trail, Fishkill Ridge, and other trails in the northern section of Hudson Highlands State Park and Fishkill Ridge Conservation Area. The area is laced with trails that are steep, rugged, and challenging in places but also offer splendid views. Because of their easy accessibility and spectacular scenery, these are some of the most popular trails in the vicinity of the Hudson.

Breakneck provides some of the most difficult and thrilling hiking in the Hudson Highlands as well as incredible views. Climbing the steep west ridge and then returning via either the red-, blue-, or yellow-marked trails makes a good half-day outing. One could make this longer by including either Sugarloaf North or Mount Taurus for a strenuous full-day hike (only the really fit and inspired should attempt this). Breakneck Ridge is one of the most popular hiking destinations in the entire book.

Like Mount Taurus, Breakneck is part of Hudson Highlands State Park. The best access is from the parking area on 9D just north of the tunnel. There is also a Metro-North train stop about a half mile north of the tunnel, with a larger parking area, convenient for those returning on the red-marked trail and yellow-marked Wilkinson Memorial Trail. The train stop, incidentally, has the best closeup view of Bannerman's Island. Thanks to a grant from the Greenway Conservancy, an observation deck was added in May 1998.

The trailhead for the white-marked Breakneck Ridge Trail is just south of the parking lot, to the right of the tunnel. The trail begins its ascent to the right of the power lines. After a hundred feet or so, two unmarked trails enter the main trail from the right. These lead a short distance to an open area with dramatic views of the Hudson River and Storm King Mountain. Next to the open area is a stone structure that shelters a manhole leading to the Catskill Aqueduct, which plunges more than a thousand feet beneath the river at this point. The largest of New York City's aqueducts, it took twenty years to construct and was completed in 1917. It replaced the two earlier Croton Aqueducts, both of which proved insufficient to meet New York City's growing demand for water. The aqueduct's capacity is more than five hundred million gallons of water per day. Construction of the tunnel underneath the Hudson was the most challenging phase of the construction and once completed represented one of the greatest engineering feats of the time.

Only those who are not bothered by heights should continue. The white trail makes a sharp left, then continues more steeply up and over the tunnel, and up the ridge at a forty-five-degree angle, rising a thousand feet in less than half a mile, or about an hour of climbing. There is treacherous loose rock underfoot, and one has to scramble up in places using one's hands, but no special skills or safety equipment are required. Because the trail rarely approaches the sheer cliff face, there's little danger of falling to your death.

As one gains elevation, views to the west open up, particularly of Storm King Mountain, Cornwall, and Bannerman's Island. Stay on the marked trail. You may observe a second stone structure on the left, partially hidden in the woods, also connected with the Catskill Aqueduct. Unfortunately not everyone who visits here removes all his or her trash, and trash has a way of begetting more until a beautiful area becomes more of a garbage dump than a scenic wonder. The New York/New Jersey Trail Conference helps maintain this area with the help of volunteers, but during the summer the job can get overwhelming.

Finally, one reaches an open ledge with pitch pines and more expansive views, a good place to rest. There's a rewarding view of the Hudson Highlands Gorge that includes Little Stony Point, the gentle, forest-covered slopes of Mount Taurus, Constitution Island and Marsh, and West Point. There's also a closeup view of the magnificent Breakneck precipice, hundreds of feet of sheer blackened granite. During the nineteenth century building stone was blasted from this cliff, as it was from nearby Mount Taurus and Little Stony Point. Looking straight down can make you dizzy, so be extra careful. An alternate trail to the left avoids the more difficult rock scrambling.

A second ledge is reached, with more views and a good place to rest and admire the scenery. Turkey vultures are often seen circling below. They build nests right on the face of the cliff and launch themselves in almost the same manner as hang gliders. Distant echoes of traffic from Route 9D below and periodic trains can be heard. Hundreds of feet straight below one can see the Breakneck Lodge, a mere toy house from this distance.

The trail zigzags to the right, to the top of the first hump; then there's a brief descent. Then one climbs steeply over more rocks to the second bare rock hump. Off the trail to the left is a view north of Newburgh Bay, Sugarloaf North, Bannerman's Island, the Newburgh/Beacon Bridge, and Dennings Point.

Descend again into a thickly wooded trough and climb more steep rocks. There's a dramatic view westward of the second hump and Storm King in the distance. On the right the yellow-marked Undercliff Trail makes its steep descent beneath tall rock cliffs. It continues approximately one-half mile down to the valley, crossing Breakneck Brook and the Brook Trail. From there it continues a mile and a half up to the summit of Mount Taurus. Climbing both peaks this way will take more than half a day.

Finally, after a mile of climbing the Breakneck Ridge Trail and a twelve-hundred-foot ascent, the trail levels out at the crest. There's a swamp on the right populated by spring peepers and bull frogs. From here on the trail follows a true ridge, with steep slopes on either side. There are many open spots with views to the east of Fahnestock Park and north to Lake Surprise and Mount Beacon. After another quarter mile or so, descend either the red-marked Bypass Trail to the left or just beyond, the blue-marked Notch Trail to the right in order to loop back to the beginning. Both trails are relatively easy.

One can continue on, following the ridge all the way to the Fishkill Ridge Conservation Area northwest of North Beacon Mountain. This route is about nine miles from Route 9D to the end, off Mountain Avenue in Beacon. It is a very strenuous hike with plenty of ascents and descents and takes a full day. It is also very rewarding, with lots of excellent views and pretty forest scenery. Those with vehicles will need to spot cars at both ends.

Just beyond the intersection with the Notch Trail, the Breakneck Ridge Trail, now marked with white-and-blue blazes, descends and intersects an old woods road, which it continues to follow northward. You'll pass an unmarked spur trail on the right, which leads to a view looking east of Lake Surprise. The Breakneck Ridge Trail climbs a steep rocky slope to an open view on bare summit rocks with a glimpse of the river on the right, along with Mount Taurus, Breakneck Ridge, Sugarloaf, Crow's Nest, Newburgh, the Newburgh/Beacon Bridge, and the Shawangunks and Catskills in the distance. The trail then descends. About a half hour from the Notch Trail intersection, the white-and-blue-marked trail forks. The left-hand blue-marked Notch Trail goes a short distance and intersects the yellow-marked Wilkinson Memorial Trail. The Wilkinson Trail continues west, slowly descending down to the drainage of Cascade Brook, then climbing Sugarloaf North and descending to Route 9D. When included with the Breakneck Ridge hike, this makes an excellent five-and-a-half-mile-long loop.

From the last intersection with the Notch Trail, go right. The Breakneck Ridge Trail continues northeast as a narrow white-marked path, climbing up to Sunset Point. Just before reaching the tree-covered summit, a view south reveals Breakneck Ridge, the Hudson Highlands Gorge, Schunemunk Mountain, and in clear weather, the skyscrapers of Manhattan. The trail descends steeply about five hundred feet to the valley of Squirrel Hollow Brook, where unfortunately, there's much evidence of

ATV damage in the area. The trail then enters city of Beacon property and ascends steeply to the summit of South Beacon Mountain 1,600 feet, the highest peak in the Hudson Highlands. Just beyond is a bullet-hole-dotted fire tower, reputedly safe to climb, but not for those who have problems with heights. There are great views from the top of the tower of Storm King, Breakneck Ridge, Manhattan in the distance, Schunemunk, and the Ramapos beyond.

Cross a fire-damaged landscape and descend northeast to another intersection with the yellow-marked Wilkinson Trail, and also with the red-marked Casino Trail. This trail leads west for about a quarter of a mile to a dirt road and another quarter of a mile through area of scrub oaks and pitch pines to the summit of North Beacon, 1,531 feet. From here there are excellent views north of the cities of Newburgh and Beacon, the Newburgh/Beacon Bridge, and the Hudson. In the area are numerous radio towers, ruins of an old casino and inclined railway, built in 1902 by the Otis Elevator Company and advertised as the world's steepest. It ceased operating in 1977. Efforts are under way to restore the Mount Beacon inclined railroad. For information write to the Mount Beacon Incline Railway Restoration Society, P.O. Box 1248, Beacon, NY 12508. Mount Beacon's summit was used during the 1920s to film silent Westerns and Civil War movies. Nearby, there's also a stone obelisk that commemorates Mount Beacon's use, during the Revolutionary War, for signal fires that warned the patriots of approaching British warships and helped link New England with the rest of the colonies—hence the mountain's name. The area of North Beacon Mountain and the Beacon Reservoir has seen centuries of human use and is crisscrossed by a myriad of informal trails and dirt roads. There's also considerable ATV damage as well as littering in spots. It's impossible to describe each of the trails, many of which are not marked, but it's an area well worth exploring, and, thanks to Scenic Hudson, all of it is open to the public.

An unmarked roadway leads north from the intersection to the Mount Beacon Reservoir, follows the east shore of the reservoir to the dam, and continues north, entering the Fishkill Ridge Conservation Area, 1,024 acres owned by the Scenic Hudson Land Trust, Inc., and leased to OPRHP. The roadway descends alongside the drainage of Dry Brook for about a half mile to an intersection with the white-marked Fishkill Ridge Trail on the left. One can follow the Fishkill Ridge Trail west down to Mountain Avenue in the city of Beacon, about three-quarters of a mile, where there's parking.

From the beginning of the Breakneck Ridge Trail on 9D, go north, about 0.3 miles from the tunnel. There's a small parking area on the right side of the road and the beginning of the yellow-marked Wilkinson Memorial Trail. There's additional parking across the road as well as the Metro-North Breakneck train stop. Following the Wilkinson Memorial Trail, you'll have a very strenuous eight miles to Route 9, with numerous ascents and descents. But there are also great views and forest scenery, making this a rewarding full day of hiking if you choose to complete the entire trail. Shorter versions and loop hikes are possible. For example, just hiking to and from Sugarloaf North, which has exceptional views, would take an hour and a half to two hours.

The trail begins as a pleasant wide path through dense foliage, zigzagging as it ascends. Then it turns left (north). After one-half mile it crosses a lovely stream via a wooden bridge. Here it intersects the red-marked Breakneck Bypass Trail (red dots on white), climbing directly east 0.8 miles to Breakneck Ridge, which is a useful route for loop hikes. The Wilkinson Trail continues uphill in a northeasterly direction. After a few minutes, the wide path veers right and continues, while the yellow-marked trail makes a sharp left turn and crosses a deep ravine with another stream. There's no bridge this time. The trail continues to ascend moderately as it approaches the base of Sugarloaf North's summit. It then climbs steeply to the right on rock steps and then sharply to the left and through a cleft in the rock, where some moderate rock scrambling is involved, though nothing of a technical nature. Just beyond is the 900-foot summit of Sugarloaf North. The top has been ravaged by a recent fire, but is making an excellent recovery. There are three splendid viewpoints. The first, sheltered as it is from the wind, is probably the best. It displays a wonderful panorama of Breakneck, Storm King, and the narrow gorge of the Hudson. Across the river are Schunemunk, Cornwall, New Windsor, Plum Point, and Newburgh. There's an excellent bird's-eye view of Bannerman's Island from this vantage. Hawks and buzzards gliding in the wind are a common sight. A skeletal tree standing in the foreground like a modern sculpture adds a picturesque element to the scene. This is a very popular spot for individuals and groups and on a pleasant weekend day can be quite crowded. There are two more views beyond, looking west and north of Dennings Point, the Newburgh/Beacon Bridge, the Shawangunks, and the Catskills.

From the summit of Sugarloaf North, the trail veers sharply right, then left, and then makes a steep three-hundred-foot descent to an open field, formerly a farm, where it crosses another old woods road. The trail then follows the south side of rock-strewn Cascade Brook, which often dries up in summer, a beautiful and unusually quiet place with many hemlock trees giving it a wild feel. After a half mile the trail, now marked with alternating white and yellow disks, crosses the stream and then a dirt road, and begins a gradual ascent to an unnamed summit that yields southward views of Breakneck Ridge . . . and finally a superb open view overlooking Melzingah Reservoir, with Newburgh, Dennings Point, and the Newburgh/Beacon Bridge, Stewart Airport, and the Shawangunks and Catskills. Just beyond is another view looking north of the city of Beacon, with Danskammer Point in the distance. The trail briefly descends and reaches the intersection with the blue-marked Notch Trail, continuing left as a yellow-and-blue-marked trail, descending northward into the valley of Squirrel Hollow Brook. After a half mile, or fifteen to twenty minutes, you arrive at Squirrel Hollow Brook. Cross the stream and reach the intersection with a dirt-and-gravel four-wheel-drive road. The blue-marked Notch Trail goes left, descending toward the Melzingah Reservoir and eventually Route 9D. The yellow-marked Wilkinson Memorial Trail goes right, ascending about a half mile to the intersection with the white-marked Breakneck Ridge Trail.

Continue northward on the wide path that's presently unmarked, following the Squirrel Hollow drainage. After a short distance a cairn (rock pile) marks where the Breakneck Ridge Trail departs on the left. The Wilkinson Memorial Trail continues a gradual ascent another half mile to the intersection with the red-marked Casino Trail, and makes a sharp right and a brief ascent to the Schofield Ridge and an excellent view south of Breakneck Ridge and the Hudson Highlands Gorge. Continue north with scrub oak overgrowing the trail in places. Watch for blazes. Follow the trail to a bald hump with a superb view east of Lake Valhalla and the Cold Spring Reservoir, and west of South Beacon Mountain with its tall fire tower, the Beacon Reservoir, the Hudson River beyond to the west, Breakneck Ridge, Storm King Mountain, and the spires of Manhattan in the far distance.

The trail descends and climbs to another view west of the Beacon Reservoir, North Beacon Mountain, and the Hudson. The trail then continues fairly level for two-thirds of a mile, or twenty minutes, and enters the Fishkill Ridge Conservation Area, owned by Scenic Hudson Land Trust, Inc., acquired in 1992, and managed by the Taconic Region of the OPRHP as an extension of Hudson Highlands State Park.

The trail climbs to another open view, this time east of Hell Hollow, and south all the way to the Tappan Zee and on a clear day, Manhattan. The trail then descends west and then north and east, zigzagging into Hell Hollow and an intersection with a dirt road. The Wilkinson Trail continues its descent to the right here, a mile and a half to its entrance to the private land of a gun club. Permission must be obtained from neighbors, but according to reports is rarely denied civil-looking individuals and groups. One can also descend westward on the dirt road, a little more than half a mile to its intersection with the white-marked Fishkill Ridge Trail to its entrance on Mountain Avenue in the city of Beacon. See above for description of this exit.

One last hike is certainly worth mentioning: A moderately strenuous seven-mile-long loop, through the Fishkill Ridge Conservation Area, over Lamb's Hill and Bald Hill, via the white-marked Fishkill Ridge Trail, is quite rewarding for its excellent views. To get to the trailhead, go north on Route 9D to the intersection of Howland Avenue with Wolcott. Continue north one-half mile to Main Street. Go right on Main, which becomes Mountain Avenue. Follow one-quarter of a mile to a narrow unmarked road on the right (there's a No Outlet sign). If you're driving, park along the side of the road and walk to the end of the road, where there's a barrier. A city of Beacon water storage tank is on the left. The white-marked trail begins here. The trail quickly enters a cool primeval dark ravine with large mature hemlocks, northern hardwoods, and narrow beams of light penetrating the forest canopy. Follow the trail as it ascends parallel to Dry Brook. After one-half mile, the trail crosses the stream to the left of a series of enchanting cascades.

Switchback up the steep side of the gully. Cross the gully and continue northeast. The trail finally levels as you reach a large hemlock grove. A dirt road appears ahead. Cross the road, and go left on a bridge over a ravine. The trail veers to the right and up a steep slope with oaks and hickories. Partial views of the river appear on the left. The trail gets steeper, to forty-five degrees. The footing is unstable, and you'll have to use your hands on bare rock and branches in places. Finally the view opens up as you reach the bare summit. The view includes the city of Beacon below, the Hudson, Newburgh, the Newburgh/Beacon Bridge, North and South Beacon Mountains, Danskammer Point to the north, and the Shawangunks and Catskills in the distance. There are numerous pitch pines, laurels, and shrub oaks in the vicinity.

Descend a small wooded ravine. The trail levels, then descends to a second, larger ravine. Then it crosses a stone fence and switchbacks up to another bare summit, Lamb's Hill, with a view north as far as Poughkeepsie. Smooth summit rocks display evidence of glaciation. Descend on a gentle but rocky slope to a dirt road (called Dozer Junction, for a bulldozer wreck parked nearby). The white-marked trail continues south a short distance to a view overlooking Hell Hollow. The trail then bends to the left (north) and continues for approximately one mile to another fine open view, part of Bald Hill. From here you can see south and west to Lake Valhalla and the Hudson in the distance. Continue north, with a partial view looking west from the col of Beacon with the Hudson in the background. Follow the trail to a second view looking south and west similar to the one before. Nearby the trail intersects an old woods road that can be followed west approximately one mile to a trailhead in Glenham.

The Fishkill Ridge Trail bends sharply to the right and continues south, eventually intersecting the Wilkinson Memorial Trail. From there an unmarked dirt road will take you back all the way to Mountain Road, just east of where you started. Or you can follow the Fishkill Ridge Trail down Dry Brook to the beginning.

BREAKNECK TO THE BEACON WATERFRONT

About 6.2 miles, mostly on Route 9D, with excellent views of the river at the beginning and end. There are opportunities to visit the historic Madame Brett Homestead and other sites in the city of Beacon, as well as wonderful hiking opportunities at Dennings Point and in Hudson Highlands State Park and the Fishkill Ridge Conservation Area.

From the Breakneck tunnel, continue north on Route 9D more than three and a half miles to the city of Beacon, where route 9D becomes Howland Avenue. Beacon is a small former industrial center trying hard to make a comeback from a depressed economy. It enjoys a magnificent setting between wide Newburgh Bay and the Hudson Highlands, with Storm King, Breakneck, and Bannerman's Island familiar landmarks to the south, as well as access to some of the region's best hiking trails. Beacon is the longtime residence of folksinger, activist, and founder of Clearwater Pete Seeger. It was also used as the primary setting for the 1994 Paul Newman film *Nobody's Fool.*

Beacon was first settled by Francis Rombout and his partner, Gulian Verplanck, who in 1682 bought eighty-five thousand acres—all the land they could see from the summit of Mount Beacon—from the Native Americans. Rombout's share was inherited by Roger Brett and his wife, Rombout's daughter, Chatharyna, who later became the sole heir when Brett died. The Beacon area saw a lot of activity during the Revolutionary War, when Mount Beacon was used as a reconnaissance signal and outpost. During the last years of the war, there were large encampments nearby of Continental Army troops, and Washington had his headquarters across the river in Newburgh.

Later, Beacon was created by the merger of two former villages, Mattewan and Fishkill Landing. During the nineteenth century it became an important manufacturing center, particularly for textiles. Beacon was incorporated as a city in 1913. Today most of its industries are closed. Many residents are employed in two huge state correctional facilities located just east of here. IBM, located in East Fishkill, also employs a large number of people. Many take advantage of Beacon's train station to commute into Manhattan. Restored nineteenth-century buildings at the east end of Main Street are enjoying a revival and now contain a number of antique shops and cafés. Efforts are under way to improve Beacon's waterfront, much of which remains undeveloped. There are spectacular river views and access from Beacon's Waterfront Park as well as Dennings Point. The Newburgh/Beacon Bridge also provides amazing views and walking opportunities (see chapter 11). Beacon has one of the most ambitious trail plans of any riverfront town or city. It includes linking Madame Brett Mill Park with Dennings Point and the Beacon waterfront with a 1.7-mile paved path suitable for bikes and wheelchairs. Beacon's Metro-North station, located on the waterfront, provides regular service and easy access from New York City. At present, the hiking trails are some distance from the station.

From the intersection of Route 9D and Slocum Road, you can detour on Route 9D 0.6 miles to Craig House, a private psychiatric hospital, on the left. The ornate Victorian mansion was built in 1859 by shipping magnate and philanthropist Joseph Howland, who named the house Tioranda. It was designed by Richard Morris Hunt, who later designed such lavish homes as Vanderbilt's Biltmore, in North Carolina, and the base of the Statue of Liberty.

Follow Slocum Road 0.5 miles to a T-intersection with South Avenue. Go left on South Avenue 0.1 miles as it descends to a small bridge over Fishkill Creek, closed to automobile traffic. Cross the bridge, and just beyond on the right is a parking area and entrance to Scenic Hudson's 23.8-acre Madame Brett Mill Park and the half-mile-long Fishkill Creek Trail. Fishkill Creek is one of the larger tributaries of the Hudson south of Albany, the second longest stream in Dutchess County. The trail begins as a wide level path. Follow it to the creek and a view of Tioranda Falls, where Madame Brett's mill was located. The trail passes a sluice gate and ascends an old concrete spillway barrier. The trail then enters a more idyllic wooded area by the slow-moving creek, climbs a steep bluff, and follows the edge of the bluff, finally emerging in a vacant lot. There are abandoned factory buildings straight ahead with no-trespassing signs. To return you must backtrack the whole way. To follow the creek south, use the new pedestrian boardwalk, which begins by the south side of the bridge. It cleverly bypasses an old abandoned hat factory. The boardwalk leads to a small parking area from which an unmarked trail continues for another half mile through dense foliage, parallel to the creek, with occasional views of the marsh at the mouth of the creek, opposite Dennings Point (see below for a description). There are plans for this trail to eventually reach Dennings Point and link with the Beacon waterfront. For information call Scenic Hudson at 914-473-4440.

After leaving the park, continue north. Go through the narrow railroad tunnel and detour right on Tioranda Avenue approximately one mile to visit the Madame Brett Homestead and Beacon's restored downtown area.

The Madame Brett Homestead is located at 50 Van Nydeck Avenue. Make a left one block before you reach Main Street. The historic house is on the left. Originally built in 1709, it is Dutchess County's oldest surviving residence. The original owners were Chatharyna Rombout Brett and her husband, Roger Brett. Following her husband's early death, Chatharyna Brett became a dynamic businesswoman dealing in real estate, milling grain and lumber, operating sloops, and so on. She established a cooperative storehouse on the river for produce going to New York City. She ended up selling much of the twenty-eight thousand acres she inherited from her father, which encouraged more settlement and business activity in the region. She was so well respected that she was referred to as Madame Brett. In 1715 prosperity enabled her to expand the house to its present size. She is buried at the churchyard in Fishkill. Washington, Lafayette, von Steuben, and other patriots were guests of her granddaughter Hannah Brett Scheck. The exterior of the house, which remained in the family for 140 years, features scalloped red cedar shingles. Parts of the interior were updated, depending on need and the fashion of the times. Purchased by the Daughters of the American Revolution in 1954, it is now on the National Register of Historic Places. The interior has a huge collection of furnishings, many belonging to the family, including eighteenth-century china, Madame Brett's original ceramicware, her saddle and shoes, as well as a few of her original furnishings. Frances Rombout's grandfather clock, dating back to the seventeenth century and brought over from Europe, is included in the collection. In addition there's a room with a huge doll collection; another room devoted to Robert Fulton, who married into the family; and a punchbowl Lafayette gave the Brinkerhoff family. Outdoors is the Marion Brinkerhoff Formal Garden, in the Dutch style with flowers and gravel paths. Nearby is a lovely brook and woods with wildflowers. It is open from May through December on the first Sunday of the month from 1:00 to 4:00 P.M. There is a small admission fee. For information call 914-831-6533.

Backtrack on Tioranda Avenue to the railroad tunnel, and continue east on South Avenue, which makes a sharp right. Follow the road north for about 0.3 miles to the intersection with Sargent Avenue and then another half mile to the intersection with Dennings Avenue. Go left on Dennings, one-half mile to end of the road, right by the railroad tracks and Beacon's sewage treatment plant on the left. This is the entrance to Dennings Point, a sixty-six-acre peninsula north and west of the mouth of Fishkill Creek, owned and managed by the New York State Department of Conservation, which acquired the land in 1988. The area was a burial site for the Wiccapee and Shenandoah Indians. The site of a ferry operation during the Revolutionary War, in 1785 it was purchased by William Dennings, a New York City merchant. His family lived on the southern part of the peninsula. The northern third of the peninsula later became an industrial area, producing bricks and other building materials, and wire. For the most part it has returned to its natural state and is heavily wooded. It is one of the few wild public access points along the river. There are secluded beaches, wildlife, and excellent views of the river and surrounding area. The site does not appear to get many visitors. There is only one small sign notifying that this is state land and stating the rules of visitation. Dogs must be leashed, and no bikes are permitted.

To enter the property, follow the dirt road past the barrier. Go south about a quarter of a mile, parallel to the Metro-North tracks. The road bends right and crosses a bridge over the tracks. A short distance beyond, the road crosses Conrail tracks. Just past the tracks there's a private residence on the right (no trespassing). The road continues to an intersection with another trail and veers left (south), passing an old abandoned Pin Ticket factory, which produced paper clips, on the left. Straight ahead, a trail leads to the waterfront and a view of the mouth of Fishkill Creek, a designated Significant Coastal Fish and Wildlife Habitat. This area includes shallows, mudflats, and some marshland. It's an important spawning area for anadromous fish including alewives, blueback herring, white perch, striped bass, and tomcod. There are large numbers of resident fish, too, including largemouth bass, bluegills, and brown bullheads. Blue crabs, herons, and turtles also inhabit the area. It is an important feeding site for migrating ospreys and a breeding site for least bitterns. Rare aquatic plants like the estuary beggar-tick, subulate arrowhead, and kidney leaf mud plantain are found here. Water chestnuts are unfortunately also quite prevalent. The mouth of Fishkill Creek is a popular fishing spot; there's a panoramic view of Breakneck Ridge and Storm King to the south.

The road becomes a trail, which divides into a mile-and-a-half-long loop around the peninsula, marked with white markers and well maintained. Give yourself at least an hour to hike the entire trail, more if you choose to stop at one of the many lovely vistas. If you take the left branch, you'll pass many wild raspberry bushes with plentiful fruit. Enter dense forest with oaks and black birch trees and partial views of the river on the left. Chipmunks, squirrels, rabbits, and deer are abundant. After about a quarter of a mile you'll pass ruins on the left. The trail continues south to the end of the peninsula. There are side trails to a pebble-and-sand beach strewn with driftwood and wonderful views south of Breakneck and Storm King, Bannerman's Island, Newburgh, and New Windsor across the way and north toward the Newburgh/Beacon Bridge. The trail continues north, eventually joining the other branch just west of the abandoned factory. Return from here the same way you entered.

From the entrance to Dennings Point, backtrack north on Dennings Avenue to the intersection with Wolcott Avenue. Continue west and north. Wolcott Avenue branches off Route 9D and heads straight for the Metro-North train station and the Beacon Waterfront Park, a landscaped peninsula jutting westward into the river. The park has recreational facilities, benches, and great views south of Breakneck and Storm King, Newburgh across the river, and the Newburgh/Beacon Bridge. Nearby is the headquarters of the Beacon Sloop Club and the old ferry dock, from which there was regular service across the river to Newburgh from 1743 to the completion of the Newburgh/Beacon Bridge in 1963. The twenty-one-acre area of former industrial land south of the train station has been purchased by Scenic Hudson. The environmental organization plans to clean up the property and develop it for recreation and commercial use, including a riverfront promenade and trail connections to nearby Dennings Point.

11 Mid-Hudson West
CORNWALL TO ATHENS

Having cleared the formidable Highlands, one descends into a less rugged landscape that many consider to be the valley proper. Geologically it's underlain by sedimentary rock from the early Paleozoic era, part of the Hudson/Mohawk Lowlands. The rock beds are intensely folded, faulted, and most (where exposed, severely weathered) often buried under thick glacial deposits. Generally the shale, which is softer, is found in the valleys and ravines, while the harder sandstones form the hills and ridges. A band of dolomitic limestone (composed of magnesium carbonate) stretches from just north of Newburgh east to just south of Marlboro, where it crosses the Hudson.

Although the landscape is gentler than that of the Highlands and Palisades, local erosion has created steep bluffs and hills and narrow ravines in places, so travel—whether on foot or by bike—often isn't quite as mellow as one might expect. A couple of miles west of the river, there's a broken line of ridges between New Windsor and Kingston, sometimes referred to as the Marlboro Mountains. Composed of harder, more weather-resistant rock, they rise hundreds of feet. Despite the intrusions of radio towers and antennas, these ridges are cloaked with thick forests and, especially in the area west of West Park and Esopus, still maintain much of their primitive character. Bears are often sighted here. From Kingston north, the Allegheny Plateau, an area of Silurian and Devonian sedimentary rocks, many of them fossil bearing, comes within a mile of the river's west shore and parallels it north into the Capital region. The most prominent feature of this plateau is the Catskill Mountains, which tower higher than four thousand feet to the west and form an imposing backdrop.

The river itself presents a startling contrast in images, from more than a mile and a half wide at Newburgh Bay to the relatively narrow Lange Rack, or Long Reach (named by Robert Juet), a section less than half a mile wide between Danskammer and Crum Elbow. Stretching four and a half miles between Kingston and Ulster Landing Park are the Flats, a very shallow bar located in midriver, and a popular spawning ground for shad, striped bass, and white perch. Unlike the Highlands, much of this section of the river has been developed. Small cities, large villages, and tiny hamlets line the shore, but unlike areas to the south, suburbs are not the rule. Less-developed areas exist between the communities and these areas are essentially rural in character. Orchards and vineyards, prevalent in places, are one of the main attractions of this area, as are the many fruit and vegetable stands along the roadways in season. Much of the land is second- and third-generation mixed deciduous forest that sports a rich profusion of plant and animal life: Deer, wild turkeys, opossums, foxes, coyotes, racoon, muskrat, snapping turtles, herons, egrets, and hawks are among the wildlife you may observe. Sanctuaries such as John Burroughs, Ramshorn/Livingston, and Esopus Meadows exist for their protection.

The west side of the mid-Hudson was never the home of large estates as were other parts of the Hudson region. During colonial times this area attracted large numbers of settlers seeking their own plots of land to farm. Today the area abounds in historical sites: the Gomez-Mill House, the oldest surviving Jewish residence in North America; the Hasbrouck House, Washington's headquarters in Newburgh during the final years of the Revolutionary War; the New Windsor Cantonment, the last encampment of the Continental Army; the Senate House in Kingston, the site of New York State's first government; and Slabsides, the cabin John Burroughs, one of America's leading naturalists and authors of the nineteenth century, built and used as a retreat. Both Newburgh and Catskill have historical districts where superb examples of a variety of nineteenth-century architectural styles may be observed. Kingston has both the Stockade, with many fine remnants of an eighteenth-century colonial community preserved, and the Rondout, once a leading Hudson River port. Both are now urban cultural parks. Those interested in antiques should check out the village of Saugerties. Lighthouses are another attraction along this section of the river.

In this section most of the paths follow back roads through countryside that is particularly excellent for biking. The segments between West Park and Kingston and Catskill and Athens are especially scenic. Except for a few community parks, most of the land in this section is privately owned. Therefore, no extensive network of walking trails yet exists like those found in other sections. However, recent land acquisitions by private groups like Scenic Hudson, including Shaupeneak Ridge, Esopus Meadows, Saugerties Lighthouse Park, the Ramshorn/Livingston Sanctuary, and the Cohotate Preserve have opened up areas to easy, nonstrenuous hiking and strolling. Many of these sites are not well known, and thus you may enjoy a degree of solitude you might be hard-pressed to find in other areas along the river. The Mid-Hudson, Rip Van Winkle, and Newburgh/Beacon Bridges are all open to pedestrians and bicycles and provide rewarding views of the river. From West Park north, the west bank of the river is not burdened with the presence of railroad tracks, making this one of the very best sections for visiting the river's shoreline.

Shortline provides regular daily bus service from the Port Authority Terminal in Manhattan to Vails Gate and Newburgh. For information call 1-800-631-8405. Adirondack Trailways provides daily bus service from Newburgh to Kingston, via 9W, with stops in Marlboro, Highland, West Park, Esopus, and Port Ewen. There's also daily service from the Port Authority Terminal in Manhattan direct to Kingston, Saugerties, and Catskill, as well as weekday service from Catskill to Athens. For information call 1-800-858-8555. Metro-North provides regular daily train service to Beacon and Poughkeepsie on the east side of the Hudson. For information call 1-800-METRO-INFO.

For information about dining, accommodations, and events, contact Orange County Tourism, 914-294-5151, ext. 1647; the Ulster County Public Information Office, 1-800-DIAL UCO; the Greene County Tourism and Information Center, 518-943-3223; or 1-800-355-CATS.

The Route

CORNWALL TO NEWBURGH

A distance of 3.3 miles on roads, passing Moodna Creek, a Significant Coastal Fish and Wildlife Habitat, and Kowawese Unique Area, with its fine beach and excellent views of Newburgh Bay and the Highlands. Add another 5.6 miles if you do a detour loop through Vails Gate and New Windsor to see the historical sites there connected with the American Revolution.

Beginning in the heart of Cornwall-on-Hudson (described in chapter 9), from the gazebo at the corner of Hudson Lane and River Road, make a right turn onto River Road, descending the hill. You'll encounter a brief view of Newburgh Bay on the left with the Newburgh/Beacon Bridge in the distance, and then reach the intersection of Shore Drive. A right turn here would take you to beautiful Cornwall Landing Park, which unfortunately is only open to town residents. Go left on Shore Drive. There are glimpses of wetlands along the mouth of Moodna Creek on the right. In the nineteenth century, its name was changed from Murderers Creek (according to legend, in the seventeenth century a female settler and her child were murdered and their bodies dumped in the creek), to the more "romantic" Moodna Creek through the efforts of Nathaniel Willis, who also changed the names of Storm King Mountain and Mount Taurus. The wetlands are part of the Moodna Creek Significant Coastal Fish and Wildlife Habitat Area, home of several state-listed endangered and special-concern species. From along the railroad tracks on the right, one may gain a better view of these wetlands. Bird-watching is reported to be particularly excellent. Some 135 species have been recorded here within a single year. In the spring, herons, least bitterns, belted kingfishers, woodcocks, pileated woodpeckers, ducks, hawks, kingbirds, swallows, owls, sandpipers, and wrens breed in the area. Teals, turkey vultures, ospreys, terns, thrushes, and grosbeaks may also be seen migrating through. In late summer, herons, bald eagles, and northern harriers are possible postbreeding dropins. At low tide in late summer to early autumn, plovers, sandpipers, wrens, and waxwings are often observed. In late fall, cormorants, gulls, peregrine falcons, kestrels and other hawks, vireos, warblers, loons, brants, geese, ducks, and golden eagles visit. In the wintertime, grebes, coots, goldfinches, and sparrows may be sighted. Moodna Creek is a spawning ground for largemouth bass, bluegills, and brown bullheads. Snapping turtles, muskrat, and raccoon also inhabit the marsh.

At 0.9 miles from the beginning, you'll reach the intersection with Route 9W. On the right, across the bridge over Moodna Creek, is the sixty-two-acre Nicholl Farm, a property owned and managed by Scenic Hudson since 1996. It contains a partially restored 1735 homestead of one of George Washington's lieutenants. The property was used as headquarters by officers of the Continental Army between 1780 and 1781. It is not officially open to the public at present. Native artifacts covering the entire prehistory of the area were excavated in the vicinity, including a Woodland age burial site. For information call Scenic Hudson at 914-473-4440.

From this intersection you can begin a very worthwhile detour that takes you to a number of historical sites from the period of the Revolutionary War when this area served as an encampment for troops of Washington's Continental Army. If you decide to do that, cross 9W at the flashing red light. *Be very careful!* There are four lanes of traffic, and this is a dangerous intersection. Continue west on Forge Hill Road for 1.4 miles till you come to the entrance to Knox Headquarters on the left.

Knox Headquarters, a state-designated historic site, is located near the corner of Forge Hill Road and Route 94. The stone house of John El-

lison, built in 1754 with a one-story clapboard wing added later, was occupied during the Revolutionary War by officers of the Continental Army
including Gens. Henry Knox, Nathanael Greene, and Horatio Gates. Ellison operated a gristmill (its ruins are nearby) and supplied grain and
wood to the Continental Army. A turnpike to Goshen once ran through
this property, and colonial farmers used it to bring their grain to Ellison's mill. The flour was then transported a short distance to a family-
owned dock on the river, where it was shipped via sloop to New York City.
The downstairs of the house has a wide gracious hall, high-ceilinged
rooms, and tall, twelve-pane windows, all reflecting the affluence of the
owner. The residence has period furnishings and is set up as it might
have been when it was an officers' headquarters.

On the grounds of Knox Headquarters is the Jane Colden Native
Plant Sanctuary, named after America's first female botanist, which features many varieties of wildflowers. An unmarked, unmaintained walking trail follows the boulder-strewn stream as it descends through a quiet
wooded area past the gristmill ruins and lovely forest scenery. The
grounds are closed in the winter. The house is open Wednesdays and
Sundays from 1:00 to 5:00 P.M., from June through Labor Day. Call 914-
561-5498 for admission fees and other information.

Just beyond Knox Headquarters, you'll reach the intersection of
Route 94, Quassaick Boulevard. There's a light. Make a left and continue
a short distance to the infamous Five Corners, a busy commercial intersection in the heart of Vails Gate. For a short detour to the Edmonston
House, go straight on 94. The house is on the right just before you reach
the Thruway underpass.

The Edmonston House is a restored 1755 stone house that includes
a blacksmith shop, slave quarters, and other exhibits, including ones on
Gen. Arthur St. Clair, who used it as a headquarters during the Revolu-
tionary War. The house now serves as the headquarters of the Temple
Hill Association, a group dedicated to preserving Revolutionary War sites.
It is open Sundays from 2:00 to 5:00 P.M. from July through September.
Admission is free. Call 914-561-5073 for information.

Backtrack to the Five Corners, and go west on Temple Hill Road,
Route 300. This is part of the "Freedom Trail" the just-released Iranian
hostages took on their way to ceremonies at West Point in January 1981.
Follow Temple Hill Road for 1.1 miles to the New Windsor Cantonment
on the right. The 120-acres are a state-designated historic site.

In 1782, following the American victory in Yorktown, six thousand
to eight thousand troops of the Northern Continental Army and five hundred civilians, including women and children, camped in the vicinity
while peace negotiations took place in Paris. The encampment was ideally

situated north of the Hudson Highlands and the fortress at West Point, and opposite Mount Beacon. It was also near abundant food resources in the Hudson Valley, and it was a position from which Washington could threaten British-held New York City in case peace negotiations should fail. The troops camped here until the war officially ended.

During this period, in which there was little military action, some important events took place nonetheless. General Washington firmly rejected the idea of becoming king of the new republic. In the Newburgh Address, he won the sympathy of his officers—disgruntled at not being paid, they were conspiring to overthrow the Continental Congress—and established the principal of civilian authority over military command. It was also here that Washington created the Order of the Purple Heart.

Among the replica structures on display at the cantonment is the Temple or Public Building. It served as a meeting place, and religious services were held there. The Mountainville, or Old Officers, Hut is the only surviving structure built by the Continental Army. It was purchased at the end of the war, moved, and served as a residence for 150 years until the state acquired it and moved the hut to its present site.

The cantonment includes a Visitors' Center and small museum. Both have displays depicting the history of the site and the life of Continental Army troops. Included are artifacts, documents, the first Purple Heart award, one of Baron von Steuben's drill manuals, a collection of original eighteenth-century artillery pieces, including a huge British thirty-two-pounder, a wonderful diorama of a regiment of the Continental Army on the march, and a film about the site. Staff on hand dressed in authentic uniforms engage in various crafts, demonstrate weaponry, and perform other daily activities of the Continental Army soldiers. The cantonment is open Wednesdays through Saturdays from 10:00 A.M. to 5:00 P.M. and Sundays from 1:00 to 5:00 P.M., from mid-April through October. There is a small admission fee, also good for Washington's Headquarters in Newburgh, should you wish to visit both sites in the same day. Call 914-561-1765 for information.

Just beyond the entrance to the New Windsor Cantonment, on the left is the Last Encampment. Parking is just off the road. Operated by the Temple Hill Association, the Last Encampment includes excavated foundations of dozens of the 572 huts constructed by Continental Army troops during their stay here. Full-size wooden replicas of two of the huts are on display. These include exhibits, artifacts excavated on the site, and an educational film. There is a picnic ground nearby and a 167-acre nature preserve with mature forests populated by sugar maples, tulip trees, poplars, red oaks, hickories, beeches, dogwoods, five sisters, poison ivy, spicebush, and barberry. There are meadows and old fields with relatively new growth of vines and brambles, including blackberry, Atlantis, honeysuckle, red cedar, and various young trees, wild onions, stump sprouts, and grasses. A large interior wetland can easily be seen from a two-story observation tower. Here you can observe red maples, black swamp ash, willows, purple loosestrife, common reeds, and various ferns. Along the edges of the wetland you'll see skunk cabbage and ferns, and you might spot jack-in-the-pulpit. Animals known to frequent the preserve include red foxes, white-tail deer, gray squirrels, raccoon, chipmunks, moles, woodchucks, rabbit, field mice, opossums, garter snakes, black rat snakes, and racers, various turtles (box, snapping, painted, and spotted), and amphibians (bullfrogs, green frogs, spring peepers, and common toads). A number of birds may also be seen including wild turkeys, tree sparrows, starlings, mourning doves, juncos, cardinals, mockingbirds, robins, grackles, cedar waxwings, woodpeckers, wrens, flickers, redwing blackbirds, and red-tailed hawks. An easy mile-long nature trail provides an excellent way to explore the preserve. Bones of an Ice Age mastodon were also excavated nearby. Open daily from dawn till dusk, the Last Encampment should be avoided in the middle of summer, when bugs are a major annoyance. The huts are open Tuesdays through Sundays, 10:00 A.M. to 5:00 P.M., from April 19 through October. Admission is free. Call 914-561-5073 for information.

From the entrance to the Last Encampment, continue west on Temple Hill Road. Slightly more than a half mile on the left is the Brewster House (there's a state historical marker). Built in 1762 by Deacon Samuel Brewster for his son, Timothy, the stonehouse served as the quarters of Chaplain Joel Barlow of the Continental Army during the Revolutionary War. It is now a restaurant.

At 0.8 miles west of the Last Encampment, you arrive at the intersection of Union Avenue (there's a light). Make a sharp right onto Union Avenue and head east. After one mile Union Avenue begins to descend, with a dramatic view of the Hudson and the Highlands in the distance. Less than a half mile beyond, you'll reach the intersection of Route 32 (there's a light here, too). Cross Route 32 and continue another mile, passing the Higby House (state historical marker) on the left. In October 1777, following the fall of Forts Clinton and Montgomery, a British courier, Daniel Taylor, was sent north through patriot lines to convey a message from Gen. Sir Henry Clinton to General Burgoyne. He was captured by the patriots near Hurley, and one Dr. Morse Higby was summoned to retrieve a silver bullet Taylor swallowed when he was apprehended. The bullet Higby removed from Taylor's stomach contained a cryptic message. Taylor was later hanged in Hurley as a spy.

Continue east on Union Avenue, passing a cemetery on both sides of the road. Less than half a mile later, you'll reach the intersection of Route 94 and another light. Continue straight another 0.4 miles to Route 9W and another light. Cross the highway and bear right. Just beyond is the intersection with River Road. Go left.

If you continue on the main route, from the intersection of Shore Drive and Route 9W, make a right onto 9W, crossing a bridge over Moodna Creek and passing the Nicholl Farm Site on the right (see description above). Continue north about one-half mile to just past a trailer park on the right. Beyond it is narrow Plum Point Lane, the entrance to Kowawese Unique Area at Plum Point, named after the Native American tribe that once inhabited the area. Kowawese is a 102-acre park owned by New York State and managed by Orange County. It was purchased by the state through funds provided by the 1986 Environmental Bond Act and finally opened to the public in October 1996. There is an extensive beach suitable for walking at low tide (swimming is forbidden). The remains of an old barge dock, picnic grounds, fishing, and wonderful panoramic views of Newburgh Bay, Cornwall, Storm King, Breakneck and Fishkill Ridge, and the Newburgh/Beacon Bridge to the north are among the attractions. Plum Point is also an excellent launching site for canoes and kayaks, and supposedly great for wind surfing.

The site was originally settled in 1680 by Patrick MacGregor. During the Revolutionary War, a line of chevaux-de-frises (sharpened timbers designed to gouge the hulls of ships), was stretched between here and Bannerman's Island to block the passage of British warships. Plum Point was also the site of an American battery of cannon. In 1778, neither was effective in stopping or slowing down the British, who sailed past on their way north to burn Kingston. On their return a few days later, the battery fired on them again in what was a largely symbolic gesture of defiance.

There are portable toilet facilities. A Visitors' Center, with rest rooms and historical and natural history exhibits, is planned to open in the summer of 1999. A network of trails is scheduled to open at the same time. Kowawese is open daily from dawn till dusk. It is closed in the winter. Admission is free.

Continue north on 9W another 0.3 miles. Make a right onto River Road. After another 0.3 miles, you'll reach the intersection with the detour. Continue north on River Road. After another half mile you'll pass storage tanks on the right and a state historical marker indicating the former site of the Newburgh Glassworks. Between 1867 and 1872 rock quarried from nearby Storm King Mountain was used here to manufacture such glass products as bottles, pocket flasks, and insulation materials. Continue 0.8 miles from the sign and you'll enter the City of Newburgh, where River Road becomes Marine Boulevard.

CITY OF NEWBURGH TO THE
NEWBURGH/BEACON BRIDGE

A walk or bike of 2.6 miles along the riverfront, with many open views and access to the river. Optional side trips include Washington's Headquarters, the Newburgh Historic District, and across the Newburgh/Beacon Bridge.

Newburgh is located on the west side of Newburgh Bay, mostly on a plateau rising three hundred feet above the river. This once very important riverport and commercial center has many historical sites, such as the Crawford House and Washington's Headquarters. It was the birthplace and home of Andrew Jackson Downing (1815–1852), one of the most renowned and influential American landscape architects, who counted Calvert Vaux, Frederick Clark Withers, and Frederick Law Olmsted among his protégés. Newburgh has a large state-designated historic district, with exquisite examples of nineteenth-century architecture, including many designed by Vaux, Withers, and Alexander Jackson Davis. The city boasts spectacular views of the river and the Hudson Highlands, especially along the waterfront and from the Newburgh/Beacon Bridge, which is popular with both pedestrians and bicyclists.

First described by Henry Hudson in 1609 as an excellent place to build a town, Newburgh was settled in 1709 by German immigrants led by Lutheran minister Joshua Kocherthal, from the Rhineland-Palatinate. They named their community after their hometown in Germany, Neuerberg-on-the Rhine. Most of these early settlers had emigrated elsewhere by 1762. Their place was taken by Scots and English, who renamed the town Newburgh, in honor of Newburgh-on-Tay, a Scottish town.

Following the American victory at Yorktown during the Revolutionary War, Newburgh served as Washington's headquarters from March 1782 to August 1783. Meanwhile the Continental Army camped nearby in New Windsor and Fishkill. Washington and his army stayed here while awaiting the outcome of peace negotiations in Paris that finally brought the war to a close.

Following the Revolutionary War, Newburgh developed as a shipping and trading center for the rich agricultural lands farther west. The construction of the Newburgh/Cochecton Turnpike improved Newburgh's access to agricultural produce and increased its importance as a shipping center. In the early nineteenth century Newburgh became an international seaport, for traders in china and ivory, as well as an important whaling port. It was also a major steamboat landing, and many famous Hudson River steamers were constructed in its shipyards. Shipping entrepreneurs like David Crawford, whose Greek Revival home is now a

BALMVILLE

Newburgh/Beacon Bridge

9W

84

Grand Ave

Marine Blvd

North St

HUDSON RIVER

NEWBURGH

Mount St Mary's College

Liberty St

Grand St

Montgomery St

Crawford House

1713 Cemetery

HISTORIC DISTRICT

South St

DOWNING PARK

Third St

Dutch Reformed Church

Newburgh City Club

Newburgh Landing

Courthouse Square

First St

Montgomery St Station

Broadway

Washington Ave

9W

Washington Headquarters

NEW WINDSOR

9W

River Rd

HUDSON RIVER

approximately $\frac{1}{2}$ mile

museum; his business partner, Thomas Powell, after whose wife, Mary, the famous steamboat was named; and Homer Ramsdell, who married Powell's daughter and later took over his business were among Newburgh's wealthiest and most powerful citizens. Besides shipping, they also invested in roads, railroads, and industry.

Renowned landscape architect Andrew Jackson Downing lived and worked in Newburgh in the mid-eighteen hundreds, as did his younger associates Vaux, Olmsted, and Withers. Downing was more famous for his influential writings than he was for his finished creations, and unfortunately little of his work remains in Newburgh. Highland Gardens, the beautiful estate he designed and lived in, was torn down in the 1930s. It was located just west of the intersection of Montgomery Street and Marine Boulevard. A chimney, the only surviving remnant from the mansion, is in the backyard of the Crawford House. Downing Park in Newburgh was designed by Vaux and Olmsted (their last joint project), as a memorial to Downing following his tragic death in a steamboat accident on the river. Many of the Gothic Revival–style homes and buildings designed by Vaux and Withers can still be seen in Newburgh's Historic District and vicinity (see below).

By the mid-nineteenth century Newburgh had become an important industrial center, with many factories producing a rich assortment of goods. Newburgh was incorporated as a city in 1865. In 1884, thanks to the efforts of Thomas Edison, Newburgh became the first community outside New York City to be wired for electricity. Newburgh, like many other Hudson River cities and towns, has seen its role as a commercial, trade, and industrial center decline in the twentieth century. Since after World War I businesses and industry have been steadily vacating the riverfront. The cessation of ferry service in 1963, following the construction of the Newburgh/Beacon Bridge and competition from stores and malls in the outskirts, led to the total abandonment of the riverfront commercial district, which was subsequently leveled by urban renewal. Today efforts are under way to revitalize Newburgh. Easy highway access to New York and other East Coast cities, a great location on the river, and the presence of nearby Stewart International Airport may yet boost the economy. With historic sites and neighborhoods, as well as impressive views of the Hudson, Newburgh has much to offer the visitor. The town unfortunately also has a reputation for crime. Visitors should exercise proper caution, especially at night, and avoid certain sections such as South Street and Lander Street.

Just west of Newburgh, next to Stewart Airport, is the 7,500-acre Stewart Buffer Zone. Some 6,200 acres of this undeveloped open-space property, managed by the DEC, are open to the public. It has lowland forests, fields, and wetlands. While there are no views of the river, there are excellent opportunities for hiking and biking along the myriad old roadways. There are no marked paths. This area has been threatened by plans calling for development. For information contact the Stewart Park and Reserve Coalition (SPARC) at Box 90, Blooming Grove, NY 10914, or call 914-564-3014.

Trailways and Shortline bus companies have a terminal located on Route 17K, close to the Thruway interchange, but unfortunately far from the city center. Trailways also makes a stop on Broadway near the intersection of Route 32 and 9W. There's a train station across the river in Beacon that's served by Metro-North. The best motel accommodations are located by the Thruway, but there are also some bed-and-breakfast establishments located in the area.

From the city limits go north on Marine Boulevard approximately one mile to the second light, Washington Street. Go left, up the hill two blocks to Washington's Headquarters at 84 Liberty Street, a state-designated historic site. The house was originally built in 1724 and enlarged in 1750–1752 when it was purchased by Jonathan Hasbrouck, a wealthy Huguenot merchant and miller. It is a typical Dutch colonial–style residence with a low roof, but it is also similar to the Huguenot stone houses in New Paltz, where Hasbrouck was from. Washington and his wife, Martha, rented it from April 1782 to August 1783, from Hasbrouck's widow. It served as both residence and headquarters for Washington, and it was his longest occupancy of any site during the war. Besides the Washingtons a number of aides, servants, and guests also resided here.

Anyone expecting a palace where this country's major VIP stayed is bound to be disappointed. Washington described the low ceilings and sparsely furnished and decorated quarters here as "confined," but he preferred to set a positive example for his fellow officers and troops. Only the parlor, located in the newer part of the house, where Martha Washington entertained guests, reflects some English style and elegance. Today the rooms are furnished with original eighteenth-century pieces and reproductions as it might have appeared during Washington's stay. Included is the original Dutch-style jambless fireplace and a desk Washington used in the Ellison House.

New York State purchased the home from the Hasbrouck family in 1850, the very first public preservation effort by a state or federal agency. The museum displays an original chain and boom from the West Point iron chain that stretched across the Hudson during the war, one of the original links of the Fort Montgomery chain, and an original section of a cheval-de-frise. All these were used to defend against British warships attempting to sail up the Hudson. There are other exhibits related to the

headquarters site, officers' decorations, documents, articles, and artifacts depicting the life of Revolutionary War soldiers, and eighteenth-century furnishings. There is a short educational film. The museum is where
house tours originate. The block-size park that surrounds the house and
museum has excellent river views. There's a limestone monument called
Tower of Victory, a statue dedicated to the Minutemen, and the grave of
a Revolutionary War soldier. The headquarters is open from mid-April to
late October, Wednesdays through Saturdays from 10:00 A.M. to 5:00 P.M.,
and Sundays from 1:00 P.M. to 5:00 P.M.. There is a small admission fee,
good for the New Windsor Cantonment as well. Call 914–562–1195 for
information.

From the corner of Washington Street, continue north on Marine
Boulevard 0.4 miles to Second Street. A right turn will bring you to Newburgh Landing, a waterfront park, the site of festivals and special events,
including a farmers' market. Sightseeing cruises aboard the *Pride of the
Hudson* depart from here.

If you go left up Second Street, you will be in the heart of the Newburgh Historic District. Like the waterfront, much of this area had deteriorated and was condemned for demolition. However, efforts like those
of Elizabeth Lyon in 1974 saved historic homes from the wrecking ball.
The district includes beautiful homes from the nineteenth century, practically all of them privately owned. A large number have already been restored. Many have excellent views of the Hudson, and many feature lovely
gardens. The open-house tours held twice a year in December and June
are events not to be missed. Call the Crawford House for information.

The area around Courthouse Square and Second and Grand Streets
includes many buildings of architectural note, such as the brick Greek
Revival–style Newburgh Courthouse, built in 1841 and designed by Thor-
ton Niven, and the First Methodist Church on Third Street, a mid-nineteenth-century Gothic Revival, designed by Rembrant Lockwood. Alexander
Jackson Davis designed the Saint George Episcopal Church in 1819, and
the Dutch Reformed Church in 1830 on Third and Grand, which many consider to be one of the finest examples of Greek Revival churches in America. It is unfortunately now in a dilapidated state. In 1998 Hillary Clinton
spoke here about restoring the church and other historical landmarks. At
112–120 First Street is Quality Row, designed by Niven and Pollard. There's
an old 1713 cemetery between Liberty and Grand Streets and South and
Clinton Streets. The ramshackle clapboard structure in the northwest corner of the cemetery, facing Liberty Street, was the eighteenth-century
Weigand Tavern.

A. J. Downing's protégés Vaux and Withers remained in Newburgh
following the architect's death and designed many of the city's most

beautiful homes, buildings, and churches in the romantic Gothic Revival style. The distinctive picturesque residence at 196 Montgomery Street, built in 1875, and today restored in its original colors, was designed by Vaux. So was the 1857 country house at 333 Grand Street, beautifully displayed in bright storybook colors. The Child Care Center at 182 Grand Street and the Saint Patrick's Rectory at 55 Grand Street were designed by Vaux and Withers. The ornate Newburgh City Club at 120 Grand Street, currently being renovated, and the large residence at 55 Broad Street, beautifully restored as luxury apartments, were designed by Vaux and Downing. Calvary Presbyterian at 120 South Street and Grand, the Seventh-Day Adventist Church at 259 Grand, and homes at 264 and 268 Grand were designed by Frederick C. Withers.

The Selah Reeve House at 131 South Street was built in 1780 as a merchant's house and also served as a Masonic temple. It was admired by many in the nineteenth century for its romantic views of the river and surrounding countryside. The Montgomery Street Station on the west side of Montgomery Street between South Street and Second Street was one of the world's first central electric stations. It was built by Thomas Edison's Electric Illuminating Company in 1884.

The stunning brick Victorian homes lining Montgomery Street are one of the highlights of Newburgh's Historic District. Also located there is the Crawford House at 189 Montgomery Street, the headquarters of the Historical Society of Newburgh Bay. The 1830 Greek Revival mansion was built by David Crawford, a prosperous steamboat operator and veteran naval officer from the War of 1812. The residence is modeled after English country houses of the Palladian tradition. The attic story projects over the portico and is supported by four forty-foot-high Ionic columns. The house contains Empire period antiques, marble fireplaces, an unsupported flying staircase, a child's room with dolls and toys, and exhibits on Hudson River steamships and sloops, including scale models of the *Clermont* and *Mary Powell*. There are guided tours from June through October, on Sundays from 1:00 to 4:00 P.M. and by appointment. There is a small admission fee. For information call 914-561-2585.

From the corner of Second Street, continue north on Marine Boulevard as it veers to the left, uphill and away from the river. After just less than a mile, make a right turn onto Grand Street. You soon leave the Newburgh city limits and enter Balmville, a residential community. There are many fine homes here, built in the nineteenth century on landscaped properties overlooking the Hudson. After 0.3 miles, you'll see the pedestrian entrance to the Newburgh/Beacon Bridge on the left, with parking along the roadside on the right.

The Newburgh/Beacon Bridge, the Hudson's newest bridge, opened on November 6, 1963, and is 7,855 feet long and 252 feet high. The bridge took two years to construct. I-84 crosses it. The bridge began as a single span, but the fact that four lanes of traffic at either end were suddenly squeezed into two caused frequent bottlenecks, most notably during the Woodstock Festival in August 1969, when traffic was backed up for several miles. A second span was completed in 1980. The pedestrian walkway is approximately two miles long. It is the longest such walkway across the Hudson and a designated part of the Greeway Trail. From here you can walk, or walk your bicycle, to Beacon and the eastern shore of the Hudson. The walk can be exhilarating or excruciating depending on your state of fitness and the wind and weather conditions. The magnificent view looking south, of Newburgh Bay, Breakneck Ridge, and Storm King, is unsurpassed. Observing the massive steel structure of the bridge itself and the river 192 feet below is also an experience. The pedestrian walkway is open year round, from dawn till dusk.

BALMVILLE TO WEST PARK

This twenty-three-mile-long segment of the route is mostly on back roads, trying hard to avoid commercial 9W. As it is you get to experience some quieter, less traveled stretches. Views of the river are infrequent. The best ones are along River Road, just north of Balmville, and from the Mid-Hudson Bridge and neighboring Johnson Iorio Memorial Park. The area between Marlboro and Highland is the region's leading producer of fruit and wine. Visitors may want to stop at one of the many roadside markets or sample wines at a local vineyard. The Gomez-Mill House, south of Marlboro, is also well worth visiting.

From the Newburgh/Beacon Bridge overpass, continue north on Grand Street, passing the Daniel B. St. John House at 40 Grand Avenue, on your right. The Gothic Revival home, with a fine river view, built in 1856 and designed by Frederick Withers, is a private residence. Just under a mile past the bridge, the road veers to the left and arrives at an intersection in front of the Balmville Tree. The giant tree, surrounded by a protective fence, has a circumference of twenty-five feet, five inches and is reported to have been a seedling in 1699. However, the claim that it is the oldest tree in Orange County is probably not true since pitch pines in the Shawangunks have been dated as older.

At the tree, make a sharp right onto Sloan Road, follow it 0.4 miles, then make another right onto River Road. A short distance beyond on the left is Morningside, a fine example of a country seat, designed by Frederick Withers and built in 1859. This stunning Gothic Revival home is nestled on a hillside and unfortunately is only partially visible. A replica of the mansion's library is on display in the Period Room exhibition in the American Wing at the Metropolitan Museum of Art in New York City. This private residence features lovely grounds that incorporate elements of Downing's romantic landscape design. Giant specimen trees, including copper beech, are present.

After less than a half mile on River Road, you pass a number of lavish modern homes on the right with river views. Views of the river continue uninterrupted for the next two miles. After three miles you'll pass a huge power-generating plant on the right. Nearby is Danskammer Point, which according to traditions takes its name from the Dutch words for "devil's dance hall." It is reputed to have been the site of native ceremonial dances performed prior to hunting or fishing expeditions, or warfare. These ceremonies were first observed by Henry Hudson and later more fully described by Lt. Pieter Couwenhoven, who commanded a detachment of Dutch volunteers and Long Island Indians during the Second Esopus War, in 1663. The ceremonies apparently continued to be held until the beginning of the eighteenth century.

After Danskammer Point, the road veers sharply left. Continue another 0.6 miles to a corner by Cedar Hill Cemetery. Andrew Jackson Downing is buried here, in section 46. From River Road, make a sharp right onto Old Post Road. Go about one and a half miles, and make a left onto Mill House Road. Follow Mill House Road for approximately half a mile. On the right is the Gomez Mill House.

The Gomez Mill House was built in 1714 by Luis Moses Gomez, a prosperous Jewish immigrant from Spain whose family, faced with expulsion in 1492, had ostensibly "converted" to Catholicism but for many years continued to practice their Jewish religion and customs in secret. During the Inquisition even converts faced persecution, however, and the family fled to the Caribbean and eventually settled in New York City, where they joined a small community of Spanish and Portuguese Jews who had taken up residence there. Gomez became a wealthy trader, building and owning New York City's first synagogue. In 1714 he purchased six thousand acres of land in the Hudson Valley and moved there and built this fortresslike house with three-foot-thick stone walls. There he lived part-time for the next thirty years with his sons, selling the land and trading with the Esopus Indians. He also built a sawmill on a nearby stream, which came to be known as Jew's Creek. The home was later purchased by Wolfert Ecker, a Dutch American who served as a lieutenant in the Revolutionary War. Ecker added a second story made of bricks manufactured by slaves near Roseton. The house served as a meeting place for patriots during the war. Later Ecker replaced the sawmill with a gristmill and established a landing on the Hudson and a ferry and shipping line to carry freight downriver to New York City.

In the early twentieth century the famous papermaker and craftsman Dard Hunter lived here. He built an Old English–style mill with a thatched roof, which has been recently restored. The home was purchased by the Starin family after World War II. With great effort Mildred Starin restored the home and had it designated a National Historic Landmark. Continuously inhabited for 281 years, the Gomez Mill House is the oldest manor house in Orange County as well as the oldest surviving Jewish home in North America. Mostly original period furnishings from the past three centuries are on display, including decorative Jewish ceremonial pieces. There are tours and a small admission fee. Open from April 20 through October 27, Wednesdays, Saturdays, and Sundays from 10:00 A.M. to 4:00 P.M. For reservations or information call 914-236-3126 or fax 914-236-3365.

From the intersection of Mill House Road and 9W, go right (north) onto 9W and continue one mile into the small village of Marlboro. Perched on a bluff overlooking the falls and valley of the Old Man's Kill where it enters the Hudson, this eclectic-looking village was formerly an active steamboat landing and shipping center for agricultural produce. Today fruit growing remains the primary activity, and the area's many orchards and vineyards are the main attraction for visitors. The town has several restaurants. The hills west of the town are very picturesque. A remarkable view of the Hudson with the falls of the Old Man's Kill plunging in the foreground may be observed from the dining room of the Raccoon Saloon.

Continue on 9W north through the village. After 0.9 miles, off to the right is the Lewis Dubois House, built in 1757. Colonel Dubois, the original owner, was an officer during the Revolutionary War and was visited here by General Washington. Cannonballs have been discovered on the property, which was fired upon by the British on their way to Kingston in 1777. The home is privately owned and not open to the public.

A half mile farther up the road, 9W widens to three lanes and climbs a hill. Just before the crest of the hill, look behind you on the left side of 9W for an extensive view of the Hudson, with Fishkill Ridge in the distance. On the left is a broad pastoral view of orchards and vineyards.

After another mile and a half, turn right onto South Road. There's a sign for Milton on the corner. On South Road you immediately pass a 1760 one-story stone house on the right, the Micajiah Lewis Homestead, beautifully restored as a private residence. At 0.6 miles make a right turn onto Maple Road, and after another 0.3 miles, you'll reach a T-intersection with Dock Road, paved with bricks. Detour right, downhill, a short distance to the Kedeem Fruit Warehouse and an open view of the river, right across from the IBM plant.

Backtrack up Dock Road and continue uphill a short distance to the intersection opposite the post office in the center of the small hamlet of Milton. One mile west of Milton on the Milton Turnpike is the Hudson Valley Materials Exchange, a nonprofit recycling center open to the public. It's worthwhile for shopping and investigating creative ways to reduce the waste stream. Call 914-795-5507 for information and hours.

Go right, onto Milton Road. After 0.1 mile you'll pass a lovely orchard on the right. Beautiful nineteenth-century homes line both sides of the road for the next 1.1 miles, an idyllic rural ambience, until you reach busy 9W again. Make a right onto 9W. Continue north one and a half miles, passing Illinois Mountain on the left, a prominent hill more than nine hundred feet high, composed of harder, erosion-resistant Ordovician sandstone, the highest point in the Marlboro Mountains. It is privately owned and off limits to the public.

Now 9W widens to four lanes, passing a shopping center on the right. Beyond it is the exit for the Mid-Hudson Bridge. Just beyond that, make a right onto Haviland Road. There's a sign for Johnson Iorio Park on the corner.

Down the road 0.3 miles, you'll pass the unmarked entrance to the Poughkeepsie Railroad Bridge on the left. Begun in 1873 and completed in 1889, the bridge was the first span across the Hudson south of Albany. It is 5,280 feet long and 212 feet above the river. A 1974 fire destroyed a large section of track and rendered the bridge useless for train traffic. It was never repaired and has been closed ever since. Some officials have attempted to remove what they consider to be an eyesore, but there has been a popular effort to save the bridge and turn it into a pedestrian walkway. Tours were being conducted on a regular basis but were halted by legal challenges. For information call 914-454-9649/1110.

Continue to the end of Haviland Road where it enters a gate and tiny Johnson Iorio Memorial Park, named for two soldiers killed in the Vietnam War. There are picnic tables and benches, with an open view of the river with the Mid-Hudson Bridge and Poughkeepsie across the way. This is also the entrance to the pedestrian walkway for the Mid-Hudson Bridge.

Designed by Ralph Modjeski (1861–1940), one of the leading bridge designers of his day, the Mid-Hudson Bridge is a three-thousand-foot-long steel suspension span. It opened in 1930 and towers 135 feet above the river. The pedestrian walkway has great views looking north. One can walk or bike from here to Poughkeepsie and the east shore of the Hudson.

Backtrack 0.2 miles to the River Road intersection. Make a right onto River Road and descend the steep hill. You'll pass underneath the Pough-keepsie Railroad Bridge. Make a right onto Mile Hill Road and continue the steep descent another 0.2 miles to a T-intersection. Go left on Oakes Road, and cross the railroad tracks. There's a view of the river and the Mid-Hudson Bridge towering overhead to the right. You'll pass a restaurant on the right and a marina. A ferry here to Poughkeepsie was bombarded by the British in 1778 on their way north to Kingston. This area, part of the village of Highland waterfront, is planned for redevelopment including more recreational use. The road bears left and crosses the tracks again, then climbs a steady incline. A little more than half a mile beyond the tracks, make a sharp right onto Belvue Road. The road bends right and climbs more steeply, finally leveling out with partial views of the river through the trees. Continue north through a wooded residential area interspersed with undeveloped deciduous forest. A mile and a half from the intersection, make a right onto Red Top Road. This road bends sharply to the left and continues two miles to an intersection with Route 9W.

Route 9W is four lanes of divided highway here, with a nice wide shoulder. Go right, north. After one-half mile there's a view of the river looking north. After another mile the road narrows to two lanes. The tiny hamlet of West Park is reached after traveling another half mile.

WEST PARK TO KINGSTON

The eight miles of this segment, all of which are on 9W and River Road, are practically untouched by commercial blight and are the most scenic in this chapter, particularly the section along River Road from which there are excellent views of the Hudson. For hikers there are worthwhile side trips to the Burroughs Sanctuary, Shaupeneak Ridge, Black Creek Forest, and Esopus Meadows, all private preserves open to the public. A visit to the Klyne Esopus Museum will acquaint visitors with the history of this area.

West Park is a lovely little hamlet where much of the choice riverfront land is owned by various Catholic orders. There are many glimpses of the river through the trees. Areas of conifer forests just a mile west of 9W, in and around the Burroughs Sanctuary, have an incredibly wild feel, totally unexpected here smack in the middle of a long-populated area.

West Park gains most of its fame from its association with the naturalist John Burroughs. Born in Roxbury, New York, in the Catskills, Burroughs moved to West Park in 1873, and built his home, called Riverby,

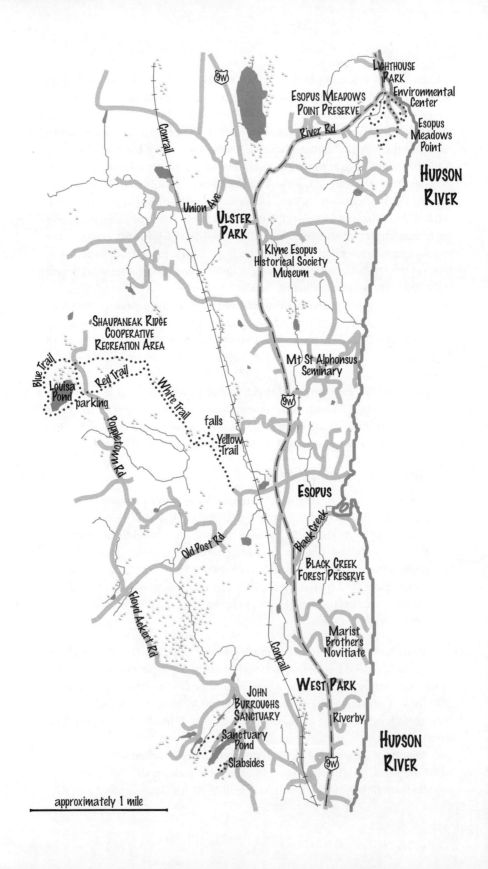

Conrail

9W

Esopus Meadows
Point Preserve

LIGHTHOUSE
PARK

Environmental
Center

Esopus
Meadows
Point

River Rd

HUDSON
RIVER

Union Ave

ULSTER
PARK

Klyne Esopus
Historical Society
Museum

SHAUPANEAK RIDGE
COOPERATIVE
RECREATION AREA

Mt St Alphonsus
Seminary

Blue Trail

Red Trail

Louisa
Pond

parking

White Trail

9W

falls

Poppletown Rd

Yellow
Trail

ESOPUS

Black Creek

Old Post Rd

BLACK CREEK
FOREST PRESERVE

Floyd Ackert Rd

Marist
Brothers
Novitiate

Conrail

WEST PARK

JOHN
BURROUGHS
SANCTUARY

Riverby

HUDSON
RIVER

Sanctuary
Pond

Slabsides

9W

approximately 1 mile

there. Riverby was a nine-acre working farm where Burroughs raised grapes and spent the rest of his life. Besides his writing and agrarian pursuits, he also worked as a bank examiner for the federal government and later as West Park's first postmaster. At his nearby Bark Study, overlooking the Hudson, he composed many of his famous works. His admiration of nature and his fascination with it in all its complexity reflect the romantic sentiments of the late nineteenth century. He wrote nature essays, travelogues, scientific treatises, literary criticism, and political and social commentary. At his best he successfully blended science with art. Burroughs was visited here by students, writers, reporters, scientists, and such luminaries as Theodore Roosevelt, John Muir, Oscar Wilde, Thomas Edison, Henry Ford, and Walt Whitman. Ironically, Burroughs grew weary of the view of the Hudson from Riverby, preferring the intimacy of small streams to the grandeur of a great river. In 1895 he built a rustic cabin nearby, known as Slabsides, which he used a retreat. Slabsides is located at the John Burroughs Sanctuary. Those interested in learning more about the life of this fascinating personality should read the marvelous biography written by Edward J. Renahan, Jr., available in paperback from Black Dome Press.

From the beginning of West Park, continue north on 9W, 0.7 miles, crossing a bridge over the West Shore railroad tracks. Here the railroad leaves the shore of the Hudson and continues an inland course northward toward Albany. At the bottom of the hill is the intersection with Floyd Ackert Road. Detour left, cross the railroad tracks, and continue uphill, approximately one mile west of 9W to the entrance to the John Burroughs Sanctuary on the left side of the road. The 174-acre nature preserve is owned and operated by the John Burroughs Memorial Association, a private nonprofit group that, in addition to managing the preserve, runs scheduled outings. The preserve is thickly forested with secondary growth. Oaks and hickories are prevalent in the warmer drier areas. In the moister, cooler spots, such northern hardwoods as maples and birches as well as large hemlock stands can be seen. Some 142 species of birds have been sighted in the preserve, including a number of hawk species that breed in the vicinity, also ruffed grouse, cuckoos, owls, whippoorwills, various woodpecker species, wrens, wood thrushes, eastern bluebirds, gnatcatchers, vireos, warblers, and ovenbirds. There's abundant other wildlife as well, including beaver, deer, foxes, and the occasional bear. Frogs are particularly plentiful in shallow woodland pools, and their singing is noteworthy in the early spring, sometimes before all the snow has melted. There are hiking, biking, and cross-country ski trails.

The main feature of the preserve is Slabsides, John Burroughs's picturesque cabin. The cabin is still simply furnished with pieces Burroughs made by hand with materials he found nearby in the forest. Slabsides is a designated National Historic Site. Nearby is a swamp Burroughs used to grow celery, and there's a two-hundred-yard-long nature trail that leads to a spring that supplied the naturalist with water. A brochure, available at the cabin, corresponds to ten numbered stations along the way.

To get to Slabsides from Floyd Ackert Road, go left on Burroughs Drive, a little more than a quarter mile to a sign for Slabsides on the right. Cars can park on the road here. Walk or bike a hundred yards on a dirt road to Slabsides. The nature trail is just beyond.

A couple of hundred yards past Burroughs Drive is the preserve's second entrance, on the left. There's a gate and a sign for the preserve. You may park right off Floyd Ackert Road. Hike or bike through hemlock stands up the dirt road called Pond Lane. After a quarter mile you'll reach human-made Sanctuary Pond on the left. Just before the pond is a turnoff for the Alfred Adams Connector Trail, which skirts the north end of the pond and continues one-third of a mile east to Burroughs Drive.

Continuing south on Pond Lane, you'll pass a peninsula jutting into the pond with huge slanting slabs of Ordovician sandstone. A trail on the left goes a short distance to the end of the peninsula. There's a beaver lodge and a number of downed trees with the chew marks characteristic of the beaver's work. Follow Pond Lane south another hundred yards to the Pond House on the right, the sanctuary's headquarters. It serves as a meeting place for the John Burroughs Society and as a library for his works. Explanatory brochures for the Alfred Adams Connector Trail are located here. Just before the Pond House was the site of the Boglio Hotel, which burned in 1939. (The Pond House used to be servants' quarters for the hotel. Stone terrace walls and a statue of Bacchus remain.) The trail continues south, parallel to the pond, and then loops back through the forest to Pond Lane, across from the peninsula. The Burroughs Sanctuary is open year round and admission is free. Slabsides is open twice a year, on the third Saturday in May and the first Saturday in October. For more information call 914-338-8830 or 914-679-2642.

Nearby is Black Creek, which descends from here toward the Hudson in a beautiful series of falls. The surrounding rugged terrain has forest with relatively old growth. This was a favorite spot where Burroughs and his friend Walt Whitman used to walk.

Return to 9W and continue north. On the right is Aberdeen, the Frothinham homestead, built around 1830, an outstanding example of Greek Revival architecture. Just beyond it on the right is Riverby, the unassuming former residence of John Burroughs (mentioned above), visible from 9W only when the leaves are down.

Continue north on 9W. Less than a half mile on the right is the quaint stone Episcopal Church of the Ascension, built in 1852. The beautiful grounds have stunning views of the Hudson and Hyde Park beyond.

A little more than half a mile further up the road you'll pass the entrance to the Marist Brothers Novitiate on the right, formerly the Payne Estate, built in 1910 by Col. Oliver Hazard Payne (1842–1917), a Civil War general and later a rich stockholder in Standard Oil. The house, constructed of imported limestone, was a copy of an Italian mansion, and was designed by the firm of Carere and Hastings, which also designed the New York Public Library on Fifth Avenue in Manhattan. It is closed to the public and not visible from 9W. However, there's a good view of it from the Vanderbilt Mansion grounds across the river. The giant medieval-looking stone stables, part of the estate, can be seen on the left when the leaves are down. They were designed by Julian Burroughs, John Burroughs's son.

After another half mile, descending most of the way, the road crosses Black Creek. A 130-acre area east of 9W is owned by Scenic Hudson, which acquired the property in 1992 as the Black Creek Forest Preserve and created a two-mile-long trail network. Americorp and volunteer groups were involved in this trail-building effort. The mouth of Black Creek where it enters the Hudson is a part of the park. This park opened to the public in spring 1999. The preserve has parking, informative signboards, and a cool suspension bridge over Black Creek. For information call Scenic Hudson at 914-473-4440.

Continue north on 9W, climbing another half mile to the intersection with Old Post Road in the tiny hamlet of Esopus. Detour left on Old Post Road. Go west one-tenth of a mile, crossing the railroad tracks. The entrance to Shaupeneak Ridge Cooperative Recreation Area is on the right. There's a parking area and information kiosk, with a second parking area off Popletown Road next to Louisa Pond. Shaupeneak is a five-hundred-acre forest preserve owned and managed by Scenic Hudson, the New York State Department of Environmental Conservation, and the West Esopus Landowners Association. The property mostly comprises a steep wooded ridge of Ordovician rock, hundreds of feet high, part of the Marlboro Mountains. The plateau summit includes a clear pond in a glacially carved depression and wetland with cattails, lilies, and loosestrife. The property used to belong to a private hunting club. Hunting is still allowed with a permit. The preserve is being developed for low-impact recreation; hiking, canoeing, hunting, fishing, and bird-watching. Shaupeneak has the best hiking opportunities in this section of the Hudson region: great scenery, views, and a good workout. It is open year round and admission is free. You should take proper precautions during hunting season, however.

The White Trail heads north from the lower parking lot along the edge of a field, ascends the ridge, and links to the Yellow Trail and later the Red Loop Trail. The Yellow Trail gradually ascends through an area of old stone fences and large deciduous and hemlock trees, with a rich undergrowth of ferns, yew sprouts, and mosses. A Purple Trail detours north to a view of a small picturesque waterfall. The Yellow Trail continues to ascend, more steeply, to the left of a stream. The trail then veers to the left, finally rejoining the White Trail again. The White Trail reaches the plateau and levels out, crosses a drainage area, and continues another quarter mile to an intersection with the Red Loop Trail. Turn right on the Red Loop Trail and head for the edge of the cliff where there's a magnificent panoramic view of the Hudson and Esopus Island with Mount Saint Alphonsus Seminary in the foreground and Mills/Norrie State Park on the opposite side of the river.

The Red Loop Trail continues west, mostly level, another quarter mile to another view, this time looking north at the Catskills and the Rondout and Esopus Valleys. A short distance beyond, the trail crosses Popletown Road, where it links with the Blue Trail that circles Louisa Pond. The north side of the pond is a wetland with abundant ducks, geese, and great blue herons. Beaver are also present. The Blue Trail passes through thick stands of conifers and, after a mile, crosses the stream at the south end of the pond. Near the south end of the pond is another parking area. One could also begin here, with a number of hiking options.

Return to 9W via Old Post Road. Continue north on 9W another 0.6 miles, passing the Mount Saint Alphonsus Seminary on the right, a massive four-and-a-half-story stone structure built in 1900 by a Roman Catholic Redemptorist Order in the Romanesque style. It is barely visible through the trees and can be better observed from Shaupeneak Ridge or from Norrie Point across the river.

Half a mile north you enter the tiny hamlet of Ulster Park, passing orchards on your left, with an excellent view of Shaupeneak Ridge to the west. Another half mile on your left is the Klyne Esopus Historical Society Museum, located in a Dutch Reformed church built in 1827 out of handmade bricks. Informal exhibits include native artifacts collected locally, farm implements, and tools used in ice harvesting on the Hudson. There is a display devoted to Alton B. Parker (1852–1926), an Esopus resident who served as a justice on the New York State Supreme Court and in 1906 ran for president against Teddy Roosevelt. Another exhibit is devoted to Sojourner Truth. Born a slave in nearby Rifton around 1797,

she was auctioned off in 1806. By the time she was thirteen she had been
sold three times. She ended up with a West Park farmer named John Du-
mont, who mistreated her. In 1826 she escaped. The following year all
slaves in New York State were declared legally freed. With the help of
Quakers she sued her former master, who had sold her son into slavery
in Alabama at a time when it was illegal to sell slaves out of state. In
1828, at the Ulster County Courthouse in Kingston, she won her case;
her son was freed and returned to her. Later she became an evangelist,
touring the country. Truth worked with leaders like Abraham Lincoln
and William Lloyd Garrison. She died in 1883. The museum also has a
genealogical library. It's open Saturdays and Sundays from 1:00 P.M. to
4:00 P.M. from the third weekend in May through the third weekend in October. Call 914-338-8109 for information.

Less than a quarter mile up 9W, make a right onto River Road, a designated scenic road. The next four miles are extremely rewarding and include the best views of the river in this section of the Hudson region.
Climb a steep hill, then level off, passing an orchard on the right. On the
left there's an old one-room schoolhouse with a steeple, beautifully restored as a private residence. Just beyond, the road bends to the left and
descends with a view of the river in the distance in the winter. Often seen
walking along the road are groups of bearded men wearing plaid shirts
and trousers with suspenders and women with old-fashioned long skirts
and kerchiefs wrapped around their heads and often accompanied by
large numbers of children. These are Hutterians from the nearby Maple
Ridge Bruderhof. The Hutterians are an international Christian community founded in the 1920s in Germany. Today more than two thousand
members live in eight communal settlements or "hofs." They practice
strict Christian values (divorce, crime, drugs, violence, and premarital
sex are forbidden) and support themselves manufacturing quality children's toys. At 1.3 miles from the beginning of the road, you'll reach the
Esopus Meadows Environmental Education Center on the right.

The center is operated by Clearwater. There are exhibits here, along
with views of the river looking east of the Esopus Meadows Lighthouse
and north toward the Kingston-Rhinecliff Bridge with the Catskills in the
distance. Esopus Meadows is a broad, barely submerged square mile of
tidal flats, no more than three feet deep even at high tide. Cattle used to
graze here. It is a designated Significant Coastal Fish and Wildlife Habitat. Aquatic vegetation is plentiful, especially water chestnuts. In late
summer the tidal flats are literally paved with green. Anadromous fish
use the shallow-vegetation waters here to spawn and feed. The shortnose sturgeon, an endangered species, is one fish that breeds here.
Herons, egrets, and bitterns feed in the shallow waters. Snapping turtles

are also present. Just beyond the shallows is the main channel of the river, which drops off abruptly to a depth of sixty feet.

The lighthouse was built in 1872, replacing an earlier one completed in 1839. Like the Rondout Lighthouse, the Saugerties Lighthouse, and the Athens Lighthouse, the Esopus Meadows Lighthouse also served as a residence for the lighthouse keeper and his family. Because of its remote location in the middle of the river, it was often difficult to supply in the wintertime. It is the only remaining Hudson River lighthouse built with a wooden frame and a clapboard exterior. The lighthouse operated until 1965, when it was replaced by an automated navigational aid. In 1979 it was listed in the National Register of Historic Places. The Save the Esopus Meadows Lighthouse Commission was formed to restore and preserve this landmark. They may be contacted at P.O. Box 1290, Port Ewen, NY 12466.

Past the environmental center is the ninety-three-acre Esopus Meadows Point Preserve, which is owned and managed by Scenic Hudson. The 2.01 miles of trail in the park are designated part of the Hudson River Greenway Trail. At the environmental center parking lot there's an information board with brochures and maps. An old dirt road, part of the blue-marked Meadows Flats Trail, continues east a short distance parallel to the river, providing more views, ending at Esopus Meadows Point, a dock and picnic area. You can walk along the shore here at low tide. The Meadows Flats Trail also loops through the hilly forest terrain underlain by Ordovician shale and sandstone, past a small shale pit with a view of the river and the Esopus Meadows Lighthouse. The Klyne Esopus Trail and the Upland Forest Trail also wind through the hilly forest. Despite the lack of elevation, some trails are fairly rugged and require caution. The Klyne Esopus Kill meanders through the west side of the property, creating deep ravines. It enters the Hudson right by the signboard. There are also forest wetlands, some of which are permanent while others occur primarily in the spring or after rainy periods. Mixed deciduous trees such as hophornbeams, oaks, hickories, maples, birches, and tulip trees, as well as hemlocks and white pines are present. Deer, wild turkeys, foxes, coyotes, opossums, skunks, raccoon, and rabbit are some of the animals that might be seen here.

Just beyond the Environmental Center, on the right, is the tiny Lighthouse Park, a town of Esopus park, with parking, picnic tables, benches, and views of the river, Esopus Meadows, the lighthouse, the Kingston-Rhinecliff Bridge, and the Catskills in the distance.

River Road continues directly along the river. There's a popular fishing spot on the right 0.8 miles past Lighthouse Park, from which ducks, geese, and swans can often be observed. The road passes numerous attractive houses, many built right along the river. Finally it swings left (west) away from the river and, four miles from the beginning, rejoins Route 9W in Port Ewen.

Port Ewen was a corporate town, built in 1851 by the Pennsylvania Coal Company and named in honor of its president, John Ewen. Most of the town's fourteen hundred residents were employed in constructing the company's coal barges. During the nineteenth century the areas adjacent to Rondout were important industrial centers, and Port Ewen was a significant industrial satellite. Today it is primarily residential. The most attractive areas are east of 9W on bluffs overlooking the river. Essentially it serves as a low-key segue into Kingston.

Go right on 9W through the modest village center. After one mile the road widens to four lanes. Just beyond, there's a light at the intersection of North Broadway. Detour right here for Sleightsburg Spit Town Park. Follow North Broadway as it bends sharply to the left, with an open view of the river on the right. Descend 0.4 miles to First Street on the right. Make a right here and, a short distance later, the first left onto Everson, a dead end. On the right is Sleightsburg Spit Park. This seventy-nine-acre property (twenty-two acres are land based; the rest is marshland), was acquired by Scenic Hudson in 1994. Today it is owned and managed by the town of Esopus (officially scheduled to open in May 1999). It is located on the narrow neck of land between Rondout Creek and a shallow wetland area to the south. The Skillipot, a cable ferry, once connected this area to the Rondout, located on the opposite shore. A rough gravel road east leads to a parking area. From there a wide path continues east another quarter mile to a small wooded island accessible only at low tide. The terrain is wooded and in many places wet. A short path to the south leads to excellent views of the marsh and mudflats with characteristic plants; cattails, arrowroot, and heartleaf plantain, wading birds such as herons, and many ducks. Ospreys visit during the spring migration. There's a camouflaged shelter blind for observation. The marsh is a spawning ground for anadromous as well as resident fish. It's hoped that eventually Sleightsburg Spit will be connected by trail to the town of Esopus Beach, located one mile south.

Backtrack to 9W and the light. Go straight, crossing 9W, and follow the road 0.3 miles as it winds downhill and crosses the old suspension bridge over Rondout Creek. Completed in 1921, this was one of the earliest suspension bridges and served as a model for larger suspension bridges that came later. The bridge replaced the Skillipot cable ferry (see above). (According to stories, a female riveter—an extremely rare phenomenon in pre–World War II days–attracted the attention of spectators whenever she worked on the bridge.) From the bridge there's a wonderful view, looking east, of the Rondout neighborhood, with the Hudson in the distance. Below is Island Dock. This artificial island in the middle of Rondout Creek was once buried beneath immense piles of Pennsylvania coal, 70 to 80 feet high, awaiting transfer to barges to be shipped downriver to New York City. Canal boats docked here. Their operators also lived on them, and so this area came to resemble a small floating community. The Rondout Creek used to be the eastern terminus of the Delaware and Hudson Canal. Looking west you'll see the 150-foot-high West Shore Railroad Bridge. The 1,200-foot-long railroad bridge was built in 1883 and is still in use. As you cross the old 9W Bridge, you enter the city of Kingston.

Beautifully situated between the Hudson and the Catskill Mountains, Kingston is the largest city on the west bank of the Hudson between Newburgh and Albany, and the county seat of Ulster County. As the first capital of New York State and the site of one of its oldest colonial settlements, Kingston is very rich in history. The city is endowed with more than three hundred years of architectural heritage, including more than two dozen structures dating back to the seventeenth and eighteenth centuries. It may be useful to think of Kingston as two separate towns. There's Kingston itself, with the Stockade section (also called Uptown), its oldest part. As the name indicates, the Stockade area was once fortified. Today it's the commercial heart of the city and where most of its seventeenth- and eighteenth-century buildings and homes are located. There's also the Rondout, once a separate village that was a busy port and shipping center. It, too, has a colorful history.

The two communities merged in 1878. Both are state-designated Urban Cultural Parks with many attractions and visitors' centers. Quiet residential streets provide many opportunities for lovely walks and biking. The 3.77-mile-long Heritage Trail links the Stockade neighborhood with the Rondout. In 1997 it was designated part of the Hudson River Greenway Trail. There is also the 1.66-mile-long Greenway Trail, created by the Kingston YMCA, which links the Rondout with Kingston Point.

The Rondout area has a large assortment of restaurants and cafés, antique stores, art galleries, and boutiques as well as bed-and-breakfast accommodations. The Stockade area also has shopping and numerous food establishments. Information about dining, shopping, accommodations, and special events is available from the Urban Cultural Park Visitors' Centers (see below). Kingston also benefits from its proximity to nearby Woodstock, an art and cultural center. Trailways has a bus terminal on the corner of Washington and North Front Streets, near the Stockade area. Call 1-800-225-6815 for information on fares and schedules. Kingston Citibus has hourly service except on Sundays and major holidays. Call 914-331-3725 for information. There's also a weekend trolley service geared to visitors. The Ulster County Mini Rural Bus has daily service to Saugerties and New Paltz. Call 914-339-4910 for information. On the opposite side of the river in Rhinecliff is a train station served by Amtrak.

The Kingston area was first settled by the Europeans in 1652. Led by Thomas Chambers, they disembarked at what is now Rondout and traveled overland to the fertile lowlands along Esopus Creek to the north and west. The settlers were former tenant farmers who moved from Rensselaerswyck, near Troy, because of the political and economic restrictions of living within that patroonship. They farmed the lowlands along Esopus Creek and called their community Esopus. Esopus was the fourth permanent community in the Dutch New Netherland colony. Settlement of the area inevitably led to conflicts with the Esopus Native Americans who lived nearby and cultivated adjacent fields. After several violent clashes in which a child and a man were killed and a farm destroyed, in 1658 the settlers constructed a stockade under the guidance of Peter Stuyvesant to protect the community from raids. (Remnants of the stockade were uncovered in excavations in 1970.) Tensions between the Dutch settlers and the indigenous people continued to grow, leading to the First Esopus War in 1659, in which Esopus was besieged by hundreds of warriors for two and a half weeks. There were casualties, and prisoners were taken on both sides. Some were tortured and killed. With the help of other tribes, a peace treaty was finally signed in 1660 in which the Esopus Native Americans were forced to cede additional lands to the Dutch as well as pay restitution. Some of the tribesmen captured in the war were shipped to the Caribbean and sold into slavery. Three years of peace followed, but tensions remained high.

During this time the settlement grew, and the boundaries of the stockade expanded. The name of the community was changed to Wiltwyck, meaning "wild woods." A second village, called Nieuwe Dorp ("new town"), was constructed a mile and a half to the south, where Hurley is currently located. Most new settlers received their land either free or at low cost from the government of New Netherland, which was anxious to promote settlement.

In 1663 Wiltwyck and Nieuwe Dorp were both surprise-attacked by the Esopus. Twenty-one settlers were killed, and women and children were taken hostage. Militia counterattacked and, after more than one attempt, managed to rescue all the hostages. In the process native villages were destroyed, and a lot of their valuable cropland was burned. This led to the eventual defeat and destruction of the Esopus tribe. Again sachems from other tribes were employed to help negotiate a settlement to the conflict in 1664.

In 1664 Wiltwyck came under British control and in 1673 was re-named Kingston, though it was still more popularly referred to as Eso-pus. It was garrisoned by British troops, and there was tension between the British and the local Dutch inhabitants. The arrest of a sergeant in the citizens' militia in 1667 led to an uprising by armed civilians, which was resolved peacefully, however. The British soldiers were later rewarded by grants of farmland in the Marbletown area. Many Huguenots from France migrated to the area, where they intermarried with the Dutch and British. Kingston became one of the leading centers of wheat production in colonial America. During the French and Indian Wars, Kingston served as a base of military operations.

Just before the American Revolution, in 1775, there was an alleged conspiracy by slaves to destroy the town and massacre its citizens. About twenty slaves were caught and imprisoned.

In 1777, during the American Revolution, the New York State Senate met in Kingston in the Abraham van Gaasbeek House, while the State Assembly met nearby at Bogardus Tavern. Kingston was also the site of New York State's first constitutional convention. In July 1777, George Clinton (1739–1812) was sworn in as the first governor of New York State at the Kingston Courthouse. Two months later Chief Justice John Jay opened the first term of the New York State Supreme Court there.

Hoping to divert the Americans who had trapped General Burgoyne and his army near Saratoga, the British, under Maj. Gen. Sir John Vaughn, sailed up the Hudson in October 1778 in the armed frigate *Friendship.* Learning that Burgoyne had already surrendered, the British burned Kingston on October 16 in retribution. Vaughn called Kingston "a nursery for almost every villain in the country." The British did not remain long, however, and the town was quickly rebuilt. No longer the state capital, Kingston nevertheless continued to prosper as the center of a rich agricultural region. The building of the Ulster/Delaware Turn-pike helped open the town to new markets.

Meanwhile the tiny village of Rondout served as Kingston's port on the Hudson. Originally called Redoubt, it was later corrupted to Run-doubt and finally Rondout. The completion of the Delaware and Hudson Canal in 1828 allowed high-grade anthracite coal, mined in Pennsylva-nia, to be transported via boat to Rondout, where it was transferred to river craft and shipped down the Hudson to New York City. Rondout's prominence as a shipping center and port grew practically overnight. In addition to coal, locally quarried bluestone, cement, and bricks were shipped from here. Rondout became the most important port on the west side of the Hudson between Albany and Newburgh, as well as a leading industrial and commercial center. Rondout became the home port for the *Mary Powell,* the Hudson's most famous steamship. The town had its own opera house and a number of magnificent mansions owned by the town's elite, overlooking the community. It also had an unsavory reputation for being an unruly place with a large immigrant population, crowded shanty-towns, numerous incidents of brawling and street fighting, and more than fifty saloons.

By 1870 Rondout's population had reached ten thousand. It had out-grown neighboring Kingston, which also benefited from Rondout's growth while becoming an important railroad and manufacturing center in its own right. Rondout's bid to incorporate as a city failed, and in 1878 it merged with its smaller neighbor. Competition from the railroads even-tually forced the Delaware and Hudson Canal to close in 1904. Steamship traffic on the Hudson and rail connections from Kingston Point helped to maintain Rondout's commercial viability into the twentieth century. How-ever, the eventual decline of the railroads as well as steamship travel led to economic stagnation. Rondout continued to languish, losing popula-tion and businesses. By the 1960s urban renewal projects had leveled much of what had been the center of town. In 1970 a community group named SCORE was formed to rehabilitate the old Rondout neighborhood. In 1979 Rondout was added to the National Register of Historic Places. By the 1980s gentrification was already taking place. Kingston's Stock-ade area has undergone a similar revitalization. The loss of a huge IBM plant on the outskirts of Kingston in the early nineties was indicative of a local economy in transition. As this community transforms itself in the twenty-first century, its rich cultural heritage will certainly play a key role in efforts to attract tourists and prospective businesses.

TOURING KINGSTON ON FOOT OR BY BIKE

After crossing the old suspension bridge, go east on Abeel Street (part of the Kingston Greenway Trail). Cornell Park, which has a wonderful view of the Rondout neighborhood and the confluence of Rondout Creek with the Hudson, is located two short blocks north of this intersection at the corner of Wurts and Hunter Streets. Continue east on Abeel a short distance and make a right on Company Hill Path just before the West End Grill, which was once a synagogue and then a church. The Com-pany Hill Path led from the waterfront, uphill to the main headquarters of the Delaware and Hudson Canal Company. Workers would tread up this path to get their paychecks. The Company Hill Path continues down to West Strand, opposite West Strand Park on the right. West Strand Park

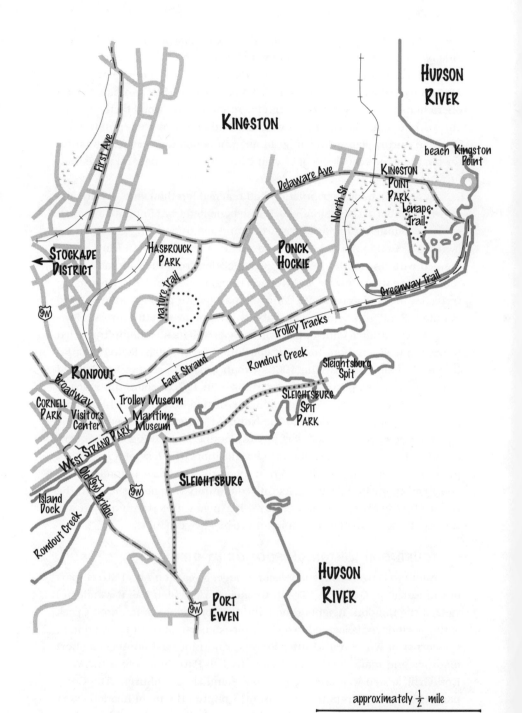

HUDSON
RIVER

KINGSTON

beach Kingston
Point

Delaware Ave

KINGSTON
POINT
PARK

North St

Lenape
Trail

First Ave

STOCKADE
DISTRICT

HASBROUCK
PARK

PONCK
HOCKIE

Greenway Trail

nature trail

9W

Trolley Tracks

East Strand

Rondout Creek

Sleightsburg
Spit

RONDOUT

Broadway

SLEIGHTSBURG
SPIT
PARK

CORNELL
PARK

Trolley Museum

Visitors
Center

Maritime
Museum

WEST STRAND PARK

Island
Dock

Old 9W Bridge

9W

SLEIGHTSBURG

Rondout Creek

HUDSON
RIVER

PORT
EWEN

9W

approximately ½ mile

is a small formal park facing Rondout Creek, with a gazebo, strolling paths, benches, and a healing circle. It is the site of summertime concerts. A number of signs point out landmarks and local history. The park also has rest rooms. Rondout Creek is often plied by pleasure boats as well as tugs and barges. The tour boat *Rip Van Winkle* docks here. This used to be a major shipbuilding area: The U.S. Navy had shipyards that during World War I built transports and later minesweepers and other ships. There's a closeup view of Island Dock just west of here.

Across from the West Strand Park is a distinctive row of residential-type brick buildings in the Italianate style, with cast-iron and round arched windows. Galleries, boutiques, and restaurants can be found on the first floors of these structures. Just beyond, at the corner of West Strand and Broadway, on the left-hand side is the Mansion House, built in 1854. It was once a luxurious hotel with a famous saloon, an important stopping-off point for steamship and stagecoach travelers. Across West Strand from the Mansion House was the Sampson Opera House, built in 1875. The first floor was a department store. Today it's the location of a restaurant. Across Broadway from the Mansion House is the Rondout Urban Cultural Park Visitors' Center. There are elaborate displays on the Rondout area's history as well as temporary exhibits. It's an excellent place to get information on the area. The phone number is 914-331-7517.

To visit Kingston's Stockade Area, which is three miles north and west of here, detour left onto Broadway and go uphill six blocks to a light and intersection with McEntee Street (this is part of the Heritage Trail). Go right on McEntee, which becomes Broadway. Broadway bends sharply to the left, passing Rondout's old wealthy neighborhood on West Chestnut Avenue on the left. Broadway continues uphill, finally leveling out and soon passing Kingston Hospital on the right. Continue west, passing Kingston's old City Hall, built in 1876, on the right and the old Andrew Carnegie–donated Library on the left, next to the high school. The City Hall building is currently (1999) being renovated. Broadway passes underneath railroad tracks. Just beyond on the left is the Ulster Performing Arts Center (UPAC), a fifteen-hundred-seat theater that is listed on the National Register of Historic Places. About a mile and a half beyond is Academy Green, a small park, on the left. It was here that Peter Stuyvesant signed a treaty with the Esopus tribe on July 15, 1660, to end the First Esopus War. On the green are bronze statues of Henry Hudson, Peter Stuyvesant, and George Clinton.

Continue straight ahead. Broadway becomes Clinton Avenue. Two and a half blocks on the right, just before the Senate House on the left, is the Stockade Area Visitors' Center, at 308 Clinton Avenue. It is located in an 1837 Federal-style house built by Thomas van Gaasbeek. There are exhibits on the Stockade area history and Kingston's architectural heritage. It is also an excellent place to get information about the Stockade area and the rest of Kingston. The phone number is 914-331-9506. An excellent brochure is available on a walking tour of the Stockade area. While the Stockade area's numerous seventeenth- and eighteenth-century stone buildings and homes are the main attraction for most visitors, you shouldn't ignore the many fine examples of nineteenth-century architecture also on display. The walking tour highlights these as well.

Right across from the Visitors' Center, on the left is the Senate House (296 Fair Street). The Dutch-style stone residence was originally built in 1676 by Col. Wessel Ten Broeck. Later it was expanded, and, under the ownership of Abraham van Gaasbeek, a large meeting room was rented and used by New York State's first senate, hence the name. The house was burned by the British in 1778 and restored the following year. Four rooms with period furnishings are open to the public: a replica of a colonial kitchen, a bedchamber, and two others, including the one where the senate met. A neighboring museum contains historical exhibits, furniture, and paintings by Kingston native John Vanderlyn, the largest collection of his work anywhere. Vanderlyn painted the panoramic *Versailles*, on display at the Metropolitan Museum of Art in New York City. The Senate House and surrounding property were acquired by New York State in 1887 to preserve as a historic site. Today it is owned and managed by the Palisades Interstate Park Commission.

The Senate House and museum are open from mid-April to October, Wednesdays through Saturdays from 10:00 A.M. to 5:00 P.M. and Sundays from 1:00 to 5:00 P.M. Call 914-338-2786 for information.

There are numerous other attractions in the Stockade area: The Old Dutch Church, still considered the mother church of the Dutch Reformed Church in America, located on the corner of Main and Wall Streets, was constructed in 1852 of native bluestone in the Renaissance Revival style. Kingston's Dutch Reform congregation dates back to 1659 and this is its fourth church. In the churchyard are gravestones dating back to 1710 including the grave of George Clinton. Inside the church, the beautiful main altar stained-glass window is by Tiffany and Company. For tours call 914-338-6759.

The Ulster County Courthouse, built in 1818, occupies the site of the earlier courthouse burned by the British in 1778, where Gen. George Clinton was sworn in as the first governor of New York State in July 1777 and John Jay was sworn in as New York's first chief justice in September of that year. The former slave Sojourner Truth won her son's freedom here in 1821, an event commemorated by a plaque in front of the courthouse.

The intersection of Crown and John Streets has eighteenth-century stone houses on all four corners. It is claimed that this is the only such intersection in the United States.

Peace Park at the corner of North Front Street and Crown Street has a wonderful mural depicting the history of Kingston as well as benches, a signboard, and a map.

Wall Street and North Front Street remain the commercial heart of the Stockade area and for the city of Kingston as a whole. They're lined with nineteenth-century brick buildings in the Italianate style. This area has been refurbished, with canopies and Victorian paint schemes added, designed by Woodstock artist John Pike.

The Fred J. Johnston Museum, located at 63 Main Street, displays furnishings and decorative arts from the early eighteenth to the early nineteenth century with an emphasis on the Federal style. The house was built in 1812 by John Sudam (1782–1835), a prominent attorney, New York state senator, and regent. Washington Irving and President Martin Van Buren were close friends of Sudam and visited him here. The museum is open from May through October, Saturdays and Sundays from 1:00 to 4:00 P.M. There is a small admission fee. Call 914-339-0720 for information.

The Volunteer Firemen's Hall and Museum of Kingston is located at 265 Fair Street. The original firehouse building was built in 1857 and is listed in the National Register of Historic Places. The museum contains the original meeting hall and memorabilia of Kingston's nineteenth-century volunteer firefighters, including a parade carriage and antique fire engines. The museum is open June to August, Wednesdays through Fridays from 11:00 A.M. to 3:00 P.M. and Saturdays from 10:00 A.M. to 4:00 P.M.; in April, May, September, and October, on Fridays from 11:00 A.M. to 3:00 P.M. and Saturdays from 10:00 A.M. to 4:00 P.M. Admission is free. Call 914-331-0866, or 914-331-4065 for information.

FROM THE RONDOUT VISITORS' CENTER TO KINGSTON POINT AND NORTH

Follow the East Strand, east, under the new 9W bridge. The Hudson River Maritime Museum, located at One Rondout Landing, is on the right. The museum is small but always has interesting exhibits on the legacy of Hudson River maritime activity, including paintings, photographs, models, artifacts, and memorabilia. Outdoors the 1898 steam tug *Mathilda*, a hundred-year-old shad boat, and a lifeboat from the steamship

Mary Powell are displayed. Each May the Shad Festival is held here. The museum, which also has a gift shop, is open from May through October. There's a small admission fee. For information call 914-338-0071.

Excursions out to the Rondout II Lighthouse aboard the *Indy 7* start here. For a small fee the boat takes guests over to Rhinecliff, and then to the lighthouse erected in 1915, where tours are given. Built to accommodate the lighthouse keeper and his family, the lighthouse has been fully restored and is maintained with the original period furnishings, illustrating the relatively comfortable but isolating life of lighthouse residents. Visitors can climb to the top of the lighthouse to see the lantern and catch the view.

Just beyond the Maritime Museum on the left is the Trolley Museum, located at 89 East Strand. It features vintage trolley cars and trolley rides on original tracks along the waterfront out to Kingston Point. It is open on weekends and holidays from Memorial Day through Columbus Day. Call 914-331-3399 for information.

Backtrack a short distance to just before the 9W bridge. A paved path goes right up the hill, east of and parallel to 9W. Make a right at the first railroad trestle on the right. Go underneath the trestle into Rondout Gardens, a housing project. Continue east between E and B buildings. Just behind C building on the right is the entrance to the High Road, an old roadway no longer in use, which now makes an excellent trail. The High Road path follows the edge of a limestone ridge through forest, with partial views of Rondout Creek below and the Hudson in the distance. The area below is largely landfill and is still subject to occasional flooding. Above on the left is Hasbrouck Park, connected by some informal paths. The High Road path runs into Yeoman Street, passing the ruins of a Spanish-style church on the left. Make the first right on East Union and then a right on Tompkins and follow two short blocks to East Strand again.

Go east a short distance on East Strand to North Street where the road makes a sharp turn to the left. Go right here instead, and walk or ride a short distance to the railroad bed. Go left, following the rail line east. A path parallel to the tracks has been cleared by the Kingston YMCA. Trolleys from the Trolley Museum use the tracks, so exercise caution, though they only go some five miles per hour. Continue for about a half mile to an open area on the right, with benches. There's a fine view from here looking south at the mouth of Rondout Creek, the Hudson, and the Rondout II Lighthouse. On the north side of the tracks is a shallow lagoon with aquatic plants. From here, on weekends and during the summer, one can hitch a ride on the trolley the rest of the way out to Kingston Point. The trolley stops at a picnic ground with an open view of the river looking east toward the village of Rhinecliff. A small bridge crosses the lagoon into Kingston Point Park.

Kingston Point Park is a formal park on the site—briefly defended by a handful of patriot militiamen—where the British landed in November 1777. Later it was the site of Dayline Park, and a hotel. It was developed in 1893 by Samuel Decker Coykendall and designed by Downing Vaux, the son of Calvert Vaux. Passengers would disembark here from steamships or ferries, and enjoy the amusement park, gamble in the casino, swim at the beach, and/or stay in the hotel, while waiting for a trolley to the Kingston train station to transfer to the Ulster Delaware Railroad, which provided service from here to the resorts in the Catskills. A small wooded island in the lagoon used to be the site of a bandstand, where music would be played to entertain the crowds. The park is in the process of restoration, thanks to the Kingston Rotary Club. The park has picnic facilities. The picnic shelter used to be a trolley stop. The Lenape Trail, marked with yellow blazes, provides a short woodland circuit to an open area above an outcrop of steeply tilting Ordovician sandstone. There's a fine view from there looking south and east of the lagoon and the Hudson River, with the Rondout II Lighthouse in the distance. The entrance to the park is an impressive iron gate.

Opposite the entrance on the right is Kingston Point Beach, a public swimming beach with a view looking north of the Kingston-Rhinecliff Bridge. Continue west to the intersection of North Street and Delaware Avenue. Go straight (west) uphill, one-half mile to Hasbrouck Park on the left. There's an elementary school on the corner, where you turn. The narrow road climbs 0.2 miles past woods and playing fields to a parking area at the very end, where there's an expansive view from the top of the Pockhockie Cliffs of the Pockhockie neighborhood and the confluence of Rondout Creek and the Hudson River. The area below was once devoted to ship- and boatyards. A nearby nature trail follows the edge of the bluff east through the woods to a second, similar view. A brochure that identifies thirty species of trees that may be seen along the trail is available at the Rondout Visitors' Center.

Backtrack to the entrance to Hasbrouck Park on Delaware Avenue. Go left (west) on Delaware Avenue, 0.4 miles to intersection with First Avenue.

KINGSTON TO SAUGERTIES

This eleven-mile segment, entirely on roads, includes a very scenic stretch on Ulster Landing Road in settings that are quite rural. Except for Chester Rider Park, one will have to detour to Ulster Landing Park to get good views of the river. Ulster Landing Park also offers hiking opportunities.

From the intersection of Delaware Avenue and First Avenue make a right onto First Avenue. Follow First Avenue north 0.4 miles to an intersection. Make a left here and then an immediate right, and continue north on First Avenue. At a point 1.7 miles north of the intersection with Delaware Avenue, First Avenue passes a quarry and climbs a hill with a limited view of the river. It then descends and enters the small hamlet of East Kingston, 0.6 miles beyond which First Avenue bends sharply to the left and joins Route 32. Make a right onto Route 32. Just beyond on the right is Ulster Landing Road. Turn right onto Ulster Landing Road. Continue 0.9 miles to Chester Rider Park on the right. Owned and operated by the New York State Department of Environmental Conservation and the New York State Power Authority, it's used primarily as a boat launch, but it has an excellent view of the Hudson with the Kingston-Rhinecliff Bridge towering overhead to the north.

From Chester Rider Park, continue north on Ulster Landing Road another half mile, passing underneath the Kingston-Rhinecliff Bridge. The Kingston-Rhinecliff Bridge does not allow pedestrian access. It will permit bicycles, but the owners must have a notarized statement assuming all responsibility for any accidents. Because it is quite narrow, very high above the river, subject to strong gusts of wind, and really not built for bicycle traffic, I would strongly recommend against attempting it. If you're still interested, contact the New York State Bridge Authority at 914-691-7245.

Continue north on Ulster Landing Road another mile past the bridge to the intersection with Kulack Road. Go right on Ulster Landing Road, and follow 1.4 scenic miles to Ulster Landing Park on the right. This is a county park, open to the public. It has limited hours and charges admission. The main feature is a sandy beach that permits swimming, and a neighboring picnic ground and boat launch. There are excellent views of the river with an opportunity for leisurely strolling alongside it by shady trees. All of these are accessible by car or bike. One of the park's other features is its forestland and trails. From just south of the entrance, a half-mile-long white-marked trail winds through the forest, crosses a small stream, and eventually joins a woods road before descending past a steep ravine down to the beach. A yellow-marked trail that runs somewhat to the north of the white-marked one adds another quarter mile of interest. A short red-marked trail runs from the upper parking area down to the beach area. Two segments of a white-marked trail leave from the upper parking area: One runs from the parking area out to Ulster Landing Road, about a quarter mile, passing through a beautiful white pine grove along the way. Another segment descends to the riverfront, passing a very steep ravine and continuing north along the top of steep bluffs with many partial views of the river. Deer and wild turkeys are among the wildlife you may observe here. For information call 914-336-8484.

From the entrance to Ulster Landing Park, continue north on Ulster Landing Road, another 0.6 miles to the intersection of Flatbush Camp Road. Make a right here, and continue 0.4 miles to Turkey Point, 133 acres of mostly undeveloped hardwood forest and fields and old conifer plantations owned by New York State and managed by the Department of Environmental Conservation (DEC). The property is marked with small signs. A rough dirt-and-asphalt road with a barrier leads about a quarter mile down to the riverfront, an old docking area, and a signal light atop a tower. The dock itself is owned by the Coast Guard and currently is off limits. However, there are plans to open it to public use. There are excellent views in both directions, south as far as the Kingston-Rhinecliff Bridge. Just south of the dock are the remains of a foundation of an old Knickerbocker Ice Company icehouse. The DEC plans to develop a trail system more than two miles long for hiking, mountain biking, and cross-country skiing, which may eventually connect with Ulster Landing Park. Backcountry camping (up to three nights) will also be permitted, with some basic facilities. For information contact the DEC at 914-256-3000.

From the intersection continue west on Ulster Landing Road 0.4 miles to Route 32. Go right (north) on Route 32. One-half mile on the right is the Flatbush Reformed Church, built in 1808 of rubblestone. A carriage shed still flanks the front entrance of the church on the right. After another 1.6 miles north, you'll reach the small hamlet of Glasco, located at the eastern end of the Glasco Turnpike. It served as a shipping port for glass manufactured at Shady near Woodstock, transported overland via the turnpike, and then loaded on boats and shipped downriver to New York City. From here continue 1.5 miles north to the intersection with 9W. Go right on 9W, north 0.8 miles to the village of Saugerties.

Saugerties, one of the more attractive communities along the river, is located where Esopus Creek enters the Hudson, just after plunging over some spectacular falls. Most of the town is located on high bluffs overlooking the river. A sign welcomes you to FRIENDLY SAUGERTIES. The downtown area has more than forty antique stores, other shops, and restaurants. There are plans to reactivate ferry service between Saugerties and the village of Tivoli, located across the river. While in Saugerties, be sure to visit the Ruth Reynolds Glunt Nature Reserve.

The town was first settled by the Dutch in the late seventeenth century. By 1828 the Livingstons, who owned large tracts of forest land in the Catskills, used the falls of the Sawyers Kill and Esopus Creek to power the world's largest collection of water-driven machinery, and Saugerties became the chief lumbering and paper-milling center in the United States. Saugerties's leading role proved short-lived, however, as the neighboring forests were soon exhausted, and the timber industry relocated north, in the Adirondacks. Saugerties was also a major shipping center for bluestone quarried nearby, a popular building material.

In the late 1980s Saugerties was rocked by a controversy over a proposal to build a giant landfill on the Winston Farm just west of the town. That same site hosted the twentieth anniversary of the Woodstock Festival in 1994, which attracted hundreds of thousands of young people and veterans of the earlier festival, for three days of wild music and frolicking in the mud. Plans are to develop Winston Farm as an outdoor entertainment center.

Continue north on 9W through the historic Barclay Heights neighborhood, named after Henry Barclay (1778–1851), an early settler who founded the Trinity Church and promoted industrial development in the area. After 0.4 miles 9W makes a sharp left and then a sharp right, passing Trinity Church on the left, and then another sharp left where there's a spectacular vista on the right of the confluence of Esopus Creek below where it enters the Hudson. On the right is a view of the Catskills. Just beyond, cross Esopus Creek. Here 9W becomes Partition Street and climbs a hill 0.6 miles to the intersection of Main Street in the heart of town. Go right (east) on Main Street. After 0.2 miles, you'll pass the Dubois-Kierstede House on the left. The front lawn is decorated with lovely locust trees. This stone house was originally built in 1727 by Hezikiah Dubois. It was purchased in 1773 by Dr. Christopher Kierstede, who married Leah Dubois, a relative of the original owner. The original front door on iron strap hinges is of Dutch design. The front porch and some other features were added in the late nineteenth century. There are plans under way to open this house to the public.

Another stone house, also built in 1727, is 0.2 miles beyond on the left—the Samuel Schoonmaker Homestead. Schoonmaker was a descendent of Hendrick Jochems, one of the early settlers in the Kingston area. Samuel's son Egbert served as a captain in the Revolutionary War. The house has remained in the family ever since

Across from the Schoonmaker Homestead, make a sharp right onto Mynderse Street to visit the Ruth Reynolds Glunt Nature Reserve. At 0.2 miles on the left is a historical marker indicating that the Mynderse House is located nearby. The Mynderse House was built in 1690 and is believed to be the oldest standing house in the Saugerties area. It is unfortunately not visible from the road and is privately owned and not open to the public. Continue a short distance to the intersection with Lighthouse Road, make a left onto Lighthouse Road, and descend the hill, with a view of Esopus Creek below and to the right. After a little more than a quarter mile, you'll see the distinctive Captain John Field House on the left, perched on a hillside. Captain Field conducted a successful commercial and passenger shipping business on sloops that traveled to far-away ports in the South. It's no accident, then, that the Greek Revival architecture of this residence, built in 1836, seems to emulate the lifestyle of affluent Southerners. The two-story house has a commanding view of both the Esopus Creek shipping docks and the Hudson River.

Pass marinas on the right. After 1 mile, there's a Coast Guard station on the right, then, just beyond it on the right, a small parking area for the Glunt Nature Reserve. This gem of a park, one of the most beautiful spots along this section of the river, is owned and operated by the Saugerties Lighthouse Conservancy. The half-mile-long Lighthouse Trail goes from the parking area out to the Saugerties Lighthouse, through deciduous forests and marshes with cottonwoods and cattails. There are gorgeous vistas of the Hudson looking both north and south, and of the mouth of Esopus Creek where it enters the river. Seen just south of the lighthouse, the mouth of the creek is a spawning ground for an endangered species, the short-nosed sturgeon, as well as a nursery for striped bass, American shad, white perch, alewife, and blueback herring. It is an osprey feeding ground and a feeding and nesting site for various waterfowl. Heartleaf plantains grow in the mudflats. The trail to the lighthouse is level and relatively easy except for a few muddy spots; signs warn that the trail may be flooded during high tide.

Originally built in 1838, the Saugerties Lighthouse was replaced in 1868 by the present brick structure, which operates now as a bed-and-breakfast and as a museum. It is connected to the mainland by a crude pier composed of landfill. There are public tours Saturdays, Sundays, and holidays, from Memorial Day through Labor Day, from 2:00 P.M. to 5:00 P.M. There is a small admission fee. Call 914-246-9170/4380 for information.

Backtrack 1 mile on Lighthouse Road, uphill, to the intersection of Mynderse Road, no sign. Make a right turn onto Mynderse Road and continue uphill and then level, 0.3 miles to the intersection with 9W. Make a right onto 9W and continue north. At 0.2 miles on the right is Seamon's Park, which is famous for its brilliant chrysanthemum display, running for three weeks from the first Sunday in October. The park also has a partially restored gristmill, dating from 1750, on Sawyers Creek.

SAUGERTIES TO ATHENS

Eighteen and a half miles through mostly rural countryside on back roads with a number of fine views along the way, as well as hiking opportunities at the Ramshorn/Livingston Sanctuary and the Cohotate Preserve. Catskill and Athens have lovely riverfront parks, and houses and buildings of historical interest.

Cross Sawyers Creek and continue north 0.8 miles to the turnoff for Malden-on-Hudson. Go right here, and continue one-half mile to the small hamlet. Like Rondout and Saugerties, Malden was once a great shipping port for bluestone. Bluestone is a kind of dark gray sandstone quarried in the nearby Catskill Mountains. During the nineteenth century it was used for paving sidewalks and in the construction of houses and other buildings. By the 1920s the use of concrete made bluestone as a paving material obsolete, and its use declined though it's still used for decorative purposes. Malden-on-Hudson was once the home of John Bigelow (1817–1911). Between 1848 and 1861 Bigelow shared with William Cullen Bryant the ownership and editing of the *New York Evening Post*. He was a vigorous free-trade advocate and abolitionist whose editorials won great notoriety. He served as minister to France from 1865 to 1866 and is credited with preventing France from granting recognition to the Confederacy.

Go right, and then make another sharp right and descend toward the river, bearing left. There's a park along the waterfront with views, but it's privately owned. Bear left again and begin ascent. After one-half mile you'll reach the main road again, and a stop sign. There's a cannon from the Spanish-American War on the left in a small recreation park. Go straight, another 0.2 miles, till you reach 9W.

Make a right onto 9W. Continue north 1.6 miles to the small hamlet of West Camp. There's a state historic marker and a commemorative plaque. Saint Paul's Lutheran Church replaced an earlier one constructed nearby in 1710 by the Germans. West Camp was one of two Hudson Valley sites, where, in 1710, thousands of immigrants from the German Rhineland-Palatinate settled (the other site was across the river, in what is now Germantown). In the early eighteenth century the Palatinate had been devastated by war and famine. As part of an English plan to break the Swedish monopoly on the production of tar, pitch, and turpentine, essential products for the maintenance of the Royal Navy, the Palatine Germans were lured to the New York colony to produce mass quantities of these materials—the single largest migration to the New World in colonial times.

Turning out these products meant stripping the bark from pine trees, felling them, and roasting the stripped logs until the resins could be gathered and shipped. In return for their labor, the German farmers were promised free passage to the New World, supplies, and eventually land. They found this kind of work unappealing, however, and for a number of reasons, production fell far short of expectations. After two years support for the project waned, and it was abandoned. The Palatine Germans were told they would have to fend for themselves. A few remained in the area, some becoming tenant farmers on the Livingston Estate, and others dispersed, settling in such places as Rhinebeck, the Schoharie Valley, and New Jersey.

There's a light 0.6 miles beyond West Camp. Bear right, go underneath the railroad bridge, and then left. At 0.4 miles from the light, you'll reach the small village of Smith's Landing. Continue north another 0.6 miles to a second light; here 9W narrows to one lane, bearing left. The roadway squeezes though another railroad bridge, then bears right. At 1.8 miles past the second light, there's a view of Inbocht Bay on the right. A half mile beyond, make a right onto Embought Road. Cross the railroad tracks, and head east toward the river. After 0.8 miles the road bends sharply left (north), with an excellent view of the river on the right-hand side. Archaeological excavations nearby at Lotus Point revealed a Native American presence here in the transitional period between the Archaic and Woodland stages. Continue north, passing forest wetlands on the left and agricultural land, slowly gaining in elevation. At 2.7 miles from the turn, you'll reach the village of Catskill.

Catskill is situated between the Catskill Mountains and the Hudson River. The county seat of Greene County, it was once an important commercial center, river port, and tourist destination, gateway to the Catskill Mountain House. Today it is mostly a quiet unassuming place, whose architecture provides hints of its once-bustling past. It is alleged to be one of the homes of Rip Van Winkle. It was also home to Samuel Wilson, who became famous as the model for Uncle Sam, and Thomas Cole, one of the most renowned Hudson River painters. Catskill has a wonderful sampling of nineteenth-century architectural styles in beautiful residential neighborhoods on bluffs overlooking the river. Dutchman Landing Park on the waterfront provides the best views of the river in this community. Walkers should also be sure to visit the Ramshorn/Livingston Sanctuary.

The Catskill area contains evidence of habitation for thousands of years up to the time of Dutch settlement. The first recorded European settlement was that of Claes Uylenspiegal, a fur trader, and Hans Vos, who established a mill on the Vosenkill before 1650. The early Dutch settlement was called Het Strand ("the beach"). The town grew in the late eighteenth century as New Englanders, who had settled across the river in Hudson, noted the advantages of Catskill's location and began migrating to this side of the river. These New Englanders established Catskill as a major shipping and trading port as well as a center for whaling. The town was incorporated in 1806. Completion of the Susquehanna Turnpike in 1800 was a strong impetus for growth, making Catskill an important east-west trading route. Produce was also shipped downriver from here to New York City. The nearby Catskill Mountains provided a ready source of timber for local sawmills and shipment south via the water. The tanning industry, which developed in the Catskills in the early nineteenth century, was another factor behind Catskill's growth. By 1836 the port of Catskill was shipping substantial quatities of grain, butter, hay, potash, tallow, shingles, lumber, and leather.

Thomas Cole settled here in 1825 and painted the surrounding countryside—works that were highly influential in the field of landscape painting and for nineteenth-century American art as a whole. His home at 218 Spring Street, where he resided from 1836 until his death in 1848, is a designated National Historic Landmark. Plans are to restore it. Cole's paintings also helped advertise the region to potential visitors, many of whom came to visit the nearby Catskill Mountain House, then one of the world's premier resorts. The Grant House and the Prospect Park Hotel, both located by the river here, were less expensive alternatives that middle-class guests could afford.

From the village limits, continue north on Embought Road 1.2 miles to Grandview Avenue. Make a right onto Grandview, passing some nineteenth-century mansions, interspersed with modern homes, part of a designated National Historic District. At 0.8 miles you'll reach a quiet traffic circle. Go straight another tenth of a mile to the parking area for the Ramshorn/Livingston Sanctuary. The sanctuary is a 353-acre nature preserve that includes one of the largest tidal swamp forests on the Hudson. It is a designated Significant Coastal Fish and Wildlife Habitat. Created by Scenic Hudson and the Northern Catskills Audubon Society, it is owned and operated by both groups. There are no actual views of the river from here, but it's a pleasant place to walk on easy trails and experience a variety of different habitats, including marshlands with cattails, tidal swamps with red maples and sumac, tidal creeks, former agricultural lands with many wildflowers, and upland hardwood forests with ferns, hemlocks, maples, white pines, cedars, walnuts, and hickories. One may observe wildlife such as rabbit, foxes, coyotes, beaver, and snapping turtles. Birds are plentiful and include wild turkeys, red-tailed hawks, woodpeckers, redwing blackbirds, various species of ducks, and different varieties of songbirds, such as robins, wood thrushes, crows, jays, chickadees, and sparrows. An old farm road travels 0.6 miles through old agricultural lands and young forest to a small wooden bridge over Ramshorn Creek, from where tidal marshes can be observed. Beyond the bridge the road becomes a trail that makes a couple of loops through an upland forest area. A brochure, available at the entrance, provides explanations for the numbered signposts you encounter along the trails. An observation tower for viewing the marsh is planned. It's reported the swamp forest and Ramshorn Creek are also excellent for canoeing. The park is open from dawn to dusk. Call Scenic Hudson for information at 914-473-4440.

From the sanctuary entrance, backtrack one-tenth of a mile to the traffic circle. Go right on West Main Street. The road bears left and descends to Catskill Creek. At 0.4 miles you'll pass the old abandoned Union Cotton Mill on the right, a two-story brick factory built in 1860. After 0.2 miles you'll pass the Uncle Sam House on the left. The house was built in 1790 and in 1807 was the site of the wedding of Martin Van Buren, the eighth president of the United States, to Hannah Hoer. From 1817 to 1824, the house was the residence of Samuel Wilson, who during the War of 1812 became known as Uncle Sam, one of our nation's best-loved icons.

Just beyond the house is the intersection with Bridge Street. Make a right onto Bridge Street, and cross Catskill Creek. Catskill Creek is an important tributary of the Hudson, whose source is high up in the Catskills. The lower reach, up to the bridge, provides a sheltered environment for boats, and marinas line its banks.

At the third right after the bridge, make a right onto Main Street. The impressive Greene County Courthouse is on the left-hand corner. Go east, passing an interesting row of Victorian buildings on the right. After 0.8 miles on Main you'll reach Dutchman's Landing Park on the left, next to a water treatment plant. Dutchman's Landing is a fairly large landscaped park with benches, picnic tables, a gazebo, a snack bar, and a paved walkway along the Hudson. There are excellent views of the river, particularly looking north toward the Rip Van Winkle Bridge.

Backtrack 0.2 miles to River Street. Make a right onto River Street, which goes north one block and then bends to the left and becomes Broad Street. Follow Broad a short distance to the end of the street. Climb the long stairway up the hill (carry your bike) to where Broad Street continues. Follow Broad Street to Greene Street. Make a right onto Greene, and then another right onto Harrison. Pass the Saint Anthony's Friary on the right. This was formerly the Prospect Park Hotel, built in 1860. During the latter half of the nineteenth century, it was one of the leading resorts in the Catskills. (A model of the hotel can be seen at the Bronck House Museum near Coxsackie.)

Harrison Street bends sharply left and becomes Prospect Street. Continue until you reach William Street, 0.6 miles north of the staircase. Prospect and William are a designated National Historic District. Go right on William to Woodland Avenue, and make a left onto Woodland. Then turn right onto High Street, which then curves left and becomes Colewood Avenue. Continue north a short distance, soon reaching the intersection with the approach to the Rip Van Winkle Bridge, which is located just east on the right. Completed in 1935, the bridge is 5,041 feet long, with a main span of about 800 feet. There is a pedestrian walkway on the south side of the bridge and views of Olana—the home of Hudson River painter Frederick Church—the mouth of Catskill Creek, and the distant Catskill Mountains. Rogers Island, below (more visible from the north side of the bridge), has one of the Hudson's largest tidal swamp forests. The island is a designated Significant Coastal Fish and Wildlife Habitat and is managed by the DEC as a wildlife management area. Public use is discouraged.

At the intersection for the bridge, continue north and descend toward the river. A half mile past the bridge, there are partial views of the river through the trees. About a mile north of the bridge intersection, the road turns sharply to the left and becomes Hamburg Road, ascending a very steep hill. If you're riding a bike, you may have to walk it here. After another 0.6 miles you'll reach the intersection of Route 385. Make a right turn onto 385. Go north 0.9 miles, to the entrance to Cohotate Preserve and the Greene County Environmental Education Center, on the right.

The Cohotate Preserve is certainly one of the loveliest parks along the Hudson. It includes three thousand feet of frontage on the river; the site of a nineteenth-century icehouse and dock, which are still visible; marshlands; a deep ravine; and rugged hillsides that are 100 percent forested. Forty species of trees are present including hemlocks, white pines, oaks, hickories, maples, birches, cottonwoods, sassafras, and elms. There is also abundant wildlife including rabbit, squirrels, chipmunks, skunks, opossums, foxes, coyotes, muskrat, deer, box turtles, wild turkeys, various songbirds, woodpeckers, great blue herons, geese, ducks, gulls, rails, bitterns, sandpipers, and terns. Some 2.5 miles of trails descend from the parking area down to the river shoreline and the old dock. Along the waterfront trail there are frequent partial views through the trees, but the best views are from the old icehouse site, where one can observe tidal flats with characteristic marsh plants and the river itself with the Rip Van Winkle Bridge to the south and the city of Hudson across the way. Along the trails are interpretive signs and exhibits pertaining to the history and natural history of the area. This park is the product of the efforts of many groups and individuals including the Iroquois Pipeline Land Preservation and Enhancement Program, the Hudson River Improvement Fund, the Forest Stewardship Program, the Greene County legislature, and former state senator Charles Cook.

From the Cohotate Preserve continue north on 385 0.4 miles to a partial view of the river on the right. One mile beyond, there's a more open view on the right, with Mount Merino across the way and Olana in the distance. Continue north 0.2 miles, passing underneath power lines. At 0.6 miles beyond the power lines, you'll pass another view of the river on the right, with the city of Hudson and the Athens Lighthouse, built in 1874, prominent in your view. Here you enter the village of Athens.

Athens is a small attractive village with a beautiful riverfront park, a number of historical homes and buildings, and a pleasantly quiet laid-back atmosphere. Athens is so tranquil it almost seems to belong to a different century. Located to the west of Athens is one of the most significant Paleo-Indian sites in northeastern North America, and probably the most prominent archaeological site in the Hudson region. At this site, estimated to be about eleven thousand years old, prehistoric nomadic hunters quarried flint, which they used to manufacture spearheads. They also likely butchered game on the site. Other sites in the area cover the entire span of Native American presence in the region. Athens was obviously a favorable location for human habitation.

Andrian van Loon, a Walloon who migrated down from Canada, purchased land from the natives in the late seventeenth century. The Zion Lutheran Church was first organized here in 1703. The Reverend Justus Falkner was the first Lutheran minister ordained in North America. In the early nineteenth century, Athens was discovered by New Englanders who had settled across the river in Hudson. Athens became a thriving seaport and whaling and shipbuilding center. It was incorporated in 1805. The characteristic Greek Revival architecture of Athens's older homes reflected the culture and affluence of many of its citizens. The town's fortunes waned with the rise of steamboat traffic and competition from other river towns. Undamaged by later development, many of Athens's older homes and buildings survive—though often in disrepair—attesting to the town's once-glorious past. There's a former opera house in the Brooks Building on Second Street, now an antique center.

From the edge of town one immediately encounters the Jan van Loon House on the left, a Dutch-style stone house built in 1706, reputed to be the oldest in the area. Above on the hill is the Haight–Gently–Van Loon Mansion, built in 1812 in the Federal style and wonderfully restored, one of the elaborate residences in which the prosperous town's elite lived. Both homes are privately owned and not open to the public.

Continue north on 385 a short distance, passing the beautifully re-stored Northrup House on the left. Built in 1803, it served as the resi-dence of Issac Northrup, one of the New Englanders who founded the town. Across from the Northrup House, make a right, and go one block east toward the river. The road veers to the left and becomes North Wa-ter Street. Lovely Riverfront Park is on the right. The park has wonder-ful views of the Athens Lighthouse, the city of Hudson across the way, Mount Merino, and the Rip Van Winkle Bridge to the south. North of the park are marinas. Across from the park are a few eating establishments. The most prominent building facing the park is the Stewart House, built in 1883 by Hardy Stewart, a well-to-do local businessman. In 1987 it was used in the filming of the movie *Ironweed,* starring Jack Nicholson and Meryl Streep. Following the filming the building was completely re-stored and now serves as a restaurant and inn.

12 Mid-Hudson East

BEACON TO HUDSON

This long section takes in a lot of appealing countryside, superb views of the Hudson River looking west, often with the Catskill Mountains in the distance providing a dramatic backdrop. There are also a multitude of great estates, now historic sites, which are among the most renowned in the whole region. These include the Young/Morse Estate, Val-Kill, the FDR estate, the Vanderbilt Mansion, the Mills Mansion, Wilderstein, Montgomery Place, Clermont, and Olana. In 1990, the thirty-two-square-mile area between Staatsburg and Germantown was recognized by the U.S. Department of the Interior as a National Historic Landmark District. Hudson River Heritage is dedicated to the promotion and preservation of the Historic Landmark District. They may be contacted at P.O. Box 287, Rhinebeck, NY 12572, or call 914-876-2474.

Attractive communities like Rhinebeck and Tivoli cater to visitors, with shops, restaurants, and galleries. The areas north of Hyde Park are already acclaimed as popular scenic bike routes. A number of the large estates have excellent hiking trails. The Hyde Park Trail, which connects the FDR estate with Val-Kill and the Vanderbilt Mansion, is a superb walkers' route. There's also fine walking along the river by Norrie Point, and in the forest and by marshes in the Tivoli Bay National Estuarine Research Reserve.

The topography of this section is relatively gentle. However, steep hills and bluffs and deep ravines can create rugged local conditions. Generally, though, the routes in this section don't have severe elevation gains, and most are rated as relatively easy. This section is part of the Hudson/Mohawk Lowlands, an area of sedimentary rock—primarily black shale and gray sandstone—deposited in seas during the Ordovician period. These rockbeds were greatly disturbed and folded during the Taconian Orogeny. The harder sandstone often forms the ridges, while the softer shales erode into valleys and ravines. A sizable area north of New Hamburg and south of Poughkeepsie is underlain by dolomitic limestone, which is heavily quarried as a building material. A small area of Devonian limestone and shale, part of the Allegheny Plateau, occurs on Becraft Mountain, just southeast of the city of Hudson. It, too, is heavily quarried.

The Mid-Hudson East area was settled by English and German immigrants during the late seventeenth and eighteenth centuries. Forests that once covered the area were cleared for timber and cropland. The area became a rich agricultural (primarily wheat-producing) region. Poughkeepsie and Hudson were important ports and commercial centers supporting, among other things, a thriving whale industry. Later, with the introduction of rail service, they became industrial centers producing a host of products including textiles and machinery.

During the nineteenth century much of the riverfront was lined with the great estates of the Hudson Valley's most prominent and powerful families, especially the Livingstons in the area north of Staatsburg. These properties were often landscaped in the romantic style, following the influence of noted landscape architect Andrew Jackson Downing. Around the turn of the century the area became fashionable and attracted America's wealthiest entrepreneurs, such as Vanderbilt and John Jacob Astor, who built fabulous estates.

Following World War I, the area fell out of fashion as a home for the rich, and many of the great estates were sold. Some were donated and later opened to the public as historic sites. Agriculture also declined throughout the twentieth century, and much former agricultural land, which hasn't been developed, has returned to a patchwork of fields and forest. In the latter half of the twentieth century, the southern half of this section has increasingly been affected by the growth and expansion of the New York Metropolitan Area. This has led to a large increase in population and accelerated residential and commercial development, particularly along the corridor that lines Route 9 south of Poughkeepsie, an area that more and more is coming to resemble the infamous strip development along Route 17 in New Jersey. That growth appears to be heading northward, and Route 9 was recently widened as far north as Hyde Park. However, much of the area still retains its rural charm.

Metro-North has regular express train service to Beacon, New Hamburg, and Poughkeepsie. For information call 1-800-638-7646. Amtrak has regular service to Rhinecliff and Hudson. For information call 1-800-USA-RAIL. Shortline Bus has regular service to Wappingers Falls, Poughkeepsie, Hyde Park, Staatsburg, and Rhinebeck. For information call 1-800-631-8405. Adirondack Trailways also has regular service to Pough-keepsie. For information call 1-800-858-8555. The Dutchess County Loop Bus provides local bus service throughout the county. For information call 914-485-4690.

For information about accommodations and dining, call the Dutchess County Tourism Promotion Agency at 914-463-4000 or 1-800-445-3131 or Columbia County Tourism at 518-828-3375 or 1-800-724-1846.

The Route

BEACON TO BOWDOIN PARK

A distance of 9.8 miles, mostly on back roads, with an optional side trip to Mount Gulian. This route includes Stony Point Environmental Center and the hamlets of Chelsea and New Hamburg.

From the Beacon waterfront cross the bridge over the tracks, and go left on Beekman Street. Climb a hill 0.4 miles to a traffic light and go left (north) on Route 9D. Continue north another 0.7 miles, passing the pedestrian and bike entrance to the Newburgh/Beacon Bridge on the left (see description in chapter 11). Cross the bridge over I-84, and just beyond is a sign for Mount Gulian Historic Site on the left. To visit, make a left and then immediately another left onto Sterling Street, and go 0.3 miles through an apartment complex. Mount Gulian is on the right.

Mount Gulian is a replica of a Dutch-style colonial residence that served as the headquarters for Baron Friedrich von Steuben, the Prussian who was a general in the Continental Army during the final year of the Revolutionary War. It includes displays of eighteenth-century colonial family life and memorabilia from the Society of the Cincinnati, the first U.S. veterans' organization, which was begun here. The property has a small view of the river. Open April through June and September through December, Wednesdays and Sundays from 1:00 to 5:00 P.M., and July through August, Wednesdays through Sundays from 10:00 A.M. to 5:00 P.M. Call 914-831-8172.

From Route 9D continue north another 1.5 miles to the entrance of Stony Kill on the left. Stony Kill is a 756-acre historic farm and environmental center operated by the New York State DEC. There's a 1740 stone farmhouse on the property, and an 1836 manor house. The property was farmed continuously for three hundred years. Now much of the land is returning to its natural state. The woods, fields, and ponds have poke-weed, Queen Anne's lace, goldenrod, asters, and touch-me-nots, red maple swamps, and old nurseries of Norway and white pine. There are approximately three miles of relatively easy (as long as they're not over-grown) hiking trails, natural history programs, and exhibits. Call 914-831-8780 for information.

From the first entrance to Stony Kill, continue north on Route 9D another mile to an intersection with a light. Go left (west) on Broadway Avenue 1.4 miles to a T-intersection in the hamlet of Chelsea, and go right on Market Street. There's a marina on the left and an open view of the Hudson with Danskammer Point and the monstrous hulk of Central Hudson's coal/oil power facility prominent in your view.

Continue north 1.6 miles on Market Street, climbing a hill. Then make a left onto Wheeler Hill Road, which ascends for half a mile and then crests, descends, and veers right. After 1.1 miles on Wheeler Hill Road, make a left onto very narrow Old Troy Road, which winds its way down along a ravine, and after 0.2 miles passes an old eighteenth-century stone colonial house on the right, with a view of the river on the left, including the mouth of Wappingers Creek, one of the Hudson's larger tributaries south of Albany. It is also the largest stream in Dutchess County and for its first mile is tidal. About a third of a mile beyond, intersect Old Hopewell Road. Go left, cross the bridge over Wappingers Creek, and enter New Hamburg, a small residential riverside community, bisected by the railroad. There's a Metro-North station here with regular service. A greenway trail, extending from the village to Bowdoin Park via the firehouse, is currently being developed. The New Hamburg Greenway Trail will connect to the Wappingers Greenway Trail. For more information and maps, contact Ed Philips, recreation director of the town of Poughkeepsie Parks and Recreation Department, at 914-485-3628. Just east of town and within easy walking distance is the 90-acre Reese Sanctuary, owned by the National Audubon Society, a woodland corridor along the north side of Wappingers Creek Estuary. There's a mile-and-a-half-long trail beginning from the playground off Main Street. The trail runs parallel to the creek, with partial views of where it empties into the Hudson. It's hoped that this trail will eventually provide a continuous link between the New Hamburg Greenway Trail and the Wappingers Greenway Trail.

From New Hamburg go north 0.6 miles on Main Street, which becomes Channingville Road. Then make a left onto Sheafe Road, which continues north. After another 0.7 miles arrive at the entrance to Bowdoin Park on the left. Bowdoin Park is a 301-acre Dutchess County park. Formerly an estate, it includes a wide assortment of recreational facilities, including a playground and picnicking. From the main parking area there's a good view of the river and Central Hudson's coal/oil power plant. Though much of the park is intensively developed, one of its better-kept secrets is its miles of wonderful hiking trails. The trails are well kept, for the most part well marked, and traverse a variety of scenery, including various kinds of forest and meadows. The Edna C. Macmahan Nature Trail provides a gorgeous open view of the river at Indian Rock. Indian Rock and another site at the north end of the park were rock shelters where artifacts including knives, scrapers, various projectile points, hammers, pottery shards, and bone and shell fragments, some more than 5,500 years old, were excavated. Exposures of white and gray rock throughout the park are the Pine Plains Dolostone, similar to limestone except that it has been partially replaced by magnesium carbonate. There's an inlet of the Hudson at the southern end of the park, just past the soccer field, also reachable by trail. Kingfishers, blue herons, mallards, and geese may be observed there. The pond is inhabited by painted turtles and snapping turtles. For more information call 914-298-4600.

BOWDOIN PARK TO LOCUST GROVE

About 6.4 miles, mostly on back roads, including Bowdoin Park and Locust Grove. (The route goes out of its way to avoid a particularly treacherous stretch of Route 9. The last mile and a half on Route 9, through a very commercialized section, is a designated bike route.)

From the entrance to Bowdoin Park, continue north on Sheafe Road. After 1.1 miles you'll pass the former entrance to an estate that once belonged to George Clinton. Continue north. The area just west of here is the huge Clinton Point Quarry, operated by the New York Trap Rock Corporation, which quarries dolostone for building materials. The quarry is one of the largest in New York State. A little more that two miles north of Bowdoin Park, Sheafe Road comes to a fork with three-way stop signs. Take the left-hand fork, Old Post Road, a short distance past a mobile-home park on the left, and make a left onto Camelot Drive. Go west 0.6 miles on Camelot Drive. The road then bends sharply to the right and becomes South Drive. Make the first left onto Mockingbird Lane, and follow around the circle, 0.4 miles to Nassau Drive, and make another left. Continue north one-half mile to Sheraton Drive, after the second stop sign. Make a left on Sheraton, and continue 0.4 miles west to a fork. Take the left-hand fork, still Sheraton, a short distance to the end, where you intersect Barnegat Road. Go right (the only option), and continue north one-half mile to IBM Road, right across from the huge IBM plant. Make a right here, and follow east to Route 9. There's a light.

Make a left onto Route 9 and head north. There's a sidewalk for pedestrians. After 0.3 miles cross underneath the overpass for Spackenkill Road and continue north, passing large shopping centers on both sides of the road. Just 1.2 miles north of the Spackenkill Road overpass, you'll reach the entrance to the Samuel Morse Estate on the left.

The Samuel Morse Estate, Locust Grove (a registered National Historic Landmark), was the summer residence of Samuel Finley Breese Morse, an accomplished portrait painter, photographer, and teacher as well as inventor of the telegraph. Morse purchased Locust Grove in 1846 and, with the help of his friend Alexander Jackson Davis, designed and built new additions to the original 1830 Federal-style house, including a four-story tower. Davis also helped design the grounds, combining both formal and natural elements. Following Morse's death in 1871, the estate was purchased in 1901 by W. H. Young. The house and property were donated by Miss Annette Young. Renovations were completed in 1980, and now the home and estate are open to the public. Most of the objects on display in the house belonged to the Young family and reflect life at the turn of the century. Included are Duncan Phyfe, Chippendale, and Queen Anne–style furnishings, early-twentieth-century children's toys, a dollhouse, and a music box. Morse's billiard table as well as some of his paintings and sketches are also on display. The works of Hudson River artist Sanford Gifford and prints by western artist George Catlin may be seen. In the basement is a small museum devoted to Morse, including a replica of his original 1835 telegraph as well as later versions, and a copy of his obituary from the *New York Times*, which reads in part: "Professor Morse died last night at 6 o'clock. Few people have ever lived to whom all departments of industry owe a greater debt than the man we are now called on to record."

The 150-acre estate includes beautiful formal gardens and forest land left in its natural state: the Annette Innis Young Memorial Wildlife Sanctuary. The topography is varied, with tall bluffs, steep slopes, deep ravines, and plateaus. Most of the property is forested, with hemlocks, oaks, tulip trees, and other varieties. There are a pond and two coves, created when the railroad cut off these inlets from the Hudson's main channel, which are inhabited by lovely water lilies as well as water chestnuts. Wildlife in the sanctuary includes deer, squirrels, opossums, foxes, rabbit, raccoon, muskrat, and coyotes. Birds that may be seen include ducks, woodpeckers, grouse, great blue herons, warblers, finches, vireos, and thrushes. There are three miles of trails. Most are quite easy, well marked, and graded. Some are a little more challenging. A free map and guide are available from a kiosk just north of the house. Two highlights are a small waterfall, seen from the Cascade Trail, and an open panorama of the Hudson north toward the Mid-Hudson Bridge, seen from the Saw Mill Trail. A new visitors' center is under construction.

The Samuel Morse Historic Site is open from May through November and on three weekends in December, from 10:00 A.M. to 4:00 P.M. There is a charge for house tours. No bikes or pets are allowed. Call 914-454-4500 for information.

LOCUST GROVE TO THE FDR ESTATE (HYDE PARK)

Eight miles, through the city of Poughkeepsie, through historic neighborhoods, and along the waterfront. The last section, north of the city, is along busy Route 9, which fortunately has a wide shoulder. This segment includes the Poughkeepsie Rural Cemetery, Springside, Kaal Rock Park, and Victor C. Waryas Park. It also passes Marist College and the Culinary Institute of America. There's an optional side trip to Val-Kill, Eleanor Roosevelt's onetime home.

From the entrance of the Samuel Morse Historic Site, continue north on Route 9, 0.8 miles. On the left is the entrance to the Poughkeepsie Rural Cemetery, which dates from 1852, when there was a popular movement to create parklike environments for the deceased. Enjoyed by guests who visited them, nineteenth-century cemeteries became the forerunners of our public park system. Cemeteries like this one are also places of history, where many famous personages from the Poughkeepsie area are buried, including Matthew Vassar; the Smith brothers of cough drop fame, and the Smiley brothers, who founded the Mohonk Mountain House. Also noteworthy are the beautiful sundial, designed by the Tiffany Studios in New York, and a 1904 trolley-stop shelter, both located near the main entrance. There are excellent views of the Hudson from many vantage points in the cemetery, especially the Whittier Mausoleum.

Poughkeepsie is located approximately halfway between New York City and Albany, and its central location was a primary reason behind its growth. It is the largest city on the Hudson between Yonkers and Albany. Two of the Hudson's most important environmental organizations are located here: Clearwater and Scenic Hudson. Poughkeepsie was also the home of the Smith Brothers. When in Poughkeepsie you may want to visit the city's historic neighborhoods, and such sites as the Cunneen Hackett Cultural Center at 9 and 12 Vassar Street, the 1765 Clinton House at 549 Main Street (914-471-1630), and the 1767 Glebe House at 635 Main Street (914-454-0605). Both the Clinton House and the Glebe House are operated by the Dutchess County Historical Society. Vassar College and Marist College are located nearby.

Vassar College was founded in 1861 as America's first four-year women's college by Matthew Vassar (1792–1868), the owner of a successful brewery located on the Poughkeepsie waterfront. The college turned coed in 1969. The campus with its stately buildings, beautiful

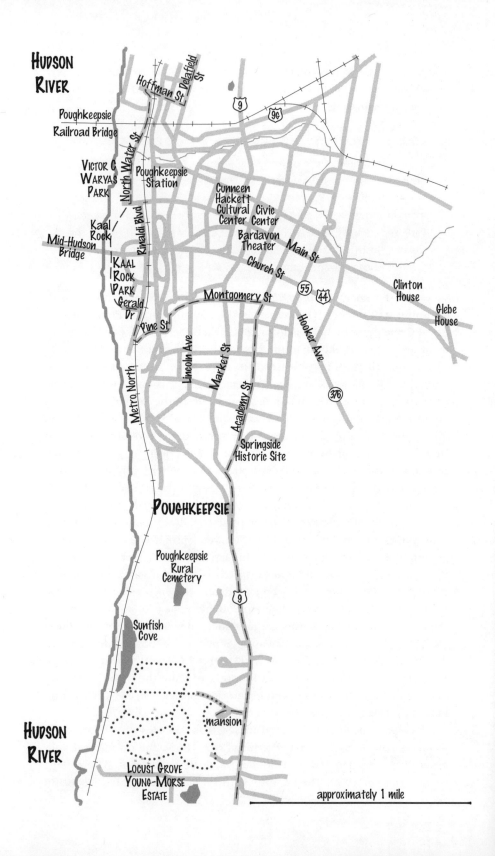

grounds, and flower gardens is well worth visiting. Also located on the Vassar campus is the Warthin Geology Museum, with displays of rocks, minerals, and fossils; and the small but magnificent Frances Lehman Loeb Art Center. It has an outstanding collection of Asian, African, European, and American art including many fine works by artists of the Hudson River School, including Thomas Cole, Frederick Church, George Innes, Albert Bierstadt, Sanford Gifford, and Asher Brown Durand. Call 914-437-5243 for information. The Vassar campus is located east of town in the suburb of Arlington.

Poughkeepsie was originally inhabited by Native Americans of the Wappinger Confederacy, who named it for a stream that represented the halfway point along the path between Hudson Ford, near Albany, and Manhattan. The land was sold to Dutch settlers in 1683. William Prendergast, the leader of the 1754 armed rebellion by Hudson Valley tenant farmers against the manor lords, was arrested and tried here. He was sentenced to be hanged, but according to legend his wife rode, alone on horseback, all the way to New York City, where she persuaded the governor to pardon her husband. She then rode all the way back to Poughkeepsie, arriving just before her husband would have been hanged, thus saving his life.

During the Revolutionary War, American warships used to defend the river from the British were constructed here. After the burning of Kingston, Poughkeepsie served as the temporary capital of New York State, and two legislative sessions were held here in 1778. The Clear Everitt home served as the governor's residence and is today referred to as the Clinton House. In June 1787 the New York convention to ratify the U.S. Constitution met here and ratified it by a close vote. Alexander Hamilton, John Jay, George Clinton, and Chancellor Livingston were among the delegates who attended the convention. In 1824 the city was visited by Lafayette as part of his United States tour. Here as elsewhere the visit was marked by large-scale celebrations.

Poughkeepsie was incorporated as a village in 1799. The completion of the Dutchess Turnpike in 1808 from Poughkeepsie to Sharon, Connecticut, made Poughkeepsie an important commercial center and river port, with a fleet of eight one-hundred-ton-capacity sloops sailing weekly to New York, loaded with flour and grain. One-third of New York City's flour came from Dutchess County, and Poughkeepsie was the main shipping point. In 1814 Poughkeepsie became the first steamboat terminal between New York and Albany.

During the 1830s Poughkeepsie was a major whaling port. In 1849 the New York Central reached Poughkeepsie, and regular train service began. By the 1850s diverse industries sprang up along the waterfront, including foundries, carpet manufacturing, shipbuilding, farm equipment, and the Smith Brothers cough drops. The city's wealthy inhabitants built fabulous mansions in the Academy and Mill Street area. The Bardavon, a magnificent opera house that rivaled the elegance of the finest opera houses in Europe, opened here in 1869. It has continued operating as a multipurpose theater ever since. Poughkeepsie was incorporated as a city in 1854. In 1886 a railroad bridge was constructed here, the first bridge across the Hudson south of Albany. Between 1895 and 1950 Poughkeepsie was the site of the Intercollegiate Racing Association's annual Regatta on the Hudson.

During the twentieth century Poughkeepsie and its waterfront experienced the same kind of economic and environmental decline suffered by most cities along the Hudson. Much of the riverfront area was leveled as part of urban renewal projects, replaced with residential and commercial projects that lack character. Construction of the Route 9 bypass slashed a huge swath through the heart of the waterfront section, limiting access to the river. Like other riverfront communities, Poughkeepsie is attempting a comeback, made more difficult by recent downsizing at the nearby IBM plant, one of the area's major employers. The central area does have a flourishing nightclub scene and restaurants. Use caution at night, because drug dealing and crime are also rampant.

Poughkeepsie's waterfront is currently accessible through Victor C. Waryas and Kaal Rock Parks (see below). A continuous trail along the river from the Poughkeepsie Rural Cemetery to the campus of Marist College is planned.

Poughkeepsie is served by regular train and bus service. Both Metro-North and Amtrak trains stop at the Poughkeepsie station, which is very convenient to the waterfront. The City of Poughleepsie Transit provides daily bus service around the city. For information call 914-454-4118. The Dutchess County Loop Bus provides service around town and to other local communities. Shortline and Adirondack Trailways provide long-distance service. The main shopping area is on Route 9, south of town. There are restaurants and clubs not far from the waterfront, near the train station. For more information about Poughkeepsie, including accommodations and dining, contact the Poughkeepsie Area Chamber of Commerce at 914-454-1700.

From the Poughkeepsie Rural Cemetery, continue north 0.2 miles, passing underneath Route 9, and up Academy Street. Climb a hill and continue another 0.2 miles to the entrance of Springside on the right. Twenty-acre Springside is a National Designated Landmark. It was originally a forty-four-acre ornamental farm, used as a summer home by Matthew Vassar. In 1850 Vassar commissioned renowned landscape architect Andrew Jackson Downing to design the property. Downing's design contrasted the gentle, rounded forms of hills and mature trees with more dramatic elements of rock outcrops and gnarled tree trunks. The estate included a cottage, barn, carriage house, icehouse, dairy, conservatory, gardener's cottage, log cabin, and deer shelter. Downing drowned in a steamboat accident before Springside was complete. Springside is the last unaltered surviving example of Downing's work. However, any visitor expecting a landscaped park will be disappointed. Practically all the original structures have been removed or are in ruins, and everything is quite overgrown. There are a substantial number of downed trees on the property and many of the original carriage trails are mere traces. It's a wild oasis in the midst of an urban setting, an adventurous place to wander around in, with some impressive trees to marvel at. The original gatehouse still stands, facing Academy Street. There are tours. Call 914-454-2060 for information. Work is under way to restore this landmark.

From Springside continue north 0.6 miles through the historic Academy Street neighborhood, with many fine nineteenth-century mansions, representing different styles from Greek Revival to Victorian Gothic. Most are in excellent condition and are private residences. Make a left at the second light, onto Montgomery Street. Go west two blocks to the intersection with Market. There's a light. The headquarters of Clearwater, Inc., the environmental group, is on the opposite corner right behind a small park with a fountain. Continue west a short distance to the corner of Lincoln Avenue and another light. Continue straight on Pine Street, which winds downhill, crossing underneath Route 9 and then the railroad tracks. Just beyond the second tunnel, you'll reach the intersection with Rinaldi Boulevard. Go right on Rinaldi. Then make a left on Gerald Drive, right across from the Laurel Street overpass. Follow a short distance to a roadway on the left, which leads down to the parking area and Kaal Rock Park.

Kaal Rock Park is named for the promontory jutting into the river just north of the Mid-Hudson Bridge, the most impressive landmark along the Poughkeepsie waterfront. The "rock" is a mix of sharply folded layers of sedimentary rock, part of a moving mass of rock that was pushed eastward into a deep basin during the Taconian Orogeny during the early Paleozoic age. There's a walkway that extends about a thousand feet south along the river to an old sewage treatment plant. It also continues north underneath the Mid-Hudson Bridge. There are impressive views of the river and the bridge towering high above.

From the north end of the park, Kaal Rock looms ahead. Though it is not officially part of the park, it is city-owned property. It sees a fair amount of informal use and a trail ascends it. The area is maintained through volunteer efforts. The views from the top of the bluff are the best of the entire waterfront. Much of the area is wooded. A dirt road continues east to a cul-de-sac. From here one can cut north across the grass, down a gentle slope into Victor C. Waryas Park, which is located north of Main Street and west and north of the Poughkeepsie train station. The north end of the park is a large open area used informally for parking. The park includes a boat ramp, floating dock, tugboat dock, playgrounds, picnic areas, rest rooms, and a snack bar. There are superb views of the river and both the Mid-Hudson Bridge to the south and the Poughkeepsie Railroad Bridge to the north.

From the park continue north on North Water Street, crossing a stream and passing underneath the impressive ironwork of the Poughkeepsie Railroad Bridge towering overhead. Continue north to the intersection with Dutchess Avenue. Make a right onto Dutchess Avenue, and cross a bridge over the railroad tracks and Route 9. After the bridge, you'll reach a T-intersection. Make a left and then an immediate right onto Hoffman Street. Go east, uphill to the intersection with Delafield Street. Make a left on Delafield and continue one-half mile to the intersection with Route 9. Enter Route 9 and pass the entrance to Marist College on the left. Marist is a four-year liberal arts college with more than four thousand students. The school plans to develop its riverfront area as Longview Park and connect it by trail to Poughkeepsie's waterfront area.

After another 0.9 miles you'll pass the Hudson River Psychiatric Center on the right. Continue north on Route 9 another mile, passing the Culinary Institute of America on the left. The Culinary Institute, a private organization, was founded in 1946 in New Haven, Connecticut, and relocated here in 1972 on the site of a former Jesuit monastery. It is the premier U.S. school for chefs, and restaurants are proud to have graduates manning their kitchens. There are four excellent, though pricey, restaurants on campus, operated by students and faculty. For reservations call 914-452-9600.

Continue another 1.8 miles north on Route 9 from the Culinary Institute to the village of Hyde Park. The entrance to the FDR estate is on the left. Hyde Park, originally called Stoutenburgh, after Jacobus Stoutenburg, who lived here in 1741, was later named after the estate on which the Vanderbilt Mansion was built, and was officially established in 1821. With the FDR estate and Val-Kill on the south end of town and the Vanderbilt Mansion on the north end, connected by the Hyde Park Trail, there is plenty to attract visitors here. The village itself is an unfortunate clash of quaint nineteenth-century Victorian charm and twentieth-century suburban tackiness, and has all the attributes of a minor tourist trap. The walking tour manages to avoid the ugly strip development and those on bikes can pass through quickly.

Hyde Park is served by Shortline Bus. For more information about accommodations, dining, and so on, call the Hyde Park Chamber of Commerce at 914-229-8612.

Springwood, the FDR estate, was the home of Franklin Delano Roosevelt, thirty-second president of the United States. He was born here in 1882 and spent much of his life here. While he was governor of New York State (1928–1932) and president (1932 till his death in 1944), Springwood served as a frequent refuge from the pressures of political office. He is buried in the family rose garden along with his wife, Eleanor.

A portion of the original house dates back to the early 1800s. Purchased by the Roosevelt family in 1867, it was remodeled and expanded until it reached its present form in 1916. The home was designated a National Historic Site in 1944, following FDR's death, and was formally dedicated in 1946. Springwood and the 188 acres that surround it are owned and operated by the National Park Service. The excellent library/museum includes a superb collection of memorabilia from every stage of FDR's fascinating life, beautifully displayed, including interactive exhibits, a replica of the White House War Room, his car, ship model collection, as well as a room devoted to Mrs. Roosevelt. Roosevelt's depression-era programs and his role as wartime leader get special attention in the exhibits.

The house includes original furnishings. Most interesting are the three master bedrooms: FDR's, his wife's, and his mother's, side by side. The only disappointing thing is the view of the Hudson. Trees have blocked most of it, and what's left is barely a glimpse.

The FDR House and library/museum are open from 9:00 A.M. to 5:00 P.M. every day from May 19 through October 31; Wednesdays through Sundays the rest of the year. There's an admission for the museum and house tour. Children under seventeen are admitted free. For information, call 914-229-9115.

THE FDR ESTATE TO MILLS/NORRIE STATE PARK

For bicyclists or walkers wishing a shortcut, this 5.3-mile-long route is the best alternative. It is primarily on Route 9, part of Bike Route 9, a designated segment of the Hudson River Valley Greenway Trail. Unfortunately it passes a lot of unsightly strip development in Hyde Park, and you can count on plenty of traffic most of the way. An optional side trip to the Vanderbilt Mansion and Bard Rock would provide lovely river views and sites of historical interest.

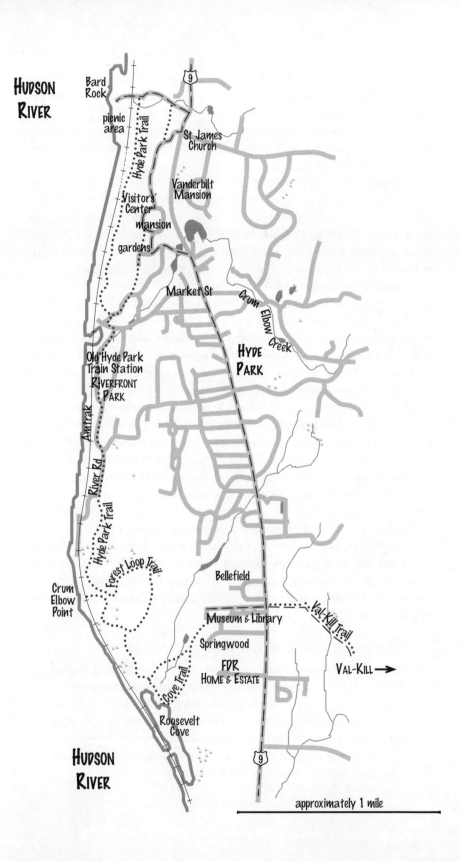

HUDSON
RIVER

Bard
Rock

picnic
area

St James
Church

Hyde Park Trail

Visitor's
Center

Vanderbilt
Mansion

mansion

gardens

Market St

Crum Elbow Creek

HYDE
PARK

Old Hyde Park
Train Station

RIVERFRONT
PARK

Amtrak

River Rd

Hyde Park Trail

Forest Loop Trail

Bellefield

Museum & Library

Val-Kill Trail

VAL-KILL →

Crum
Elbow
Point

Springwood

FDR
HOME & ESTATE

Cove Trail

Roosevelt
Cove

HUDSON
RIVER

approximately 1 mile

From the FDR estate continue north on Route 9 into the heart of Hyde Park's commercial strip. At 0.9 miles you'll pass the stone Stoutenburgh House on the right, which today serves as a restaurant. After another 1.2 miles you'll pass the main entrance to the Vanderbilt Estate on the left.

The Vanderbilt Estate comprises 211 acres. In 1895, during the period known as the Gilded Age, Frederick William Vanderbilt—the grandson of Commodore Cornelius Vanderbilt, who had founded the family fortune in shipping and railroads—purchased the land. The original mansion on the site was torn down and replaced by an opulent fifty-four-room structure built in the Italian Renaissance style by Follim McKim of McKim, Mead & White, the leading U.S. architectural firm of the time. The influence of McKim's partner Stanford White is apparent in rooms on the first floor. The interior of marble columns, gold leaf, plaster, and carved wood is a composite of Continental styles lavishly reproduced, using original period pieces—statues, tapestries, and furniture—imported from Europe as well as finely crafted reproductions. The home and estate were maintained on a year-round basis by a staff of sixty, each of whom was paid $1.50 a day, three times the going rate. Vanderbilt added other buildings, gardens, and greenhouses to the property. Much of the land was cultivated, and Vanderbilt was a serious competitor at the Dutchess County Fair for his livestock, produce, and flowers. The Vanderbilts also owned a town house on Fifth Avenue in New York City as well as other homes in Bar Harbor, Maine; Newport, Rhode Island; and the Adirondacks. They only stayed in Hyde Park a few weeks in the spring and fall and during the winter, when they would sleigh-ride on the property. Many parties and gala events were held here. Neighbors included other families of prominence and wealth.

The house and estate were donated to the government and designated a National Historic Site in 1940, two years after Frederick William's death. Today it is owned and managed by the National Park Service.

The mansion is open from 9:00 A.M. to 5:00 P.M., Wednesdays through Sundays from May through October, and is closed on Thanksgiving, Christmas, and New Year's. For a small admission fee there's a self-guided tour of the mansion; children under seventeen are admitted free. (If you're fortunate, there may be a guided-tour group present you can hook up with.) Concerts and other special events are also held here. Admission to the grounds is free, and they're open year-round. There are superb open views of the Hudson (see below). Bicyclists may consider an optional side trip to Bard Rock on the river, which also has excellent views. For information call 914-229-9115.

From the entrance to the Vanderbilt Mansion, continue north on

Route 9. Just beyond the entrance you'll cross a bridge over lovely Crum Elbow Creek. About 0.4 miles north on the right is Saint James Episcopal Church, where the Roosevelts worshiped, and just beyond it on the left is the north entrance to the Vanderbilt Estate. Continue north on Route 9, passing the Dominican Boys Home on the left and the Anderson School a third of a mile beyond.

At 3.2 miles north of the Vanderbilt Mansion entrance, you'll reach the turnoff for Mills/Norrie State Park, also on the left. This thousand-acre recreation area, owned and operated by the New York State OPRHP, is one of the few large tracts of public land along the Hudson where the tracks do not run alongside the river. Thus three miles of the original shoreline have been preserved and are accessible. Most of the park is woodland in a seminatural state with planted trees, remnants of when the land was part of an estate. There is hiking, biking, horseback riding, cross-country skiing in winter, and one of the Hudson's few public camp-grounds with facilities for tent camping as well as bungalows. It is open all year. There is no admission charge. Call 914-889-4646 for information. For camping reservations call 1-800-456-CAMP.

Val-Kill and the FDR and Vanderbilt estates are all connected by the Hyde Park Trail, an 8.5-mile-long trail system that links these major attractions. The trail was the result of a partnership of many individuals and organizations, including the National Park Service River and Trails Program, the Greenway Heritage Conservancy, and the NYSOPRHP. It is well marked with a logo of a tulip poplar, FDR's favorite tree. More than four and a quarter miles of the Hyde Park Trail are designated part of the Hudson River Valley Greenway. For information about the trail, including an excellent brochure with a map, contact the Hyde Park Recreation Department at 914-229-8086.

FDR ESTATE TO VAL-KILL VIA THE HYDE PARK TRAIL

A walkers' and bikers' route. The marked trail starts in the parking area for the FDR estate, and heads east along the driveway out to Route 9. The trail crosses Route 9 (there's a trail marker on the opposite side), turns right (south) a short distance, then makes a left into the woods and continues east. Follow the path through the woods, east, approximately 2 miles to Route 9G. You'll come out just south of the entrance to Val-Kill, on the opposite side of the road. Another half-mile walk will bring you to the Val-Kill residence.

Val-Kill was the residence of Eleanor Roosevelt (1884–1962). It is the only National Historic Site dedicated to a first lady. The property was a favorite retreat of the Roosevelt family and was also visited by such foreign heads of state as Winston Churchill. A cottage in the Dutch colonial style was constructed in 1925, which Mrs. Roosevelt used as a refuge from public life as well as from her dominating mother-in-law, Sara Delano. With friends Mrs. Roosevelt built a second, larger cottage, used for ten years as a crafts factory to employ local residents making Early American–style furniture. The business failed during the Great Depression. Following FDR's death in 1944, Val-Kill became Mrs. Roosevelt's home. She led a very public life in support of social programs, women's rights, and world peace. Such luminaries as John F. Kennedy, Nikita Khrushchev, Adlai Stevenson, Haile Selassie, and Jawaharfal Nehru all paid her visits here. After her death the house and property were threatened by development, but in 1977 it was designated a National Historic Site.

The home is uniquely modest and stands in sharp contrast to the Hudson region's more lavish residences. It has many of Mrs. Roosevelt's personal mementos. The grounds are lovely and include 1.25 miles of trails, a large pond, gardens, woodlands, and fields. It is also connected to the FDR estate by a 2.5-mile-long trail (see above). There's a guided tour of the home and a video, and self-guided tours of the grounds are available. Admission is charged for guided tours. Open 9:00 A.M. to 5:00 P.M., seven days a week, May 19 through October 31; weekends only the rest of the year. Call 914-229-9115 for information.

FDR ESTATE TO THE VANDERBILT MANSION VIA THE HYDE PARK TRAIL

A walkers' route. From the museum/library, where there's a map of the trail, follow the marked path south, to the right of the FDR mansion.

The trail descends past a field on the left, with a rear view of the mansion overhead. Continue to a fork. Go right on the wide carriage path. (The Hyde Park Trail is also the Cove Trail at this point.) The trail continues its descent. Pass an attractive small pond and dam with falls, on the right. Cross the stream, and proceed through mixed deciduous forest with red ash trees, maples, and oaks, and many old-growth hemlocks present. The trail forks again. The Cove Trail continues left to Roosevelt Cove, an inlet of the Hudson, separated from the main channel by the railroad tracks, which has turned into a marsh where you may observe cattails, spatterdock, arrowhead, and other typical marsh plants as well as bird life. The Hyde Park Trail continues right as the Forest Trail. Climb a small hill with thin, steeply tilted beds of Ordovician gray sandstone and shale exposed on the right. The trail veers right (north). Pass a small seasonal shallow pool on the left, covered with duckweed. Skunk cabbage, marsh marigolds, and ferns are also present.

Reach another fork, and the Forest Trail Loop continues right. The Hyde Park Trail goes left, crosses another small stream, and then climbs past more shale outcrops. Enter a lighter area of smaller and younger deciduous trees with dense undergrowth. There are partial views of the river through the trees. The trail veers to the right again. At the next fork you meet the Forest Trail Loop again on the right. The Hyde Park Trail continues left, leaving the national park. A short distance beyond, there's another fork. The fork to the left goes a short way to a pedestrian bridge over the railroad tracks to Crum Elbow Point, on the river, with excellent views. The distance from the FDR Visitors' Center to Crum Elbow Point is 1.2 miles.

The Hyde Park Trail continues north through open parklike woods with low ground cover and partial views of the river on the left through the trees. Having come 1.25 miles from the FDR mansion, you reach a roadway. Follow the markers through a pleasant residential neighborhood, past houses with river views. Pass a four-acre town riverfront park on the left with a picnic area, playground, and a map of the Hyde Park Trail. The Old Hyde Park Train Station on the left, built in 1914, was designed by the architectural firm of Warren and Wetmore, which also designed Grand Central Station in New York. It is on the National Register of Historic Places. The station closed in 1960. Continue 0.2 miles to the intersection of Dock Road, go left across a stone bridge over Crum Elbow Creek with huge falls. The entrance to Vanderbilt Estate is on the right.

The Hyde Park Trail passes the lower gatehouse on the left, and just beyond leaves the roadway and goes left on a wide dirt carriage path, clearly marked. This path continues for about 1.25 miles to the entrance of Bard Rock. Along the way you'll pass through mixed deciduous forest with dense stands of mature hemlocks. You might see a woodpecker or two; squirrels and chipmunks are abundant. The Vanderbilt Mansion is on the right, on top of the hill covered with tall grass and wildflowers. You'll reach a T-intersection. Go left and over the bridge across the railway, and enter Bard Rock, a popular spot for sunning and picnicking, with superb views of the river, especially looking north with Shaupeneak Ridge, Esopus Island, and the Catskills in the distance.

Backtrack over the bridge and continue straight (east) on the road, gradually ascending. The trail veers to the right off the road, past a field, and climbs to the top of the ridge and a grove of hemlocks. The trail splits here. Go straight, continuing south along the ridge to superior views looking north with a wonderful patchwork of fields and forests in the foreground and Shaupeneak Ridge and the Catskills in the background. Just beyond is the Visitors' Center and gift shop, and just beyond them is the Vanderbilt Mansion, described above. If you continue past the mansion, there are lovely formal gardens in the Italian Renaissance style, with fountains and statues.

NORRIE POINT ENTRANCE TO THE MILLS MANSION

A bikers' and walkers' route. Approximately 3 miles, mostly on paved park roads and quiet old roads with no vehicular access. Views of the river at Norrie Point and just before the Mills Mansion. There are steep, rugged sections mainly suited to mountain bikes. The primary features of this segment are the Norrie Point Visitors' Center and the Mills Mansion, a state-owned historic site.

At the entrance to Mills/Norrie State Park, make an immediate left on a paved road and continue, passing through a narrow tunnel under the railroad tracks, approximately 0.4 miles. Just past the tunnel there's a T-intersection. Go left, passing a marsh on the left, then a cove on the right, followed by a marina on the right. Just past the marina is the Norrie Point Visitors' Center, about half a mile from the T-intersection.

The Norrie Point Visitors' Center, operated by Dutchess County Community College, has exceptional views of the Hudson in all directions. Esopus Island lies across the way, and the massive stone structure on the opposite shore at the foot of Shaupeneak Ridge is the Mount Saint Alphonsus Seminary. The Catskills may be observed in the distance to the north. I have seen harbor seals next to the island, and birds such as cormorants are plentiful. The Visitors' Center has a small aquarium exhibit displaying different types of river habitats and their characteristic fish. Other (mounted and stuffed) creatures are displayed in the museum. There are also rest rooms and vending machines. Call 914-889-4830 for information about the center.

From the Norrie Point Visitors' Center, backtrack one-half mile on the road, passing the marina on the left, rest rooms on the right, and finally the intersection you came out on. Continue straight (north), a short distance to an intersection with another road. Go straight and climb a hill to another intersection. Signs indicate a camping area to the left. Go right (the sign indicates a picnic area), and follow a short distance to the end of the road and a picnic/parking area with rest rooms, 0.85 miles from Norrie Point. The road becomes a wide dirt path (with blue markers), and continues north. It does not permit vehicular access beyond this point. Follow the dirt road as it runs parallel to the river for about a quarter of

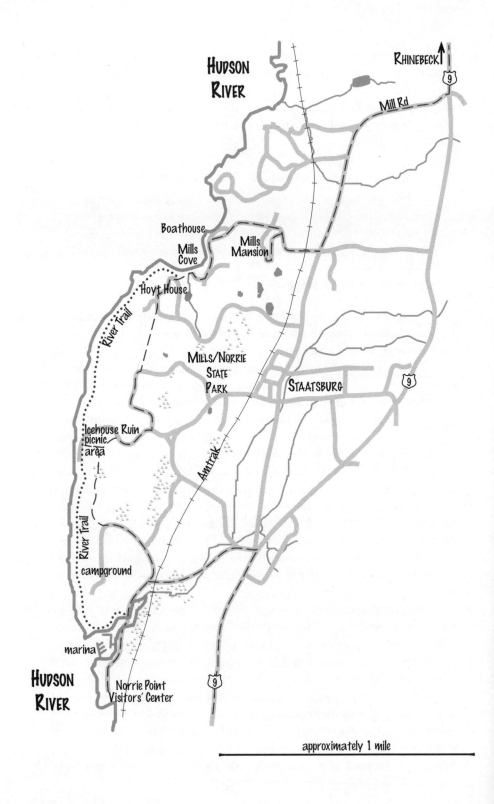

HUDSON
RIVER

RHINEBECK
9

Mill Rd

Boathouse

Mills
Cove

Mills
Mansion

Hoyt House

River Trail

MILLS/NORRIE
STATE
PARK

STAATSBURG

9

Icehouse Ruin
picnic
area

Amtrak

River Trail

campground

marina

9

HUDSON
RIVER

Norrie Point
Visitors' Center

approximately 1 mile

a mile. There are no views of the river here except in winter, but the walk or ride through the forest is pleasant. The road makes a sharp turn to the right and climbs a steep hill, intersecting a paved road by a memorial to Louis Gordon Norrie; the land was donated to the people of Hyde Park in his memory. You can make a short detour here, left, down the paved road to where it ends by the Hudson, to a picnic area with fine views of the river, including Shaupeneak Ridge and the foundation of what was once an icehouse.

The blue-marked trail continues north beyond the intersection with the memorial. Follow it a short distance. By an old stone tower on the left, the trail bends sharply right and soon intersects the paved road again. Go left, and follow the paved road a very short distance. The trail leaves the roadway on the left (clearly marked with a metal barrier and blue markers). Follow the trail (an excellent old road) north. The trail soon bends to the left and then to the right. It continues north another quarter of a mile and reaches another intersection. The main road forks to the right. Instead, continue straight (north), on a wide dirt-and-gravel path with blue markers. After another quarter mile you'll pass the Hoyt House on the left, a Gothic Revival–style house built in 1855, designed by Calvert Vaux, who also designed the grounds (now wild and over-grown), following the principles of his partner and mentor Andrew Jackson Downing. Unfortunately it has not been restored.

The road continues north, descends, and reaches Mills Cove with a spectacular open view, looking north, of the Esopus Meadows Lighthouse and the Catskills in the distance. Just before the cove the white trail intersects on the left. Continue on past the gardener's house on the right, the former home of the superintendent of the property, now a private residence. The road forks. Go left, along the cove, with the huge lawn on the right and the Mills Mansion at the top of the hill. Pass the boathouse. The road turns to the right and ascends the hill toward the mansion. The lawn has great views and is excellent for sunbathing and picnicking.

The Mills Mansion is the single largest state-owned historic building. It has sixty-five rooms and fourteen baths and was built in 1895 in the beaux-arts style. The property earlier belonged to Morgan Lewis, the third governor of New York State and his wife, Gertrude Livingston, who purchased the sixteen hundred acres in 1792. Almost the entire estate was cultivated by tenant farmers including the area that is presently the lawn. Ruth Livingston Mills, Lewis's great-granddaughter, and her husband, Ogden Mills, a wealthy financier and philanthropist, took over the property in 1890. They converted the estate into an English landscape garden, designed to enhance and romanticize the beautiful characteristics of the natural setting, and enlarged the home into its present form.

The Millses had other homes as well in New York City; Newport, Rhode Island; and France, and only lived here in the spring and fall. Ruth was very socially conscious and held extravagant parties in the huge dining room. The mansion is lavishly decorated with antiques, paintings, tapestries, and oriental porcelains and is a superb representation of life in the Gilded Age. It is open from April 15 through Labor Day, Wednesdays through Saturdays, from 10:00 A.M. to 4:30 P.M., and Sundays from noon to 4:30 P.M.; and September and October from Wednesdays through Saturdays, noon to 4:30 P.M. There are guided tours every half hour. Admission is free. Call 914-889-8851 for information.

NORRIE POINT TO THE MILLS MANSION

A walkers' route. For walkers, the primary feature of this route is the 2.66-mile-long River Trail, which runs right along the Hudson from the small cove just north of the Norrie Point Marina to the larger cove near the Mills Mansion. It is designated part of the Hudson River Greenway Trail. The River Trail is the longest trail along the Hudson on the eastern bank of the river and provides a rare glimpse of what the Hudson's predevelopment shoreline would have looked like. Secluded beaches, sheer cliffs, hemlocks and cedars clinging to the rocks, blooming columbines, and wonderful vistas are some of the features you'll encounter along the way. The trail is narrow and steep in places, and you should exercise extreme caution along the tops of cliffs. You can return via the blue-marked trail described above. The entire loop is about 4 miles and should take two to two and a half hours.

From Norrie Point Visitors' Center, backtrack north past the marina. Cross the bridge, and turn left off the road. There's no sign or marker here, but the route is obvious. The River Trail climbs around the point past cottages. Just beyond the cottages, you'll pass the campground, off to the right. After you walk about a mile, the trail approaches the river from a bluff. Just beyond is a picnic area with views (described above) and the ruins of the icehouse. The trail continues north through a more spectacular section, running along the top of tall precipitous bluffs, with outcrops of steeply tilted shale and sandstone. Hemlocks are plentiful. There are many excellent vistas. Watch your step because of sheer dropoffs. A few side trails lead to pebble beaches along the shoreline. The trail finally reaches a dirt road and beach at Mills Cove (see above for description of the rest of the route).

There are two suggested routes from Mills Mansion to Ferncliff Forest. One goes through the village of Rhinebeck; the other follows the river more closely and goes through the village of Rhinecliff. Both routes are mostly on quiet, scenic country roads, with only a brief stretch on a main highway. Hiking trails are accessible from these roads at Wilderstein and Ferncliff Forest. Both routes have much to offer in terms of rural ambience and historic sites.

MILLS MANSION TO FERNCLIFF FOREST

A distance of 8.6 miles through the village of Rhinebeck.

From the Mills Mansion, continue east. Cross the bridge over the railroad tracks just before the main entrance. At the gate (there's a Do Not Enter sign) turn left on Mill Road. There's a golf course on the right, a tall stone fence on the left. The road bends to the right with fields on both sides of the road. About 0.7 miles from the Mills Mansion entrance, Mill Road reaches an intersection with busy Route 9. Go left (north) on Route 9, 0.8 miles to the intersection with South Mill Road. There's a sign for Linwood on the corner. Go left (west) on the road 0.6 miles, descending to a bridge over Fallsburg Creek. South Mill Road climbs briefly to a view of the Hudson and Vanderburgh Cove, a mature cattail marsh, and descends to a second bridge 0.3 miles after the first. Just before the bridge, a short trail leads to the Landsman Kill, a stream with exposed mudflats at low tide and characteristic marsh plants like arrowroot, spatterdock, and pickerelweed. Just beyond the bridge on the north side of the creek is a small stone cottage where the famous novelist Thomas Wolfe stayed for two months in the early 1920s as a guest of his friend, estate owner Ollin Dow, while he was working on *Of Time and the River.* Cross the bridge, and climb the hill on a winding road. One-half mile from the bridge you'll pass Linwood on the left, a religious sanctuary. Use of the beautiful grounds is by permission only.

South Mill Road forks 0.7 miles north of Linwood. Go right on Mill Road. Mill Road is part of the Sixteen Mile Historic District, which includes nearly forty houses built by Beekman and Livingston family members. Most of the properties (few of them visible from the road) are landscaped in the romantic style of A. J. Downing. Continue north 2.4 miles to the intersection of Route 9. Across the street is the Quitman House.

A parsonage built in 1798, the Quitman House now serves as a museum of Rhinebeck history, with permanent and changing displays. It is open from May 18 through October 27, from 1:00 to 4:00 P.M. on weekends. There's a small admission charge for adults. Call 914-876-4902 for information.

From the intersection of Mill Road and Route 9, go left and cross the Landsman Kill again. This stream powered mills during the eighteenth

century. Just 0.3 miles beyond is the main intersection of the village of
Rhinebeck. On the left is the Beekman Arms Hotel.

Rhinebeck was named after the Rhine River. William Beekman was
a Dutch immigrant who purchased the land from the Esopus in 1647.
His grandson Henry settled Rhinebeck in 1716 with immigrants from the
Rhineland-Palatinate (see chapter 11). The King's Highway between New
York City and Albany passed through Rhinebeck, which became an important stage stop. Established in 1766 to accommodate travelers, the
Beekman Arms is reputed to be the oldest continuously operating hotel
in the United States. For information about rates and accommodations,
call 914-876-7077.

The town grew, and by 1846 many of its houses and buildings, some
of which survive today, were being designed in the popular Greek Revival
style. Rhinebeck also has some of the region's finest examples of Victorian architecture. The Rhinebeck area has long been a magnet for big-city
"refugees." Recent years have brought considerable gentrification to the
village and now tourists flock there. The main attraction outside the village is the famous Rhinebeck Aerodrome, where one can see restored antique aircraft. The weekend air shows, from June through October, are
spectacular not-to-be missed entertainment. Call 914-758-8610 for information. Cafés, boutiques, antique shops, and upscale craft shops line
the busy village streets. Upstate Films, which shows avant-garde and foreign films, and the Omega Institute, a major New Age education and spiritual center, have added to the area's diverse cultural attractions.
Rhinebeck has some of the best dining in the region. There are also a
number of bed-and-breakfasts and private campgrounds in the area. For
information about accommodations and dining in the Rhinebeck Area,
contact the Rhinebeck Chamber of Commerce at 914-876-4778.

Just north of the village's main intersection, you'll pass the Delamatier House on the left. Built in 1844, the Delamatier House is a charming Gothic Revival–style residence designed by Alexander Jackson Davis.
It now serves as a bed-and-breakfast and conference center. One-half
mile north of the main intersection, go left on Old Post Road and continue one-half mile to a fork. Go left on Mt. Rutsen Road, and continue
north 1.2 miles. The main entrance to Ferncliff Forest is on the left.

MILLS MANSION TO FERNCLIFF FOREST VIA RHINECLIFF

A distance of 8.5 miles, mostly on back roads, passing the Wilderstein
Estate.

Follow the same 3.6-mile route from the Mills Mansion to the corner
of South Mill Road and Morton Road. From there, go left 0.3 miles on

Morton Road. On the left side of the road is the entrance to Wilderstein, a registered National Historic Site. Wilderstein is an interesting and unusual Victorian mansion built in 1852 by Thomas Suckley, a descendant of the Beekman and Livingston families, who made his fortune through the family export trade and real estate investments. Suckley named the property "Wilderstein" ("wild man's stone"), in reference to a Native American petroglyph found nearby. The thirty-five acres of land overlooking the Hudson were landscaped by Calvert Vaux to enhance their natural beauty. The mansion was enlarged in 1888 in the Queen Anne style, including a third floor, a large veranda, and a dramatic five-story circular tower.

The interior of the mansion, designed by Joseph Burr Tiffany, displays beautiful oak, mahogany, and cherry woodwork and lovely stained glass. Every room features a different theme. One has Louis XVI–style furnishings. The house, which had deteriorated greatly, is currently being restored. Margaret Suckley (1891–1991), the last family member to live at Wilderstein, worked as an archivist for her distant cousin Franklin Delano Roosevelt. She became a good friend and gave him his famous Scottish terrier Fala, about whom she later wrote a book. Her diaries and correspondence with FDR were later published in Geoffrey C. Ward's *Closest Companion.*

There are carriage paths and trails for walkers to enjoy the scenery. Calvert Vaux planted European larches, red oaks, silver maples, sycamores, gingkoes, catalpas, and black locusts around the house. The steep wooded slopes are populated by white pines, hemlocks, basswoods, hickories, maples, sweet gums, black walnuts, oaks, dogwoods, black cherries, and elms. Wildflowers like asters, goldenrods, chickories, ragweeds, trout lilies, jack-in-the-pulpits, blue hepaticas, white wood anemones, and such shrubs as honeysuckle, blackberry, spicebush, and viburnum may be observed in the woods and fields. Deer, woodchucks, rabbit, squirrels, and chipmunks are common. Ruffed grouse, wild turkeys, robins, and mockingbirds are among the many species of birds seen here. There are excellent views of the Hudson from Umbrella and Cove Points, with the Catskills in the distance. From these sites one can also observe Suckley Cove in the foreground, an inlet of the Hudson turned into marshland, with sweet flag, cattails, and purple loosestrife, muskrat, bitterns, geese, ducks, swans, teals, herons, kingfishers, ospreys, and redwing blackbirds.

Owned and operated by Wilderstein Preservation, a private nonprofit group, Wilderstein is open from May through October, Thursdays through Sundays, from 12:00 to 4:00 P.M. There is a small admission fee for tours. Iced tea and cookies are served on the veranda in late afternoon. For information call 914-876-4818.

From the entrance to Wilderstein, continue north on Morton Road. The road bends right and then left, and 1.9 miles north of Wilderstein, enters the tiny village of Rhinecliff. It is a very pleasant interlude: a mostly residential riverfront community of attractive, modest homes and fine views. Rhinecliff was purchased by the Kipp family from the Esopus in 1686. There's a railroad station here served by Amtrak. The Long Dock was the former terminal of the Rondout/Rhinecliff Ferry. There are a couple of restaurants here, on Shatzell Avenue, and a bar that features live bands.

A half mile past the train station, the road bends sharply right and becomes Rhinecliff Road. This section of road is far busier than the section south of Rhinecliff. Continue east 0.4 miles to the intersection of River Road. Go left (north) through beautiful countryside, passing the Ferncliff Nursing Home on the left after 1.1 miles. After another 0.7 miles there's a yellow trail marker on the right side of the road. Walkers may enter here. This is part of the 192-acre Ferncliff Game Refuge and Forest Preserve. The property served as a Methodist retreat in the late nineteenth century (remnants of old foundations survive), and was later purchased by John Jacob Astor as part of his 2,800-acre estate. Astor died when the *Titanic* sank in 1912. The land was donated by his descendants in 1963, and in 1983 Ferncliff Forest, Inc., a private nonprofit group, was established to manage the preserve. There are mature mixed deciduous forests, including large stands of hemlocks, a pond, and wetlands. There are also a couple of miles of marked trails that would take up to two hours to explore. When I was there in July 1997, some of the trails were overgrown and suffered storm damage: downed trees. Though views of the Hudson are limited, this is the best stretch of wild forest between Mills/Norrie State Park and Tivoli Bay, and it's the only place to camp if you're hiking through. A short quarter-mile hike up the yellow-marked East Tower Trail brings you to the 350-foot summit of Mount Rutsen, where there used to be an observation tower. The trail descends as a wide path another quarter mile, passing a lean-to on the right and reaching the light-blue-marked North Pond Trail. Go right on the wide path to Mount Rutsen Pond, where there's a second lean-to with a water pump, sheltered picnic area, and fire pit. The pond is populated by bullfrogs and other amphibians and, very likely, turtles and fish. Birds are also plentiful as well as deer, chipmunks, and squirrels. From the pond a brief walk south on a wide dirt track brings you out to Mount Rutsen Road and the preserve's main entrance.

For information about camping in Ferncliff Forest (there's no fee, but reservations are required), contact the Fraleigh Agency at 914-876-7035 or Staley's Real Estate at 914-876-3196. Both are located in Rhinebeck.

FERNCLIFF FOREST TO MONTGOMERY PLACE

A walk or bike of 3.8 miles on quiet country roads with an optional side trip to Poet's Walk.

From the main entrance to Ferncliff Forest, follow Mount Rutsen Road north a half mile to the intersection with River Road. Veer right, and continue north on River Road another 0.7 miles to the intersection with Route 199. The next section of River Road, though it has no views of the Hudson, is exceptionally charming, shaded by locust trees and lined with stone fences and bright orange daylilies that bloom in late June. Continue north on River Road, and 0.6 miles past the intersection with Route 199, you'll see the entrance to Poet's Walk on the left.

Poet's Walk Romantic Landscape Park is owned and managed by Scenic Hudson. The 120-acre park contains open fields separated by a patchwork of forests and offers impressive views of the Hudson River and Catskill Mountains beyond. There's an information pavilion just beyond the parking area, which also has a bike rack. Maps and brochures are available to the public, including poetry to contemplate while strolling the grounds. Rustic wooden benches, wide paths, and two gazebos add to the picturesque environment. Wonderful scenery, great views, and easy trails make Poet's Walk a very popular destination and certainly one of the highlights of anyone's visit to the region. The land was first purchased from the Native Americans by Col. Peter Schuyler of Albany in 1685 and sold in 1715 to Henry Beekman, the founder of Rhinebeck. Beekman divided the property and leased it to Palatine immigrants. In 1811 the land was purchased by John Armstrong (1758–1843), husband of one of Chancellor Livingston's sisters. Armstrong served in the Revolutionary War and was one of the officers at the New Windsor Cantonment who plotted a military coup against the Continental Congress over unpaid wages. Washington personally quelled the rebellion. No one was punished, and Armstrong went on to serve as a senator, ambassador to France (Napoleon presented him with a gift of prized Merino sheep), brigadier general, and secretary of war. The property was landscaped in the English romantic style by architect Hans Jacob Ehlers, a competitor of A. J. Downing. Landscape features evoked images from nineteenth-century romantic poems. Supposedly Washington Irving and the poet Fitz-Greene Halleck walked the property, hence the name. Armstrong's daughter married into the Astor family, and her daughter married into the Delano family. The property was named "Steen Valetje," Dutch for "little stony falls," after a stream on the property.

On the left side of the road 0.3 miles north of Poet's Walk is a state historical marker indicating the site of Rokeby, General Armstrong's

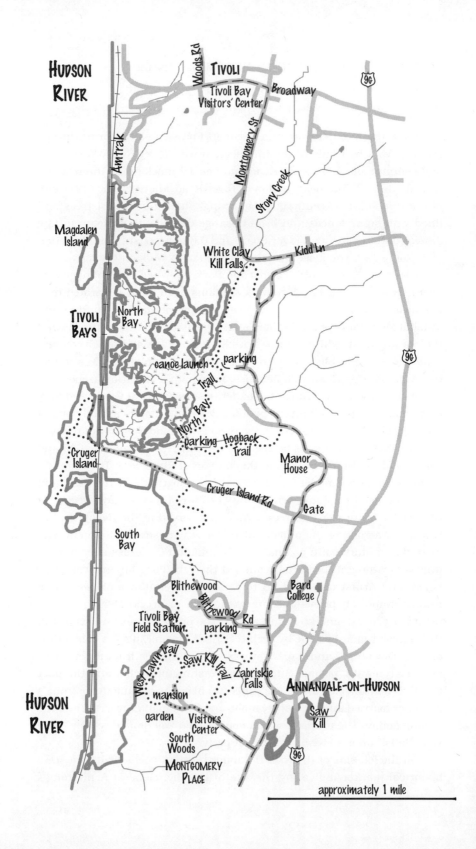

residence, built in 1815, later the home of William Astor, who in 1866 was distinguished as the wealthiest man in America. Descendants of the Astor family still reside there; it is not open to the public.

Another 1.2 miles north along River Road brings you to the intersection of Dock Road. A left brings you down to Barrytown and the river. The small hamlet of Barrytown is a headquarters for the Reverend Moon's Unification Church. It is also headquarters for the Hudson River Ice Yacht Racing Club. Racing sail-powered iceboats was popular in the nineteenth century. The sport was revived about thirty years ago and today is practiced by a number of enthusiasts. Some of the new-model iceboats can travel at speeds of up to seventy miles per hour. Continue straight on River Road, passing the attractive Saint John the Evangelist Episcopal Church of Barrytown on the right. Another half mile brings you to the entrance to Montgomery Place on the left. Go a short distance west on a wide dirt road, passing a farm market open in summer from July 1, and vineyards and orchards.

Montgomery Place is owned by Historic Hudson Valley. The original Federal-style mansion was built in 1805 by the sister of Chancellor Livingston and widow of Gen. Richard Montgomery, a British officer who was with General Wolfe when he died at the Battle of Quebec, which ended the French and Indian Wars. Twenty years later, in 1775, during the Revolutionary War, Montgomery died leading American troops in an unsuccessful assault on the same town. On leaving his young wife, Janet, at the home of General Schuyler near Saratoga, to embark on his fateful last campaign into Canada, he reputedly kissed her and said, "You shall never blush for your Montgomery." Montgomery was the first American general to die in the Revolutionary War. Built by his widow in his honor, Montgomery Place was originally called Château de Montgomery. Janet Montgomery led a quiet life and never remarried. Edward Livingston (1764–1836), Chancellor Livingston's brother, purchased the property. The home was later redesigned and enlarged by Alexander Jackson Davis, the entrance porch and veranda added, and the interior remodeled. The grounds were landscaped in the romantic tradition, influenced by A. J. Downing. The estate continued to serve as a Livingston family summer home and retreat.

The mansion contains a large collection of furniture and art objects from three centuries of the Livingston family, including numerous family portraits. Particularly noteworthy is the room devoted to General Montgomery and his memorabilia, and a set of imported leather chairs from France, a housewarming gift from Chancellor Livingston. On the west side of the mansion there's a steep slope and superb view of the river, the Catskills in the distance, and Tivoli Bay to the north. This is a wonderful place to picnic and admire the vista. The tour of the mansion and grounds takes approximately one hour. Some parts of the grounds are landscaped, and others were intentionally left wild. One of the highlights is a huge three-hundred-year-old tulip tree. There are formal herb, perennial, and rose gardens developed in the 1920s by amateur horticulturist Violetta Delafield, the wife of Gen. Ross Delafield. (General Delafield was another Livingston descendant.) Also noteworthy is the so-called Rough Garden, a woodland path that links the other gardens with the main house that features lush displays of ferns, rhododendrons, dogwoods, and many colorful flowers.

A pair of curving paths designed by Edward Livingston in the romantic style have been restored as the West Lawn Trail and the Saw Kill Trail. The West Lawn Trail begins at the north end of the mansion, following a wooded ridge that gradually descends into a deciduous forest of maple and oak trees and a stand of hemlocks below and opposite the house. It then leaves the woods passing an artificial pond with water lilies, amphibians, and fish and continues up the hill toward the mansion past a site where prehistoric artifacts were excavated, finally ending at the south side of the mansion, a total of just over a quarter of a mile. The Saw Kill Trail branches from the West Lawn Trail a short distance north of the house. It descends through a ravine with a seasonal brook and hemlocks, birches, and beeches until it reaches the Saw Kill, a small tributary of the Hudson. A power plant was erected here in the 1920s to use the power of the stream to generate electricity to meet the estate's energy needs. The trail begins to ascend as a lovely carriage road through an old mature forest of white pine and aspen, finally ending at the Visitors' Center, a total distance of about three-quarters of a mile. A map and guides are available at the Visitors' Center. Just west of the Visitors' Center are the South Woods, a picturesque grove of very mature hemlock and spruce trees dating back to colonial times, reputed to be the oldest forest grove in the Hudson Valley.

Montgomery Place is open from April to October, Wednesdays through Mondays from 10:00 A.M. to 5:00 P.M. and until sunset on summer weekends. It is open weekends only in November, December, and March. Closed January and February. There's an admission fee for tours of the house and grounds, a smaller fee for the grounds only. Buy tickets at the Visitors' Center, where the tours originate. There are also a gift shop and rest rooms. For information call 914-758-5461.

MONTGOMERY PLACE TO THE VILLAGE OF TIVOLI

There are two possible routes for walkers; the first one is also the recommended route for bicyclists and is about four miles. There's an optional side trip to Blithewood, which has an excellent view of the river. Both routes traverse the campus of Bard College and the Tivoli Bay National Estuarine Research Reserve, and the second route includes a worthwhile side venture to Cruger Island.

From the Montgomery Place entrance, go north on River Road, soon crossing the Saw Kill on a small bridge. Just beyond, the road splits as you enter the village of Annandale. Bear left on Annandale Road, and continue north another 0.3 miles to the entrance to Bard College. Bard College is a small attractive campus located on the two-thousand-acre former estate of Robert B. Ward, a prominent banker. It was founded in 1860 by Dr. John Bard as Saint Stephens College for the sons of Episcopal clergymen. In 1920 it became a unit of Columbia University, and in 1945 it became independent again. The Bard campus is an eclectic mix of old and new structures. The college boasts excellent programs in literature and the arts. A classical music festival held every summer is world renowned. There is also a graduate program in environmental studies. The Tivoli Bay Field Station, built in 1972, used for research and for classrooms, is operated by Bard College; the New York State Department of Environmental Conservation, as part of the Hudson River National Estuarine Research Reserve; and Hudsonia, a private nonprofit corporation founded to promote better scientific understanding of human-environmental interactions in the Hudson Valley. One should take care not to disturb the researchers there who are busy at work.

A short distance past the entrance to the college there's an intersection for Blithewood Road. Go left on Blithewood, 0.2 miles to another intersection, and continue all the way to the end of Blithewood Road, about 0.4 miles to the mansion. Blithewood was built in 1900 by A. C. Zabriskie on the site of an earlier mansion built by Armstrong in 1795, which was called Mill Hill; it burned in 1877. Today, Blithewood is home to the Jerome Levy Economics Institute, affiliated with Bard. There are excellent views from here of the Hudson, Tivoli's South Bay, and Cruger Island, and there's a lovely Italian-style formal garden overlooking the river, one of the Hudson's most romantic spots.

Backtrack to Annandale Road. Continue north about 0.6 miles through the campus on an excellent pedestrian and bike path that parallels Annandale Road. The road makes a sharp right in front of a medieval-style gatehouse. Go to the left side of the gatehouse and follow the roadway in front of the Manor House Mansion, a large two-story stucco Tudor-style home built in 1918, which now serves as an administrative center. Just beyond it on the left, a narrow asphalt track leads across the lawn with excellent views of the Catskills. Continue north to a barrier. At this point you enter the New York State Department of Environmental Conservation's Tivoli Bay National Estuarine Research Reserve, part of the National Estuarine Research Reserve System. The entire reserve is 1,468 acres of various forest habitats, fields, intertidal cattail marshes, tidal creeks, and tidal pools. It is the largest undeveloped tidal freshwater wetland complex on the Hudson and serves as an important spawning ground and feeding area for striped bass, killifish, alewife, and blueback herring. Blue crabs, muskrat, and snapping turtles also inhabit the marsh. The 800 acres of woodlands are home to deer, wild turkeys, ruffed grouse, squirrels, and an occasional black bear.

The road continues north for about a mile, passing fields on the left and entering a forested area with small shallow ponds. The road intersects another road right after crossing through another barrier. A short detour left down the hill brings you to the Stony Creek Canoe Launch and a superb view of the North Bay, with the Catskills in the distance.

Construction of the railway in 1850 cut off Tivoli's both North and South Bays from the Hudson's main channel but allowed the river to flood them twice a day, depositing sediment. Marshes formed, and decaying plant material gradually accumulated forming thick muck. Aquatic plants such as cattails, spatterdock, wild rice, Phragmites, and purple loosestrife inhabit the marsh. Willows, pickerelweed, dogwood, and marsh marigolds are common along the shore. Bird life is plentiful, though easier to observe from a canoe; early spring and late summer are the best times. Least bitterns, Virginia rails, long-billed marsh wrens, gray catbirds, yellow warblers, common yellowthroats, redwing blackbirds, northern orioles, American goldfinches, various sparrows, and pileated woodpeckers are among the species you might observe. During the spring and autumn migration great blue and green herons, American bitterns, numerous duck and geese species, swans, ospreys, and ruby-throated hummingbirds can be seen. In February and March a bald eagle sighting is possible.

From the intersection continue right, slightly less than a 0.7 miles, to Kidd Lane. From the road entrance (there's a Tivoli Bay sign, small parking area, and an information kiosk). The road bends sharply to the right, crosses Stony Creek, and continues north for another mile, becoming Montgomery Street and passing numerous attractive Victorian houses as it enters the village of Tivoli.

Tivoli was formerly known as Red Hook Landing, a stop for Hudson River sloops and the site of a ferry between Red Hook Landing and Saugerties. In 1798, a Frenchman, Pierre de Labigarre, tried to establish a utopian community here and renamed the town after a village in Italy. The utopian community was a financial failure, but the village continued to prosper as a river port and later as a railroad stop. The village was incorporated in 1872. During the twentieth century, it suffered economic decline as the railroad station closed and Route 9G bypassed the village center. Since the late 1980s there's been a bit of a revival, which continues up to today. Tivoli has been able to take advantage of its location north of Tivoli Bay and Bard College, and south of Clermont, and just east of the Hudson River to attract visitors and new residents. The community plans to reestablish ferry service with the village of Saugerties. There are also plans to develop a park on its waterfront and a Tivoli Commons Park on four acres of land around the historic Watts Depeyster Fireman's Hall, with trail links to the Kaatsbaan International Dance Center and the Tivoli Bay Wildlife Management Center. Nobody's Bikes, a community-sponsored project in Tivoli and neighboring Red Hook, begun in 1997, tries to increase ridership and awareness of alternative transportation. They provide a fleet of recycled bikes in good working order for residents and visitors to borrow at no charge. These are available at a number of handy locations throughout the village and should be returned by the end of the day. Nobody's Bikes also sponsors workshops on bike maintenance and safety, as well as community rides and an Earn-a-Bike program. For more information contact Catherine Gould-Martin at 914-758-9105 or Andy Bicking at 914-757-5484. A number of new shops, including a thriving artists' co-op at 60 Broadway, which is open on weekends and has changing exhibits (914-757-2667), and a variety of very good restaurants and cafés, make Tivoli an excellent stopover. Despite all the new growth and activity, the atmosphere here remains very laid-back. Visitors should check out the Tivoli Bay Visitors' Center located in the historic Watts Depeyster Firemen's Hall along with the library and town offices. The Visitors' Center has educational displays and a computer program. It is open from noon to 4:00 P.M. on weekends.

BARD COLLEGE TO THE VILLAGE OF TIVOLI

A walker's route. This route is almost entirely on trails through woods that skirt Tivoli's South and North Bays. It is only slightly longer than the bikers' route. It also includes a very worthwhile side trip to Cruger Island, one of the most scenic and secluded spots along the entire river, also a designated National Historic Site. The length of this stretch is a little over four miles and should take two to two and a half hours, but add at least two miles and an additional hour and a half if you visit Cruger Island.

From the corner of Blithewood and Annandale Roads, make a left onto Blithewood. Then make another left at the first road to the Bard

College water plant. Just beyond, the road becomes a wide carriage path and enters a young forest with oaks, maples, ash trees, white pines, and hemlocks. Follow a short distance to the Saw Kill. This is a popular walk for Bard students. The trail makes a sharp right and passes lovely Zabriskie Falls on the left. You're now on the South Bay Trail. The trail narrows, then crosses a boardwalk past a wetland area with purple loosestrife, spicebush, alder, silky dogwood, and elderberry. There's a pond with a dam. Plants in the pond include water chestnut, water celery, waterweed, and duckweed. Various fish, including largemouth bass, American eel, bullheads, bluegill sunfish, and redfin pickerel inhabit the pond, as do aquatic snails, a number of painted turtles, an occasional snapping turtle, and water snakes. On the opposite shore is the Montgomery Place property. Continue east, passing a parking area on the right. One could also access the trail from here. Just beyond, the trail intersects a dirt road that leads to the Tivoli Bay Field Station. The trail leaves the road on the left over a small brick bridge and descends a ravine with the Saw Kill cascading below on the left. Aquatic insects such as mayflies and stone flies inhabit this section of the stream as well as minnows. Continue to descend through the steeply sloping forest. The ornamental ground cover is periwinkle, also called myrtle. It has pale blue flowers in the spring. This beautiful exotic plant is one of the many remnants of when this area was landscaped as part of the large nineteenth-century Mill Hill Estate, designed by A. J. Downing.

Follow the trail down to the shore of Tivoli's South Bay. In the mid-eighteenth century a sawmill operated here. This is a very shallow inlet that becomes a mudflat at low tide. Alewives, suckers, and smelts spawn in these waters. White perch, striped bass, and largemouth bass enter the cove to feed on crayfish, scuds, and other invertebrates. Continue north intersecting the road to the field station again. Just before the field station, the trail veers to the left, into woods comprising mixed hardwoods: oaks, maples, beeches, hickories, as well as some hemlocks. Such woodland wildflowers as hepaticas, pink spring beauties, trilliums, yellow trout lilies, anemones, spicebush, wild ginger, and jack-in-the pulpits may be seen blooming in the spring.

The trail continues north, skirting the shore of the South Bay with partial views through the trees. Cross two wooden bridges over seasonal streams, and then reach an intersection. A spur trail to the left leads to Blithewood Point and a superb open view of the South Bay, with the Kingston-Rhinecliff Bridge, Cruger Island, and the Catskills in the distance. South Bay comprises one of the two Tivoli Bays, which are part of the Hudson River National Estuarine Sanctuary/Research Reserve. South Bay, primarily shallows and mudflats, is separated from the Hudson's main channel by the railroad embankment. It is separated from the North Bay by a causeway. From June to September, South Bay is covered with a dense mat of vegetation made up mostly of water chestnuts. Wild rice, arrowheads, smartweed, pickerelweed, and bulrushes are some of the other plant inhabitants of South Bay. Great blue herons, bitterns, ducks, geese, gulls, cormorants, red-tailed hawks, and ospreys have all been observed in the vicinity. Continue right, uphill and away from the river, soon reaching an open lawn and the sprawling Blithewood mansion and garden on the right. The huge maple tree has been certified as the largest (in circumference) in New York State.

Continue across the lawn, bearing left, to its northwest corner. The trail continues here as a wide carriage path, descending through a dark hemlock grove with Christmas ferns, sugar maples, and oaks, soon crossing another wooden bridge over a small stream. Spicebush and witch hazel grow in the vicinity; in blossom, they attract bees and hummingbirds. Pass an inlet of the bay on the left with cattails and shallows or mudflats beyond. Just north is another spur trail on the left, leading to a twin-humped point and more open views. Continue north, skirting the bay, with more partial views through the trees. The trail then veers right and left and arrives at an open meadow, Bartlett Field. Bear left a short distance to the southwest corner of the field. Enter the woods again on a wide carriage road, veering to the right. Descend to another small seasonal stream, crossing it on another small wooden bridge. Climb to the right and soon reach Cruger Island Road and the Tivoli Bay Wildlife Management Area, owned and operated by New York State. Getting this far should take approximately one hour.

From the intersection, go left on Cruger Island Road 0.1 miles to another intersection. To visit Cruger Island, continue straight (west) about one-half mile on the Cruger Island Trail, crossing the pedestrians-only causeway that separates Tivoli Bay's North and South Bays. The causeway was built around 1800, leading to a sloop dock located on the North Bay. Flooded at high tide, the causeway remains wet even at low tide. Except in winter, walkers may want the benefit of rubber sandals to make the journey in comfort. The causeway is populated with such shrubs as red maple and ash, in places, indicating a swamp habitat as opposed to a marsh, where grasses and aquatic plants would proliferate.

From the causeway you'll reach the railroad tracks. Cross them carefully: High-speed Amtrak trains come through here several times a day, and it's easy to underestimate the speed of their approach. Look both ways and if you see any, wait. Just beyond the tracks is Cruger Island, which you've already discovered is connected to the shore by the tracks and the causeway. The mile-long island, which doesn't see many visitors, has unmarked hiking trails, great views and beaches, and an interesting mix of native and nonnative plants, many of them flowering. Cruger Island is one of the best secluded spots on the Hudson Estuary.

From the tracks a narrow woodland path leads to the northernmost tip of the island, where there is a beach, a pleasant meadow, and excellent views looking across the Hudson at the village of Glasco, with the Catskill Mountains in the distance. The trail then bends southward with more views for about a mile, past a few more beaches, some ruins of an old estate, and finally to the southernmost tip of the island with an open view of the river and the Kingston-Rhinecliff Bridge in the distance. Toads, salamanders, and frogs breed in shallow pools on the island.

Cruger Island was heavily used by Native Americans, as evidenced by a number of shell middens and other archaeological sites. The island was purchased in 1835 by John Church Cruger, who landscaped it, planting trees, flowers, and shrubs, some of which survive today. He also built a replica of a Mayan temple on the tiny island off Cruger Island's southern tip, designed to re-create the romantic atmosphere of Thomas Cole's paintings. In the 1950s Cruger Island served as a camp for poor children.

Backtrack across the causeway to the intersection. Go left (north) a short distance, through ashes, larches, tulip trees, trilliums, and ferns, to a parking area. On the left side a trail leads a short distance to a canoe launch and an open view of the North Bay.

From the east side of the parking area, follow the trail, which enters the forest and soon splits. The right-hand fork becomes the Hogback Trail. The left-hand fork becomes the mile-long North Bay Trail, which skirts the eastern shore of North Bay, crossing bluffs and deep ravines. Excellent brand-new wooden bridges span the ravines. Between the third and fourth bridges, climb a steep bluff to a panoramic view of the North Bay. After the fourth bridge, cross a lovely stream bounded by mature hemlocks, and finally arrive at the Stony Creek Canoe Launch and a second open view of the North Bay. From here the North Bay Trail leads northeast, following the southern bank of Stony Creek (also known as White Clay Kill), through some large stands of hemlock, gradually ascending, and passing the dramatic White Clay Kill Falls just before reaching Kidd Lane by the bridge. Continue left, north on Kidd Lane, 1 mile, which brings you into the heart of the village of Tivoli.

TIVOLI TO CLERMONT

This 2-mile segment, entirely on quiet paved roads, is suitable for both walkers and bicyclists (walkers will take approximately one hour). Though there are no views of the river, the last mile and a quarter, through dark hemlock forests, is beautiful.

From the corner of Montgomery Street and Broadway in the heart of the village of Tivoli, go left (west), passing the Artists' Co-op on the left, the Watts Depeyster Firemen's Hall, and Saint Paul's Protestant Episcopal Church, a Victorian Gothic ediface designed in 1868 by Robert E. Livingston, a grandson of Chancellor Livingston. After 0.3 miles make a right onto Woods Road and continue north. Passing a condo development on the right, Woods Road enters a peaceful, scenic forested area with little development and many large hemlocks and other trees. You'll see the entrance to Clermont State Historic Site on the left, 1.7 miles from the intersection with Broadway.

Clermont is maintained by the Taconic State Park and Recreation Commission. The Georgian-style brick house was originally built between 1730 to 1750 by the son of Robert Livingston (1654–1728), who had amassed the huge 160,000-acre estate known as Livingston Manor. His son, also named Robert (1688–1775), inherited 13,000 acres from his father. His son, another Robert (1718–1775), was a member of the Stamp Act Congress and New York's Committee of Correspondence. His son, Robert R. Livingston (1746–1813), was one of the five men selected to draft the Declaration of Independence. Clermont was burned by the British in 1777 because of the Livingstons' prorevolutionary activities.

Robert rebuilt the house between 1779 and 1782. He went on to serve as the first U. S. minister of foreign affairs (secretary of state), and was later ambassador to France, where he helped negotiate the Louisiana Purchase. As chancellor of New York State, he administered the oath of office to George Washington when he became president. Chancellor Livingston also experimented with raising crop yields and sheep breeding, and introduced the merino breed into the United States. In France he met Robert Fulton. Together they developed America's first practical steam vessel, popularly referred to as the *Clermont,* which also stopped here on its maiden voyage between New York and Albany.

The house and estate saw many guests, including George and Martha Washington, Lafayette, and Washington Irving. The north wing was added in 1802 and the south wing in 1830. The steep château-style roof was added in 1874 as servants' quarters, and the house was further enlarged in 1893 to a total of forty-four rooms. The Livingston family continued to reside here until 1962, when the house was donated to the state. It was designated a National Historic Landmark in 1973. The outdoor gardens were created by Alice Delafield Clarkson Livingston, the last private owner of Clermont. The house is furnished and decorated by three centuries of Livingston inhabitants with a strong emphasis on late-eighteenth- and early-nineteenth-century decor. The Visitors' Center has exhibits and a brief educational film on the Livingstons. There's a small fee for the house tour, which explains the history of the Livingston clan. The mansion and Visitors' Center are open from April 15 through Labor Day, Wednesdays through Saturdays from 10:00 A.M. to 5:00 P.M. and Sundays from noon to 5:00 P.M. There are rest rooms and a drinking fountain and picnic area. Special events, including a spectacular Fourth of July fireworks celebration and concert, are held here. For more information call 518-537-4240.

Besides its obvious value as a historic site and an opportunity to learn about one of the Hudson region's more prominent families, Clermont offers superb views of the Hudson as well as walking trails. The vista looking across the river at Saugerties and the Malden-on-Hudson Lighthouse, with the Catskills in the distance, is one of the most famous and most photographed views along the entire river. Clermont's 485 acres are open year round from 8:30 A.M. to sunset. The 1.06-mile-long Riverfront Trail begins at the parking lot and heads south for about a quarter of a mile along a bluff overlooking the river, with partial views through the horse chestnuts, black walnuts, tulip trees, hemlocks, oaks, and locust trees that grow there. Wildflowers such as goldenrod may be observed in old crop fields. The trail loops around and connects with other trails, some on carriage roads. Cross-country skiing is possible in winter. There's mountain biking and horseback riding on the wider trails.

CLERMONT TO HUDSON

A distance of 14.1 miles, except for a short stretch through Olana, entirely on roads. The landscape is primarily rural, and there are many scenic agrarian vistas and distant views of the Catskills. The Hudson is best viewed from waterfront parks in Cheviot and North Germantown and along Northern Boulevard, at Olana, and along Mount Merino Road. Besides the trip itself, Olana is the obvious big attraction along this segment. However, the historic city of Hudson has much to commend it and makes an excellent stopover.

From the entrance of Clermont, continue north on Woods Road, 0.3 miles to an intersection. Woods Road turns left. Follow it north for 2.6 miles through tranquil countryside to the corner of Roundtop and Cheviot Roads. Detour left one-half mile down to the waterfront and over the railroad tracks to a tiny park with a picnic table and dock and a fine view of the river. Across the way is a cement plant and the tiny hamlet of Smith's Landing. The Catskill Mountains can be seen in the distance. Cheviot is a small attractive residential community. On the way back to Woods Road, you'll pass an old cemetery on the left and a state historical marker noting the location of East Camp, one of the two main sites where thou-

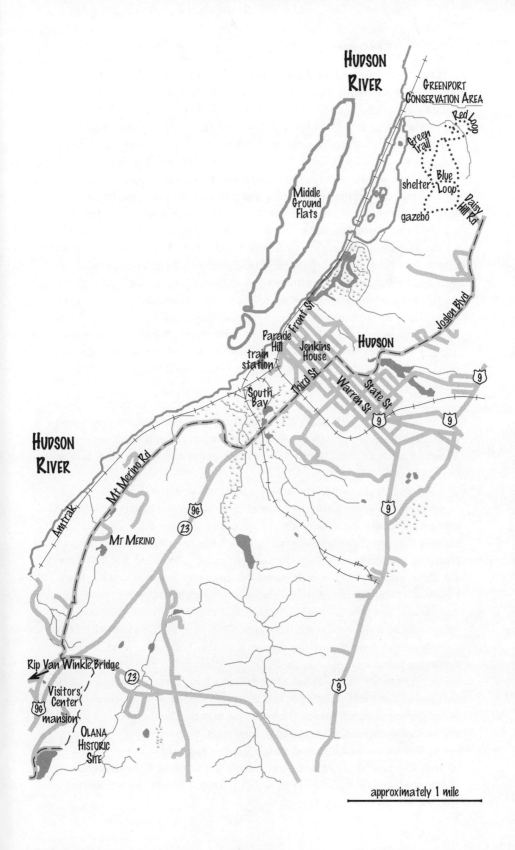

HUDSON
RIVER

GREENPORT
CONSERVATION AREA

Red Loop

Green Trail

shelter

Blue Loop

gazebo

Daisy Hill Rd

Middle
Ground
Flats

Joslen Blvd

Parade Hill

Front St

train station

Jenkins House

HUDSON

9

South Bay

Third St

Warren St

State St

9

9

HUDSON
RIVER

Mt Merino Rd

9G

23

9

Amtrak

Mt Merino

9

Rip Van Winkle Bridge

23

Visitors' Center

9G

mansion

OLANA
HISTORIC
SITE

9

approximately 1 mile

sands of Palatine immigrants were settled to produce turpentine and other naval stores for the Royal Navy in 1710 (see chapter 11).

From the intersection of Woods Road, continue north another mile to its end at Route 9G. Go north on Route 9G through the small hamlet of Germantown, continue 1 mile and make a left on Northern Boulevard. Follow this quiet road 0.4 miles as it winds through the pleasant residential community of North Germantown. Detour left on Anchorage Road and follow it 0.2 miles as it winds down to the river. Cross the railroad tracks to Ernest R. Lasker Jr. Park located on the waterfront. It is primarily a boat-launching site. There's a fine view of the river looking north as far as Olana and south as far as Saugerties. A number of cement plants, a tiny unnamed island, and Inbocht Bay can be seen opposite as well as the Catskill Mountains in the distance. Backtrack to Northern Boulevard and continue north with some fine views of the river along the way. The road continues another 1.4 miles to Route 9G.

Go left (north) on 9G, and continue another mile and a half, crossing the Roecliff Jansen's Kill. Just beyond on the left is a historical marker denoting the site of Robert Livingston's first manor house built in 1699. It burned in 1800.

After another 2.4 miles north on 9G you arrive at the entrance road to Olana on the right. Climb the steep road, passing a shale quarry and a pond on the right, and sighting the mansion on top of the hill to the left. The road ascends the hill. Walkers may shortcut across the field, but be careful of ticks.

Olana, a state-owned historic site, was the home and property of the famed Hudson River painter Frederick Edwin Church (1826–1900). The home and 250-acre grounds were carefully designed by Church and Calvert Vaux in the romantic style. In the same way that his magnificent landscape paintings glorified the rugged beauty of nature, Church used the impressive setting and designed his property to create ideal effects. He planted thousands of trees, many of which survive today, including magnolias, dogwoods, maples, Carolina hemlocks, eastern hemlocks, white pines, basswoods, and birches. The view of the river, the surrounding countryside, and the distant Catskills is unsurpassed. Views of Church's home from its commanding position on top of the hill are also quite impressive. The Moorish style of this eccentric stone house makes this one of the most distinctive residences in the entire Hudson region if not the entire United States. The interior is typically Victorian, a pleasing juxtaposition of finely crafted furnishings, intricate woodwork, interesting decorative objects, and subtle light. A number of Church's works as well as those of other artists, the artist's studio, and his collection of souvenirs from around the world are displayed. Church, whose aesthetic sensibilities are evident throughout, was the prototype of the modern-day adventure traveler. Windows and hallways are arranged to capture certain views. Olana presents an outstanding portrait of nineteenth-century artistic and romantic spirit.

The house is open to tours only Wednesdays through Sundays from 10:00 A.M. to 4:00 P.M. from mid-April through Labor Day, and in September and October from noon to 4:00 P.M. A small fee is charged for tours. The grounds are free and are open daily, year round, from 8:00 A.M. to sunset. There is a Visitors' Center in the old carriage house where one buys tour tickets. There are exhibits there as well as an educational film. For information call 518-828-0135.

From the Church home, continue northeast, going right, down a steep ravine. At the north road, go left (north) less than a half mile to the park boundary on Route 23. Go left on 23 (west) a short distance to the intersection with Route 9G. Just beyond on the right is the Mount Merino Road. Turn right. Go north one-half mile to an open view of the Hudson, the Catskills, and the Rip Van Winkle Bridge. At 1.9 miles, pass underneath power lines. At 2.3 miles, the road bends sharply right, and 0.2 miles beyond, it reaches 9G again. Go left (north) here, passing a wetland area on the left, part of South Bay, once the site of the Hudson Iron Works, which converted crude iron ore into pig iron. In 1860 about sixteen thousand tons were produced here. Just beyond, you'll enter the city of Hudson. The road ascends and becomes Third Street. From the corner of Mount Merino Road to the intersection of Warren and Third Streets in the heart of the town is 0.8 miles.

Hudson, the county seat of Columbia County, is located in the center of a very scenic, mostly rural region. With Olana to the south and the Catskills to the west, there are plenty of reasons for a traveler to visit. The city has a colorful past. Warren Street, which is also the main street and the prime focus of interest, has many structures dating back to the late eighteenth and early nineteenth centuries, displaying a rich variety of architectural themes, including many in the Federal and Greek Revival styles. Some have been beautifully restored. It also has the largest concentration of antique shops in the region, as well as crafts shops, galleries, restaurants, and cafés. Parade Hill, a popular small park at the west end of Warren Street, has an excellent view of the river. It was created in 1795 by the Hudson Common Council as a pedestrian mall.

Hudson was originally the site of a small Dutch settlement called Claverack Landing. In 1783, thirty settlers from Nantucket, led by Thomas and Seth Jenkins, known as the original proprietors, purchased land here after scouting up the river. They were whalers who had suffered from raids by the British navy during the Revolutionary War as well as high taxes from the Massachusetts government for failing to join the patriot side during the war (they were Quakers and committed to nonviolence). The whalers were searching for a safe harbor for their enterprise. They returned the following summer with their ships, their families, and forerunners of prefab houses, which could be erected quickly. The town almost instantly became a major whaling port and prospered. Mills in town processed the whale blubber into oil, candles, and other products. After three years the population was already fifteen hundred, and Hudson was incorporated as the third city in New York State, after New York and Albany. Hudson later competed to become the state capital and only narrowly lost to Albany. The city continued to flourish and grow. The busy waterfront was lined with wharves, and there were five shipbuilding yards. The city's wealthy residents built tall stately homes on Warren Street.

The War of 1812 had a devastating impact on America's whaling industry. After the war the whaling industry recovered, but Hudson now had to compete with other whaling ports along the river such as Newburgh, Catskill, Athens, and Poughkeepsie. The Panic of 1837 and the introduction of new technologies and products such as kerosene reduced the need for whale-derived products and the industry as a whole declined. By 1845, the Hudson Whaling Company finally ceased operations. Hudson turned to other forms of commerce and manufacturing and continued to prosper. (At the other end of the spectrum, Columbia Street, formerly Diamond Street, was a thriving infamous bordello district for more than a hundred years, finally closed in the 1950s.) Hudson suffered the same fate as most other Hudson River cities and towns as industry in the area declined and the river's importance as a transportation thoroughfare decreased. Today the city is beginning to see something of a revival as new residents are drawn to the beauty of the region and Hudson's historical structures get a face-lift.

Hudson has regular train service via Amtrak. For information about shopping, dining, and accommodations in Hudson, call the Columbia County Chamber of Commerce at 518-828-4417.

The Robert Jenkins House at 113 Warren Street is a small historical museum owned and operated by the Daughters of the American Revolution, which purchased the home in 1900. It was built in 1811 by Robert Jenkins, who served as the third and fifth mayor of Hudson. Members of the Jenkins clan were among the original proprietors from Nantucket who settled the city. The museum is primarily a repository for an eclectic collection of antique items donated by members of the DAR. However, a few objects relate to Hudson's whaling past, including the jawbone and teeth of a sperm whale and a whaling captain's log. Among the antiques are a 1744 Dutch Bible, Civil War uniforms and guns, spinning wheels, china, and ornaments made of human hair. There is a small charge for tours; children under twelve are admitted free. The museum is open in July and August Sundays and Mondays from 1:00 P.M. to 3:00 P.M. There is also a genealogical library. For information call 518-828-9764 or 518-851-3950.

13 The Capital Region
ALBANY AND VICINITY

While the city of Albany is the focal point of most visits to the area, this section of the Hudson region has a lot more to offer in terms of scenery, outdoor recreation opportunities, and attractions. There are pleasant country roads to explore, unspoiled by modern intrusions, and quiet villages like Coxsackie, Stuyvesant, and Castleton-on-Hudson. Little-known nature preserves like Greenport, Papascanee Island, and Four-Mile Point provide tranquility as well as a good chance for walking and observing wildlife. There are many fine views along the river. Historic sites like Fort Crailo and the Bronck House tell a story of life during the early years of European (Dutch) settlement. And of course, there's Albany, the capital of New York State, home to museums, historic sites, interesting neighborhoods, and the beginning of the Hudson/Mohawk Bikeway.

The Capital region is part of the Hudson/Mohawk Lowlands. Geologically it is similar to the Mid-Hudson region to the south. Rising up a few miles southwest of Albany is the Helderberg Escarpment, part of the Allegheny Plateau, composed of younger sedimentary rock, primarily limestone, from the Devonian age. Glacial Lake Albany covered much of the area and left thick deposits. This section of the river is narrower, has many shallow sections, and has more islands than other sections of the river. Landfills, construction of the New York Central Railroad, and dredging operations designed to make Albany accessible to oceangoing vessels have had a major impact on the riverfront, connecting islands like Papscanee, Schodack, and Houghtaling to the shore.

When the Dutch arrived this was primarily Mahican land. The Dutch established their first permanent settlement here at Fort Orange. Trade with the Mahican in beaver pelts was the leading economic activity. Practically all the rest of the area became part of Rensselaerwyck, the large patroonship granted in 1630 to Kiliaen van Rensselaer, a pearl and diamond merchant from Amsterdam. By 1637 the patroonship expanded to more than seven hundred square miles, far beyond the boundaries of the original charter. Kiliaen never visited the New World or Rensselaerwyck, but his proved to be the only successful patroonship, and the only one to survive the end of Dutch rule. The land to the south of Rensselaerwyck later became part of the Livingston Manor. These lands were later subdivided among the numerous heirs, but large landholdings were quite prevalent well into the nineteenth century. Prominent landowning families like the Rensselaers dominated the area's political and social life for more than two hundred years. Despite the change to British rule, the Capital region remained thoroughly Dutch. At least up to the American Revolution, the Dutch language was spoken, Dutch customs and religion practiced, and the architecture was distinctly Dutch.

During colonial times the area's rich alluvial soil made it an important agricultural region, primarily producing grain. Today commerce, state government, tourism, and agriculture are the primary components of the area's economy.

For many years this section of the Hudson was the primary recipient of pollution from factories and paper mills located north, on the upper river. Pesticide and chemical fertilizer runoff from agricultural fields, and the dumping of untreated raw sewage funneled here via the Mohawk and other tributaries, made this the most polluted section of the river, earning it the nickname the Albany Pool. The Albany Pool was reputed to be oxygen dead in the summer. Thanks to antipollution efforts since the 1960s and the addition of sewage treatment plants, this section of the river is considerably cleaner than it used to be.

Amtrak provides regular daily service from New York and other communities along the Hudson to Rensselaer, opposite Albany. For information call 1-800-872-7245. Adirondack Trailways provides regular daily service to Albany from the Port Authority Terminal in Manhattan. There is also weekday service from Catskill to Coxsackie, New Baltimore, Coeymans, and Albany, with other stops in between. For information call 1-800-858-8555. Greyhound Bus Lines provide regular express service from New York City to Albany. For information call 1-800-231-2222. The Capital District Transportation Authority provides regular bus service around Albany and Rensselaer Counties. For information call 518-482-8822. Albany County Airport is serviced by six major carriers.

The Route

HUDSON TO RENSSELAER

This thirty-two-mile-long segment, which follows roads up the Hudson's eastern bank, is rewarding for its rural ambience and unspoiled scenic vistas, especially of the river and the distant Catskills and Helderberg Plateau. The section between Stuyvesant and Castleton-on-Hudson is particularly gorgeous. Between Stockport and Stuyvesant is Stockport Flats, part of the Hudson River National Estuarine Research Reserve, for the most part accessible only by water. There are places along the shore for viewing this protected area. The Greenport Conservation Area, Nutten Hook, Lewis Sywer Preserve, and Papascanee Island Preserve offer opportunities for hiking and a chance to observe wildlife and, in the case of the Lewis Sywer Preserve, to experience a rare freshwater tidal swamp forest environment. Those interested in the history of firefighting should see the American Museum of Firefighting in Hudson. To better understand the life of early Dutch settlers in the region, visit Fort Crailo in the city of Rensselaer, located in a restored Rensselaer family residence.

Beginning in the center of Hudson (the city is described in chapter 12), from the corner of Third Street and Warren Street continue north on Third Street, two blocks to State Street. Go right on State Street and follow a short distance, and make a left onto Carroll Street. Continue north to Short Street, another left. After a short distance, pass a lake on the right. The road then bends to the right and becomes Harry Howard Avenue. Go straight, passing the Fireman's Home on the left. This is also the site of American Museum of Firefighting. Exhibits include sixty-four fire engines, from early hand-pulled and horse-drawn engines to the later steam and internal combustion engines as well as special wagons with ornate decorations used solely for parades. All these items were donated. Uniforms, photos, badges, and Currier & Ives prints are among the other memorabilia on display. The museum is open daily from 9:00 A.M. to 4:30 P.M.

From the Museum of Firefighting, continue north on Harry Howard Avenue 0.4 miles. Just past the high school on the left, you will reach the intersection with Joslen Boulevard. Bear left, and continue north on Joslen. At 0.7 miles past the high school, make a left onto Daisy Hill Road to visit the Greenport Conservation Area. The Joslen Motor Lodge is opposite, and there's a small sign for the preserve on the corner. Follow Daisy Hill Road a short distance, all the way to the end of the road and a parking area.

The four hundred-acre Greenport Conservation Area includes meadows, forests, and wetlands. There are more than three and a half miles of marked walking trails and it offers some of the best scenery and hiking and cross-country skiing in this section. It is owned and managed by the Columbia County Land Conservancy, Inc.

In 1661 the land was purchased from the Mahican by a Dutch settler. The property was a dairy farm for the next three hundred years. The open meadows were used for grazing, and to grow corn and hay for livestock feed. Timber was harvested from the neighboring woodlands. Threatened by development, the land was purchased in 1992 by the Columbia Land Conservancy with additional help from the Nature Conservancy, the Lila Acheson and DeWitt Wallace Fund, and the Iroquois Gas Transmission System Land Preservation and Enhancement Program.

The two-mile-long Blue Trail begins at the information kiosk. Maps and brochures are available there, including a nature guide for the Blue Trail. This easy, fairly level trail goes around a pair of meadows that are mowed in the fall to encourage the growth of berry shrubs, herbs, and other plants. Wildlife use these plants as a food source, and they provide necessary cover for birds to nest. The trail also passes hedgerows and deciduous forest lands populated with cedars, dogwoods, a variety of oaks, black locusts, and shagbark hickories. Because of the diversity of terrain, a number of animal and plant species thrive here, including deer, foxes, rabbit, squirrels, wild turkeys, redwing blackbirds, red-tailed hawks, black rat snakes, and various songbirds. From the trail a picnic shelter offers a vista of the Catskills. A curved wooden bench in the woods provides the best vista of the Hudson and distant Catskills. There's also a rustic Adirondack-style gazebo made from native cedars with a pleasant river view.

The three-quarter-mile-long Green Trail is the most challenging of the preserve's trails. It splits from the Blue Trail at the picnic shelter, follows the edge of bluffs through forest land, and crosses some steep ravines. There are some partial views of the river and neighboring wetlands through the trees. The mile-long Red Trail, a loop that travels through woodlands and dense cedar groves and along a stream, splits off from the Blue Trail at its north end, near a rustic wooden bridge.

From the corner of Daisy Road, continue north on Joslen Boulevard 1.3 miles to the intersection with Route 9. Go left (north) on Route 9. From the hilltop there's an expansive view of the Catskills to the west and the Taconics and Berkshires to the east. Continue north on Route 9 2.4 miles, descending, and then crossing Stockport Creek. Staats Road is on the left. It goes west approximately one mile to the New York Central railroad tracks located on the river. On the right is the Staat House, which was built between 1654 and 1666 by Col. Abram Staat, making it one of the oldest surviving stone Dutch homes along the river. Substantially altered by later inhabitants, today it is a charming private residence. It replaced an earlier house that was burned by Native Americans. A state historical marker indicates that this was also one of landing sites of Henry Hudson's *Half Moon* on September 17, 1609.

Beyond the house there's parking, an expansive view of the river, and a canoe launch. This is one of the primary access points to the fifteen-hundred-acre Stockport Flats, five miles of wetlands, islands, and shorelands, which is part of the Hudson River National Estuarine Research Reserve. Hudson River Islands State Park is part of Stockport Flats. The dredging operations of the Army Corps of Engineers in 1926 deposited large quantities of dredge spoils here, filling in wetlands. The operations also formed the peninsula at Gay's Point and islands like Stockport Middle Ground. These changes created protected inlets, which encouraged the development of the extensive wetlands that exist today. Narrowleaf cattails, wild rice, spatterdock, and purple loosestrife are among the many marsh plants that may be observed here. American shad and other anadromous fish spawn here, as do smallmouth bass. Banded killifish are abundant. Ducks, great blue herons, starlings, grackles, cowbirds, redwing blackbirds, kingfishers, and swallows are among the birds you might see. Bald eagles have begun nesting near the marsh, the first instance of bald eagles nesting in the region in many decades. Turkeys, deer, and raccoon frequent the shore. For more information about Stockport Flats, contact the NYSDEC at the Bard College Field Station, 914-758-5193.

From the end of Staats Road, backtrack 0.7 miles to the intersection with Souther's Road. Go left on Souther's Road and climb the hill. After 0.9 miles there's a view of the river on the left, looking south of Stockport Middle Ground, an island that is part of Stockport Flats. Just beyond is a view north of Gay's Point, a peninsula. After another 0.3 miles, there's an intersection. The road on the left leads a short distance to a parking area at Judson Point, with views of both Stockport Middle Ground and Gay's Point as well as extensive wetlands. Continue right (east) 1 mile to a juncture with Route 9J. Bear left onto 9J, and continue north 2.4 miles to the small community of Nutten (Newton) Hook. Go left on Ferry Road, which is a narrow paved lane. Cross the railroad tracks and continue one-third of a mile to the end of the road. There's a parking area here and open views of the river. Coxsackie is right across the way. On either side of the small peninsula there are tiny beaches and the remnants of an old dock for a ferry that traversed the river between here and Coxsackie. Before the parking area, on the right (north) side of the road, there's the Federal Footpath, an unmarked but easy-to-follow hiking trail, with a sign at its beginning. The trail goes north a short distance between a steep knoll and wetland on the right, and then intersects another trail. Go left on the latter trail, up the steep knoll, climbing to about ninety feet above the river. The trail turns right and, after the summit, descends with views of the river on the left. Less than half a mile from the beginning, on the right, are ruins of the old Stack Ice House, with the powerhouse standing in excellent condition. The chimney is still intact. It is on the National Register of Historic Places. Just beyond is a picnic area with more views looking north of Coxsackie Island. You may continue from here, east on Ice House Road, back to Route 9J, or return on the first trail south that skirts between the wetland and the knoll one-third of a mile back to where you started on Ferry Road.

From the intersection of Ferry Road, continue north on Route 9J another 2.1 miles to the lovely small riverfront community of Stuyvesant. Stuyvesant was formerly the location of Kinderhook, which relocated further inland because of the prevalence of malaria in this area. It was also the birthplace of Benjamin Butler (1795–1858), an American general and acting secretary of war (1833–1838). The village of Kinderhook, located about ten miles east, is the location of a number of historic residences, some of which are open to the public, including the home of Martin Van Buren, eighth president of the United States. From 9J go left on Riverview Road, which descends to the waterfront and open views of the river. After 0.4 miles it ascends and rejoins 9J. Go left on 9J again, passing the two brick Van Schaak homes on the left. Built in the late eighteenth and early nineteenth centuries, both are in the Federal style.

There's an excellent view of the river on the left, looking south and west toward the distant Catskills, 1.2 miles north on 9J, and 0.3 miles beyond, there's another beautiful vista looking west and north. After another 0.6 miles, the road is crossed by an old railroad trestle. Continue north 0.4 miles, passing the Lewis A. Swyer Preserve at Mill Creek on the left. Just beyond on the left is a parking area.

The ninety-five-acre Lewis A. Swyer Preserve, owned and operated by the Nature Conservancy, is one of the more unusual nature preserves along the Hudson. It is primarily a swamp forest habitat and definitely worth visiting. A superb half-mile-long boardwalk trail enables guests to experience this otherwise inhospitable muddy environment and observe the dense jungle of vegetation that is present here. Parts of the swamp forest are flooded daily by the tidal river and the stream. Other parts are flooded only rarely, as in a large storm. The ground is covered with swamp cabbage and ferns, an ideal habitat for a number of plant and animal species, including rare plants like the kidney leaf mud plantain and the estuary beggar-tick. Birds include great blue herons and various ducks. The trail continues out to a small tower with a vista of an estuarine cattail marsh and the Hudson River beyond the railroad tracks.

From the Lewis A. Swyer Preserve, continue north 0.7 miles on 9J, crossing underneath a second railroad bridge. At 0.8 miles beyond the bridge, there are a number of views on the left of Houghtaling Island, which has been transformed by dredging operations into a peninsula. The northern section is referred to as Schodack Island, and the entire peninsula is part of undeveloped Castleton Islands State Park. Plans are under way to open this park for hiking and other recreation uses. In the foreground is Schodack Creek. Continue 1.2 miles and enter Rensselaer County. Continue north on 9J another 0.7 miles, passing through the tiny hamlet of Schodack Landing. Just 0.6 miles north from Schodack Landing, there's an open view of Schodack Creek, which separates most of Schodack Island from the mainland. Just under 2 miles north of Schodack Landing, Route 9J passes underneath the tall Alfred H. Smith Railroad Bridge. It is immediately followed by the 5,330-foot-long Castleton Bridge, which carries the Berkshire section of the New York State Thruway. Both bridges cross the Hudson.

A mile and a half beyond the bridges, enter the charming village of Castleton-on-Hudson. It was first settled in 1638 and incorporated in 1837. Just past the heart of town, there's a broad open view of the river and parking. Continue north on 9J 1.4 miles to a turnoff on the left. Walkers may detour here to visit Campbell Island. Papscanee Creek can still be crossed on a steel girder with a guard rail. After crossing the creek, continue east a short distance, passing a target-shooting range on the left, unfortunately quite littered with shell casings and other junk. The trail continues straight to an opening overlooking the river. One can see south as far as the Castleton Bridge and north to the Albany skyline. The shore is lined with a wall of concrete bulkheads to prevent erosion. An old road continues north another half mile, parallel to the waterfront, but ends at a No Trespassing sign.

Backtrack to 9J and continue 1 mile north on relatively flat road with a blissfully wide shoulder to Staats Island Road on the left. There's a sign for the Papscanee Island Nature Preserve on the corner. Make a left onto this smooth dirt road, cross Papscanee Creek, and continue 0.4 miles, crossing the railroad tracks. Just beyond on the right is the southern entrance to the Papscanee Island Nature Preserve. There is a small parking area and information board. This entrance is closed in the winter. The 156-acre preserve is owned by the Open Space Institute and managed by Rensselaer County. It was acquired between 1992 and 1995 after neighboring areas were threatened by development. Papscanee, formerly known as Papsichene Island, named after a Native American who sold land on the west side of the Hudson to Van Rensselaer's agents, is a onetime island that because of landfills is now connected to the mainland. The island's rich soil was cultivated by Mahican and later by Dutch settlers. Through a cooperative arrangement parts are still under cultivation today, making it one of the oldest continuously cultivated tracts of farmland in the nation.

The east side of the preserve is bordered by the railroad tracks and a wetland along Papscanee Creek. Deciduous forests, open fields, and shallow woodland pools are some of the various habitats you may encounter here. Despite its proximity to populated areas, it is a very serene place. You may not see any other people, but wildlife is fairly abundant, including snapping turtles, painted turtles, moles, shrews, voles, muskrat, mice, foxes, raccoon, weasels, mink, and deer. There have even been reports of moose and bears. Birds are especially plentiful. You might see ruffed grouse, bitterns, rails, gallinules, woodcocks, green and blue herons, teals, kestrels and various other hawk species, wild turkeys, kingfishers, warblers, finches, redwing blackbirds, grosbeaks, sparrows, ducks, and grebes. The preserve is part of the Papscanee Marsh and Creek Significant Coastal Fish and Wildlife Habitat.

From the parking lot go north on the red-marked trail a short distance to an intersection with a white-marked trail. If you have a bike you may have to walk it on the narrow trail, but this shouldn't present much of a problem. Bicyclists will find the white-marked trail easier. Following the red-marked trail, continue a short distance to an intersection with a blue-marked trail on the right. The red-marked trail ends a short distance beyond, at a riverside picnic area with a fine view of the river. Backtrack to the blue-marked trail, and continue north past a view on the left of the river with a pond in the foreground. The blue-marked trail winds through the forest for another quarter mile and intersects the white-marked trail across from the railroad tracks. Continue north, on an unmarked trail parallel to the railroad tracks, a short distance to an intersection with a dirt road. Go left on the dirt road. The road intersects another, which leads to an area that's closed because the Army Corps of Engineers uses it as a dump. Continue north on the dirt road, mostly through open fields bordered by fragrant honeysuckle. Some of these fields are still cultivated by a local family. At the north end of the preserve there are shallow woodland fens and the remnant of a railroad spur. From the south entrance to the north is approximately a mile and a half. For information about the preserve, call the Open Space Institute at 212-505-7480.

From the northern boundary of the preserve, which has ample

parking and which remains open year round, you may continue north on Sun Oil Road through an industrial area. After 1.9 miles the road bends to the right (east) and passes an open view of the Port of Albany on the left, with Albany's downtown skyline in the distance. This is an excellent place to see large oceangoing ships docking. A short distance beyond, make a left onto Riverside Avenue and go north, entering the city of Rensselaer. Rensselaer was formed by the union of three villages: East Albany, Greenbush, and Bath-on-Hudson. It's alleged to have been in Rensselaer, in 1758, during the French and Indian Wars, that Dr. Richard Shuckburgh composed "Yankee Doodle Dandy," poking fun at the local militia troops.

Continue north on Riverside Avenue 0.4 miles through an industrial area. Make a sharp left and then a sharp right. Riverside Avenue becomes Broadway. Continue north on Broadway another 1.4 miles, passing more storage tanks along the way, finally entering a residential area with nineteenth-century Victorian residences in various stages of disrepair. On the right is Fort Crailo.

Fort Crailo is a state-owned historic site, operated by the OPRHP. It was the manor house of the Rensselaer family, who built the residence in the early eighteenth century. Since it was located far from Albany, the Rensselaers took the precaution of building thick walls and installing gunports in case of attacks by Native Americans or the French. It's unlikely that the house was ever attacked. The house continued to serve as a residence of the Rensselaer family until 1829, when it underwent a number of changes. Susan Delancy Van Rensselaer Strong, a family descendant, purchased the house in 1899 and donated it to the state in 1924. Between 1929 and 1933 the house was restored to what was believed to be its original appearance and thereafter displayed as a Dutch residence. A fire in 1976 damaged the house. Because of numerous inaccuracies in the previous restoration, the house was converted to a museum of Dutch colonial history and culture.

In 1971 the construction of I-787 across the river in Albany led to the fortuitous discovery of the original Fort Orange. A tremendous number of artifacts was uncovered in the six-month excavation, many of which are now displayed at Fort Crailo. They help tell the fascinating story of Dutch life in the early days of the colony. Among the artifacts are beautiful ceramic ware and Delft tiles. There is a typical Dutch jambless fireplace. In the basement a colonial kitchen has been reconstructed. There is also an educational video. Fort Crailo is open April 15 through October 31, Wednesdays through Saturdays from 10:00 A.M. to 5:00 P.M., and Sundays from 1:00 P.M. to 5:00 P.M. There is a small admission charge. Tours are every half hour to once per hour. Across from the house is a small landscaped riverfront park with a view of Albany's downtown skyline. Call 518-463-8738 for information.

From Fort Crailo it's another half mile north on Broadway to the Dunn Memorial Bridge on the left. There's a small riverfront park at the entrance to the bridge, with benches for relaxing and admiring the view of the river and Albany across the way. Dunn Memorial Bridge has a pedestrian lane on its north side, perfect for bikes or walkers.

ATHENS TO ALBANY

This 30.5-mile segment is entirely on roads. It travels through some gorgeous rural settings most of the way, and has views of the river with the Berkshires in the distance. A very worthwhile short detour is to the peaceful Four-Mile Point Preserve, certainly one of the best places to experience the riverfront in this section. The villages of Coxsackie and Coeymans also have lovely riverfront parks worth visiting. Another worthwhile detour is to the Bronck House west of Coxsackie, an excellent place to experience more than three hundred years of local history. The city of Albany is the climax of this trip. It has a long list of attractions, some of which cater especially to those on foot or bike, as well as historic sites and museums.

From Athens Riverside Park in the village of Athens, continue north on North Water Street as far as it goes till the road bends to the left and rejoins Route 385. Continue north, passing an open view of the river after 0.2 miles and just beyond, the Van Loon House on the right, built in 1724, apparently sinking into the ground. After another 0.4 miles you'll pass the Athens State Park Boat Launch on the right. There's a shady picnic area here with views of the river. An inlet at the mouth of Murderers Creek has mudflats and characteristic aquatic plants, such as pickerelweed and spatterdock.

Cross the bridge over Murderers Creek. On the right, a sign advertises the Isabella C. Rainey Murdererskill Nature Trail. We were not able to find the trail, but readers are welcome to look for it. Route 385 climbs a hill and after less than half a mile, levels. At 1.2 miles north of Murderers Creek, there are expansive views on both sides of the road of fields on the left, with the Catskills in the distance. On the right there are partial views of the Hudson River with the Berkshires in the distance. Just 3.1 miles north of Murderers Creek, Four-Mile Point Road is on the right. A short distance down this road leads to the Four-Mile Point Preserve on the left, just as the road bends sharply to the right.

Four-Mile Point Preserve is a small (eight-acre) riverside park with fine views. Native Americans used this site as a fishing spot. Stone spools, pestles, projectile points, and scrapers have been excavated from adjoining uplands. The property was part of the Loonenburg Patent, purchased from the Native Americans in 1665. In the early nineteenth century this was the site of Lampman's Dock, where hay, straw, grain, and bricks were shipped downriver. Remains of the old dock are still visible on the shore. In the late nineteenth century the Knickerbocker Ice Company leased the dock for shipping ice. Scenic Hudson and the town of Coxsackie purchased the land, which is now managed by the town. There are two short trails, one leading to a bluff with a pair of views looking up and down the river; the other, descending to the waterfront, a tranquil beach, and a picnic area. Stockport Middle Ground (an island) is across the way, and Gay's Point and the Stockport Flats marshes (described above) are located a short distance north. These are part of the National Estuarine Research Reserve.

Continue north on 385. After another mile and a half, make a right onto Ely Street. After 0.8 miles make a right onto Reed Street in the center of the village of Coxsackie. Then make a left onto River Road, which leads to Coxsackie's Riverfront Park. The beautiful park has benches, a gazebo, picnicking, a boat launch, and expansive views of the river, including Nutten Hook across the way, Gay's Point to the south, and islands that are part of Hudson River Islands State Park. There is a board with information about the history and natural history of the area, including Stockport Flats.

The name "Coxsackie" comes from the Native American "hoot of an owl." First settled in 1663 by Pieter Bronck, it became a prosperous farming area. In 1775, a group of disgruntled local farmers met and composed a declaration of independence, a whole year before the more famous one was drafted in Philadelphia. In the nineteenth century the village was a thriving river port and an important center for cutting and shipping ice and the manufacture of bricks. The village was incorporated in 1867. Today the nearby Coxsackie Correctional Facility is the area's primary employer. The village center by the river has many interesting nineteenth-century buildings that recall a time when Coxsackie's waterfront was a busy and thriving area. It's mostly quiet now, with just a few businesses and many unoccupied buildings, but it appears ripe for new development, once the public discovers what a charming place this is.

From the riverfront park go right on Betke Boulevard, and then make a right onto Mansion Street. Mansion Street merges with and becomes Route 385. Go west on Route 385 1.1 miles to Lawrence Avenue. To visit the Bronck Museum, continue west on Route 385 another 0.9 miles to the intersection with Route 9W. Make a left, and go south on 9W 1.3

miles. The Bronck Museum, owned and operated by the Greene County Historical Society, is on the right across from the Coxsackie Correctional Facility. The original house, built in 1663, is the oldest residence in the Hudson region open to the public. Additions were later made. The house remained in the family for eight generations until 1939.

The Broncks were a Swedish family who arrived in the New World in 1639 and settled the Bronx, which was named after them. Their son, Pieter, was a seafaring character, who settled in Albany, then called Beverwyck, and operated a tavern. Records show that he was taken to court on forty occasions, mostly related to disturbing the peace, brawling, selling liquor to the Native Americans for furs, and failure to pay his debts. In 1662 he was forced to sell the tavern. With the money he got he purchased land from the Native Americans in the Coxsackie area. Under the terms of an agreement with the Dutch government (they had to approve all land purchases from the Indians), Pieter also had to settle the land. He built a small single-room stone house with a steeply slanting roof for his wife and son and their servants. The massive timber beams, made from yellow pine, are all that remain of the virgin forest that once populated this region. Pieter—no farmer and inexperienced in running a farm—died soon after settling the land. His widow and the rest of the family managed to survive the next several years as subsistence farmers. Settlers arrived and purchased land from the family. Soon the area became a rich agricultural region, producing mostly grain. Now prosperous, the family expanded the house with an addition in 1685. In 1738 there was a second addition. This four-room brick-veneer dwelling was built in the style of affluent Dutch homes in the Albany area, with the brick exterior attached to a wooden frame. All three sections of the home are connected. Little appears to have been altered inside the house since the early nineteenth century.

Some of the special features of the museum include original eighteenth-century fireplaces, wide floorboards, an original Dutch door, and eighteenth- and nineteenth-century family furnishings. There are also a number of items that belonged to the famous Hudson River School painter Thomas Cole.

In addition to the Bronck House, the museum also includes a kitchen annex, with a beehive oven and typical kitchen "appliances" of the eighteenth century. The Antiquarium is a converted Victorian horse barn, which now displays artifacts of Greene County history. The famous scale model of the Catskill Mountain House is one of the exhibits, which also includes sections of the original Corinthian-style columns from the hotel. The Dutch Barn has antique sleds and carriages on display as well as the original thick floor planks. The thirteen-sided barn, built in 1830, is the oldest documented barn of its type in New York State. Except for a single center pole, the weight of the roof rests entirely on the thirteen sides. On the grounds there are cemeteries where family members are buried, along with a separate grave area for the slaves. A research library and a gift shop are also located on the grounds. The museum is open from May 24 through October 15, Tuesdays through Saturdays from 10:00 A.M. to 4:00 P.M., and Sundays from noon to 4:00 P.M. There is a small admission charge. Tours of the house and museum are informative and engaging.

From the Bronck House backtrack north on 9W to the intersection with Route 385. Go right (east) on 385 0.9 miles. Just past the railroad tracks make a left on Lawrence Avenue. Go north on Lawrence. After 0.3 miles there's an open field on the left with a view of the Catskills. Continue north through a lovely country setting. One and a half miles north of the intersection with 385, the road crosses Sickles Creek. At 0.6 miles beyond the stream the road bends to the right and descends. A half mile later it ascends and continues north another 2.6 miles to an open view looking east with the river below (just outside our view). Continue north another 0.4 miles to the intersection of Main Street. Make a right onto Main, continue another half mile, and bear right onto Mill Street. You've now entered the small village of New Baltimore, a former sloop and barge–building and repair center. Continue north on Mill Street, with views of the river between charming nineteenth-century homes. After 0.3 miles Cornell Park appears on the right, a small landscaped riverfront park. Just beyond, make a right onto Main Street. Follow it north 0.4 miles to where it merges with Route 144. There is an open view of the river here, with Houghtaling Island in the background.

Continue north another mile on Route 144, crossing into Albany County. Just beyond, the road crosses Hannacrois Creek and soon enters the village of Coeymans. Coeymans was once a major ice-cutting center. It was first settled by Pieterse Coeymans in 1673. The major attraction is the lovely Coeymans Landing Fishing Access Site, a riverfront park. It is located one block east of the center of town. The park has a pier, boat launch and marina, playground, picnic tables, and benches. It is located across from undeveloped Schodack Island.

Backtrack to Main Street (Route 144) and continue north. After three miles cross the railroad tracks, and go underneath the New York State Thruway overpass. A little more than a mile beyond you'll reach the junction with Route 396. Continue north on Route 144 another 0.4 miles to the New York State Thruway Selkirk exit on the left. At 0.3 miles past the exit you'll enter the hamlet of Cedar Hill. Follow Route 144 another 1.2 miles, passing the Bethlehem Historical Society Museum on the left. Continue north on Route 144 another 2.2 miles. Storage tanks appear on the right. Just 0.7 miles farther a large power-generating plant is seen on the right-hand side. Railroad tracks are crossed after another 0.4 miles. At 0.6 miles after the tracks, the Empire Plaza and downtown Albany's skyline appear straight ahead. Continue north on Route 144, 0.6 miles to the junction with Route 32. Go north on Route 32, cross Normanskill Creek, and enter the city of Albany. The Port of Albany is on the right-hand side. The Normanskill was part of a route regularly taken by Mohawk trading with the Dutch at Fort Orange.

As New York State's capital and its oldest permanent settlement, Albany is a major center of historical and cultural attractions in the area. The State Capitol and the Empire Plaza are two of the city's major highlights. There are also excellent museums including the New York State Museum and the Albany Institute of Art, and historic sites such as the Schuyler Mansion, Historic Cherry Hill, and the Ten Broeck Mansion. Despite the fact that the Hudson River is largely cut off from the city by I-787, it's Albany's location on the scenic waterway that gives the city much of its allure. On the riverfront there's a lovely park and the Hudson/Mohawk Bikeway, a superb paved walking and bike trail that extends from the Dunn Memorial Bridge north along the river, providing excellent opportunities for recreation and viewing the river.

More than 250 years of Albany's history are reflected in its wealth of architecture, from old Dutch style, to Gothic Revival, to art deco, to modern. From the Capitol, probably the most expensive building in the United States in the nineteenth century, to the elaborate Empire Plaza, Albany's public buildings have reflected the grandeur of the Empire State. A number are located in Albany's Urban Cultural Park, which comprises much of the downtown area. A trip to the Urban Cultural Park Visitors' Center in Quackenbush Square will acquaint one with Albany's history and attractions. A walking or bike tour of the Urban Cultural Park will enable visitors to experience some of Albany's more interesting buildings. Visitors should also check out *Albany Architecture: A Guide to the City*, published by Mount Ida Press. The heart of the town has attractive turn-of-the-century neighborhoods, many of them restored. While downtown Albany is, for the most part, fairly quiet at night and on weekends, the bohemian neighborhood around Lark Street, between Madison and Central Avenues, has an exciting nightlife as well as shops and cafés reminiscent of Greenwich Village.

At the time of Henry Hudson's visit in 1609, the Albany area was populated by the Mahican tribe. In 1614 the Dutch established a fortified trading post called Fort Nassau on nearby Castleton Island, where the present-day Port of Albany is now located. Damaged by floods, it was

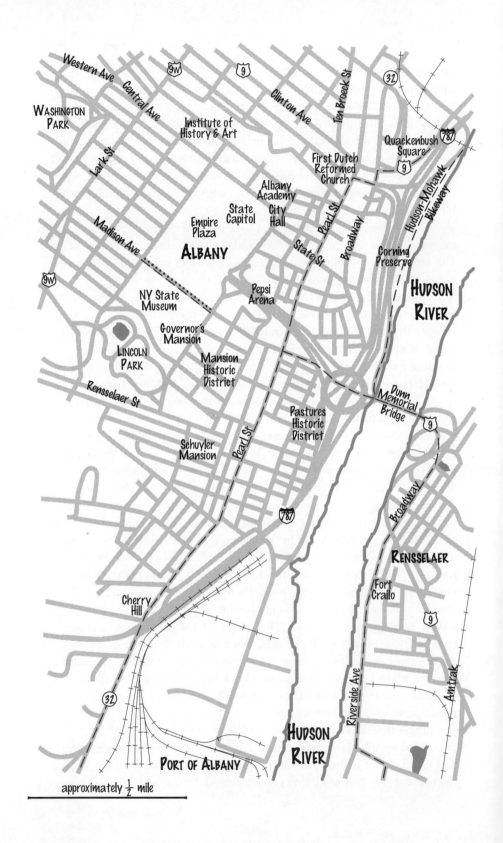

approximately ½ mile

abandoned in 1617, and Fort Orange was erected in Albany in 1624. Thirty Walloon families were settled here and became the colony's first permanent residents. Fort Orange became a significant trading post, dealing mostly in beaver pelts, which were purchased from the Mahican, who established nearby camps, then shipped downriver. In 1629 Kiliaen Van Rensselaer was granted a huge tract of land around Fort Orange, which became the Rensselaer Patroonship, named Rensselaerwyck. The Rensselaers to a large degree acted with total authority over their land, which included a settlement called Fuyck, located outside of Fort Orange. The Rensselaers were often in conflict with the Dutch West India Company and the Dutch government. Peter Stuyvesant, director general of New Netherland, challenged the Rensselaers' authority. In 1652 he legally annexed Fuyck and renamed it Beverwyck ("beaver town"), ruled by the Dutch government independent of Rensselaerwyck.

When New Netherland was conquered by the British in 1664, Beverwyck was renamed Albany, after the duke of Albany and York. Despite the change in name and government, however, Albany remained a Dutch city with an overwhelmingly Dutch population. This was reflected in the narrow gable-fronted buildings that were prevalent as well as in the culture and religion of the inhabitants. It remained so until the nineteenth century.

Located near the confluence of the Hudson and Mohawk Rivers, Albany was an important transportation hub and fur-trading post, chartered as a city in 1686. As fashions changed and the fur supply dwindled, Albany's role changed. The area around the city was settled by tenant farmers who produced primarily grain. Thus Albany became a major grain-shipping port. During the French and Indian Wars, the area north of Albany was contested by both the English and the French and their respective tribal allies. In 1675 the British built Fort Frederick on a hill overlooking the town, replacing Fort Orange. Albany's stockade fortress encircled the community and was enlarged as Albany grew. During this time there was great fear of raids by the French and the Indians. In 1690 the nearby community of Schenectady was destroyed in such a raid. Albany became a center of British military operations, with many troops encamped in the area. Following the end of the French and Indian Wars, Albany grew and prospered, expanding well beyond the stockade. Wealthy landowning families like the Rensselaers and the Schuylers built elaborate country estates outside the city. During the Revolutionary War, Albany's strategic location made it the objective of a planned three-prong invasion by the British to divide the American colonies. That plan failed, and the British were defeated in the north, near Saratoga.

In 1797 Albany became the New York State capital. The architect

Philip Hooker (1766–1836) designed many of Albany's most prominent buildings of the time, including the first State Capitol. The First Church in Albany and the Albany Academy are among the few Hooker buildings that survive today.

The city's location on the Hudson made it an important river port. In 1807 Fulton's steamship, the *Clermont,* sailed up the Hudson, arriving in Albany two days later. In 1825 the Erie and Champlain Canals were completed. The Erie Canal entered the Hudson in what is now the Corning Preserve, along Albany's waterfront. Albany became a major shipping center for Midwest grain and Adirondack timber. In the 1830s Albany was home to Herman Melville, who would later rise to fame as the author of *Moby-Dick* and other great works. In 1831 New York State's first commercial rail line began operating between Albany and Schenectady. Twenty years later, the New York Central Railroad connected Albany with New York City and Buffalo. By 1865 a railroad bridge was built across the Hudson, connecting rail lines on both sides of the river and making the city an important rail hub. Albany had its own stockyards, where eastbound cattle trains stopped for feed and water. A vivid portrait of Albany life during the Great Depression is in *Ironweed,* by Pulitzer Prize–winning local author William Kennedy. In 1932 the Port of Albany was developed to accommodate oceangoing vessels. Today it is a major entry point for grain, molasses, bananas, automobiles, and petroleum products. Grain and building materials are exported. The port's grain elevator was for many years the world's largest. Albany has an international airport and is a hub of interstate highways, connecting it to other metropolises in the Northeast, Midwest, and Canada. It is also home to a major campus of the State University of New York. State government and commerce are the city's primary employers.

For information about accommodations, dining, shopping, and special events in the Albany area, call the Albany County Convention and Visitors' Bureau, 518-434-1217 or 1-800-258-3582, or the Albany Visitors' Center at Quackenbush Square, 518-434-5132.

From the city limits continue north on South Pearl Street (Route 32). After a mile cross the I-787 overpass. Just beyond, on the left, is Historic Cherry Hill. Cherry Hill is owned and operated by Historic Cherry Hill, a nonprofit group. The Georgian-style wood-frame mansion was built in 1787 by Philip van Rensselaer and his wife, Maria, both members of the most prominent Dutch family in the area. Cherry Hill was located on a nine-hundred-acre estate of which only five acres survive today. The house remained in the family for five generations and 186 years. The last two generations, the Rankins, went to great trouble to maintain and restore the house. Emily Watkinson Rankin, the last descendant of the Rensselaers to reside in the house, donated it as a museum in 1963.

The house displays the furnishings of the Rensselaer and Rankin families and appears much as it did in Victorian times, when Emily Rankin lived here. Included are many fine eighteenth- and nineteenth-century pieces; a 1749 wooden cradle, a fold-out Chippendale couch, a banjo clock, an earhorn, silhouette portraits, charcoal carved birds, embroidery, and many Chinese items collected by a missionary daughter. In 1827 Jesse Strang, a handyman, had an affair with Elsie Whipple, a cousin of the families staying there, and murdered her husband. Strang was tried and hanged, in what was Albany's last public execution. The house is open Tuesdays through Saturdays from 10:00 A.M. to 3:00 P.M. and Sundays from 1:00 to 3:00 P.M. There is a small admission fee. For more information call 518-434-4791.

Continue north on South Pearl Street. After another 0.7 miles, you'll pass Schuyler Street on the left. Make a left onto Schuyler, and continue one block uphill to the Schuyler Mansion. The entrance is around the back, off Catherine Street. The Schuyler Mansion is a State Historic Site operated by the OPRHP. This opulent Georgian-style brick home was completed in 1764 by Philip Schuyler (1733–1804). A descendant of Albany's earliest settlers, he inherited sixteen hundred acres in the Saratoga area, which he expanded to twenty thousand. He constructed mills, a store, and a church and encouraged settlement of his property. Later he was able to acquire another eighteen thousand acres along the Mohawk. During the French and Indian Wars he served as a captain. He married Catherine, member of the prominent Rensselaer family, who resided across the river in Fort Crailo. The Schuyler Mansion was on an eighty-acre country estate, located outside the city of Albany. With large rooms, wide central hallways on both floors, tall windows, and high ceilings, it was considered to be very extravagant for its time.

During the American Revolution, Schuyler served as a delegate to the Continental Congress. That body appointed him one of the four original major generals in the Continental Army. During the war General Washington, Lafayette, Benjamin Franklin, and Benedict Arnold were among the notable public figures who visited his home. Alexander Hamilton, who married his daughter Elizabeth in 1780, was a frequent guest. Blamed for the evacuation of Fort Ticonderoga, Schuyler was court-martialed but later acquitted. Following the American victory at Saratoga, the British general Burgoyne and his staff were detained in the Schuyler home as honored prison guests. In 1781 there was a failed attempt by a party of Tories to kidnap Schuyler. After the war Schuyler served as commissioner of Indian affairs and as surveyor general of New York State. Beginning in 1780 he served several terms in the New York State Senate. Schuyler ran twice for governor but lost to George Clinton both times. In 1789 he was appointed one of New York's first two U.S. senators. Schuyler was a strong early proponent of canals.

The interior of the house is currently being restored, with colorful wallpaper in the style of Schuyler's time. Elegant eighteenth-century furnishings are on display. The Visitors' Center has exhibits on Schuyler's life. The house is open from mid-April through October, Wednesdays through Saturdays from 10:00 A.M. to 5:00 P.M., Sundays and holidays from 1:00 A.M. to 5:00 P.M. There is a small admission fee. For more information call 518-434-0834.

From the corner of Schuyler and South Pearl Streets, continue north on South Pearl Street another 0.4 miles to Madison Avenue. The area west of South Pearl and south of Madison is the Mansion Historic District, named for the executive mansion, located at 138 Eagle Street. It is the site of many fine mid-nineteenth-century homes and buildings. From this intersection one can go left (west) on Madison to the New York State Museum and Empire Plaza. Or one can go straight on South Pearl Street into downtown. To visit the waterfront, follow the directions below.

From the corner of South Pearl Street and Madison, go right (east) on Madison Avenue. The low-lying area east of South Pearl Street and south of Madison is the Pastures Historic District. While much of the district was demolished by urban renewal projects in the 1960s and 1970s, a number of restored Federal-style and Greek Revival homes and buildings from the early nineteenth century remain. Along the south side of Madison Avenue are buildings and row houses dating from 1808 to 1827. Continue east on Madison to one of the world's most confusing interchanges. Continue straight ahead right through it. Eventually you'll emerge by the water, just south of the Dunn Memorial Bridge. Pedestrian and bike access can be made from here. The bridge has fine views of the river and the downtown Albany skyline. You could also continue north on the asphalt walkway, which runs along a narrow strip between I-787 and the river. The strip gradually widens and becomes a park, the Corning Preserve, built on the site of a former thirty-two-acre shipping basin. The Erie Canal entered the Hudson River near here, and cargo was transferred from canal boats to sloops and barges for shipment downriver to New York. When in operation this was a scene of great activity. Just north of here, along the former canal, was Albany's lumber district, where timber from the Adirondacks was cut, stored, and shipped. Today the park is a pleasant oasis of green lawns, paths, benches, and a playground, open from dawn to 11:00 P.M. The paved riverfront path continues north along the Hudson as the Hudson/Mohawk Bikeway. It continues west forty miles to Schenectady and Rotterdam. Eventually it is hoped that it will parallel the New York State Barge Canal all the way to Buffalo.

Those wishing to tour downtown Albany and visit some of the sites should stop at the city's Visitors' Centers at Quackenbush Square. To get there from South Pearl and Madison, go straight, north on South Pearl, going underneath a large overpass and continuing past the Knickerbocker Arena on the left, the site of concerts and sporting events. You'll soon reach State Street, downtown Albany's main artery, with the State Capitol located at the top. South Pearl Street becomes North Pearl Street. On the southeast corner of this intersection is the Norstar Bank. The facade of the present structure, built in 1927–1928, incorporates part of the city's oldest bank, which was designed by Phillip Hooker and built in 1803. Continue north on North Pearl Street less than 0.3 miles to Clinton Square on the right. To the left at 3 Clinton Square is the home of Herman Melville, restored as a law office. There's a historical marker in the square. Also to the left of the square is the First Church in Albany (Reformed), designed by Philip Hooker and built in 1798. The church is reputed to have the oldest pulpit in the United States, brought here in 1656. The original Dutch Reformed Church, built in 1642, was located where State Street and Broadway now intersect.

Opposite the First Church, cross Wallenberg Park to the corner of Clinton Avenue and Broadway. Across Clinton and Broadway is Quackenbush Square. The Dutch-style Quackenbush House, located here, dates back to 1736 and is the oldest Dutch building left in Albany. Today it is a restaurant. Next door is the Albany Visitors' Center, located in what was part of the Quackenbush Pumping Station. Between 1890 and 1986 it was the office of the Albany Water Commission.

The Visitors' Center has excellent exhibits on the history of the city, models of Albany's more significant streets, and a planetarium with films. Maps, brochures, and other information are available. There are also walking tours of downtown Albany, which start from here on Saturdays from June through September. No reservations are required. The neighboring courtyard is quiet. It has benches and lovely shade trees, perfect for resting or snacking. For information call 518-434-5132.

Those visiting downtown Albany should also consider the following sites:

The New York State Museum is located in the Cultural Education Center, across Madison Avenue, south of the Empire Plaza. It features large exhibition halls on New York City and the Adirondacks, including a subway car and re-creation of the early-nineteenth-century port. There's also an exhibit on Native Americans with full-size replicas of a wigwam and an Iroquois long house. The Paleo-Indian West Athens site is re-created in a diorama, and there are replicas of prehistoric Ice Age mastodons. There is a children's learning center. Open daily except major holidays, from 10:00 A.M. to 5:00 P.M. Admission is free. For information call 518-474-5877.

The quarter-mile-long Governor Nelson A. Rockefeller Empire State Plaza is a two-billion-dollar complex of state offices located between the State Capitol and the New York State Museum. The indoor concourse displays a museum's worth of works of American abstract art. The impressive outdoor plaza has a reflecting pool, a sculpture by Alexander Calder, and a skating rink. The small glass structure just west of the reflecting pool is the headquarters of the Hudson Valley Greenway. The Empire Center at the Egg, a performing arts center that features dance, music, and theater, looks like something out of *Star Trek*. There's an observation deck on the forty-second floor of the Corning Tower, Albany's highest building, with views of the city, the Hudson River, and surrounding region. It is is open Mondays through Fridays from 9:00 A.M. to 3:45 P.M. and Saturdays and Sundays from 10:00 A.M. to 3:45 P.M. Admission is free. For information about the Empire Plaza call 518-474-2418.

The State Capitol, located at the top of State Street overlooking the rest of downtown, was begun in 1865. Designed in different styles by a succession of architects, it proved so expensive to build that it was officially declared complete in 1899, before a planned dome was added. The Renaissance/Romanesque structure is adorned with numerous intricate carvings. Highlights include the elaborate Million-Dollar Staircase and the legislative chambers. A small museum features flags, uniforms, seals, and other items related to New York State history. There are free guided tours hourly Mondays through Fridays from 9:00 A.M. to 4:00 P.M., Saturdays and Sundays from 10:00 A.M. to noon. For information call 518-474-2418.

The Albany Academy, located in lovely Academy Park north of the State Capitol, was built in 1813 and designed by Philip Hooker. This exquisite Federal-style building is, I believe, the most beautiful in Albany. It was originally a private school for boys, and Herman Melville was one of its students. Joseph Henry, who became the first secretary of the Smithsonian Institution in Washington, taught mathematics here. Today it houses the Albany Board of Education. Outside, facing the State Capitol is one of Albany's loveliest gardens. Just north on Elk Street is a wonderful row of Federal and Greek Revival mansions built in the 1820s and 1830s, called "Quality Row," where many of Albany's most prominent citizens resided. Just east are the Albany County Courthouse, the State Court of Appeals, and the Albany City Hall.

The Albany Institute of History & Art, located at 125 Washington Street, has exhibits mostly pertaining to Albany's artistic heritage, including a fine collection of antique furnishings, Hudson River School paintings by Cole, Durand, Church, and others, the interior of a seventeenth-century Dutch farmhouse, and an unusual collection of decorated cast-iron stoves manufactured locally. Open Wednesdays through Sundays from noon to 5:00 P.M.; it is closed on major holidays. There is a small admission fee for adults and students over twelve. For information call 518-463-4478.

The Ten Broeck Mansion, located in the heart of a run-down neighborhood, is unfortunately isolated from the rest of downtown. It is owned and operated by the Albany County Historical Association. The Federal-style country residence was built in 1797 by Gen. Abraham Ten Broeck and designed by Philip Hooker. Ten Broeck served in the American Revolution as commander of the militia and fought in the Battle of Saratoga. From 1779 to 1783 he served as Albany's mayor. His wife was Elizabeth van Rensselaer. Ten Broeck died in 1810 and his wife in 1813. Theodore Olcott, a prominent Albany banker, purchased the home in 1848 and added new features such as an indoor kitchen and bathrooms and east and west porches in the then-popular Greek Revival style. The house is supposed to have served as a station on the Underground Railroad. Heirs of Olcott presented the mansion to the Albany County Historical Society in 1948.

The home features Second Empire furnishings, a curved-door closet, a rare wax portrait of the Ten Broeck family, mourning embroidery, a child's sled bed, and memorabilia from the War of 1812. There's an outdoor formal garden, mesosequoia trees, and an old copper beech. The Ten Broeck Mansion is located at 9 Ten Broeck Place, north and west of Quackenbush Square. The house is open from mid-April to mid-December, Wednesdays through Fridays from 2:00 P.M. to 4:00 P.M. and Saturdays and Sundays from 1:00 P.M. to 4:00 P.M.; it is closed on holidays. There is a small donation. Call 518-436-9826 for information and directions.

14 Views from Afar

While the preceding chapters have focused on the areas right along the river, a number of places away from the river also offer excellent views of the Hudson and are certainly worth visiting for that and other reasons.

Black Rock Forest

Black Rock Forest Preserve is a 3,700-acre natural area open to the public. It is owned and operated by the nonprofit Black Rock Forest Consortium, comprising private and public educational and research institutions such as the American Museum of Natural History, Barnard College, Brookhaven National Laboratory, and Columbia University. Dr. Ernest Stillman donated the preserve to Harvard University in 1928 as a facility for forest management research. Harvard donated it to the Black Rock Consortium in 1989. The preserve features a high forested plateau with a dense network of marked hiking trails and unpaved roads. There are many reservoirs and peaks higher than fourteen hundred feet, including the highest summits in the Hudson Highlands west of the river.

Many of the trails are relatively easy or moderate for Hudson Highlands trails, and so the area attracts a lot of interest from a number of users. Trail maps are available at the entrance. The trails of Black Rock Forest are also covered in the New York/New Jersey Trail Conference map number 7, *West Hudson Trails*. Black Rock Forest is located just west of 9W, south of Cornwall, opposite Storm King Mountain. To get there go north on 9W, passing the scenic overlook for Storm King on the right. Continue another 0.4 miles to Mountain Road, and make a right. Make another immediate right and go through the tunnel. Continue south 0.7 miles up Reservoir Road to the parking area on the left-hand side of the road just before the barrier. Up the road a short distance, there are a sign board, brochures, and maps. A small donation is requested.

Geologically Black Rock Forest is part of the Reading Prong and similar in geology to neighboring Storm King Mountain. The reservoirs supply the communities of Cornwall and Highland Falls with drinking water and are strictly off limits. The forests of Black Rock, while impressively wild looking today, have been cut a number of times to supply fuel to heat local homes and farms, or shipped downriver to New York. Wood was also used to power the nearby ironworks at Cold Spring and also brickyards along the Hudson. The area once supported some small isolated farmers who supplemented their income cutting wood, though thin soils and relatively harsh weather made these enterprises marginal at best and none lasted more than a generation or two. Stone walls, exotic plants, and an occasional foundation are the only remnants. The use of coal and other fuels has decreased the demand for timber and so the forests have returned to Black Rock. Harvard University still utilizes Black Rock for research in forestry.

Black Rock forests are typical of the Hudson Highlands. They are dominated by oaks and hickories, though many chestnut sprouts indicate that this once was also a dominant tree. In the moist soils around streams and ponds, maples, tupelo, ash, birch, basswood, beech, poplar, and sycamore thrive. Hemlocks are prevalent in the more sheltered ravines. Pitch pine, shrub oak, and red cedar populate the more exposed rocky ridges. Beneath the forest canopy, beautiful flowering dogwood, hornbeam, witch hazel, and striped maple flourish. The forest floor is home to mountain laurel, azaleas, mapleleaf viburnum, blueberries and huckleberries, ferns, and mosses. In swamps and near ponds and streams, spicebush, chokeberry, and elderberry thrive. Many varieties of wildflowers are common in the forest, including relatively rare species like trailing arbutus. These bloom primarily in early spring.

Because of the varied terrain and many ponds, there is a great diversity of habitats and wildlife: deer, beaver, raccoon, opossums, foxes, woodchucks, rabbit, weasels, squirrels, chipmunks, rodents, bats, and snakes—including rattlesnakes and copperheads, though these are rare—snapping and painted turtles, frogs, toads, salamanders, newts, and a variety of bird life, including migrating hawks, peregrine falcons, and eagles, which may be observed in the fall.

Bicycles are not permitted in the preserve unless you're a member of the Black Rock Mountain Club (call 914-534-2966 for information). This is worth considering, since Black Rock has some of the best mountain biking in the region, and you don't have to contend with the crowds that gather at Minnewaska State Park, west of New Paltz. Vehicles are strictly prohibited. The preserve's unpaved roads see little traffic and are excellent for strolling as well as cross-country skiing in winter. Black Rock Forest is closed during deer-hunting season. The two main hiking trails are the yellow- and blue-marked Stillman Trail, which for the most part is also the Highlands Trail, and the white-marked Scenic Trail. Both are maintained by the New York/New Jersey Trail Conference, which also maintains a number of other trails in the preserve. Spy Rock (1,461 feet) is located just off the Scenic Trail. It is the highest point in the preserve. From this vantage point, during the Revolutionary War, patriot sentinels were posted to monitor British ship movements up the river. Unfortunately the view of the river is now mostly blocked by trees, but it is still a worthwhile hike.

The Stillman/Highlands Trail leads to Black Rock, one of the area's other prominent summits, for which the park is named. The rocky pitch-pine-clad peak has impressive views of the river looking north toward Newburgh Bay as well as the Catskills, Shawangunks, and Schunemunk to the west. The mile-and-a-half-long route can be completed in an hour, one way. To get there, from the parking area continue up the road a short distance to the intersection just below the Upper Reservoir. Go right on White Oak Road (no sign), crossing a brook and passing a signboard on the left with maps. Continue uphill a short distance to the intersection with the yellow-marked Stillman Trail. One can either continue along the road here or go left and follow the trail. If you follow the trail, prepare for a short, steep ascent to the summit of Mount Misery (1,268 feet). The open summit has good views looking west of forest land and hills, though none of the river.

From the top, descend to an intersection with the white-marked Scenic Trail. Go straight, west, descending to Aleck Meadow Road. (Here's where you'd end up if you'd stayed on the road, only 0.6 miles from the signboard.) Cross the road and skirt the north edge of Aleck Meadow Reservoir and a lovely view. The trail then begins a gradual winding ascent toward Black Rock, passing a number of labeled trees and the white-marked Black Rock Hollow Trail on the right, and then arriving at the 1,410-foot summit. A short trail marked with yellow footprints continues to a partial view looking north of Storm King and Breakneck. One may return the same way, or fashion a longer loop utilizing some of the preserve's other trails or roads.

Schunemunk Mountain

The northern part of this tall, nearly eight-mile-long ridge is owned and managed by the Open Space Institute, which acquired the land in 1996 from the Mountainville Conservancy of the Storm King Art Center. The 2,300-acre property was donated to the conservancy by Star Expansion Industries in 1985, which had permitted hiking on their land for many years. The conservancy includes twenty miles of hiking trails, which are maintained by the New York/New Jersey Trail Conference. The Trail Conference map number 8, *West Hudson Trails*, covers Schunemunk. Any hiking here involves serious elevation gain, and rock scrambling may be required in places.

To the Native Americans, Schunemunk meant "excellent firplace." The ridge is composed of sedimentary rock from the Devonian, with Silurian and Ordovician rock at its base. It is therefore far younger than the more-than-a-billion-year-old granite and gneiss that underlie its neighbors, the Hudson Highlands to the east. The youngest rocks, exposed along the summit ridge, are relatively hard conglomerate (also called puddingstone), large white quartz pebbles, often several inches across, in a purplish matrix rich in hematite. These were deposited on the shores of an ancient inland sea 350 million years ago by relatively swift-moving streams eroding once mighty highlands to the east. Large blocks of this conglomerate rock, referred to as megaliths, form a small maze of interesting caves and passages. The later collision of Africa and North America in the Acadian Orogeny deformed the rock beds and created faults, such as the cleft between the two parallel ridges now occupied by the densely wooded Barton Swamp. During the Ice Age glaciers ground the surface of the conglomerate flat in most places. The highest point along the ridge is 1,664 feet, taller than any of the neighboring Highlands peaks—in fact, the highest point in the region south of the Shawangunks. The relatively dry ridge top is home to prolific pitch pines, huckleberries, and blueberries. The forests are populated with red, chestnut, and American oak; wild sarsaparilla; wintergreen; and rare flowering ditany. Three species of rare moths can be observed here. It is also one of the last habitats in the state for the Allegheny woodrat. Because of its height Schunemunk is excellent for watching raptors such as red-tailed hawks and turkey vultures, particularly during migration.

There are numerous options for hiking on Schunemunk, including the eight-mile-long Jessup Trail, the Long Path, as well as many other hiking trails. Schunemunk trails are usually well marked. They're maintained by the New York/New Jersey Trail Conference. For an exciting and strenuous daylong loop trek over the top of the mountain with open views of Newburgh Bay, start from the parking lot on the north side of Taylor Road, one-half mile west of Route 32 in Mountainville. Mountainville also has Shortline bus service. From there the yellow-marked Jessup Trail follows Taylor Road west and north approximately 1 mile. The Jessup Trail then leaves the left side of the road and crosses a field. Follow the markers into the forest, where the trail intersects a woods road. Turn left and follow the road, parallel to Baby Brook. The Jessup Trail then turns right, leaves the woods road, and immediately crosses railroad tracks. Be careful! The trail then begins a steady ascent, about seven hundred feet in less than a mile, up to Taylor Hollow, where it intersects the red-on-white-marked Barton Swamp Trail. Make a sharp right onto the Barton Swamp Trail. The trail climbs up to the Western Ridge, one of the two parallel ridges that comprise Schunemunk. It is a short distance, but the climb is steep and involves scrambling on ledges. There's a superb view looking back at Newburgh Bay, Storm King, and Mount Beacon. The trail meets the Long Path, marked with turquoise blazes. Go left on the Long Path, and follow south along the crest of the narrow ridge for about two miles.

Turn left on the blue-on-white-marked Western Ridge Trail, and follow it downhill into the depression between the two ridges, where Barton Swamp is located. It intersects the red-on-white-marked Barton Swamp Trail. Go right, following the Barton Swamp Trail south a short distance. The blue-on-white-marked Western Ridge Trail then leaves the Barton Swamp Trail on the left and climbs steeply on rocks up to the Eastern Ridge, intersecting the yellow-marked Jessup Trail.

Go left (north) on the Jessup Trail. After a short distance, cross the 1,664-foot summit and continue north. A short distance north of the summit, a spur trail on the left leads to the famed megaliths, well worth exploring. Continue north another short distance to the intersection with the white-on-black-marked Dark Hollow Trail on the right, 0.4 miles north of the summit. Go right on the Dark Hollow Trail as it descends from the ridge heading east, 1.8 miles. About a quarter of the way down, there's a splendid open view of Newburgh Bay, Mount Beacon, and Storm King. The trail continues to descend, finally reaching railroad tracks. Go north along the tracks, about one hundred feet to the white-marked Sweet Clover Trail. Turn right on the Sweet Clover Trail, cross the tracks, and continue east on a dirt road. The road turns left (north) and continues till it becomes a paved private road, crosses an athletic field, and finally arrives back at the parking area where you started.

Blue Mountain Reservation

This sixteen-hundred-acre heavily forested Westchester County park lies just south of Peekskill. There are fifteen miles of marked hiking paths and bridle trails, seven miles of which are suitable for mountain bikes. The trails are rated yellow for beginners, orange for intermediate, and red for advanced. The park has four ponds and a number of recreational facilities, picnicking, rest rooms, and a lodge with dormitory accommodations groups can rent. The topography is hilly, with numerous large outcrops of igneous rocks of the Cortlandt Complex. The forest is comprised of mature stands of mixed deciduous trees with scattered small stands of hemlocks. Deer, squirrels, wild turkeys, and a number of other species of animals reside here. No hunting is allowed. The west side of the park is marred by the drone of traffic from nearby Route 9. However, that is less of problem on the more rugged east side of the park. Blue Mountain Reservation is the largest area of wild forest land in Westchester Country in close proximity to the Hudson River. To get to the park, get off Route 9 at the Welcher Avenue exit and head east one-half mile to the park entrance. The entrance is located about one mile south of the Peekskill train station. Maps are available at the entrance, which is manned during the warmer months, or by calling the park at 914-737-2194, or the Westchester County Parks Department at 914-242-PARK. The Westchester County Mountain Bike Association also has an excellent map and information about the park. The park is open year round from dawn till dusk. A parking fee is charged during the warmer months.

The park has a couple of fine views of the river. Unfortunately one of them, Spitzenberg Mountain, famed for its panoramic view of Haverstraw Bay, is off limits due to lead contamination. It is located right next to a shooting range. The other, Blue Mountain, is a moderate hour-long walk from the parking lot just past the lodge. One can also mountain bike to within a quarter mile of the view and walk the rest of the way.

To get there from the park entrance, go left right after the gate and follow the road 0.7 miles past the lodge to a parking area across from a pond. From the parking area follow a trail marked yellow/orange/green a short distance to an intersection with a yellow-marked trail. Go left here, following the yellow-marked trail north, crossing a pair of seasonal brooks and doubling back to just across from the lodge, and intersect an orange/yellow-marked trail. Head east on the orange/yellow-marked trail gently rising through scattered hemlocks. There's a ravine to the left. At the first intersection the orange-marked trail turns left. Go straight on the yellow-marked trail, passing lovely Dickey Brook on the left and soon intersecting the red-marked trail. Go right on the red-marked trail, which immediately bends to the left and climbs steeply in an area of very large rock outcrops. The red-marked trail levels and reaches an intersection with another red-marked trail. Take the left fork and continue climbing. The red-marked trail levels out again and intersects an orange/red/green-marked trail. Go right on this new trail a short distance to an intersection with a blue-marked footpath on the left. There is a sign at this intersection, The blue-marked trail climbs steeply, zigzagging its way east to an open view (west) of Peekskill Bay, Jones Point, the Indian Point Nuclear Plant, and the dramatic southern entrance to the Hudson Highlands. Dunderberg, Bear Mountain, and Anthony's Nose are a few of the many peaks visible. One can also see Iona Island and Marsh in the distance.

To return backtrack on the blue trail down to its intersection with the orange/red/green-marked trail. Go left (south) on the orange/red/green-marked trail approximately one-third of a mile to the Montrose Station Road. You'll cross an underground gas pipeline here. An orange/green-marked trail continues west from here several minutes to an intersection with a red-marked trail on the right. Continue west on the orange/green-marked trail several more minutes to an orange/red-marked trail on the left, which goes south to a pond. Continue west on the orange/green-marked trail a few more minutes, passing an orange-marked trail on the left and then descending to the parking area by the pond where you started. The return from Blue Mountain should take from thirty to forty-five minutes.

High and Little Tor

Between 829 and 832 feet (I've seen three figures listed!), High Tor is the highest peak along the Palisades Ridge. It is also the highest point along the Hudson River south of the Hudson Highlands, and the panoramic 360-degree view from the summit includes everything from Manhattan skyscrapers up to Mount Beacon, the Tappan Zee, and Haverstraw and Peekskill Bays. It is one of the finest views in the entire book. High Tor is located in 565-acre High Tor State Park, which is part of the Palisades Interstate Park. The New York/New Jersey Trail Conference map number 4B, *Hudson Palisades Trails*, covers High and Little Tor.

Part of the Palisades Ridge, High Tor is composed of the same Triassic diabase rock characteristic of this formation. High Tor was used by the patriots as a reconnaissance post during the American Revolution. Like much of the rest of the ridge, it was threatened by quarry operations, and in 1936 was the subject of the eponymous award-winning Maxwell

Anderson play, *High Tor,* about the menace quarrying posed to the mountain. Soon afterward much of the mountain was purchased by a number of groups, including the New York/New Jersey Trail Conference, and presented to the Palisades Park Commission in 1943. A fifty-four-acre former vineyard was recently added to the south side of High Tor State Park, thanks to the efforts of Scenic Hudson. This site includes meadows, fields, a pond, and remains of an eighteenth-century farmhouse.

High Tor State Park is located west of Haverstraw and south of West Haverstraw (both are served by Shortline Bus). The entrance to the park from Short Clove Road is no longer open. There is a large traprock quarry there operated by Tilcon. To climb High Tor there are a couple of options. The first is by far the shortest one to the summit, but it's also the steeper and more strenuous of the two (about 600 feet of elevation gain to the summit) and includes a bit of rock scrambling. Finding the trailhead is one of the bigger challenges. From the corner of 9W and Route 304, continue north on 9W another mile and a half to the intersection of Short Clove Road on the left. There's a light. Continue north another half mile to the trailhead for the Deer Path on the left. It is poorly marked, and there's no parking. The Northern Riverview Healthcare Center is located just beyond on the same side of the road.

The Deer Path Trail is marked with fading white paint blazes. It climbs uphill a short distance, then turns sharply to the left and continues its very steep ascent for a long quarter of a mile. Finally, it reaches the ridge, turns to the right, and joins the Long Path, marked with turquoise blazes. Go right and follow the Long Path as it makes a steep ascent on bare rock up to the first disappointment: You're not on the summit! There is a view looking south toward the Tappan Zee, DeForest Lake, and Manhattan skyscrapers, and west toward Haverstraw Bay and Westchester. Catch your breath and continue up to a second rocky rise, less steep than the first, but there's a more expansive vista once you reach the top, including the Tilcon mine, and a view as far north as Peekskill and the beginning of the Hudson Highlands. However, this proves not to be the summit either.

The trail continues west. There's another steep, scrambling climb to another false summit. However, the true summit is an easy jaunt from here. Relish the 360-degree view described above. There are foundation remains of a former airways beacon. This is also an excellent location for observing the autumn hawk migration described in the section on Hook Mountain. The deep grooves in the diabase bedrock you see are the result of the hot magma cooling.

The trail continues west on the exposed summit, then veers sharply to the left and makes a short steep descent to a dirt fire road, heavily damaged by four-wheel drives or ATVs. The Long Path follows this mostly level road the rest of the way north to the Central Highway, a distance of about three miles, passing mostly young forest of oak, hickory, red maple, birch, ash, and dogwoods. There are scattered groves of hemlocks and mountain laurel along the way. About two miles west of High Tor is Little Tor (710 feet), another exposed rocky summit. The view from here, mostly north and west, is not as expansive, but includes the Palisades Ridge, West Haverstraw, Haverstraw and Peekskill Bays, and the southern flank of the Hudson Highlands. There's a fine example of a glacial erratic (a boulder transported by the glacier, probably from the Hudson Highlands in this case) on the summit. Little Tor is located just north of the Long Path, reached by an obvious, though unmarked, trail. There is a sign at its juncture with the Long Path. Continue west another mile. Just before reaching the Central Highway, the Long Path crosses underneath power lines. At the Central Highway there's a parking area. The Long Path continues west from here into South Mountain County Park.

To get to the Central Highway, go west on Route 202 from its intersection with 9W in West Haverstraw. There's a cemetery on the corner. After 1.6 miles make a left onto Central Highway, and go south and uphill to the crest of the ridge, just under a mile. There's parking on the left for the Long Path. The trail is gated to prevent vehicular traffic.

The Catskills

The Catskills provide the highest topography in the region, much of the most dramatic mountain scenery, the largest areas of undeveloped forest land, and hundreds of miles of hiking trails, including some of the region's most challenging. The Catskills themselves provide a dramatic backdrop for many of the region's most celebrated scenic views. Sweeping vistas of long stretches of the river and surrounding valley can be seen from the tops of some of the range's highest peaks. Thirty-five Catskill peaks are higher than 3,500 feet. (The highest, Slide Mountain, [4,180 feet], is the tallest peak in New York State outside the Adirondacks.) The 3,500 Club is composed of enthusiasts who've climbed all thirty-five of them. They lead outings for those wanting to attempt that feat. Be forewarned, though, many of their hikes involve a considerable amount of bushwhacking and winter ascents. They can be reached via the NY/NJ Trail Conference.

This chapter focuses on the eastern flank of the Catskills, referred to as the Escarpment. The Escarpment is distinguished by a rapid rise in elevation above the Hudson Valley to the east. Kaaterskill High Point (3,655 feet) is the highest point in this section, but much of the Escarpment is above 2,000 feet. A number of trails traverse the Escarpment, including segments of the Devil's Path, the Long Path, and the Escarpment Trail. This "wall" of mountains is only broken in two places by Plattekill Cove, and north of it, Kaaterskill Clove. These steep dramatic valleys cut through the Escarpment with sheer cliffs and numerous waterfalls, providing some of the most spectacular scenery in the entire Catskill Range. The area around North Lake, once the site of the famous Catskill Mountain House, is justly popular for scenery, views, and trails that often are not overly strenuous, and has been attracting visitors for nearly two centuries. Two nearby towns, Woodstock and Palenville, both have regular bus service via Adirondack Trailways. Call 1-800-858-8555 for fares and schedules.

Ironically, the Catskills are not a true mountain range, but an elevated part of the Allegheny Plateau composed of sandstones, conglomerates, and shales deposited in river deltas during the Devonian period, approximately 350 million years ago. The mountainlike appearance of the region was created over millions of years by the erosion of streams as well as by glacial activity. The harder, more erosion-resistant conglomerate caps the summits of the range's highest peaks. The glaciers probably carved the steep east-facing slopes of the Escarpment.

The Catskills are heavily wooded in most places with second- or third-generation forests. In fact, rocky areas largely devoid of vegetation (fairly common in the Hudson Highlands) are rare in the Catskills. The slopes and valleys, once primarily clothed with hemlocks, today are home to northern hardwoods such as beech, birch, and maples, as well as hemlock and white pine. Southern-ranging oak, hickory, and tulip trees may also be found, especially at lower elevations and valleys. Generally, the higher the elevation, the more affinity the vegetation has with northern forests. Boreal forests of red spruce balsam fir, similar to ones found in northern Canada, occur on the tops of the highest peaks. Balsam trees often occur in dense stands that are nearly impossible to bushwhack through. Paper birch, mountain ash, and red cherry also occur in high mountaintop environments. Porcupines are usually prevalent, feeding primarily on tree bark. Plants in boreal environments are very sensitive to any disturbance, particularly trampling, and recover very slowly. It may take many years to overcome damage.

For the most part the same animal species that inhabit the rest of the region can be found here in the Catskills. However, certain larger mammals like bobcats and bears, more common here than elsewhere, are not frequently seen because of their nocturnal habits. Mink, otter, and fishers are some of the rare mammals that inhabit the Catskills.

Land disputes and the mountains' harsh topography at first

discouraged settlement. They remained a largely, unmapped, primeval wilderness until the early nineteenth century. As a wilderness area in close proximity to the Hudson Valley and centers of human population, the Catskills inspired a certain mystique and folklore, such as the legend of Rip Van Winkle. They also inspired artists like Thomas Cole of the Hudson River School, who glorified the Catskills as a prime example of nature's rugged beauty.

Once the Hudson Valley had been largely stripped of forests, the Catskills became a source of timber for fuel and construction. Also, tannin, a substance in the bark of hemlock trees, was essential for tanning hides. Large numbers of hemlocks were required to produce small quantities of tannin. During the nineteenth century, a number of tanneries were located in the Catskills, close to the source of hemlock trees as well as waterpower. This industry of cutting trees and processing leather employed thousands and encouraged settlement of the area. Quarrying of bluestone and marginal forms of agriculture were also briefly practiced here. Once the supply of hemlock trees was exhausted, however, the tanning industry rapidly declined and disappeared from the region.

Since the early nineteenth century the Catskills have been a popular resort area. Fresh mountain air, supposed to be essential in promoting health, as well as spectacular scenery and natural environments, attracted guests throughout the nineteenth century to opulent resorts like the Catskill Mountain House. The Catskill Mountain House was founded in 1824 along the edge of the Escarpment, near North Lake. It was also near Kaaterskill Falls, one of the best-known scenic wonders of the time. The Greek Revival–style hotel, with thirteen Corinthian-style columns, was advertised as standing 3,000 above sea level, but actually it was at only 2,200 feet. Under the management of Charles Beach, it grew to three hundred rooms and became the leading luxury resort hotel in the region and one of the most famous in America. The hotel could be seen towering high above the Hudson River. Guests would travel upriver by boat or train, disembark at the village of Catskill, and ride a carriage up to the hotel. In 1892 an inclined railroad was installed to make the hotel more accessible. The scenic terrain around the hotel was popular with guests and was the subject of many of the Hudson River School painters' most famous works. While the original building is gone, an impressive model of the hotel may be viewed at the Bronck House Museum, near Coxsackie.

The success of the Catskill Mountain House encouraged others to build mountaintop resorts with views. Among them were the Overlook Mountain House, opened in 1880, the highest of the mountain houses; and the Hotel Kaaterskill, located on South Mountain overlooking the

Catskill Mountain House, by far the largest and most modern of the great mountaintop resorts. Competition eventually doomed all the mountaintop resorts, however. Also, high operating costs made it difficult to maintain their profitability. As the population grew more mobile, the mountaintop resorts had to compete with resorts outside the region. Eventually they fell out of fashion and closed. Only the Mohonk Mountain House near New Paltz is still operating today.

Destruction of the great forests of the Catskills and Adirondacks and the resulting increase in soil erosion, flooding, and contamination of drinking water supplies led to concern about protection of such watersheds. In 1894 the New York State Constitution was amended to protect the Adirondacks, as well as seven hundred thousand acres in the Catskills, creating the Catskill Forest Preserve. A quarter of a million of those acres were eventually purchased by the state as open-space land. Recent agreements between New York City and Catskill communities will result in further protection of Catskill watershed lands.

Catskill trails are generally well marked and maintained by the NY/NJ Trail Conference. However, they are frequently steep and rugged and, because of the often dramatic changes of elevation, require that users be prepared for sharp changes in weather conditions. Much of the state land is open for backcountry camping (see the rules in the How To section). In the winter, trails may be ascended with snowshoes or crampons. Opportunities for cross-country skiing also abound. The Trail Conference publishes an excellent series of maps that display most of the marked trails in the Catskills. The Catskill Trail maps number 40, *North Lake Area*, and number 41, *Northeast Catskills*, cover this section. Detailed hiking guides are published by the Trail Conference as well as the Adirondack Mountain Club.

A good place to start to explore the Catskill Escarpment is the beautiful village of Woodstock, located about ten miles northwest of Kingston. Woodstock is a major tourist center, with the region's largest concentration of art galleries and crafts shops, as well as those catering to New Age fashions. Contrary to popular belief Woodstock was not the location of the famous sixties festival, though many of the town's retail establishments use the festival as a marketing ploy. However, Woodstock has been an artists' colony since the early 1900s. In addition to the shops and galleries, there are a number of fine restaurants and cafés as well as bed-and-breakfast accommodations in the area. Woodstock is served by Adirondack Trailways Bus, which stops at the Village Green in the center of town.

Go north from the Village Green on Rock City Road, about a half mile to the four-way intersection with the Glasco Turnpike. Continue north, mostly uphill, on Meads Mountain Road, about 1.5 miles, to a parking area on the right-hand side of the road for the Overlook Spur Trail, marked with red. This popular 2.5-mile-long jeep trail rises fourteen hundred feet to the summit of Overlook Mountain, 3,140 feet. The grade is steady to the intersection with the blue-marked Overlook Trail, located near the ruins of the old Overlook Hotel. Continue east on a nearly level trail, passing a superb open view on the right of the Hudson Valley and the river. From the hotel ruins, the trail continues east one-half mile to the summit. An old fire tower located here is unfortunately off limits.

Backtrack to the intersection of the blue-marked Overlook Trail and go right (north). After one-half mile, you'll pass a spring on the right. Continue north. Notice the large number of mountain laurel. These are common along the east side of the Catskills, but largely absent from the rest of the range. Less than a mile north of the spring, a yellow-marked spur trail on the left descends one-half mile down to Echo Lake, one of the few high mountain lakes in the Catskills. There are designated campsites and a lean-to there. Unfortunately the view of the lake is marred by a huge antenna.

From the intersection of the Echo Lake Trail, continue north on the Overlook Trail for another 2.25 miles to the Devil's Kitchen Lean-to. It is located by a small stream. A short distance beyond, the Overlook Trail intersects the red-marked Devil's Path. The 26-mile-long Devil's Path is one of the Catskills' most famous trails. It climbs five of the Catskills' highest summits and is renowned for its difficulty as well as for its spectacular views.

Go right on the Devil's Path, which continues west and north as a fairly level trail in this section for just 1.5 miles to the intersection with the blue-marked Jimmy Dolan Notch Trail on the left. That trail ascends the summits of Indian Head Mountain and Twin Mountain; both are also located on the Devil's Path. At this point you join the Long Path. Go right (north) on the Devil's Path (also the Long Path), and continue one-half mile, descending to the end of Prediger Road. Follow the road north, less than a half mile, to Platte Clove Road.

Go east on Platte Clove Road for a little more than a mile, passing the Hutterian Bruderhof on the left (it used to be the New York City Police Camp), to the trailhead for a snowmobile trail located on the left-hand side of the road. This is also part of the Long Path and is marked with blue plastic markers. Just east, on the south side of Platte Clove Road, there's a small parking area. This section of Platte Clove Road, which follows the precipitous edge overlooking the steep cliffs of Devil's Kitchen and Plattekill Clove, is one of the most scenic and thrilling rides in this part of the state. It is closed in winter.

Follow the wide snowmobile trail (an old woods road) north for about a mile as it gradually ascends, crossing private land owned by the Catskill Center, a local conservation organization, and eventually entering state-owned land. As the trail veers sharply to the left, an unmarked but well defined path veers to the right. Follow this trail a short distance, crossing a stream and continuing nearly a mile, passing through a grove of pitch pine (which occurs in only a few places along the eastern edge of the Catskills, but which is largely absent from the rest of the range). The trail ends at Huckleberry Point, a stunning view located on top of sandstone ledges, looking south, of Plattekill Clove, Plattekill Mountain, and the Hudson Valley and the river below as far as the Hudson Highlands.

To continue north, backtrack to the snowmobile trail. The snowmobile trail enters an old hemlock grove and crosses a small stream. It then begins a steep ascent up to three thousand feet of elevation, where it levels, passing more hemlock groves. This area tends to flood in the spring, making travel difficult. A mile north of where the trail levels, the snowmobile trail separates from the Long Path, which continues north from here.

To climb to the summit of Kaaterskill High Peak, continue straight on the snowmobile trail a short distance, reaching a junction with the southern loop of this trail, which circles Kaaterskill High Peak and neighboring Round Top. Go right. Just beyond, an unofficial trail marked with blue paint blazes appears on the left. Follow this trail south as it climbs steeply over rocks and forested slopes, finally reaching the summit plateau, densely covered with balsam trees and other plants characteristic of the northern boreal forests described above. Cross the plateau, a short distance. The trail then begins to descend, leaving the boreal forest and entering a deciduous forest of northern hardwoods. After several minutes the trail arrives at an open rock ledge and grassy clearing with an expansive view looking south of Plattekill Clove, Indian Head, and Twin Mountains, the Hudson Valley, and the river. If you wish to continue south, the trail makes a very steep descent from here and eventually intersects the southern loop of the snowmobile trail. Go left and follow it north back to the Long Path, passing the wreck of a small plane right in the middle of the trail.

From the intersection described above, the Long Path continues north and east, descending one-half mile and intersecting an old woods road, which it follows eastward. Continue for another half mile, passing Buttermilk Falls on the left, with a fine view of Kaaterskill Clove to the north and South Mountain. A half mile beyond is Wildcat Falls, which has another excellent view of Kaaterskill Clove as well as the Hudson Valley and the river in the distance, from the top of the falls. The Long Path continues its long descent down to Malden Avenue in Palenville. The last half mile, which is on private land, is marked with turquoise paint blazes.

Turn left on Malden Avenue, and continue less than a half mile west out to Route 23A, crossing Kaaterskill Creek. Go right, east on 23A, usually busy with traffic, 0.7 miles to a trailhead on the left side of the road, marked with yellow blazes. Follow the trail, which is actually a bridle path, north and west, uphill for about 3.25 miles to a junction with the blue-marked Escarpment Trail. A worthwhile detour from here goes left, 0.3 miles, to Inspiration Point, with fine open views looking south of Kaaterskill Clove, Kaaterskill High Peak and Roundtop, and the Hudson Valley to the east and the river. To continue north on the Escarpment Trail (part of the Long Path), from the intersection with the bridle path, go right, uphill, about one-half mile to the intersection with the red-marked Schutt Road Trail. The intersection is near the 2,460-foot summit of South Mountain. The Schutt Road Trail on the left leads to the top of famed Kaaterskill Falls, about 2.5 miles away. In a large clearing north of the trail is the former site of the huge sprawling Kaaterskill Hotel, which occupied South Mountain's summit. It was destroyed by a spectacular fire in 1924.

Continue right (northeast) on the blue-marked Escarpment Trail for slightly more than one-half mile to an intersection with a red-marked trail on the left, a shortcut to the Catskill Mountain House site. Instead, go right on the blue-marked Escarpment Trail, which soon leads to a pair of fine 180-degree views at Split Rock and Boulder Rock. The Hudson Valley and the river are seen two thousand feet below. The Escarpment Trail continues north, eventually rejoined by the red-marked shortcut. It then makes a steep quarter-mile descent to a clearing where the Catskill Mountain House once stood. There is a commemorative plaque, but otherwise little remains of the hotel (besides the fine view), which finally closed in 1942. The by-then-dilapidated building was sold to the state and razed in 1963 as an alleged fire hazard. A dirt road leads down to North Lake Campground, a beach, and the main entrance to this area.

Continue north on the Escarpment Trail one-quarter mile to a large parking area. Follow markers north. Unmarked trails on the left lead to the campground. At 0.4 miles past the parking area, the trail reaches Artist Rock, a superb view from a series of open ledges, looking east, of the Hudson Valley and the river. After another half mile, the trail starts to climb in an area of steep rock cliffs. An intersection with a yellow-marked trail on the right is reached. This short quarter-mile spur leads to Sunset Rock, one of the most magnificent and celebrated views in the Catskills, overlooking North Lake, that also includes the site of the former Catskill Mountain House, South Mountain, Kaaterskill High Peak,

Roundtop, and of course the Hudson Valley and the river. This scene was captured in all its glory in numerous paintings of the Hudson River School.

Backtrack to the Escarpment Trail, and continue north a short distance to Newman's Ledge, which has a fine open view looking east toward the Hudson Valley and the river. The trail continues north, climbing a half mile to an intersection with a yellow-marked Rock Shelter Trail on the left. A short distance uphill on that trail leads to Badman's Cave, a sizable rock shelter. The yellow-marked trail also leads to the Mary's Glen Trail and to the main entrance to the North Lake Campground.

From this intersection the Escarpment Trail continues to climb north and west 0.7 miles to an intersection with the red-marked Mary's Glen Trail. From here, the Escarpment Trail turns right and climbs steeply, bypassing a former section of the trail, even steeper and badly eroded, finally reaching the nearly three-thousand-foot-high ridge. Boreal forest trees and plants can be seen here in this windy exposed place. The trail turns to the left and ascends the rocky slope up to North Point. This is one of the most expansive views in the entire region. One can see north all the way to Albany and south all the way to the Hudson Highlands, an amazing stretch of river and valley.

Kykuit

No guidebook to the Hudson would be complete without mention of this eighty-seven-acre estate where three generations of the Rockefeller family resided. Fortunately, in the spring of 1994 Kykuit (the name comes from words meaning "lookout" in Dutch) was opened to the public, and those who can afford the rather steep admission can enjoy its panoramic views of the river as well as its gardens and its marvelous art collection. Kykuit is located in Pocantico Hills, northeast of Tarrytown.

The original three-thousand-acre estate was purchased by John D. Rockefeller Sr. (1839–1937) in 1893. Rockefeller, the famous owner of Standard Oil, became America's first billionaire. In 1906 the original rather unpretentious house was built. In 1911 John senior retired, and the house was turned over to his son, John D. Rockefeller Jr. (1874–1960). John senior continued to reside there until his death. John junior hired the architect William Wells Bosworth (who had previously worked in an architectural firm with Frederick Law Olmsted) to remodel the exterior of the home in the resplendent beaux-arts style and landscape the grounds using many classical influences. Sixty-year-old beech trees were planted, with reserves in case the originals died or fell in a storm, and additional floors were built onto the mansion. However, he left the first two floors of the house relatively untouched. One of John junior's sons, Nelson Rockefeller (1908–1979), the four-term governor of New York State (1958–1973), who also served as vice president (1974–1977) under Gerald Ford, owned the house from 1963 till his death.

It is the art collection that is the real highlight here. Many outdoor works are beautifully situated in formal garden settings with an incredible backdrop of the Hudson River and Palisades. The collection includes the outdoor statue *Oceanus,* the Greek river god, dedicated to the great rivers of the world, including the Hudson, the Nile, the Ganges, and the Euphrates. There are also outstanding modern pieces by some of the twentieth century's most famous artists: Henry Moore, Constantin Brancusi, Alberto Giacometti, Calder, and Lipchitz. Indoors there is a sculpture by Rodin, a stunning Tang Dynasty bodhisattva with a picturesque window view of the Hudson in the background, and many fine Asian ceramic pieces. The downstairs galleries are packed with works by Calder and George Segal, sketches and tapestries by Picasso, and paintings by Robert Motherwell, Andy Warhol, and countless others.

Kykuit is a property of the National Trust for Historic Preservation. Historic Hudson Valley operates the visitation program. Two-hour tours of the estate originate at Philipsburg Manor; they include the house, gardens, and the coach barn, where the family's collection of antique carriages, automobiles, and saddles is on display. Reservations are almost a necessity for this popular tourist destination, which is open daily from April to November. Call 914-631-9491 for information and reservations.

RECOMMENDED READING

GENERAL

Adams, Arthur G. *The Hudson: A Guidebook to the River.* Albany: State University of New York Press, 1981.

Boyle, Robert H. *The Hudson River: A Natural and Unnatural History.* New York: W.W. Norton Company. Rev. ed. 1979.

Stanne, Stephan P., Roger G. Panetta, and Brian E. Forist. *The Hudson: An Illustrated Guide to the River.* New Brunswick, N.J.: Rutgers University Press, 1996.

GEOLOGY

Isachsen, Y. W., E. Landing, J. M. Lauber, L. V. Rickard, and W. B. Rogers, eds. *Geology of New York: A Simplified Account.* Albany: State University of New York, 1991.

Schuberth, Christopher J. *The Geology of New York City and Environs.* Garden City, N.Y.: American Museum of Natural History Press, 1968.

NATURAL HISTORY AND ECOLOGY

Barbour, Anita, and Spider Barbour. *Wild Flora of the Northeast.* Woodstock, N.Y.: Overlook Press, 1991.

Boyce Thompson Institute for Plant Research. *An Atlas of Biological Resources of the Hudson Estuary.* Yonkers, N.Y.: Boyce Thompson Institute for Plant Research, 1977.

Hudsonia. *Manual for the Identification of Biodiversity Resources in the Hudson River Greenway Corridor.* Annandale, N.Y.: Hudsonia, forthcoming.

Kiviat, Erik. *Hudson River East Bank Natural Areas: Clermont to Norrie.* Arlington, Va.: The Nature Conservancy, 1978.

Kricher, John C., and Gordon Morrison. *Ecology of Eastern Forests,* Peterson Field Guide Series, vol. 45. New York: Houghton Mifflin Company, 1988.

New York Department of Environmental Conservation. *Hudson River Field Guide to Plants of Freshwater Tidal Wetlands.* Illustrated by Linda Beckwith Mc-Closkey. Albany: New York Department of Environmental Conservation, 1998.

New York Department of State/Division of Coastal Resources and Waterfront Revitalization, and the Nature Conservancy. *Hudson River Significant Tidal Habitats: A Guide to the Functions, Values, and Protection of the River's Natural Resources.* Albany, N.Y.: New York Department of State/Division of Coastal Resources and Waterfront Revitalization, and the Nature Conservancy, 1990.

NATIVE AMERICAN LIFE ALONG THE HUDSON

Dunn, Shirley W. *The Mohicans and Their Land 1609–1730.* Fleischmanns, N.Y.: Purple Mountain Press, 1994.

Funk, Robert E. *Recent Contributions to Hudson Valley Prehistory.* Albany, N.Y.: State University of New York Press, State Department of Education, Memoir 22, November 1976.

Ruttenber, E. M. *Indian Tribes of Hudson's River.* Vol. 1, *To 1700.* Saugerties, N.Y.: Hope Farm Press, 1992.

Ruttenber, E. M. *Indian Tribes of Hudson's River.* Vol. 2, *1700–1850.* Saugerties, N.Y.: Hope Farm Press, 1992.

HISTORY

Adams, Arthur G. *The Hudson Through the Years.* 3rd ed. New York: Fordham University Press, 1996.

Carmer, Carl. *The Hudson.* 1939. Reprint, 1974. New York: Fordham University Press.

Cronon, William. *Changes in the Land: Indians, Colonists, and the Ecology of New England.* New York: Hill & Wang, 1983.

Dunwell, Frances F. *The Hudson Highlands.* New York: Columbia University Press, 1991.

Ellis, David M., James A. Frost, Harold C. Syrett, and Harry F. Carmen. *A History of New York State.* Ithaca, N.Y.: Cornell University Press, 1957. Reprint, 1967.

Kammen, Michael. *Colonial New York: A History.* New York: Charles Scribner's Sons, 1975.

Renehan, Edward J. Jr. *John Burroughs: An American Naturalist.* Hensonville, N.Y.: Black Dome Press, 1992, 1998.

Williams-Myers, Albert James. *Long Hammering: Essays on the Forging of an African American Presence in the Hudson River Valley to the Early Twentieth Century.* Trenton, N.J.: African World Press, 1994.

HUDSON RIVER IN LITERATURE AND FIRSTHAND ACCOUNTS

Marranca, Bonnie, ed. *A Hudson Valley Reader.* Woodstock, N.Y.: Overlook Press, 1991. Reprint, 1995.

Van Zandt, Roland, ed. *Chronicles of the Hudson: Three Centuries of Travel & Adventure.* Hensonville, N.Y., Black Dome Press, 1992.

LOCAL AREAS

Burrows, Edwin J., and Mike Wallace. *Gotham: A History of New York City to 1898.* New York: Oxford Univesity Press, 1999.

Fried, Marc B. *The Early History of Kingston & Ulster County, N.Y.* Kingston, N.Y.: Ulster County Historical Society, 1975.

Serrao, John. *The Wild Palisades of the Hudson.* Westwood, N.J.: Lind Publications, 1986.

Steuding, Bob. *Rondout—A Hudson River Port.* Fleischmanns, N.Y.: Purple Mountain Press, 1995.

Waite, Diana S., ed. *Albany Architecture: A Guide to the City.* Albany: Mount Ida Press, 1993.

HIKING AND BIKING

Bridge, Raymond. *Bike Touring: The Sierra Club Guide to Outings on Wheels.* San Francisco, Calif.: Sierra Club Books, 1979.

Fletcher, Colin. *The Complete Walker III.* New York: Alfred A. Knopf, 1984.

OTHER GUIDEBOOKS

Anderson, Katherine S., and Peggy Turco. *Walks and Rambles in Westchester and Fairfield Counties: A Nature Lover's Guide to 36 Parks and Sanctuaries.* 2nd ed. Woodstock, Vt.: Backcountry Publications, 1993.

Chazin, Daniel D., field ed. *Appalachian Trail Guide to New York–New Jersey.* 21st ed. Harpers Ferry, W.Va.: Appalachian Trail Conference, 1999.

Kick, Peter, Barbara McMartin, and James M. Long. *Fifty Hikes in the Hudson Valley: From the Catskills to the Taconics, and from Ramapos to the Helderbergs.* 2nd ed. Woodstock, Vt.: Backcountry Publications, 1995.

McAllister, Lee, and Myron Steven Ochman. *Hiking the Catskills: A Guide for Exploring the Natural Beauty of America's Romantic and Magical Mountains on the Trail and "Off the Beaten Path."* New York: New York/New Jersey Trail Conference, 1989.

Michaels, Joanne, and Mary-Margaret Barile. *The Hudson Valley and Catskill Mountains: An Explorers Guide.* 2nd ed. Woodstock, Vt.: Countryman Press, 1996.

Mulligan, Tim. *The Travelers' Guide to the Hudson River Valley from Saratoga Springs to New York City.* 3rd ed. New York: Random House, 1995.

Myles, William. *Harriman Trails: A Guide and History.* Rev. ed. New York: New York/New Jersey Trail Conference, 1994.

New York/New Jersey Trail Conference. *New York Walk Book.* 6th ed. New York: New York/New Jersey Trail Conference, 1998.

New York/New Jersey Trail Conference. *Guide to the Long Path.* 4th ed. New York: New York/New Jersey Trail Conference, 1996.

Stone, Howard. *Twenty-five Bicycle Tours in the Hudson Valley: Scenic Rides from Saratoga to Northern Westchester County.* Woodstock, Vt.: Backcountry Publications, 1996.

Turco, Peggy. *Walks & Rambles in Dutchess and Putnam Counties: A Guide to Ecology and History in Eastern Hudson Valley Parks.* Woodstock, Vt.: Countryman Press, 1990.

———. *Walks and Rambles in the Western Hudson Valley: Landscape, Ecology & Folklore in Orange & Ulster Counties.* Woodstock, Vt.: Backcountry Publications, 1996.

INDEX

Acadian Orogeny, 16, 17, 389
acid rain, 83, 86
Adirondack Forest Preserve, 74, 397
Adirondack Mountain Club, 113, 397
Adirondack Mountains, 9, 120, 161,
  227, 312, 382, 383, 394
African Americans, 49, 55–56, 62–63,
  75, 159, 165–166
agriculture, 48, 52, 54, 63–64, 66,
  76, 81–83, 153, 160, 277, 281,
  289, 322, 365, 367
air pollution, 86
Albany, city of, 9, 11, 17, 23, 27, 38,
  43, 44, 50, 51, 52, 53, 57, 63, 65,
  66, 67, 69, 76, 80, 95, 120, 122,
  123, 269, 293, 300, 303, 324, 327,
  329, 344, 357, 362, 364, 365, 370,
  372, 373, 375, 377–385, 401;
  Albany Academy, 380, 384; Albany
  County Airport, 365; Albany
  County Convention and Visitors'
  Bureau, 380; Albany County Historical Society, 385; Albany Institute of History and Art, 69, 377,
  385; Beverwyck, 48, 375, 379;
  Corning Preserve, 380, 382; Corning Tower, 384; Empire State Plaza,
  377, 382, 383, 384; First Church
  (Reformed), 380, 383; Fort Frederick, 379; Fort Nassau, 44, 377; Fort
  Orange, 44, 46, 47, 50, 365, 372,
  377, 379; Fuyck, 379; Historic
  Cherry Hill, 377, 380–381; Hudson-
  Mohawk Bikeway, 116, 377,
  382–383; Lark Street neighborhood, 377; Mansion Historic District, 382; New York State Capitol,
  377, 383, 384; New York State
  Museum, 38, 42, 50, 377, 382,
  383–384; Pastures Historic District,
  382; Port of Albany, 10, 77, 372,
  377, 380; Quackenbush Square,
  377, 380, 383, 385; "Quality Row,"
  384; Schuyler Mansion State Historic Site, 57, 377, 381–382; Ten
  Broeck Mansion, 69, 377, 385;
  tours, 383, Urban Cultural Park,
  95, 377; Visitors' Center, 377, 380,
  383
Albany County, 122, 365
Albany Pool, 365
Alleghenian Orogeny, 15, 18
Allegheny Plateau, 15, 17, 18, 273,
  364, 395
all-terrain vehicles (ATVs), 90,
  263–264, 393–394
American Revolution, 57–61, 62, 63,
  67, 132–133, 138, 152, 162, 170,

ABOUT THE AUTHOR

JEFFREY PERLS is a freelance writer, environmentalist, and outings leader.